GW01340256

CAXTON
ENGLISH
THESAURUS

CAXTON EDITIONS

First published in Great Britain by
CAXTON EDITIONS
an imprint of
the Caxton Book Company Ltd
16 Connaught Street
Marble Arch
London W2 2AF

This edition copyright
© 1999 CAXTON EDITIONS

Prepared and designed
for Caxton Editions by
Superlaunch Limited
PO Box 207
Abingdon
Oxfordshire OX13 6TA

Consultant editors Simon Image
and Bruce Howard

All rights reserved. No part of this publication
may be reproduced, stored in a retrieval system,
or transmitted in any form or by any means,
electronic, mechanical, photocopying, recording
or otherwise, without the prior permission in writing
of the copyright holder.

ISBN 1 84067 072 X

A copy of the CIP data for this book is available from
the British Library upon request

Printed and bound in India

A

abandon vb abjure, desert, drop, evacuate, forsake, forswear, leave, quit; abdicate, cede, forgo, give up, let go, renounce, resign, surrender, relinquish, yield, waive; * n careless, freedom, impulse, wildness.

abandoned adj deserted, discarded, dropped, forsaken, left, outcast, rejected; corrupt, depraved, dissolute, profligate, reprobate, sinful, unprincipled.

abate vb decrease, diminish, lessen, moderate, reduce, relax, slacken; deduct, rebate, remit; allay, alleviate, appease, calm, compose, dull, mitigate, moderate, quiet, soften, soothe, tranquillise.

abbreviate vb abridge, compress, condense, contract, curtail, cut, reduce, shorten.

abbreviation n abridgment, compression, condensation, contraction, curtailment, reduction, shortening.

abdicate vb abandon, cede, forgo, give up, quit, relinquish, renounce, resign, retire.

aberration n deviation, rambling, wandering; abnormality, anomaly, eccentricity, irregularity, peculiarity; delusion, hallucination, illusion, instability.

abhor vb abominate, detest, execrate, hate, loathe.

abhorrent adj hateful, horrifying, loathsome, noxious, odious, repellent, repugnant, repulsive.

abide vb lodge, rest, sojourn, stay, stop, tarry, wait; dwell, live, reside; bear, persevere, persist, remain; endure, last, suffer, tolerate; (with **by**) conform to, fulfil, keep to, persist in.

abiding adj constant, continuing, durable, enduring, lasting, permanent, unchanging.

ability n ableness, aptitude, dexterity, facility, knack, skill, talent; competence; capability, capacity, faculty.

able adj accomplished, adroit, clever, expert, proficient, qualified, skilful, talented, versed; competent, effective, efficient, fitted; capable, gifted, powerful, talented.

ablution n bath, cleansing, purification, shower, wash.

abnormal adj aberrant, eccentric, exceptional, irregular, odd, peculiar, singular, strange, unnatural, unusual, weird.

abolish vb abrogate, annul, cancel, eliminate, invalidate, nullify, quash, repeal, rescind, revoke; annihilate, destroy, end, eradicate, extirpate, extinguish, obliterate, overthrow, suppress, terminate.

abominable adj accursed, contemptible, detestable, execrable, hellish, horrid, odious; abhorrent, detestable, disgusting, foul, loathsome, nauseous, obnoxious, repugnant, repulsive, revolting; vile, wretched.

abortive adj fruitless, futile, idle, ineffectual, unavailing, unsuccessful, useless, vain.

about prep around, encircling, round, surrounding; near; concerning, referring to, regarding, relating to, relative to, respecting, touching, with respect to; all over, over, through; * adv approximately, around, nearing, nearly.

above adj aforementioned, aforesaid, foregoing, preceding, previous, prior; * adv aloft, overhead; before; of a higher rank; * prep higher than, on top of, over; beyond, superior.

aboveboard adj candid, frank, honest, open, straightforward, truthful, upright; * adv candidly, openly, sincerely.

abrupt adj broken, rough; precipitous, steep; hasty, precipitate, sudden, unexpected; blunt, brusque, curt, discourteous; harsh.

absence n non-appearance,

ABSENT

non-attendance; abstraction, distraction, inattention, preoccupation, reverie; default, defect, deficiency, lack.

absent *adj* away, elsewhere, gone, missing, not present; abstracted, daydreaming, inattentive, lost, musing, preoccupied.

absolute *adj* complete, perfect, supreme, unconditional, unlimited, unqualified, unrestricted; authoritative, autocratic, despotic; actual, categorical, certain, decided, genuine, positive, unequivocal.

absolutely *adv* completely, definitely, unconditionally; actually, infallibly, positively, surely, truly, unquestionably.

absorb *vb* assimilate, drink in, imbibe, soak up; consume, devour, engorge, engulf, take in; engage, engross, fix, immerse, occupy, rivet.

abstain *vb* avoid, cease, deny oneself, forbear, refrain, refuse, stop, withhold.

abstemious *adj* abstinent, frugal self-denying, sober, temperate.

abstinence *n* abstemiousness, avoidance, moderation, self-denial, sobriety, teetotalism, temperance.

abstract *vb* detach, dissociate, isolate, separate; steal, take; abbreviate, abridge, epitomise; * *adj* separate, unrelated; abstracted, occult, recondite, subtle; * *n* abridgment, condensation, digest, précis, selection, summary, synopsis.

abstracted *adj* absent-minded, dreamy, inattentive, preoccupied.

absurd *adj* foolish, idiotic, incongruous, irrational, ludicrous, nonsensical, preposterous, ridiculous, senseless, silly, stupid, unreasonable.

abundant *adj* ample, bountiful, copious, exuberant, full, lavish, luxuriant, overflowing, plentiful, rich, teeming.

abuse *vb* desecrate, dishonour, misapply, misuse, violate, wrong; harm, hurt, ill-treat, injure, maltreat, manhandle; blame, calumniate, defame, disparage, lampoon, lash, malign, revile, slander, traduce, upbraid, vilify; * *n* desecration, dishonour, ill-use, misuse, perversion, pollution, profanation; maltreatment, outrage; defamation, insults, invective, opprobrium, reviling, vilification.

abusive *adj* condemnatory, contumelious, denunciatory, injurious, insulting, offensive, opprobrious, reproachful, reviling, rude, vituperative.

academic *adj* collegiate, lettered, scholastic; * *n* academician, don, fellow, scholar, student, teacher, tutor.

accede *vb* accept, admit, agree, assent, comply, concede, concur, consent, endorse, grant.

accelerate *vb* expedite, forward, hasten, hurry, pick up, precipitate, quicken, speed, step up.

accentuate *vb* accent, emphasise, stress; highlight, underline, underscore.

accept *vb* acquire, gain, get, obtain, receive, take; accede, acknowledge, acquiesce, admit, agree to, approve, embrace.

acceptable *adj* agreeable, gratifying, pleasant, pleasing, welcome.

access *vb* broach, enter, open; * *n* approach, avenue, entrance, entry, passage; admission, admittance; (medical) attack, fit, onset.

accession *n* addition, extension, increase; succession.

accessory *adj* abetting, adjunct, aiding, ancillary, assisting, contributory; subordinate, supplemental; * *n* abettor, accomplice, assistant, associate, confederate, helper; accompaniment; frill, supplement, trimming.

ACTION

accident n calamity, casualty, disaster, incident, mischance, misfortune, mishap; chance.
accidental adj casual, chance, contingent, unintended; adventitious, incidental.
acclimatise vb accustom, adapt, adjust, habituate, inure, naturalise, season.
accommodate vb contain, hold, oblige, serve, supply; adapt, fit; adjust, compose, harmonise, reconcile, settle.
accompany vb attend, chaperone, convoy, escort, follow, go with.
accomplice n abettor, accessory, ally, assistant, associate, confederate, helper, partner.
accomplish vb achieve, attain, bring about, carry out, complete, consummate, do, effect, execute, fulfil, perform; conclude, finish.
accomplished adj achieved, completed, done, effected, executed, finished, fulfilled, realised; consummate, educated, finished, practised, proficient, skilful, versed; polished.
accord vb allow, concede, deign, give, grant, vouchsafe; agree, assent, concur, correspond, harmonise, tally; * n agreement, concord, conformity, harmony, unanimity, unison.
account vb appraise, assess, estimate, judge, rate; (with **for**) explain, justify, rationalise; * n inventory, register, score; bill, book, charge; reckoning, score, tally; chronicle, description, detail, narrative, recital, relation, report, statement; consideration, ground, motive, reason, regard, sake; consequence, distinction, importance, note, repute, worth.
accountable adj amenable, answerable, liable, responsible.
accumulate vb amass, build up, collect, gather, grow, hoard, increase, stockpile, store.
accurate adj careful, close, correct, exact, faithful, nice, precise, regular, strict, true, truthful.
accuse vb arraign, censure, charge, impeach, indict, tax.
ace n master, virtuoso; (cards, dice) one spot, single point; * adj expert, fine, outstanding, superb.
ache vb hurt, pain, smart, suffer, throb, twinge.
achieve vb accomplish, acquire, attain, complete, consummate, do, effect, execute, finish, fulfil, perform, realise; acquire, gain, get, obtain, win.
acid adj pungent, sharp, sour, tart, vinegary.
acknowledge vb recognise; accept, admit, allow, concede, grant; confess, own, profess.
acquaint vb familiarise; apprise, enlighten, disclose, inform, notify, tell.
acquaintance n companionship, familiarity, fellowship, intimacy knowledge; associate.
acquire vb achieve, attain, earn, gain, gather, get, obtain, procure, realise, secure, win.
acquit vb absolve, clear, discharge, exculpate, exonerate, liberate, pardon, pay, release, set free, settle.
acrimonious adj bitter, caustic, censorious, churlish, crabbed, petulant, sarcastic, severe, sharp, spiteful, testy, virulent.
act vb do, execute, function, make, operate, work; enact, perform; * n achievement, deed, exploit, feat, performance; bill, decree, enactment, law, ordinance, statute.
acting adj interim, provisional, substitute, temporary; * n enacting, impersonation, performance, portrayal, theatre; counterfeiting, dissimulation, pretence.
action n achievement, activity, deed, exertion, exploit, feat; litigation, prosecution; battle, combat, conflict, encounter, engagement, operation.

active *adj* effective, living, operative; bustling, busy, diligent, industrious; alert, energetic, lively, nimble, quick, sprightly, vigorous.

actual *adj* certain, genuine, real, substantial, tangible, true, present, tangible; absolute, categorical, positive.

acumen *n* acuteness, astuteness, discernment, ingenuity, keenness, sagacity, sharpness, shrewdness.

acute *adj* pointed, sharp; astute, discerning, ingenious, intelligent, keen, penetrating, piercing, sharp, smart, subtle; distressing, fierce, intense, piercing, poignant, severe, violent; sharp, shrill.

adapt *vb* accommodate, adjust, conform, fit, qualify, suit.

add *vb* adjoin, affix, annex, append, attach, sum up, total.

addict *vb* accustom, apply, dedicate, devote, habituate; * *n* devotee, enthusiast, fan; junkie, user.

addition *n* accession, enlargement, extension, increase, supplement; adjunct, appendage, appendix, extra.

address *n* abode, domicile, dwelling, home, location, residence; discourse, lecture, oration, sermon, speech; adroitness, art, dexterity, expertness, skill; * *vb* accost, apply (oneself to), court, direct.

adequate *adj* capable, competent, requisite, satisfactory, sufficient, suitable.

adhere *vb* cleave, cling, cohere, hold fast, stick.

adherent *adj* adhering, clinging, sticking; * *n* devotee, disciple, follower, partisan, supporter.

adhesive *adj* clinging, sticking; glutinous, gummy, sticky, tenacious; * *n* cement, glue, paste.

adjacent *adj* adjoining, bordering, contiguous, near, neighbouring, touching.

adjourn *vb* defer, delay, postpone, interrupt, prorogue, suspend.

adjunct *n* addition, appendage, attachment, auxiliary.

adjust *vb* adapt, arrange, dispose, rectify; regulate, set right, settle, suit; compose, harmonise, reconcile; adapt, fit.

administer *vb* contribute, dispense; conduct, control, direct, govern, manage, oversee, superintend.

admirable *adj* wonderful; excellent, fine, rare.

admiration *n* affection, approbation, approval, astonishment, delight, esteem, regard.

admire *vb* approve, esteem, respect; adore, prize.

admissible *adj* allowable, lawful, passable, permissible.

admission *n* access, admittance, entrance, introduction; acceptance, acknowledgement, allowance, avowal, concession.

admit *vb* let in, receive; agree to, accept, acknowledge, concede, confess; allow.

adopt *vb* appropriate, assume; accept, espouse, maintain, support; father, foster.

adore *vb* worship; esteem, honour, idolise, love, revere, venerate.

adorn *vb* array, bedeck, decorate, embellish, enhance, enrich, festoon, grace, ornament.

adult *adj* grown-up, mature, ripe; * *n* grown-up (person).

adulterate *vb* contaminate, corrupt, debase, deteriorate, vitiate, water down.

advance *adj* beforehand, forward, leading; * *vb* send forward; elevate, promote; benefit, forward, further, improve, promote; adduce, allege, offer; increase; proceed, progress; grow, improve, prosper, thrive; * *n* progress; advancement, growth, promotion, rise; offer, proposal.

advantage *n* ascendancy, precedence, pre-eminence, superiority, upper hand;

benefit, blessing, gain, profit; interest; convenience, prerogative, privilege.

advantageous *adj* beneficial, favourable, profitable, worthwhile.

advent *n* approach, arrival, coming, visitation.

adventure *vb* dare, hazard, imperil, risk, venture; * *n* chance, contingency, venture; contingency, incident, occurrence.

adventurous *adj* bold, courageous, daring, doughty; foolhardy, headstrong, rash, reckless; dangerous, hazardous, perilous.

adversary *n* antagonist, enemy, foe, opponent.

adverse *adj* conflicting, contrary, opposing; antagonistic, hostile, inimical, unfavourable, unpropitious; unfortunate, unlucky, untoward.

advertise *vb* advise, announce, declare, inform, proclaim, publish.

advice *n* admonition, counsel, suggestion, recommendation; information, intelligence, notice, notification.

advisable *adj* apt, advantageous, desirable, expedient, fit, prudent.

advise *vb* admonish, commend, counsel, recommend, suggest, urge; acquaint, apprise, inform, notify.

adviser *n* coach, counsellor, director, guide, instructor.

advocate *vb* countenance, defend, favour, justify, support, uphold; * *n* apologist, defender, patron, pleader, supporter; (law) attorney, barrister, counsel, lawyer, solicitor.

affable *adj* amiable, congenial, communicative, cordial, friendly, frank, free, sociable, social; complaisant, courteous, civil, obliging, polite, urbane.

affair *n* business, circumstance, concern, matter, question; event, incident, occurrence, proceeding, transaction; battle, combat, conflict, encounter, engagement, skirmish.

affect *vb* act upon, alter, change, influence, modify, transform; concern, interest, regard, relate; overcome, touch; aspire to; adopt, assume, feign.

affection *n* bent, bias, feeling, inclination, passion, proclivity, propensity; attachment, endearment, fondness, kindness, love, warmth.

affectionate *adj* attached, devoted, fond, kind, loving, sympathetic, tender.

affirm *vb* assert, asseverate, aver, declare, state; confirm, ratify.

affliction *n* adversity, calamity, misfortune; depression, distress, grief, misery, plague, scourge, sorrow, trial, tribulation, woe, wretchedness.

affluent *adj* abundant, bounteous, plenteous; moneyed, opulent, rich, wealthy.

afford *vb* furnish, produce, supply, yield; bestow, confer, give, grant, impart, offer; bear, support.

affray *n* brawl, conflict, feud, fight, mêlée, quarrel, scuffle, skirmish, struggle.

affront *vb* abuse, insult, outrage; annoy, displease, offend, pique, provoke, vex; * *n* insult, outrage, vexation, wrong.

afraid *adj* aghast, alarmed, anxious, apprehensive, frightened, scared.

after *prep* later than; behind, following; according to; because of, in imitation of; * *adj* ensuing, following, later, succeeding, successive, subsequent; aft, rear, tail; * *adv* afterwards, later, next, since, subsequently.

again *adv* afresh, anew, another time, once more; besides, further, moreover.

against *prep* adverse to, contrary to, resisting; abutting, close to, facing, fronting, off, opposite to; in expectation of; in compensation for, to

age vb decline, grow old, mature; * n aeon, date, epoch, period, time; decline, old age, senility; antiquity.

agent n actor, doer, executor, operator, performer; active element, cause, attorney, broker, commissioner, factor, intermediary, manager.

aggravate vb heighten, increase, worsen; colour, exaggerate, magnify; enrage, irritate, provoke, tease.

aggressive adj assailing, assaulting, attacking, invading, offensive; self-assertive.

aggrieve vb afflict, hurt, pain; abuse, impose, injure, oppress, wrong.

aghast adj appalled, dismayed, frightened, horrified, terrified; amazed, astonished.

agile adj active, alert, brisk, lively, nimble, prompt, ready.

agitate vb disturb, jar, rock, shake, trouble; disquiet, excite, ferment, rouse, trouble; confuse, discontent, fluster, flutter; canvass, debate, discuss, investigate.

agitation n concussion, shaking, succession; commotion, convulsion, disturbance, ferment, jarring, storm, tumult, turmoil; distraction, excitement, perturbation, ruffle, tremor, trepidation; debate, discussion.

agony n anguish, distress.

agree vb accord, harmonise, unite; accede, acquiesce, assent, comply, concur, subscribe; contract, covenant, engage, promise; compound, compromise; cohere, conform, correspond, match, suit.

agreement n accordance, compliance, concord, harmony, union; bargain, compatibility, contract, pact, treaty.

aid vb assist, help, serve, support; advance, facilitate, further, promote; * n assistance, help, patronage; subsidy, succour, relief.

ailment n disease, illness, sickness.

aim vb direct, level, point; design, intend, mean, purpose, seek; * n bearing, course, direction; object, view; reason.

air vb expose, display, ventilate; * n breeze; appearance, manner; melody, tune.

alarm vb daunt, frighten, startle, terrify; * n alarm-bell, tocsin, warning; fear, fright, terror.

alert adj awake, circumspect, vigilant, watchful, wary; active, lively, quick, prompt, ready, sprightly, spry. * vb alarm, arouse, caution, forewarn, signal; * n alarm, signal, warning.

alien adj foreign, not native; differing, estranged, remote, separated; * n foreigner, stranger.

alike adj akin, analogous, corresponding, duplicate, resembling, similar; * adv equally.

alive adj animate, breathing, live; aware, responsive, susceptible; brisk, cheerful, lively, sprightly.

allay vb appease, calm, compose; alleviate, assuage, moderate, solace, temper.

allege vb affirm, assert, declare, say; adduce, advance, assign, produce, quote.

allegiance n duty, homage; fealty, fidelity, loyalty.

alliance n affinity, intermarriage, relation; coalition, confederacy, league, treaty, union; affiliation, relationship.

allow vb acknowledge, admit, concede, confess, own; authorise, let, permit; suffer, tolerate; relinquish, spare; approve, sanction; abate, remit.

allure n appeal, attraction, lure, temptation.

ally vb combine, connect, join, marry, unite; * n assistant, associate, colleague, friend, partner.

almighty *adj* all-powerful, omnipotent.
alone *adj* companionless, deserted, forsaken, isolated, lonely, single, sole, solitary.
along *adv* lengthwise; forward, onward; beside, together.
alter *vb* change, conform, modify, shift, turn, transform, transmit, vary.
alternate *vb* fluctuate, oscillate, vacillate, vary, waver; change, interchange, reciprocate; intermit, revolve; relieve, take turns; * *adj* intermittent, periodic; alternative, equivalent, substitute; reciprocal; * *n* deputy, proxy, replacement, representative, substitute.
alternative *adj* another, different, substitute; * *n* choice, option, preference.
although *conj* albeit, even if, for all that, notwithstanding, though.
altitude *n* elevation, height, loftiness.
altogether *adv* completely, entirely, totally, utterly.
always *adv* continually, eternally, ever, perpetually, unceasingly.
amass *vb* accumulate, aggregate, collect, gather, scrape together.
amaze *vb* astonish, astound, bewilder, bowl over, confound, dumbfound, perplex, stagger.
ambiguous *adj* dubious, doubtful, enigmatic, equivocal, uncertain, indefinite, obscure, vague.
ambitious *adj* aspiring, avid, eager.
amenable *adj* acquiescent, agreeable, responsive, susceptible.
amend *vb* better, correct, improve, mend, redress, reform.
amends *npl* atonement, compensation, expiation, recompense, reparation, restitution.
amiable *adj* attractive, benign, charming, genial, good-natured, harmonious, lovable, pleasant, sweet, winning.
amicable *adj* amiable, cordial, friendly, kindly, peaceable.
amiss *adj* erroneous, inaccurate, incorrect, improper, wrong; * *adv* erroneously, inaccurately, wrongly.
amorous *adj* ardent, enamoured, fond, longing, loving, tender; erotic, impassioned.
amount *n* aggregate, sum, total.
ample *adj* broad, capacious, extended, extensive, large, roomy, spacious; abundant, copious, generous, liberal, plentiful.
amuse *vb* beguile, charm, cheer, divert, enliven, entertain, gladden, relax, solace.
analysis *n* dissection, separation.
anarchy *n* chaos, confusion, disorder, misrule, lawlessness.
ancestor *n* forebear, forefather.
ancestry *n* family, house, lineage; descent, genealogy, pedigree, stock.
anchor *vb* fasten, fix, secure, take firm hold; * *n* (nautical) ground tackle; security, stay.
ancient *adj* old, primitive; antiquated, archaic, obsolete.
angelic *adj* adorable, celestial, cherubic, heavenly, saintly, seraphic; entrancing, enrapturing, rapturous.
anger *vb* chafe, displease, enrage, gall, infuriate, irritate, madden; * *n* choler, exasperation, fury, indignation, ire, rage, spleen, wrath.
angry *adj* chafed, exasperated, furious, incensed, irritated, nettled, provoked, resentful.
anguish *n* agony, distress, grief, rack, torment, torture.
animate *vb* inform, quicken, vitalise, vivify; fortify, invigorate; activate, enliven, excite, heat, kindle, rouse, stimulate, stir; * *adj* alive, breathing, lively, organic, quick.
animosity *n* bad blood, bitterness, enmity, grudge, hatred, hostility, rancour, spleen,

virulence.

annex vb affix, append, attach, tag, tack; connect, join, unite.

annoy vb badger, chafe, disquiet, disturb, fret, irk, irritate, molest, pain, pester, trouble, vex, worry.

annul vb abolish, abrogate, cancel, countermand, nullify, overrule, quash, repeal, reverse, revoke.

anoint vb consecrate, oil, sanctify.

anonymous adj nameless, unacknowledged, unsigned.

answer vb fulfil, rejoin, respond, satisfy; * n rejoinder, reply, response, retort; rebuttal, refutation.

answerable adj accountable, liable, responsible.

antagonism n contradiction, discordance, dissonance, opposition.

anterior adj antecedent, foregoing, preceding, prior; forefront.

anticipation n apprehension, contemplation, expectation, hope, prospect; expectancy, foretaste, preconception, presentiment.

antipathy n abhorrence, aversion, disgust, detestation, hatred, horror, loathing, repugnance.

antique adj ancient, bygone, old, old-fashioned, superannuated.

anxiety n apprehension, concern, disquiet, fear, foreboding, misgiving, trouble, uneasiness, worry.

anxious adj apprehensive, solicitous, uneasy, unquiet, worried.

apathetic adj dull, impassive, inert, listless, obtuse, sluggish, torpid.

aplomb n composure, confidence, equanimity, self-confidence.

apologetic adj exculpatory, excusatory; defensive.

apology n defence, justification, vindication; excuse, plea, reparation.

apostle n messenger, missionary, preacher; advocate, follower, supporter.

appal vb affright, alarm, dismay, frighten, horrify, scare, shock.

apparent adj discernible, perceptible, visible; evident, manifest, obvious, open, patent, plain; ostensible, seeming, superficial.

apparition n appearance, epiphany, manifestation; ghost, phantom, spectre, spirit, vision.

appeal vb entreat, implore, invoke, request, solicit; * n application, entreaty, solicitation, suit.

appear vb emerge; break, open; arise, occur; look, seem, show.

appearance n advent, arrival, coming; form, shape; colour, fashion, guise, pretence; air, aspect, complexion, demeanour, manner, mien.

append vb attach, fasten, hang; add, annex, subjoin, tack, tag.

appetite n craving, desire, longing, lust, passion; gusto, relish, zest; hunger.

applaud vb acclaim, approve, cheer, clap, commend, extol.

application n emollient, lotion, ointment, poultice, wash; exercise, practice, use; appeal, petition, request, solicitation, suit; assiduity, diligence, effort, industry.

apply vb bestow, lay upon; convert, employ, exercise, use; address, dedicate, devote.

appoint vb establish, prescribe; bid, command, decree, direct, order, require; allot, assign, delegate, depute, settle; constitute, create, name, nominate; equip, furnish.

appreciate vb esteem, estimate, rate, value.

apprehend vb arrest, capture, catch, detain, seize, take; conceive, imagine, regard, view; perceive, realise, see, take in; fear; conceive, hold,

imagine, presume, understand.
approach *vb* advance, come close; resemble; * *n* advance, advent; approximation, convergence, tendency; entrance, way.
appropriate *vb* adopt, arrogate, assume; allot, apportion, assign, devote; apply, convert; * *adj* adapted, apt, befitting, fit, opportune, seemly, suitable.
approve *vb* appreciate, commend, esteem, like, recommend; confirm, countenance, justify, ratify, sustain.
approximate *vb* approach, resemble; * *adj* approaching; almost exact, inexact, rough.
apt *adj* applicable, apposite, appropriate, befitting, fit, germane; disposed, inclined, liable, prone, subject; able, adroit, clever, dextrous, handy, prompt, ready, skilful.
aptitude *n* ability, address, adroitness, capacity, readiness; applicability, appropriateness, fitness, pertinence, suitability; inclination, tendency.
arch *adj* chief, leading, prime, primary, principal; knowing, frolicsome, mirthful, playful, roguish, sly.
ardent *adj* burning, fiery, hot; eager, earnest, fervent, impassioned, passionate, zealous.
ardour *n* glow, heat, warmth; eagerness, enthusiasm, fervour, heat, passion, zeal.
arduous *adj* difficult, fatiguing, hard, laborious, onerous, wearisome; steep, uphill.
area *n* circle, circuit, district, domain, field, range, realm, region, tract.
argue *vb* plead, reason upon; debate, dispute; imply, indicate, mean, prove; contest, debate, discuss.
arise *vb* ascend, mount, soar, tower; appear, emerge, spring; begin, originate; rebel, revolt, rise; come, emanate, ensue, flow, issue, proceed, result.

arm *vb* array, equip, furnish; clothe, fortify, protect, strengthen.
army *n* battalions, force, legions, troops; host, multitude, throng.
around *prep* about, encircling, encompassing, surrounding; * *adv* about, approximately, nearly, practically, thereabouts.
arouse *vb* animate, awaken, excite, kindle, provoke, stimulate, whet.
arrange *vb* array, class, classify, dispose, distribute, group, rank; adjust, settle; concoct, construct, devise, plan.
arrest *vb* check, delay, detain, hinder, hold, interrupt, obstruct, restrain, stop; apprehend, capture, catch, seize, take; catch, engage, engross, fix, occupy, secure, rivet; * *n* check, detention, interruption, obstruction, restraint, stay, stop; apprehension, capture, detention, seizure.
arrive *vb* attain, come, get to, reach.
arrogance *n* assumption, disdain, haughtiness, insolence, loftiness, lordliness, pride, scornfulness, superciliousness.
art *n* craft; adroitness, aptitude, dexterity, ingenuity, knack, sagacity, skill; artifice, astuteness, craft, finesse, subtlety.
artful *adj* crafty, cunning, disingenuous, sly, tricky, wily.
article *n* essay, paper, piece; commodity, object, substance, thing; clause, division, head, item, paragraph, portion.
artificial *adj* counterfeit, sham, spurious; assumed, affected, constrained, forced, laboured.
artless *adj* ignorant, rude, unskilful, untaught; natural, plain, simple; candid, frank, guileless, honest, plain, unaffected, simple, sincere, truthful.
ascend *vb* arise, climb, mount.
ascertain *vb* determine, establish,

ASHAMED

verify; discover, find out.
ashamed *adj* abashed, confused.
ask *vb* inquire, interrogate, question; adjure, beg, crave, desire, entreat, implore, invite; inquire, petition, request, solicit, seek.
aspect *n* air, bearing, countenance, expression, look, mien, visage; appearance, attitude, posture, situation, state, view; angle, direction, outlook, prospect.
asperity *n* acerbity, bitterness, harshness, sternness, severity; acrimony, causticity, corrosiveness, sharpness, sourness, tartness; roughness.
aspersion *n* calumny, censure, defamation, detraction, slander, vituperation; reproach.
aspiration *n* aim, ambition, craving, desire, hope, longing.
assassinate *vb* kill, murder, slay.
assault *vb* assail, attack, charge, invade; * *n* aggression, attack, incursion, invasion, onslaught; storm.
assemble *vb* congregate, convene, convoke, gather, levy, muster; congregate, foregather.
assembly *n* company, collection, concourse, congregation, gathering, meeting, throng; caucus, congress, conclave, convention, convocation, legislature, meeting, synod.
assent *vb* accede, acquiesce, agree, concur; * *n* accord, acquiescence, approval, approbation, consent.
assertion *n* affirmation, allegation, asseveration, declaration, position, remark, statement, word; defence, emphasis, maintenance, support, vindication.
assess *vb* appraise, estimate, rate, value; determine.
assign *vb* allot, appoint, apportion, appropriate; fix; designate, determine, specify; adduce, advance, give, grant.
assist *vb* abet, aid, befriend, further, help, patronise, promote, second, support, sustain; aid, relieve, succour; relieve, spell.
associate *vb* affiliate, combine, conjoin, couple, link, relate, yoke; consort, fraternise, mingle; * *n* companion, comrade, familiar; ally, confederate, friend, partner, fellow.
association *n* combination, confederation, connection, society.
assort *vb* arrange, class, classify, file, group, rank; agree, consort, suit.
assume *vb* take; counterfeit, feign, pretend, sham; arrogate, usurp; beg, imply, postulate, posit, presuppose, suppose, simulate.
assurance *n* certainty, conviction, persuasion, security, surety, warrant; engagement, pledge, promise; assertion; confidence, courage, firmness, intrepidity; arrogance, effrontery.
astonish *vb* amaze, astound, confound, dumbfound, overwhelm, startle, surprise.
astute *adj* acute, cunning, discerning, intelligent, penetrating, perspicacious, quick, sharp, shrewd.
athletic *adj* brawny, muscular, powerful, robust, sinewy, strong, sturdy.
atonement *n* amends, expiation, propitiation, reparation.
atrocity *n* depravity, enormity, ferocity, savagery, villainy.
attach *vb* affix, annex, connect, fasten, join, hitch, tie; captivate, endear, win; (legal) distress, distrain, seize.
attack *vb* assail, assault, invade, set upon, storm, tackle; censure, criticise, impugn; * *n* aggression, assault, charge, offensive, onslaught, raid.
attain *vb* accomplish, achieve, acquire, secure; arrive at, come to, reach.
attempt *vb* endeavour, seek, strive, try; assault, attack; * *n*

attend vb accompany, escort, guard, protect, watch; minister to, serve, wait on; hear, harken, listen; serve, wait.

attention n care, circumspection, heed, observation, regard, watch; application, study; civility, courtesy, deference, politeness, regard, respect; courtship, devotion, suit.

attentive adj careful, civil, considerate, courteous, heedful, mindful, observant, watchful.

attire vb accoutre, apparel, array, clothe, dress, robe; * n clothes, clothing, costume, dress, garb, gear, habiliment, outfit, trapping, vestment, wardrobe.

attitude n pose, position, posture; aspect, conjuncture, condition, phase, standing, state.

attract vb draw, pull; allure, captivate, charm, decoy, enamour, entice, engage, fascinate, invite, win.

attribute vb ascribe, assign, impute; * n characteristic, peculiarity, property, quality.

audacity n boldness, courage, daring, fearlessness, intrepidity; effrontery, impudence, presumption.

austere adj ascetic, formal, hard, relentless, rigid, rigorous, severe, stern, stiff, strict, uncompromising, unrelenting.

authentic adj genuine, real, true, unadulterated, uncorrupted, veritable; accurate, reliable, trustworthy.

authority n dominion, empire, government, jurisdiction, power, sovereignty; ascendency, control, rule, supremacy, sway; permit, sanction, warranty; connoisseur, expert, master witness.

authorise vb empower, enable, entitle; allow, approve, confirm, permit, ratify, sanction.

auxiliary adj aiding, ancillary, assisting, subsidiary; * n ally, assistant, confederate, help.

available adj accessible, applicable, profitable, useful.

avenge vb punish, retaliate, revenge.

averse adj disinclined, indisposed, opposed, unwilling.

aversion n antipathy, dislike, reluctance, repugnance.

avid adj eager, greedy, voracious.

avoid vb dodge, elude, escape, eschew, shun; refrain from.

awaken vb arouse, excite, incite, kindle, provoke, stimulate; begin; be excited.

award vb adjudge, allot, assign, grant; * n adjudication, allotment, assignment, decree, determination, gift, judgment.

aware adj acquainted, apprised, conscious, conversant, informed, knowing, sensible.

away adv absent; * adj at a distance; elsewhere.

awe vb cow, daunt, intimidate; * n dread, fear, reverence.

awful adj august, awesome, grand, inspired, portentous, tremendous; alarming, dire, dreadful, frightful.

awkward adj bungling, clumsy, inept, maladroit; lumbering, ungainly, unmanageable; boorish; inconvenient, unsuitable.

B

baby vb coddle, cosset, indulge, mollycoddle, pamper, spoil; * adj babyish, childish, infantile, puerile; diminutive, miniature, pocket-sized, small-scale; * n babe, child, infant, suckling, nurseling; chicken, coward, milksop, namby-pamby, weakling; miniature; innocent.

back vb abet, aid, favour, second, support, sustain; go back, retreat, withdraw; * adj hindmost; * adv in return; in consideration; ago, gone, since; aside, away, behind, by; abaft, astern, backwards, hindwards, rearwards; * n end, hind part, posterior, rear.

backward adj disinclined, hesitating, indisposed, loath, reluctant, unwilling; dull, slow, sluggish, stolid, stupid; * adv behind, rearward.

bad adj baleful, baneful, detrimental, evil, harmful, hurtful, injurious, noxious, pernicious, unwholesome, vicious; abandoned, corrupt, depraved, immoral, sinful, unprincipled, wicked; unhappy; miserable; discouraging, distressing, sad; mean, shabby, scurvy, vile, wretched; defective, inferior, imperfect, incompetent, poor, hard, heavy, serious, severe.

badge n brand, emblem, mark, sign, symbol, token.

badger vb annoy, bait, bother, hector, harry, nag, pester, persecute, tease, torment, trouble, worry.

baffle vb balk, block, check, circumvent, foil, frustrate, thwart; bewilder, confound, disconcert, perplex.

bait vb harry, tease, worry; * n allurement, decoy, enticement, lure, temptation.

balance vb equilibrate, pose, (nautical) trim; compare, weigh; compensate, counteract; adjust, equalise, square; * n equilibrium; excess, remainder, residue, surplus.

bald adj bare, naked, uncovered; dull, inelegant, meagre, prosaic, tame, unadorned.

ban vb interdict, outlaw; anathematise, curse, execrate; * n edict, proclamation; anathema, curse, denunciation, execration; interdiction, penalty, prohibition.

band vb belt, bind, cinch, encircle, gird, girdle; ally, associate, combine, connect, join, league; bar, streak, stripe, striate, vein; * n crew, gang, horde, troop; ensemble, group, orchestra; ligament, ligature, tie; bond, chain, cord; bandage, belt, binding, cincture, girth, tourniquet.

bandit n brigand, freebooter, gangster, outlaw, robber.

bang vb beat, knock, maul, pummel, pound, strike, thrash, thump; slam; resound, ring; * n clang, clangour; blow, knock, lick, thump, whack.

bank vb incline, slope, tilt; deposit, keep, save; rely; * n embankment, escarpment, knoll, mound; border, bound, brink, margin, rim, strand; course, row, tier; depository, fund, reserve, savings.

banner n colours, ensign, flag, pennon, standard, streamer.

bar vb exclude, obstruct, prevent, prohibit, restrain, stop; * n pole, rail, rod; barricade, obstacle, stop; bank, sandbar, shallow, shoal, spit; (legal) barristers, counsel, court, tribunal.

barbaric adj barbarous, rude, savage, uncivilised, untamed; coarse, gaudy, outlandish, uncouth, untamed, wild.

bare vb denude, depilate, divest, strip, unsheathe; disclose, open, reveal, show; * adj denuded, exposed, naked, nude, stripped, unclothed, uncovered, undressed, unsheltered; alone, simple; bald, plain, unadorned, unfurnished; empty, destitute, meagre, minimal, poor.

bargain vb agree, bid, contract, covenant, dicker, horse-trade, make terms, offer, negotiate, trade (off), undercut; auction, convey, sell, transfer; * n agreement, compact, contract, stipulation, terms, treaty; proceeds, prize, reward, trophy.

barren *adj* childless, infecund, sterile; (botany) acarpous; bare, infertile, unproductive; ineffectual, unfruitful.
barricade *vb* block up, fortify, protect, obstruct; * *n* barrier, obstruction, palisade.
barrier *n* bar, hindrance, impediment, obstacle, obstruction.
barter *vb* bargain, exchange, trade, traffic.
base *vb* establish, found, ground; * *n* foundation, substructure, underpinning; pedestal, plinth, stand; centre, headquarters; starting point; bottom, foot, foundation, ground; * *adj* cheap, inferior; counterfeit, false, spurious; shameful, worthless.
bashful *adj* diffident, shy, timid.
basis *n* base, bottom, foundation, fundament, ground.
batch *vb* assemble, bunch, bundle, collect, gather, group; * *n* amount, lot, quantity.
bathe *vb* immerse, lave, wash; cover, drench, flood, suffuse; * *n* bath, shower, swim.
batter *vb* beat, pelt; break, bruise, demolish, destroy, shatter, shiver, smash; abrade, deface, disfigure, mar; * *n* dough, paste; (sport) batsman, striker.
battle *vb* contend, contest, engage, fight, strive, struggle; * *n* action, brush, combat, conflict, engagement, fight, fray, skirmish.
bawl *vb* clamour, cry, howl, roar, shout, squall, yell.
beam *vb* beacon, gleam, glisten, shine; * *n* gleam, ray, streak; baulk, girder, joist, scantling, stud, timber.
bear *vb* support, sustain, uphold; carry, convey, transport; abide, brook, endure, stand, suffer, tolerate; carry on, keep up, maintain; produce; * *n* crosspatch, grumbler, moaner; (finance) speculator.
bearing *n* air, behaviour, demeanour, deportment, conduct, carriage, mien, port; aim, connection, course, dependency, direction, relation; endurance, patience, suffering; bringing forth, producing; (engineering) bed, receptacle, socket.
beastly *adj* brutish, ignoble, low, sensual, vile.
beat *vb* bang, baste, batter, belabour, buffet, cane, cudgel, drub, hammer, hit, knock, maul, pummel, pound, pulverise; bruise, punch, strike, thrash, thump, whack, whip; conquer, defeat, overcome, rout, subdue, vanquish; pulsate, throb; * *adj* baffled, confounded, mystified, nonplussed, perplexed, puzzled, stumped; exhausted, tired out, worn out; defeated; * *n* blow, stroke; beating, pulsation, throb; metre, rhythm; circuit, course, round.
beautiful *adj* comely, fair, fine, handsome, lovely.
beautify *vb* adorn, array, bedeck, deck, decorate, embellish, garnish, grace, ornament.
beauty *n* elegance, grace, symmetry; attractiveness, comeliness, fairness, loveliness.
become *vb* change to, get, go, wax; adorn, befit, grace, set off, suit.
becoming *adj* appropriate, congruous, decent, decorous, fit, proper, right, suitable; graceful, neat, pretty.
bed *vb* embed, establish, imbed, implant, inset, plant; house, lodge; * *n* berth, bunk, cot, couch; channel, hollow; base, foundation, receptacle, support, underlay; accumulation, layer, seam, stratum, vein.
befool *vb* bamboozle, beguile, cheat, circumvent, delude, deceive, dupe, fool, hoax, infatuate, trick.
befriend *vb* aid, benefit, countenance, encourage, favour, help, patronise.

beg *vb* adjure, ask, beseech, conjure, crave, entreat, implore, importune, pray, supplicate.

begin *vb* arise, commence, enter, open; inaugurate, originate, start.

beginning *n* commencement, dawn, emergence, inception, start, rise; origin, source.

behaviour *n* air, bearing, comportment, conduct, demeanour, manner, manners, mien, port.

behind *prep* abaft, after, following; * *adv* abaft, aft, astern, rearward; * *adj* arrested, backward, checked, retarded; after, behind; * *n* rear, tail; back, back side, reverse; bottom, buttocks, posterior, rump.

behold *vb* consider, contemplate, eye, observe, regard, see, view.

being *n* actuality, existence, reality, subsistence; core, essence, heart.

belief *n* assurance, confidence, conviction, trust; acceptance, assent, credence, credit; creed, dogma, faith, tenet.

bellow *vb* bawl, clamour, cry, howl, vociferate, yell.

bend *vb* bow, crook, curve, deflect; direct, incline, turn; bend, dispose, influence, persuade, subdue; (marine) fasten, make fast; crook, deflect, deviate, diverge, swerve; bow; condescend, deign, stoop; * *n* angle, arcuation, crook, curvature, curve, elbow.

beneath *prep* below, under, underneath; unbecoming; * *adv* below, underneath.

beneficial *adj* advantageous, favourable, profitable, salutary, serviceable, useful, wholesome.

benefit *vb* befriend, help, serve; advantage, profit; * *n* favour, good turn, kindness, service; account, advantage, behalf, gain, good, profit, utility.

benevolent *adj* altruistic, benign, charitable, generous, kind, kind-hearted, liberal, obliging, philanthropic.

benign *adj* amiable, amicable, beneficent, benevolent, friendly, gentle, good, gracious, humane, kindly, obliging.

bent *adj* angled, angular, bowed, crooked, curved, deflected, embowed, flexed, twisted; inclined, prone, minded; * *n* bias, inclination, leaning, partiality, predilection, proclivity, propensity.

beside, besides *adv* additionally, also, further, furthermore, in addition, more, moreover, too, yet.

besiege *vb* beset, blockade, encircle, encompass, surround.

best *vb* better, exceed, excel, predominate, rival, surpass; beat, defeat; * *adj* chief, first, foremost, highest, leading, utmost; * *adv* excellently; extremely, greatly; * *n* choice, cream, flower, pick.

bet *vb* gamble, hazard, lay, pledge, stake, wager; * *n* gamble, hazard, stake, wager.

betray *vb* be false to, break, violate; blab, discover, divulge, expose, reveal, show, tell; betoken, display, expose, imply, indicate, manifest, reveal; beguile, delude, lure, mislead; ruin, seduce.

better *vb* advance, amend, correct, exceed, improve, promote, rectify, reform; * *adj* bigger, fitter, greater, larger, preferable; * *n* advantage, superiority, upper hand, victory; improvement.

beware *vb* avoid, heed, look out, mind.

bewilder *vb* confound, confuse, daze, distract, embarrass, muddle, mystify, nonplus, perplex, puzzle.

bewitch *vb* captivate, charm, enchant, enrapture, fascinate, spellbind.

beyond *prep* above, before, farther, over, past, remote.

bias *vb* bend, dispose, incline,

influence, prejudice; * n bent, inclination, leaning, penchant, predilection, proclivity, propensity, slant, tendency.
bicker vb dispute, jangle, quarrel, spar, spat, squabble, wrangle; play.
bid vb charge, command, direct, enjoin, order, require, summon; ask, call, invite, request; offer, proffer, tender; * n bidding, offer, proposal.
big adj bumper, bulking, bulky, great, huge, large, massive; important, imposing; inflated, swollen; fecund, productive, teeming.
bigoted adj dogmatic, intolerant, obstinate, narrow-minded, prejudiced.
bill vb charge, invoice; advertise, boost, promote, publicise; programme; * n account, reckoning; advertisement, banner, hoarding, placard, poster; playbill, programme, schedule; bill of exchange, money; account, reckoning.
billow vb surge, wave; heave, roll, surge, swell; * n roller, surge, swell, wave.
bind vb confine, enchain, fetter, restrict; bandage, tie up, wrap; fasten, lash, pinion, secure, tie, truss; hold, oblige, obligate, pledge; contract, shrink.
birth n ancestry, blood, descent, lineage, race; being, creation, offspring, production, progeny.
bit n atom, crumb, fragment, morsel, mouthful, piece, scrap; grain, jot, mite, tittle, whit; minute, moment, second.
bite vb champ, chew, gnaw; burn, make smart, sting; catch, clutch, grasp, grip; bamboozle, cheat, cozen, deceive, defraud, gull, mislead, outwit, overreach, trick; * n grasp, hold; punch, relish, spice, pungency, tang, zest; lick, sip, taste; crick, nip, pain, pang, sting.
bitter adj acrid; dire, merciless, relentless, ruthless; harsh, stern; calamitous, distressing, galling, grievous, poignant, sore, sorrowful.
black adj dark, ebony, inky, jet, sable, swarthy; dingy, dusky, murky, pitchy; calamitous, dark, depressing, disastrous, dismal, forbidding, gloomy, melancholy, mournful, sombre.
blacken vb darken; deface, soil, sully; asperse, calumniate, defame, revile, slander, traduce.
blame vb accuse, censure, condemn, disapprove, reflect upon, reprehend, reproach, reprove; * n condemnation, disapproval, dispraise, reprehension, reproach, reproof; defect, fault, guilt, misdeed, sin, wrong.
bland adj balmy, gentle, mild, soft; affable, amiable, kindly, mild, suave.
blank adj bare, empty, vacuous, void; amazed, confounded, confused, dumbfounded; absolute, complete, entire, mere, perfect, pure, simple, unabated, unadulterated, unmixed, utter, perfect.
blare vb blazon, blow, peal, trumpet; * n blast, clang, peal.
blasphemy n impiousness, sacrilege; profanity, swearing.
blast vb annihilate, blight, destroy, kill, ruin, wither; burst, kill; * n blow, gust, squall; clang, peal; burst, discharge, explosion.
blaze vb blazon, proclaim, publish; burn, flame, glow; * n flame, flare, flash, glow, light.
bleak adj bare, exposed; biting, chill, cold, piercing, raw; cheerless, desolate, dreary.
blemish vb blur, injure, mar, spot, stain, tarnish; asperse, calumniate, malign, revile, slander, vilify; * n blot, blur, defect, disfigurement, fault, flaw, imperfection, soil, spot, stain, tarnish; dishonour, reproach, stain, taint.
blend vb amalgamate, coalesce, combine, commingle, fuse,

mingle, mix, unite; * n amalgamation, combination, fusion, mixture, union.

bless vb beatify, delight, gladden; adore, exalt, extol, glorify, praise.

blind vb darken, deprive of sight; blindfold, hoodwink; * adj eyeless, sightless, unseeing; ignorant, injudicious, purblind, unenlightened; concealed, confused, dark, dim, hidden, intricate, labyrinthine, obscure, private, remote; headlong, thoughtless; blank, closed, shut; * n cover, screen, shade, shutter; blinker; concealment, feint, pretext, ruse, stratagem, subterfuge.

blink vb bat, nictate, wink; flicker, flutter, gleam, glitter, intermit, twinkle; avoid, disregard, evade, ignore, overlook, pass over; * n glance, glimpse, sight, view, wink, gleam, glimmer, twinkle.

bliss n beatification, blessedness, ecstasy, felicity, happiness, heaven, joy, transport.

block vb arrest, bar, blockade, check, choke, hinder, impede, jam, obstruct, stop; form, mould, shape; brace; * n lump; blockhead, dunce, fool; pulley, tackle; execution, scaffold; jam, obstruction, stoppage.

blood n children, descendants, offspring, posterity, progeny; family, house, kin, kindred, relations; consanguinity, kinship, lineage; courage, disposition, feelings, passion, temper.

bloom vb blossom, flower; thrive, prosper; * n blossom, blossoming, efflorescence, florescence; delicacy; flush, freshness, heyday, prime; flush, glow, rose.

blot vb cancel, efface, erase, expunge, obliterate, rub out; deface, obscure, spot, stain, sully; disgrace, tarnish; * n blur, erasure; blemish, blur, spot, stain.

blow n bang, beat, buffet, dab, impact, knock, pat, punch, rap, slam, stroke, wallop, buffet, impact; calamity, disaster, misfortune; blast, gust, squall, storm, wind; * vb breathe, gasp, pant, puff; flow, move, stream.

blue adj azure, cerulean, cobalt, indigo, sapphire, ultramarine; livid; dejected, depressed, dispirited, downcast, glum, melancholic, melancholy, sad.

bluff adj abrupt, blustering, coarse, frank, good-natured, open; abrupt, precipitous, sheer, steep; * n cliff, headland; deceit, deception, feint, fraud, lie; * vb deceive, defraud, lie, mislead.

blunder vb err, flounder, mistake; stumble; * n error, fault, mistake.

blunt adj dull, edgeless, obtuse, pointless, unsharpened; insensible, thick-witted; abrupt, bluff, downright, outspoken, unceremonious; * vb deaden, dull, numb.

blur vb darken, dim, obscure; blemish, blot, spot, stain, sully; * n blemish, blot, soil, spot, stain; disgrace, smear.

blush vb colour, flush, glow, redden; * n bloom, flush, glow, reddening.

boast vb bluster, brag, crack, flourish, crow, vaunt; * n boasting, bombast, brag, bravado, bombast, swaggering.

bodily adj carnal, corporeal, physical; * adv altogether, entirely, wholly.

body n carcass, corpse, remains; stem, torso, trunk; bulk, corpus; being, mortal creature, person; assemblage, band, company, corporation, corps, coterie, force, society, troop; consistency, substance.

boil vb agitate, bubble, foam, froth, rage, simmer; * n ebullience.

boisterous adj roaring, stormy; loud, noisy, obstreperous,

BRAVE

tumultuous.
bold *adj* adventurous, audacious, courageous; brave, daring, dauntless, doughty, gallant, hardy, heroic, intrepid, manful, manly, spirited, stouthearted, undaunted, valiant; assured, self-reliant; assuming, forward, impertinent, pushing, rude, saucy; conspicuous, projecting, striking; abrupt, prominent, steep.
bolt *vb* abscond, dash, flee, fly; * *n* arrow, dart, missile, shaft; thunderbolt
bond *vb* bind, connect, fuse, glue, join; * *adj* captive, enslaved, subjugated; * *n* band, cord, fastening, ligament, ligature, link; captivity, constraint, fetters, prison, shackle; attachment, attraction, connection, link, tie, union; obligation, pledge, promise.
bonus *n* gift, premium, reward.
book *vb* bespeak, engage, reserve; programme; list, log, record, register; * *n* booklet, brochure, handbook, manual, monograph, pamphlet, tract, volume, work.
booty *n* loot, pillage, plunder.
border *vb* bound, edge, fringe, line, march, rim, skirt; abut, adjoin, conjoin, connect, neighbour; * *n* brim, brink, edge, fringe, margin, rim, verge; boundary, confine, frontier, limit, outskirts.
bore *vb* annoy, fatigue, tire, trouble, weary, worry; drill, perforate, pierce, sink, tunnel; * *n* bother, pest, worry; calibre, hole, tunnel.
borrow *vb* take and return, use temporarily; appropriate; dissemble, simulate.
boss *vb* command, direct, employ, run; * *n* employer, foreman, master, overseer.
bother *vb* annoy, disturb, molest, pester, plague, tease, vex, worry; * *n* annoyance, plague, vexation.
bottom *vb* build, establish, found; * *adj* base, basic, ground, lowermost, lowest, undermost; * *n* base, basis, foot, foundation, groundwork; meadow, valley; fundament, seat; grounds, lees, sediment.
bounce *vb* bound, jump, leap, rebound, spring; * *n* knock; bound, jump, leap, spring.
bound *adj* assured, certain, decided, determined, resolute; confined, restricted; pledged, promised; beholden, obliged; * *vb* border, circumscribe, confine, limit, restrict, terminate; jump, leap, lope, spring; * *n* confine, edge, limit, march, margin, term, verge; bounce, jump, leap, vault.
boundary *n* border, circuit, circumference, limit, march, periphery, term.
boundless *adj* endless, infinite, limitless, unbounded, unconfined, unlimited, vast.
bow *n* (marine) prow, stern; bend, bulge, convex, curve, flexion; bob, curtsy, genuflection, greeting, obeisance; coming out, debut, introduction; * *vb* arc, bend, buckle, crook, curve, droop, yield; crush, depress, subdue; curtsy, genuflect, submit.
box *vb* fight, hit, spar; barrel, crate, pack; * *n* blow, buffet, spar; case, chest, container, crate, trunk.
boy *n* lad, stripling, youth.
brace *vb* make tight, tighten; buttress, fortify, reinforce, strengthen, support, truss; * *n* pair; clamp, girder, prop, shore, stay, support, tie, truss.
branch *vb* diverge, fork, ramify, spread; * *n* bough, limb, shoot, sprig, twig; arm, fork, spur; department, part, portion, section, subdivision.
brand *vb* denounce, stigmatise; mark; * *n* firebrand, torch; lightning flash; mark, stamp; blot, reproach, stain, stigma.
brave *vb* dare, defy; * *adj* bold, courageous, fearless, intrepid.

bravery n courage, daring, fearlessness, gallantry.

brawl vb bicker, dispute, jangle, quarrel, squabble; * n broil, dispute, feud, fray, jangle, quarrel, row, squabble, uproar.

brawny adj athletic, lusty, muscular, powerful, robust, stalwart, strong, sturdy.

breach n break, chasm, crack, disruption, flaw, fracture, opening, rent, rupture; alienation, difference, disagreement, split.

break vb crack, disrupt, fracture, part, rend, sever; batter, burst, crush, shatter, splinter; cashier, degrade, discard, dismiss; disobey, infringe, transgress, violate; intermit, stop; open, unfold; * n breach, chasm, gap, rip, rupture; break-up, crash, debacle.

breath n exhaling, inhaling, pant, sigh, respiration; animation, existence, life; respite, rest; breathing space, instant.

breathe vb live, exist; emit, exhale, give out; express, indicate, manifest, show.

breed vb bear, beget, engender, produce; bring up, nourish, nurture, raise, rear; discipline, educate, instruct, nurture, rear, teach; generate, originate; * n extraction, family, lineage, pedigree, race, strain.

brevity n briefness, conciseness, curtness, pithiness, shortness, terseness.

bribe vb buy, corrupt, influence, pay off, suborn; * n allurement, corruption, enticement, pay off, subornation.

bridle vb curb, control, govern, restrain, shy away; * n check, control, curb.

brief vb give directions, direct, instruct; summarise; delineate, describe, draft, outline, sketch; (law) retain; * adj concise, curt, laconic, pithy, short, succinct, terse; short, temporary, transient; * n breviary, briefing, epitome, summary, syllabus; (law) precept, writ.

bright adj blazing, brilliant, dazzling, gleaming, light, luminous, radiant, shining, sparkling, sunny; clear, cloudless, lambent, lucid; famous, glorious, illustrious; acute, ingenious, intelligent, keen; cheering, encouraging, exhilarating, favourable, inspiring, propitious; cheerful, genial, happy, lively, merry, pleasant, smiling, vivacious.

brilliant adj beaming, bright, effulgent, gleaming, glittering, lustrous, radiant, resplendent, sparkling, splendid; celebrated, distinguished, famous, glorious, renowned; dazzling, decided, signal, striking.

brim n border, brink, edge, rim, margin, verge; bank, border, margin, shore.

bring vb bear, convey, fetch; accompany, attend, conduct, convoy, lead; gain, get, obtain, produce.

brisk adj active, alert, agile, lively, nimble, quick, smart, spirited.

broad adj ample, expansive, extensive, large, spacious, sweeping, vast, wide; liberal, tolerant; diffused, spread; coarse, indecent, indelicate, unrefined.

broken adj fractured, rent, ruptured, separated, severed, shattered, shivered, torn; exhausted, feeble, shattered, spent, wasted; defective, halting, imperfect, stumbling; contrite, humble, lowly, penitent; abrupt, precipitous, rough.

brook vb abide, bear, endure, suffer, tolerate; * n burn, beck, creek, rivulet, streamlet.

brotherly adj affectionate, amicable, friendly, fraternal, kind.

bruise vb contuse, crunch; batter, break, pound, pulverise;

batter, deface; * *n* blemish, contusion, swelling.

brush *vb* buff, clean, polish, sweep, wipe; groom, rub down; caress, flick, glance, graze, scrape, touch; * *n* broom; action, collision, contest, conflict, encounter, fight.

brutal *adj* barbaric, barbarous, brutish, cruel, ferocious, inhuman, ruthless, savage; brusque, impolite, harsh, rude, rough, truculent.

brute *n* barbarian, beast, monster, ogre, savage; animal, beast, creature; * *adj* carnal, physical; bestial, gross.

bubble *vb* boil, effervesce, foam; * *n* bead, fluid, globule; trifle; cheat, delusion, hoax.

bud *vb* burgeon, germinate, push, shoot, sprout, vegetate; * *n* burgeon, germ, shoot, sprout.

budget *vb* allocate, cost, estimate; * *n* account, estimate, funds, resources; bag, bundle, parcel, roll; assortment, batch, collection, set.

build *vb* construct, erect, establish, fabricate, fashion, rear; * *n* body, figure, form, frame, physique; construction.

bulk *n* dimension, mass, size; amplitude, bulkiness, massiveness; majority, mass.

bully *vb* browbeat, bulldoze, domineer, hector, overbear; * *n* blusterer, browbeater, hector, swaggerer, tyrant.

bump *vb* collide, knock, strike, thump; * *n* blow, jar, jolt, shock, thump; protuberance, swelling.

bunch *vb* assemble, collect, crowd, group, herd, pack; * *n* bulge, bundle, hump, knob, lump, protuberance; hand; assortment, batch, collection, group, lot, parcel, set; knot.

bundle *vb* bale, pack, package, parcel, wrap; * *n* bale, batch, bunch, collection, pack, package, packet, parcel, roll.

burden *vb* encumber, grieve, load, oppress, overload, saddle, surcharge, try; * *n* capacity, cargo, lading, load, tonnage, weight; affliction, charge, encumbrance, impediment, grievance, sorrow, trial, trouble; point, substance, tenor.

burn *n* beck, brook, gill, rill, rivulet, runnel, runlet, stream; scald, scorch, singe; sunburn; * *vb* blaze, conflagrate, fire, ignite, inflame, kindle, light; cremate, incinerate; scald, scorch, singe; boil, cook, roast, seethe, simmer, stew, swelter, toast; bronze, sunburn, tan; bake, desiccate, dry, parch, sear, shrivel; glow, incandesce, tingle, warm.

burst *vb* break open, be rent, explode, shatter, split open; * *adj* broken, punctured, ruptured, shattered, split; * *n* break, breakage, breach, fracture, rupture; blast, blowup, discharge, detonation, explosion; spurt; blaze, flare; cloudburst, downpour; bang, crack, crash, sound; salvo, spray, volley; outburst, outbreak; blaze, eruption.

bury *vb* entomb, inhume, conceal, hide, secrete.

business *n* calling, employment, occupation, profession, vocation; commerce, dealing, trade; affair, concern, matter, transaction, undertaking; duty, office, task, work.

bustle *vb* fuss, hurry, scurry; * *n* ado, commotion, flurry, fuss, hurry, hustle, stir, tumult.

busy *vb* devote, employ, engage, occupy, spend, work; * *adj* employed, engaged, occupied; active, diligent, engrossed, industrious, working; agile, brisk, nimble, spry; meddling, officious.

but *conj* except, excepting, further, still, unless, yet; * *adv* even, notwithstanding, still, yet.

butchery *n* carnage, massacre,

murder, slaughter.
butt *vb* bunt, push, shove, shunt, strike; impose, interfere, intrude, invade, obtrude; abut, adjoin, connect, neighbour; * *n* end, remainder, stump; buttocks, rump; buck, push, shove, shunt, thrust; aim, goal, mark, object, point, target; dupe, gull, victim.

C

cackle *vb* giggle, laugh, titter; babble, chatter, gabble palaver, prattle, titter; * *n* babble, chatter, giggle, prattle, snigger.
cage *vb* confine, imprison, incarcerate; * *n* pen, pound.
calamity *n* adversity, affliction, blow, casualty, catastrophe, disaster, distress, downfall, evil, mischance, misery, misfortune, reverse, ruin, trial, visitation.
calculate *vb* cast, compute, count, estimate, rate, reckon, weigh; tell.
calibre *n* bore, capacity, diameter, gauge; ability, capacity, faculty, gifts, scope, talent.
call *vb* christen, denominate, designate, entitle, name, phrase, style; bid, invite, summons; assemble, convoke; cry, exclaim; arouse, proclaim, shout, waken; appoint, ordain; * *n* cry, outcry, voice; appeal, summons; claim, demand, summons; appointment, invitation.
callous *adj* hard, indurated; apathetic, dull, indifferent, insensible, inured, obdurate; sluggish, torpid, unfeeling.
calm *vb* allay, becalm, compose, hush, lull, smooth, still, tranquillise; appease, assuage, moderate, mollify, quiet, soften, soothe, tranquillise; * *adj* mild, peaceful, placid, quiet, reposeful, serene, smooth, still, unruffled; cool, controlled, impassive, imperturbable, sedate, self-possessed, unperturbed, unruffled, untroubled; * *n* lull; equanimity, peace, placidity, quiet, serenity, stillness, tranquillity.
camp *vb* bivouac, lodge, pitch, tent; * *n* bivouac, laager; circle, clique, faction, group, junta, party, ring, set; * *adj* affected, effeminate, mannered.
canal *n* channel, duct, pipe, tube.
cancel *vb* blot, efface, erase, obliterate; annul, nullify, quash, repeal, revoke.
candid *adj* fair, impartial, just, unbiased, unprejudiced; frank, free, guileless, honest, ingenuous, open, plain, sincere, straightforward.
candidate *n* applicant, aspirant, competitor, contender, probationer.
candour *n* fairness, impartiality, justice; frankness, honesty, ingenuousness, openness, straightforwardness, truthfulness.
canon *n* catalogue, criterion, formula, law, regulation, rule, standard, statute.
canvass *vb* agitate, debate, discuss, dispute; examine, investigate, scrutinise, sift; * *n* debate, discussion, dispute; examination, scrutiny, sifting.
cap *vb* cover, surmount; crown, finish; exceed, surpass, transcend; match, parallel; * *n* beret, head-cover; acme, chief, crown, head, peak, perfection, pitch, summit, top.
capable *adj* adapted, fitted, qualified, suited; able, clever, competent, efficient, gifted, intelligent, sagacious, skilful.
capacious *adj* ample, broad, comprehensive, extensive, generous, large, roomy, spacious.
capacity *n* amplitude, magnitude, volume; brains, calibre, discernment, faculty, genius,

gift, parts, power, talent, wit; ability, capability, calibre, cleverness, efficiency, skill; character, function, office, position, post, province, sphere.

capital *adj* cardinal, chief, essential, important, main, major, pre-eminent, principal, prominent; fatal; excellent, first-class, good, prime, splendid; * *n* chief city, seat; money, investments, stock.

capsize *vb* overturn, upset.

captain *vb* command, direct, head, lead, manage, officer, preside; * *n* chief, commander, leader, master, soldier.

captivate *vb* allure, attract, bewitch, catch, charm, enamour, enchant, fascinate, gain, hypnotise, infatuate, win.

captivity *n* confinement, durance, duress, imprisonment; bondage, servitude, slavery, subjection, vassalage.

capture *vb* apprehend, arrest, catch, seize; * *n* apprehension, arrest, catch, imprisonment, seizure; prize.

cardinal *adj* capital, central, chief, essential, first, leading, main, pre-eminent, principal, vital.

care *n* anxiety, concern, perplexity, trouble, solicitude, worry; attention, carefulness, circumspection, regard, vigilance, wariness; charge, custody, keep, superintendence; burden, charge, concern.

careful *adj* anxious, solicitous; concerned, troubled; attentive, heedful, mindful, regardful; canny, cautious, circumspect, discreet, vigilant, watchful.

careless *adj* carefree, nonchalant, unapprehensive, unperplexed, unsolicitous, untroubled; heedless, incautious negligent, regardless, thoughtless, unobservant, unconsidered, unthinking.

caress *vb* coddle, cuddle, cosset, embrace, fondle, kiss, pet; * *n* cuddle, embrace, hug, kiss.

caricature *vb* burlesque, parody, take off, travesty; * *n* burlesque, farce, parody, take-off, travesty.

carriage *n* conveyance, vehicle; air, bearing, behaviour, conduct, demeanour, front, mien, port.

carry *vb* bear, convey, transfer, transmit, transport; impel, urge; compass, effect, gain, secure; bear up, support; involve, imply, import, signify.

carve *vb* chisel, cut, engrave, grave, hew, indent, incise, sculpture; fashion, form, shape.

case *vb* cover, encase, enclose, envelop wrap; box; * *n* capsule, sheathe; box, container, holder, receptacle; condition, plight, predicament, state; example, instance; action, argument, cause, lawsuit, suit, trial.

cast *vb* fling, hurl, pitch, send, shy, sling, throw, toss; drive, impel, thrust; lay aside, put off, shed; compute; diffuse, impart, throw; * *n* fling, throw, toss; tinge, tint; air, character, look, manner, mien, style, turn; form, mould.

caste *n* class, grade, lineage, order, race, rank, status.

castigate *vb* beat, chastise, flog, lambaste, lash, thrash, whip; chaste, correct, punish; criticise, upbraid.

castle *n* citadel, fortress, stronghold.

casual *adj* accidental, fortuitous, incidental, irregular, random, uncertain, unforeseen, unpremeditated.

casualty *n* chance, contingency, fortuity, mishap; accident, disaster, misfortune.

catastrophe *n* conclusion, consummation, end, finale, issue, termination, upshot; adversity, blow, cataclysm, debacle, disaster mischance, mishap, trial, trouble.

catch *vb* clutch, grasp, gripe, seize, snatch; apprehend,

categorical adj absolute, downright, emphatic, explicit, positive, unconditional, unqualified, unreserved.

category n class, division, head, heading, list, order, rank.

cater vb feed, furnish, provide, purvey.

cause vb breed, create, originate, produce; effect, effectuate, produce; * n agent, creator, mainspring, origin, producer, source, spring; account, consideration, ground, incentive, motive, reason; aim, end, object, purpose; action, case, suit.

caustic adj acrid, cathartic, consuming, corroding, corrosive, eating, mordant, virulent; biting, bitter, burning, cutting, sarcastic, satirical, scalding, severe, stinging.

caution vb admonish, forewarn, warn; * n care, carefulness, circumspection, forethought, heed, heedfulness, providence, wariness, vigilance; advice, injunction, warning.

cautious adj careful, circumspect, discreet, heedful, vigilant, wary, watchful.

cease vb desist, pause, refrain, stay, stop; fail; discontinue, end, terminate.

celebrate vb applaud, commend, emblazon, extol, glorify, laud, magnify, praise; commemorate, honour, keep, observe.

celebrated adj distinguished, eminent, famed, famous, glorious, illustrious, notable.

celebrity n credit, distinction, eminence, fame, glory, honour, renown, reputation, repute; lion, star.

cement vb attach, bind, join; combine, connect, solder, unite, weld; stick; * n glue, paste, solder.

cemetery n burial-ground, burying-ground, churchyard, god's acre, graveyard.

censor vb blue-pencil, cut, edit, expurgate; classify, quash, squash, suppress; * n caviller, censurer, fault finder.

censure vb abuse, blame, chide, condemn, rebuke, reprimand, reprobate, reprove, scold; * n blame, condemnation, criticism, disapprobation, disapproval, rebuke, remonstrance, reprehension, reproach, reproof.

ceremonious adj civil, lofty, stately; formal; exact, formal, punctilious, precise, stiff.

ceremony n ceremonial, form, formality, observance, solemnity, rite; parade, pomp, show.

certain adj absolute, incontestable, incontrovertible, indisputable, indubitable, inevitable, undeniable, unquestionable, unquestioned; convinced, sure, undoubting; infallible, never-failing; existing, real; constant, fixed, settled.

certify vb assure, attest, testify, vouch; ascertain, determine, verify.

chafe vb rub; anger, annoy, chagrin, enrage, exasperate, fret, gall, incense, irritate, offend, provoke, ruffle, vex; fume, rage.

chaff vb banter, deride, mock, rally, ridicule; * n husks; refuse, trash, waste.

chain vb bind, confine, fetter, manacle, restrain, shackle; enslave; * n bond, fetter, manacle, shackle.

challenge vb brave, call out, dare, defy, dispute; require; * n defiance, interrogation, question; objection.

champion vb advocate, defend,

uphold; * n defender, promoter, protector; hero, victor, warrior, winner.
chance vb befall, betide, happen, occur; * adj accidental, adventitious, casual, incidental, unexpected, unforeseen; * n accident, cast, fortune, luck; contingency, possibility; occasion, opening, opportunity; contingency, fortuity, gamble, uncertainty; hazard, jeopardy, peril, risk.
change vb alter, fluctuate, modify, vary; displace, replace, substitute; barter, commute, exchange; * n mutation, transition, turning, variance, variation; innovation, novelty, variety, vicissitude.
changeable adj alterable, inconstant, modifiable, uncertain, unsettled, unstable, unsteadfast, variable, variant; capricious, fickle, fitful, giddy, mercurial, vacillating, volatile.
channel vb chamfer, cut, flute, groove; * n canal, duct, passage; aqueduct, canal, chute, drain, flume, furrow; groove, furrow, gutter.
chant vb carol, sing, warble; intone, recite; song.
chaos n anarchy, bedlam, confusion, disorder.
character n emblem, figure, hieroglyph, ideograph, letter, mark, sign, symbol; cast, disposition, nature; individual, original, person, personage; reputation; nature, traits; eccentric, trait.
characteristic adj distinctive, peculiar, special, specific, typical; * n attribute, feature, idiosyncrasy, lineament, peculiarity, quality, trait.
charge vb burden, encumber, freight, lade, load; entrust; ascribe, lay; accuse, arraign, blame, criminate, impeach, indict, involve; bid, command, exhort, enjoin, order, require, tax; assault, attack; * n burden, cargo, freight, lading; care, custody, keeping, ward; commission, duty, trust; responsibility; direction, injunction, mandate, order, precept; instruction; cost, debit, expenditure, outlay; price, sum; assault, attack, onset, onslaught.
charitable adj beneficial, beneficent, benignant, generous, kind, liberal; considerate, lenient, mild.
charity n benevolence, benignity, good-nature, goodwill, kind-heartedness, kindness, beneficence, bounty, generosity, humanity, philanthropy; liberality.
charm vb allure, attract, bewitch, captivate, catch, delight, enamour, enchant, enrapture, fascinate, transport, win; * n enchantment, incantation, magic, sorcery, witchery; amulet, talisman; allurement, attractiveness, fascination.
chase vb follow, hunt, pursue, track; * n course, field-sport, hunt, hunting.
chaste adj clean, continent, innocent, modest, pure, undefiled, virtuous; chastened, pure, simple, unaffected.
chasten vb correct, discipline; purify, refine, subdued.
chastise vb castigate, correct, flog, lash, punish, whip; chasten, correct, discipline, humble, punish, subdue.
chastity n continence, innocence, modesty, purity, virtue; cleanness, purity; chasteness, purity, refinement, restraint, simplicity.
chatter vb babble, confabulate, gossip, prattle; * n babble, chat, gabble, patter, prattle.
cheap adj inexpensive; common, inferior, meretricious, poor.
cheat vb cozen, deceive, juggle, shuffle; bamboozle, beguile, cajole, circumvent, deceive, defraud, delude, dupe, ensnare, entrap, fool, gull, hoax,

hoodwink, inveigle, mislead, outwit, overreach, trick; * n artifice, beguilement, catch, chouse, deceit, deception, fraud, imposture, juggle, pitfall, snare, stratagem, swindle, trap, wile; deception, delusion, mockery, paste, sham, tinsel; beguiler, charlatan, cheater, cozener, impostor, knave, trickster, rogue, render, sharper, seizer, swindler, taker.

check vb block, bridle, control, counteract, curb, obstruct, repress, restrain; chide, rebuke, reprove; * n bar, barrier, block, brake, bridle, clog, control, curb, hindrance, impediment, interference, obstacle, obstruction, rebuff, restraint, stop, stopper.

cheer vb animate, encourage, enliven, gladden, inspirit; comfort, console, solace; applaud, clap; * n cheerfulness, gaiety, gladness, glee, jollity, joy, merriment, mirth; entertainment, provision, repast; acclamation, hurrah.

cheerful adj animated, airy, blithe, cheery, gay, glad, gleeful, happy, joyful, jolly, joyous, light-hearted, lively, merry, mirthful, sprightly, sunny; animating, cheering, cheery, encouraging, glad, gladdening, grateful, inspiriting, jocund.

cheerless adj dark, dejected, desolate, despondent, dismal, doleful, dreary, forlorn, gloomy, joyless, low-spirited, lugubrious, melancholy, rueful, sad, sombre, spiritless.

cherish vb comfort, nourish, nurse, nurture, support, sustain; treasure; entertain, indulge, harbour.

chew vb crunch, masticate; bite, champ, gnaw; meditate, ruminate.

chief adj first, foremost, headmost, leading, master, supreme, top; cardinal, especial, essential, grand, great, main, master, prime, principal, supreme; * n chieftain, commander; head, leader.

child n babe, baby, bantling, brat, chit, infant, nursling, wean; issue, offspring, progeny.

childish adj infantile, juvenile, puerile, young; foolish, frivolous, silly, weak.

childlike adj docile, dutiful, gentle, meek, obedient; confiding, ingenuous, innocent, simple, trustful.

chill vb dampen, depress, discourage, dishearten; * adj bleak, chilly, cold, frigid; * n chilliness, cold, frigidity; ague, shiver; damp, depression

chip vb flake, fragment, hew, pare; * n flake, fragment, paring, scrap.

choice adj excellent, exquisite, precious, rare, select, superior, unusual, valuable; careful, frugal, sparing; * n alternative, election, option, selection; favourite, preference.

choose vb adopt, co-opt, cull, designate, elect, pick, prefer, select.

chop vb cut, hack, hew; mince; shift, veer; * n slice; brand; chap, jaw.

christen vb baptise; call, dub, denominate, designate, name, term, title.

chronicle vb narrate, record, register; * n diary, journal; account, annals, history, narration, record.

chuckle vb crow, exult, giggle, laugh, titter; * n giggle, laughter, snigger, titter.

churlish adj brusque, cynical, harsh, rough, rude, snappish, snarling, surly, uncivil, waspish; ill-tempered, morose, sullen; close, closefisted, illiberal, mean, miserly, penurious, stingy.

circle vb compass, encircle, encompass, gird, girdle, ring; revolve, rotate, round, turn;

* *n* circlet, gyre, hoop, ring, rondure; circumference, periphery; globe, orb, sphere; compass; class, clique, company, coterie, fraternity, society; circuit, compass, field, province, region, sphere.

circuit *n* cycle, revolution, turn; bounds, compass, district, province, range, region, space, sphere, tract; boundary, compass; course, round, tour.

circuitous *adj* ambiguous, indirect, roundabout, tortuous, turning, winding.

circulate *vb* diffuse, disseminate, promulgate, propagate, spread.

circumference *n* boundary, circuit, girth, perimeter, periphery.

circumscribe *vb* bound, define, encircle, enclose, encompass, limit; confine, restrict.

circumspect *adj* attentive, careful, cautious, considerate, discreet, judicious, observant, prudent, vigilant, wary, watchful.

circumstance *n* accident, incident; condition, detail, event, fact, happening, occurrence, situation.

circumstantial *adj* detailed, particular; indirect, presumptive.

citizen *n* burgess, burgher, denizen, dweller, inhabitant, resident, subject, townsman.

civil *adj* civic, municipal, political; domestic; affable, civilised, complaisant, courteous, courtly, easy, gracious, obliging, polished, polite, refined, suave, urbane, well-mannered.

civility *n* affability, amiability, complaisance, courteousness, courtesy, politeness, urbanity.

civilise *vb* cultivate, educate, enlighten, humanise, improve, refine.

claim *vb* ask, assert, challenge, demand, exact, require; * *n* call, demand, requisition; pretension, privilege, right.

clamour *vb* shout, vociferate; * *n* din, exclamation, hullabaloo, noise, outcry, uproar.

clandestine *adj* concealed, covert, furtive, hidden, private, secret, sly, stealthy, surreptitious.

clap *vb* pat, slap, strike; slam; applaud, cheer; * *n* blow, knock, slap; bang, explosion, slam.

clarify *vb* cleanse, clear, depurate, explicate, purify, strain.

clash *vb* collide, crash, strike; clank, clatter, crash, rattle; contend, disagree, interfere; * *n* collision; clang, clangour, clashing, clatter, crash, rattle; contradiction, disagreement, interference, jar, opposition.

clasp *vb* clutch, entwine, grasp, grapple, grip, seize; embrace, enfold, hug; * *n* buckle, catch, hasp, hook; embrace, hug.

class *vb* arrange, classify, distribute, range, rank; * *n* form, grade, order, rank, status; group, seminar; breed, sort; category, collection, division, group.

classical *adj* first-rate, master, masterly, model, standard; Greek, Latin, Roman; attic, chaste, elegant, polished, pure.

classify *vb* arrange, categorise, class, dispose, distribute, group, pigeonhole, rank, systematise.

clatter *vb* clash, rattle; babble, clack, gabble, prattle; * *n* clattering, clutter, rattling.

clean *vb* cleanse, clear, purge, purify, rinse, scour, scrub, wash, wipe; * *adj* immaculate, spotless, unsoiled, unspotted, unstained, unsullied, white; clarified, pure, purified, unmixed; delicate, dextrous, graceful, light, neat, shapely; entire, flawless, faultless, perfect, unblemished, whole; chaste, innocent, moral, pure; * *adv* altogether, completely, entirely, perfectly, wholly.

cleanse *vb* clean, clear, purge,

CLEAR

purify, rinse, scour, scrub, wash, wipe.

clear *vb* clarify, cleanse, purify; emancipate, free, liberate; absolve, acquit, discharge, exonerate, justify, vindicate; disengage, disentangle, extricate, rid; clean up, scour, sweep; balance; free, liberate; * *adj* bright, crystalline, light, limpid, pellucid, transparent; pure, unadulterated; free, open, unobstructed; cloudless, fair, serene, sunny, unclouded, undimmed; distinct, lucid, perspicuous; apparent, distinct, indisputable, manifest, obvious, unambiguous, undeniable, unequivocal, unmistakable, unquestionable; clean, guiltless, immaculate, innocent, sinless, spotless, unblemished, undefiled, unsullied; unhampered, unimpeded, unobstructed; fluty, liquid, mellifluous, musical, sonorous.

clemency *n* mildness, softness; compassion, forgivingness, gentleness, kindness, lenience, leniency, lenity, mercifulness, mercy, mildness.

clench *vb* confirm, fasten, fix, rivet, secure.

clever *adj* able, apt, astute, talented; adroit, capable, dextrous, discerning, expert, ingenious, knowing, quick, ready, skilful, talented.

climax *vb* crown, culminate, peak; * *n* consummation, crown, culmination, peak, summit, top, zenith.

clinch *vb* clasp, clench, grapple, grasp, grip; fasten, secure; confirm, fix; * *n* catch, clutch, grasp, grip; clincher, clamp, holdfast.

cling *vb* adhere, clear; clasp, embrace, entwine.

clink *vb*, *n* chink, jingle, ring, tinkle; chime.

clip *vb* cut, shear, snip; curtail, cut, dock, pare, prune, trim; * *n* cutting, shearing; blow, lick, rap, thwack, thump.

cloak *vb* conceal, cover, hide, mask, veil; * *n* mantle; blind, cover, mask, pretext, veil.

clock *vb* mark time, measure, stopwatch; * *n* horologue, timekeeper, timepiece, watch.

clog *vb* fetter, hamper, shackle; choke, obstruct; burden, embarrass, encumber, hamper, hinder, impede, load, restrain; * *n* dead-weight, fetter, shackle; check, drawback, encumbrance, hindrance, impediment, obstruction.

close *adj* closed, confined, snug, tight; hidden, private, secret; reserved, reticent, secretive; concealed, retired, secluded, withdrawn; confined, stagnant; airless, stale, stifling, stuffy, sultry; compressed, dense, form, solid, thick; adjoining, approaching, immediately, near, nearly; attached, dear, confidential, devoted; earnest, fixed, intense, intent; accurate, exact, faithful, nice, precise, strict; closefisted, curmudgeonly, mean, miserly, niggardly, parsimonious, penurious; * *n* courtyard, enclosure, grounds, yard; end, finish, termination; * *vb* occlude, seal, shut; choke, clog, obstruct, stop; cease, complete, end, finish, terminate; coalesce; cease, conclude, finish, terminate; clinch, grapple; agree.

clothe *vb* apparel, array, attire, deck, dress; cover, endow, envelop, enwrap, invest with, swathe.

clothes *n* apparel, array, attire, clothing, costume, dress, garb, garments, gear, habits, rig, vestments, vesture.

cloud *vb* becloud, obnubilate, overcast; befog, darken, dim, obscure, shade, shadow; * *n* cirrus, cumulus, fog, haze, nebulosity, scud, vapour; army, crowd, horde, host, multitude, swarm; darkness,

COLLECT

eclipse, gloom, obscuration, obscurity.
cloudy *adj* clouded, foggy, hazy, lowering, lurid, murky, overcast; confused, dark, dim, obscure; dismal, gloomy, sullen; clouded; blurred, dimmed, muddy.
clown *n* churl, clodhopper, countryman, lubber, peasant, ploughman, swain; boor, bumpkin, fellow, lout; dolt, clodpoll, dunce, dunderhead, simpleton, thickhead; buffoon, droll, farceur, fool, harlequin, jester, pantaloon, punch, scaramouch.
club *vb* combine, unite; beat, cudgel; * *n* bat, bludgeon, cosh, cudgel, shillelagh, stick; association, company, coterie, fraternity, set, society.
clump *vb* assemble, batch, bunch, cluster, group, lump; lumber, shock, stamp, stump, trudge; * *n* assemblage, bunch, cluster, collection, group, tuft.
clumsy *adj* cumbrous, ill-made, ill-shaped, lumbering, ponderous, unwieldy; bungling, elephantine, heavy-handed, inapt, maladroit, unskilled.
cluster *vb* assemble, batch, bunch, clump, collect, gather, group, throng; * *n* batch, bunch, clump, collection, gathering, group, throng.
clutch *vb* catch, clasp, clench, clinch, grab, grapple, grasp, hold, seize, snatch, squeeze; * *n* clasp, clench, clinch, grasp, grip, hold, squeeze.
clutches *npl* claws, paws, talons; hands, power.
clutter *vb* confuse, disarrange, disorder, jumble, mess, muss; clatter; * *n* bustle, clatter, clattering; confusion, disarray, disorder, jumble, liner, mess.
coagulate *vb* clot, congeal, concrete, curdle, thicken.
coalesce *vb* amalgamate, blend, cohere, combine, commix, mix, unite; concur, fraternise.
coalition *n* alliance, association, combination, compact, confederacy, confederation, conjunction, co-partnership, league, union.
coarse *adj* crude, impure, rough; broad, gross, indecent, indelicate, ribald, vulgar; bluff, boorish, brutish, churlish, clownish, impolite, loutish, rude, unpolished; crass, inelegant.
coast *vb* flow, glide, sail, skim, slide; * *n* littoral, seaboard, seaside, shore, strand.
coat *vb* cover, spread; * *n* frock, jacket; coating, cover, covering.
coax *vb* allure, beguile, cajole, decoy, entice, persuade, soothe, wheedle.
cobble *vb* botch, bungle; mend, patch, repair.
coexistent *adj* coetaneous, simultaneous, synchronous.
coil *vb* curl, twine, twirl, twist, wind; * *n* convolution, helix, knot, roll, spiral, tendril, twirl, volute, whorl; clamour, confusion, entanglements, tumult, turmoil, uproar.
coincide *vb* cohere, correspond, square, tally; acquiesce, agree, harmonise.
cold *adj* arctic, biting, bleak, boreal, chilly, cutting, frosty, gelid, glacial, icy, nipping, polar, raw, wintry; frost-bitten, shivering; cold-blooded, dead, freezing, frigid, indifferent, passionless, phlegmatic, sluggish, stony, torpid, unconcerned, unfeeling, unresponsive, unsympathetic; dead, dull, spiritless, unaffecting, uninteresting; * *n* chill, chilliness, coldness.
collapse *vb* break down, fail, fall; * *n* depression, failure, faint, prostration, subsidence.
colleague *n* ally, assistant, associate, auxiliary, coadjutor, collaborator, confederate, cooperator, helper.
collect *vb* assemble, compile, gather; accumulate, aggregate, amass.

collected *adj* calm, composed, cool, placid, self-possessed, unperturbed.

collection *n* aggregation, assemblage, cluster, crowd, gathering, group, pack; accumulation, congeries, conglomeration, heap, lot, mass, pile, store; alms, offering, offertory.

collision *n* clash, concussion, crash, impact, impingement, shock; conflict, crashing, opposition.

collusion *n* connivance, conspiracy, coven, deceit.

colossal *adj* enormous, gigantic, Herculean, huge, immense, prodigious, vast.

colour *vb* discolour, dye, paint, stain, tinge, tint; disguise; disguise, distort, garble, misrepresent; blush, colour, flush, redden, show; * *n* hue, shade, tint, tone; paint, pigment, stain; redness, ruddiness; complexion; appearance, excuse, guise, plea, pretence, semblance.

colourless *adj* achromatic, uncoloured; blanched, hueless, livid, pale, pallid; blank, dull, expressionless, inexpressive.

comatose *adj* drowsy, insensible, lethargic, sleepy, somnolent.

comb *vb* card, curry, groom, rake, untangle; rake, ransack, rummage, scour, search; * *n* card, hatchel; harrow, rake.

combat *vb* contend, contest, fight, struggle, war; battle, oppose, resist, struggle; * *n* action, affair, battle, conflict, contest, encounter, fight.

combative *adj* belligerent, contentious, pugnacious, quarrelsome.

combination *n* association, conjunction, connection, union; alliance, cartel, coalition, confederacy, league, merger, syndicate; cabal, conspiracy, faction, ring; compound, mixture.

combine *vb* cooperate, pool, unite; amalgamate, blend, incorporate, mix.

come *vb* advance, approach; arise, ensue, follow, issue, originate, proceed; befall, happen, occur.

comely *adj* becoming, decent, decorous, seemly, suitable; beautiful, fair, handsome, personable, pretty.

comfort *vb* alleviate, animate, cheer, console, encourage, gladden, inspirit, invigorate, refresh, solace, soothe, strengthen; * *n* aid, assistance, countenance, help, support, succour; consolation, solace, relief; ease, enjoyment, peace.

comfortable *adj* acceptable, agreeable, delightful, enjoyable, grateful, gratifying, pleasant, welcome; commodious, convenient, easeful, snug.

comical *adj* amusing, droll, farcical, funny, humorous, laughable, ludicrous, sportive.

coming *adj* approaching, arising, arriving, ensuing, expected, forthcoming, future, imminent, looming, nearing, prospective, ultimate; emergent, emerging; due, owed, owing; * *n* advent, approach, arrival; apparition, appearance, disclosure, emergence, materialisation, occurrence, revelation, rising.

command *vb* bid, charge, direct, enjoin, require; control, dominate, govern, lead, rule, sway; challenge, compel, demand, exact; * *n* bidding, charge, commandment, direction, injunction, mandate, order, requisition; ascendency, authority, dominion, control, power, rule, sway, supremacy.

commander *n* captain, chief, chieftain, commandment, head, leader.

commence *vb* begin, inaugurate, initiate, open, originate, start.

commend *vb* recommend, regard for; entrust, yield; applaud, approve, extol, praise.

comment *vb* animadvert,

annotate, criticise, explain, interpret, note, remark; * *n* annotation, explanation, exposition, commentary, note; animadversion, observation.

commentator *n* annotator, critic, expounder, interpreter.

commerce *n* business, exchange, dealing, merchandising, trade, traffic.

commercial *adj* mercantile, trading.

commission *vb* authorise, empower; delegate, depute; * *n* doing, perpetration; care, charge, duty, employment, errand, task, trust; fee.

commit *vb* confide, consign, delegate, entrust; consign, deposit, lay, place, put, resign; do, perform, perpetrate; imprison; implicate, pledge.

commodity *n* goods, merchandise, produce, wares.

common *adj* collective, public; general; commonplace, customary, everyday, familiar, habitual, usual; banal, hackneyed, stale, threadbare, trite; inferior, low, ordinary, plebeian, popular, vulgar.

commotion *n* agitation, ferment, perturbation; bustle, disorder, disturbance, hurly-burly, tumult, turbulence, turmoil.

communicate *vb* confer, convey, give, impart, transmit; acquaint, declare, disclose, publish, reveal, unfold; commune, correspond.

communication *n* conveyance, disclosure, giving; commence, conference, conversation, correspondence, intercourse; announcement, information, message, news.

communicative *adj* affable, chatty, conversable, open, sociable, unreserved.

community *n* people, public, society; brotherhood, college, society; identify, likeness, sameness, similarity.

compact *n* agreement, contract, covenant, convention, pact, treaty; * *vb* compress, condense, pack, press; consolidate, unite; * *adj* close, compressed, condensed, dense, firm; brief, concise, laconic, pithy, pointed, short, succinct, terse.

companion *n* accomplice, ally, comrade, confederate, consort, crony, friend, fellow, mate; participant, partner, sharer.

companionable *adj* affable, conversable, friendly, sociable.

company *n* assemblage, assembly, band, body, circle, collection, concourse, congregation, coterie, crew, crowd, gang, gathering, group, herd, set, syndicate, troop; party; company, fellowship, guests, society, visitors; association, corporation, firm, house, partnership.

compare *vb* assimilate, collate, parallel; liken, resemble.

comparison *n* collation, compare, estimate; simile.

compass *vb* embrace, encompass, enclose, encircle, environ, surround; beset, besiege, block, invest; accomplish, achieve, attain, carry, effect, obtain, perform, realise; contrive, devise, intend, meditate, plot; * *n* bound, boundary, extent, limit, range, reach, scope; circuit, round.

compassionate *adj* benignant, clement, commiserative, kind, merciful, pitying, sympathetic, tender.

compatible *adj* accordant, agreeable to, congruous, consistent, consonant, suitable.

compel *vb* constrain, force; coerce, drive, necessitate; bend, subdue, subject.

compensation *n* pay, payment, recompense, remuneration, salary; amends, atonement, indemnification, reparation, requital, satisfaction; balance, equalisation, offset.

compete *vb* challenge, contend, contest, emulate, rival,

struggle, vie.
competence *n* ability, capableness, capacity, fitness, qualification; adequacy, adequateness, sufficiency.
competent *adj* able, capable, clever, equal, endowed; adapted, adequate, fit, sufficient, suitable.
competition *n* contest, rivalry, rivals.
compile *vb* compose, prepare; arrange, collect, select.
complain *vb* bemoan, bewail, deplore, grieve, groan, grouch, growl, lament, moan, repine.
complaint *n* grievance, grumble, lamentation, murmur, wail; ail, ailment, annoyance, disease, disorder, illness, malady, sickness; accusation, charge, information
complete *vb* accomplish, achieve, conclude, consummate, effect, end, execute, finish, fulfil, perfect, perform, realise; * *adj* clean, consummate, faultless, full, perfect, perform; all, entire, integral, total, unbroken, undiminished, unimpaired, whole; achieved, completed, concluded, consummated, ended, finished.
completion *n* accomplishing, accomplishment, conclusion, consummation, effecting, ending, execution, finishing, perfecting, performance, termination.
complex *adj* compounded, mingled, mixed; complicate, complicated, intricate, involved, knotty, mazy, tangled; * *n* complication, involute, skein, tangle, tangle; integration, network, totality, whole; compulsion, fixation, obsession, preoccupation.
complicate *vb* confuse, entangle, interweave, involve.
complication *n* complexity, confusion, entanglement, intricacy; complexus, mixture.
compliment *vb* commend, congratulate, eulogise, extol,
flatter, laud, praise; * *n* admiration, commendation, encomium, eulogy, favour, flattery, honour, praise, tribute.
component *adj* composing, constituent, constituting; * *n* constituent, element, part.
compose *vb* build, compact, compound, constitute, form, make; contrive, create, frame, imagine, invent, write; adjust, arrange, settle; appease, calm, pacify, quell, quiet, soothe, still, tranquillise.
composed *adj* calm, collected, cool, imperturbable, quiet, sedate, self-possessed, tranquil, undisturbed, unruffled.
composite *adj* amalgamated, combined, complex, mixed; integrated; * *n* admixture, amalgam, combination, composition, compound, mixture, unification.
composition *n* constitution, construction, formation, framing; compound, mixture; arrangement, combination, make-up, synthesise, union; invention, piece, production, writing; arrangement, compromise.
composure *n* calmness, coolness, equanimity, placidity, quiet, self-possession, serenity, tranquillity.
compound *vb* amalgamate, blend, combine, intermingle, mingle, mix, unite; adjust, arrange, compose, settle; * *adj* complex, composite; * *n* combination, composition, mixture; farrago, jumble, medley, olio.
comprehend *vb* comprise, contain, embrace, embody, enclose, include, involve; apprehend, conceive, grasp, know, imagine, see, understand.
comprehension *n* comprising, embracing, inclusion; domain, embrace, field, limits, province, reach, scope, sphere, sweep; connotation, force;

comprehensive *adj* all-embracing, ample, broad, compendious, extensive, full, inclusive, large, wide.
compression *n* abbreviation, condensation, constriction, contraction, squeezing; brevity, pithiness, terseness.
comprise *vb* comprehend, contain, embody, embrace, encompass, include, involve.
compromise *vb* adjust, arbitrate, arrange, compose, compound, settle; imperil, prejudice; commit, engage, pledge; agree, compound; * *n* adjustment, agreement, settlement.
compulsion *n* constraint, force, forcing, pressure, urgency.
compulsory *adj* coercive, compelling; binding, enforced, imperative, necessary, obligatory.
compute *vb* calculate, count, enumerate, estimate, measure, number, rate, reckon, sum.
comrade *n* accomplice, ally, associate, chum, companion, compeer, crony, fellow, pal.
conceal *vb* bury, cover, screen, secrete; disguise, mask.
concede *vb* grant, surrender, yield; acknowledge, admit, confess, grant.
conceit *n* belief, fancy, idea, image, imagination, notion, thought; caprice, illusion, whim; estimate, estimation, impression, opinion; conceitedness, egoism, self-complacency; priggery, self-conceit, self-esteem, vanity; crochet, quip, quirk.
conceited *adj* egotistical, opinionated, opinionative, self-conceited, vain,
conceivable *adj* imaginable; comprehensible, intelligible, rational, thinkable.
conceive *vb* create, contrive, devise, form, plan, purpose; imagine; comprehend, think, understand; assume, imagine, suppose; become pregnant.
concern *vb* affect, belong to, pertain to, regard, relate to, touch; disquiet, trouble; * *n* affair, business, matter, transaction; consequence, importance, interest, weight; anxiety, care, carefulness, solicitude, worry; business, establishment, firm, house.
concession *n* acquiescence, assent, cessation, surrender, yielding; acknowledgment, allowance, boon, grant, privilege.
concise *adj* brief, compact, compendious, compressed, condensed, crisp, laconic, pithy, pointed, pregnant, short, succinct, summary, terse.
conclude *vb* close, end, finish, terminate; deduce, infer, judge; decide, determine, judge; arrange, settle; bar, hinder, restrain, stop; decide, determine.
conclusion *n* inference; decision, judgement; close, completion, end, event, finale, termination, upshot; arrangement, closing, effecting, settlement.
conclusive *adj* clinching, convincing, decisive; final, ultimate.
concur *vb* accede, acquiesce, agree, assent, coincide, consent, harmonise; conspire, cooperate, help.
condemn *vb* adjudge, ban, convict, doom, judge, penalise; disapprove, reprobate; blame, censure, damn, deprecate, disapprove, reprove, upbraid.
condense *vb* compress, thicken; abbreviate, abridge, curtail, diminish, epitomise, reduce, summarise; liquefy.
condescend *vb* bend, deign, vouchsafe; descend, stoop.
condescension *n* affability, civility, courtesy, deference, favour, graciousness.
condition *vb* postulate, specify, stipulate; prepare, qualify,

ready, train; acclimatise, adapt, adjust, familiarise, habituate, naturalise; fix, overhaul, prepare, recondition, repair, tune; * *n* case, plight, predicament, state; class, estate, grade, rank, station; arrangement, provision, proviso, stipulation; attendant, necessity, precondition, prerequisite.

conducive *adj* conducting, contributing, instrumental, promotive, subsidiary.

conduct *vb* convoy, direct, escort, lead; command, govern, lead, preside; manage, operate; direct, lead; * *n* administration, direction, guidance, management; convoy, escort, guard; actions, behaviour, career, carriage, demeanour, manners.

confer *vb* advise, consult, converse, deliberate, discourse, talk; give, grant, vouchsafe.

confess *vb* acknowledge, avow, own; admit, concede, grant; attest, manifest, prove, show; shrive.

confession *n* acknowledgement, admission, avowal.

confide *vb* commit, consign, divulge, entrust, trust.

confidence *n* belief, certitude, dependence, faith, trust; assurance, boldness, firmness, intrepidity, self-reliance.

confident *adj* assured, certain, positive, sure: bold, undaunted.

confidential *adj* intimate, private, secret; faithful, trustworthy.

confine *vb* restrain, shut in, shut up; imprison, incarcerate, impound, jail; limit, restrict; * *n* border, boundary, limit.

confinement *n* restraint; captivity, durance, immurement, imprisonment, incarceration; childbed, delivery, lying-in.

confirm *vb* assure, fix, settle; strengthen; authenticate, avouch, countersign, endorse, substantiate, verify; bind, ratify.

confirmation *n* establishment, settlement; corroboration, proof, substantiation.

confiscate *vb* appropriate, forfeit, seize.

conflict *vb* clash, combat, contend, contest, disagree, interfere, strive, struggle. * *n* battle, combat, contention, contest, encounter, struggle; antagonism, clashing, disagreement, discord, inconsistency, interference, opposition.

conform *vb* accommodate, adapt; agree, comport, correspond, harmonise, tally.

conformation *n* accordance, agreement, conformity; configuration, figure, form, shape, structure.

confound *vb* confuse; baffle, bewilder, embarrass, mystify, nonplus, pose; amaze, astonish, astound, bewilder, dumbfound, petrify, startle, stun, stupefy, surprise; annihilate, demolish, destroy, overwhelm, ruin; abash, confuse, discompose, disconcert, shame.

confront *vb* face; challenge, contrapose, encounter, oppose.

confuse *vb* blend, confound, intermingle, mingle, mix; derange, disorder, jumble, mess, muddle; darken, perplex; befuddle, bewilder, embarrass, flurry, fluster, mystify, pose; abash, confound, disconcert, mortify, shame.

confusion *n* anarchy, chaos, clutter, confusedness, disarray, disorder, jumble, muddle; agitation, commotion, ferment, stir; astonishment, bewilderment, distraction, embarrassment, fuddle, perplexity; abashment, embarrassment, shame; annihilation, demolition, ruin.

congratulate *vb* compliment, felicitate, greet, salute.

congregate *vb* assemble, collect, convene, gather, muster;

gather, swarm, throng.

congress *n* assembly, conclave, conference, convention, convocation, council, diet, parliament.

conjecture *vb* assume, guess, hypothesis, imagine, suspect; dare say, fancy, presume; * *n* assumption, hypothesis, supposition, surmise, theory.

conjure *vb* adjure, beg, crave, entreat, implore, invoke, pray; bewitch, charm, fascinate; juggle.

connect *vb* associate, conjoin, combine, couple, interlink, join, link, unite; cohere.

connection *n* association, dependence, junction, union; commerce, intercourse; affinity, relationship; kindred, kinsman, relation, relative.

conquer *vb* beat, checkmate, crush, defeat, humble, master, overpower, overthrow, prevail, quell, rout, subdue, vanquish; overcome.

conquest *n* defeat, discomfiture, mastery, overthrow, subjection, subjugation; triumph, victor.

conscientious *adj* careful, exact, fair, faithful, honourable, incorruptible, just, scrupulous, straightforward, upright.

conscious *adj* intelligent, knowing, percipient; rational, reasoning, reflecting, thinking; awake, aware, cognisant, sensible; self-admitted.

consent *vb* agree, allow, assent, concur, permit, yield; accede, acquiesce, comply; * *n* assent, permission; accord, agreement, consensus, concord, unison; compliance.

consequential *adj* consequent, following, resulting; arrogant, conceited, inflated, pompous, self-important, self-sufficient.

conservation *n* guardianship, maintenance, preservation, protection.

conservative *adj* conservatory, moderate; preservative; reactionary; * *n* die-hard, reactionary, right-winger; moderate.

conserve *vb* keep, maintain, preserve, protect, save, uphold; * *n* confection, jam, preserve, sweetmeat.

consider *vb* attend, brood, contemplate, examine, mark, mind, ponder, reflect, revolve, weigh; care for, consult, envisage, regard; cogitate, deliberate, mediate, muse, ponder, reflect, ruminate, think; account, believe, deem, hold, judge.

considerate *adj* circumspect, deliberate, discrete, judicious, provident, serious, staid, thoughtful; forbearing, patient.

consideration *n* attention, cogitation, contemplation, deliberation, heed, meditation, pondering, reflection, regard; consequence, important, moment, significant, weight; account, ground, motive, reason, sake.

consistency *n* compactness, consistence, density, thickness; agreement, conformableness, congruity, consonance.

consistent *adj* accordant, agreeing, comfortable, congruous, consonant, correspondent, harmonious.

consolation *n* alleviation, comfort, encouragement, relieve, solace.

console *vb* assuage, calm, cheer, comfort, solace, relieve, soothe.

consolidate *vb* cement, compact, compress, condense, harden, thicken; combine, conjoin, fuse, unite.

conspicuous *adj* apparent, clear, glaring, manifest, noticeable, perceptible, plain, striking, visible; distinguished, eminent, famed, famous, marked, noted, outstanding, preeminent, prominent, remarkable.

conspiracy *n* cabal, collusion, intrigue, league, machination, plot.

conspire vb concur, conduce, cooperate; combine, contrive, devise, project; confederate, contrive, plot, scheme.

constant adj abiding, enduring, fixed, invariable, invariant, permanent, perpetual, stable, unalterable, unvaried; certain, regular, uniform; determined, firm, resolute, stanch, steady, undeviating, unmoved, unshaken; assiduous, diligent, tenacious; continuous, incessant, perpetual, sustained, unbroken; devoted, faithful, loyal, true, trusty.

consternation n alarm, awe, dread, fear, fright, horror, panic, terror.

constitute vb compose, form, make; delegate, depute, empower; enact, fix, set up.

constitution n establishment, formation, make-up, structure; characteristic, disposition, habit, peculiarity, physique, quality, spirit, temperament.

constitutional adj congenital, connate, inborn, inbred, inherent, natural, organic; lawful, legal, legitimate; * n airing, exercise, stretch, walk.

constrain vb coerce, compel, drive, force; bind, chain, curb, enthral, hold, restrain; draw, impel.

constriction n compression, constraint, contraction.

construct vb build, fabricate, erect, raise, set up; arrange, form, found, frame, institute, invent, make, originate.

consult vb advise, ask, counsel, deliberate, interrogate, question; consider.

consume vb absorb, decay, deplete, devour, dissipate, exhaust, expend, lessen, spend, squander, vanish.

consummate vb accomplish, achieve, compass, complete, conclude, effect, effectuate, end, execute, perfect, perform; * adj complete, done, effected, finished, fulfilled, perfect.

consumption n decay, decline, decrease, destruction, use, waste; emaciation.

contact vb hit, touch; approach, be heard, communicate with, reach; * n approximation, contiguity, juxtaposition, tangency, touch.

contain vb accommodate, comprehend, comprise, embody, embrace, enclose; restrain.

contaminate vb corrupt, defile, deprave, infect, poison, pollute, stain, sully, taint, vitiate.

contemplate vb behold, observe, survey; consider, dwell on, meditate on, ponder, reflect upon, study, survey, think about; design, mean, plan, purpose.

contemplation n cogitation, deliberation, meditation, reflection, speculation, study, thought; prospect, prospective, view.

contemporary adj coetaneous, coeval, coexistent, coexisting, coincident, concomitant, concurrent, current, present, simultaneous, synchronous; advanced, modernistic, progressive, up-to-date; * n coeval, compeer, fellow.

contempt n contumely, derision, despite, disdain, misprision, mockery, scorn, slight.

contemptible adj abject, base, despicable, insolent, insulting, low, mean, pitiful, scurvy, sorry, supercilious, vile.

contemptuous adj arrogant, contumelious, haughty, insolent, insulting, scornful, sneering.

contend vb battle, combat, compete, contest, fight, struggle, vie; argue, debate, dispute, litigate; affirm, calm, maintain.

content n essence, meaning, meat, stuff, substance; measure, space, volume; contentment, case, peace, satisfaction; * vb appease, delight, gladden, gratify, humour, please, satisfy, suffice; * *adj* agreeable, happy, pleased, satisfied.

contest *vb* argue, contend, controvert, debate, litigate, question; strive, struggle; compete, cope, fight, vie; * *n* altercation, controversy, difference, dispute, quarrel; affray, battle, bout, combat, conflict, encounter, fight, match, struggle, tussle; competition, contention, rivalry.

continual *adj* constant, perpetual, unceasing; endless, eternal, interminable, perennial, permanent, perpetual; constant.

continue *vb* endure, last, remain; abide, remain, stay, tarry; endure, persist, stick; extend, prolong, perpetuate, protract.

continuous *adj* connected, continued, extended, unbroken, uninterrupted.

contract *vb* abbreviate, abridge, condense, confine, diminish, epitomise, lessen, narrow, reduce; absorb, incur, get, make, take; constrict, shrink, shrivel; agree, bargain, covenant, pledge, stipulate; * *n* agreement, arrangement, bargain, bond, compact, covenant, convention, pact, stipulation, treaty.

contradict *vb* assail, challenge, controvert, deny, gainsay, impugn, traverse; abrogate, annul, belie, counter, disallow, negative; counteract, oppose, thwart.

contradictory *adj* antagonistic, contrary, incompatible, inconsistent, negating, opposite, repugnant.

contrary *adj* adverse, counter, discordant, opposed, opposing, opposite; antagonistic, repugnant, retroactive; forward, humoursome, obstinate, refractory, stubborn, unruly, wayward, perverse; * *n* converse, obverse, opposite, reverse.

contrast *vb* compare, distinguish, oppose; * *n* contrariety, difference; comparison, distinction.

contravene *vb* abrogate, annul, contradict, counteract, countervail, go against, hinder, interfere, nullify, oppose, thwart, traverse, violate.

contribute *vb* donate, give, grant, subscribe; afford, aid, furnish, supply; concur, conspire, cooperate, minister, serve.

contribution *n* addition, bestowal, bestowment, grant; gift, offering, subscription.

contrive *vb* arrange, brew, concoct, design, devise, form, frame, hatch, invent, plan, project; plan, plot, scheme; manage, make out.

control *vb* command, direct, dominate, manage, oversee, sway, regulate, rule; check, counteract, curb, check, repress, restrain; * *n* command, disposition, dominion, government, guidance, mastery, oversight, regiment, rule, superintendence, supremacy.

controversy *n* altercation, argument, debate, discussion, disputation, dispute, logomachy, polemics, strife; lawsuit.

convenience *n* fitness, propriety, suitableness; accessibility, accommodation, comfort, ease, handiness, satisfaction, serviceability, serviceableness.

convenient *adj* appropriate, fit, fitted, proper, suitable, suited; advantageous, beneficial, commodious, favourable, handy, helpful, useful.

convention *n* assembly, congress, convocation, meeting; agreement, compact, contract, pact, treaty; custom, formality, usage.

conventional *adj* agreed on, bargained for, stipulated;

accustomed, approved, customary, everyday, habitual, ordinary, orthodox, standard, traditional, usual.

conversation *n* chat, colloquy, communion, conference, converse, dialogue, discourse, interlocution, parley, talk.

converse *vb* commune, chat, confabulate, gossip, parley, talk; * *n* communication, intercourse; conversation, talk; antithesis, contrary, opposite, reverse; * *adj* adverse, contradictory, contrary, counter, opposed, opposite.

conversion *n* change, resolution, transformation; reversal, transposition.

convert *vb* alter, change, transform, transmute; reverse, transpose; apply, appropriate; * *n* catechumen, disciple, proselyte.

convey *vb* bear, bring, carry, fetch, transmit, transport, waft; alienate, cede, consign, deliver, demise, devolve, grant, sell, transfer.

convict *vb* condemn, confute, convince, sentence; * *n* criminal, culprit, felon, prisoner.

convoy *vb* accompany, attend, escort, guard, protect; * *n* attendance, escort, guard, protection.

convulse *vb* agitate, derange, disorder, disturb, shake.

convulsion *n* cramp, fit, spasm; agitation, commotion, disturbance, tumult.

cook *vb* bake, boil, broil, fry, grill, microwave, roast, steam, stir-fry; falsify.

cool *vb* chill, ice, refrigerate; abate, allay, calm, damp, quiet, temper; * *adj* calm, collected, composed, placid, sedate, quiet, staid, unexcited, unimpassioned; cold-blooded, indifferent, lukewarm, unconcerned; apathetic, chilling, frigid, repellent; bold, impertinent, impudent; * *n* chill, chilliness, coolness; calmness, composure, poise, self-possession, self-restraint.

cooperate *vb* abet, aid, assist, co-act, combine, concur, conduce, conspire, contribute, help.

cooperation *n* aid, assistance, concert, collaboration, synergy.

coordinate *vb* accord, agree, arrange, equalise, harmonise, integrate, organise, regulate, synchronise, systematise; * *adj* coequal, equal, equivalent, tantamount; synchronous; * *n* complement, counterpart, like; companion, fellow, match, mate.

cope *vb* combat, compete, contend, encounter, engage, grapple, strive, vie.

copious *adj* abundant, ample, exuberant, full, plenteous, plentiful, profuse, rich.

copy *vb* duplicate, reproduce, transcribe; follow, imitate, pattern; * *n* facsimile, replica, reproduction, transcript; archetype, model, original; manuscript, typescript.

cordial *adj* affectionate, ardent, earnest, hearty, sincere, warm, warmhearted; grateful, invigorating, pleasant, refreshing; * *n* balm, balsam, elixir, tonic; liqueur.

core *n* centre, crux, essence, heart, kernel.

corner *vb* confound, confuse, nonplus, perplex, pose, puzzle; * *n* angle, bend, cusp, elbow, joint; niche, nook, retreat.

corpse *n* body, carcass, remains, dust.

correct *vb* adjust, amend, cure, improve, mend, rectify, redress, reform, regulate, remedy; discipline; * *adj* accurate, equitable, exact, faultless, just, precise, regular, true, upright.

correction *n* amendment, improvement, redress; discipline, punishment.

correspond vb accord, agree, answer, comport, fit, match, square, suit, tally; belong; communicate.

correspondence n accord, agreement, coincidence, concurrence, conformity, fitness, harmony, match; communication, letters.

corrode vb canker, erode, gnaw; deteriorate, rust, waste; blight, envenom, poison.

corrosive adj acrid, biting, consuming, cathartic, caustic, corroding, eroding, violent; consuming, corroding, gnawing, mordant, wasting; blighting, cankerous, carking, embittering, poisoning.

corrupt vb putrefy, putrid, render; contaminate, infect, pollute, spoil, taint; degrade, demoralise, deprave, pervert, vitiate; adulterate, falsify; bribe, entice; * adj infected, putrid, rotten, spoiled, tainted, unsound; abandoned, dissolute, profligate, vicious, wicked; bribable.

corruption n putrefaction, putrescence; adulteration, contamination, defilement, infection, perversion; demoralisation, depravation, depravity, laxity, wickedness; bribery, dishonesty.

cost vb absorb, consume; * n amount, charge, expenditure, expense, price; costliness, preciousness, splendour, sumptuousness; damage, detriment, sacrifice, suffering.

costly adj expensive, high-priced, gorgeous, luxurious, precious, rich, splendid, valuable.

cosy adj comfortable, easy, snug; chatty, conversable, talkative.

couch vb lie, recline; crouch, squat; bend down, stoop; cover up, hide; lay, level; * n bed, divan, settee, settle, sofa.

council n advisers, cabinet, ministry; assembly, conclave, convention, convocation, diet, meeting, parliament, synod.

counsel vb admonish, caution, recommend, warn; * n counsel; advice, caution, instruction, opinion, recommendation, suggestion; deliberation; advocate, barrister, counsellor, lawyer.

count vb enumerate, number, score; calculate, cast, estimate, reckon; account, consider, deem, esteem, hold, regard; tell; * n reckoning, tally.

countenance vb abet, aid, approve, assist, befriend, favour, sanction, support; * n aspect, look; aid, approbation, assistance, encouragement, favour, patronage, sanction.

counteract vb check, contravene, counter, defeat, frustrate, hinder, oppose, resist, thwart; annul, countervail, offset.

counterfeit vb forge, imitate; fake, feign, pretend, simulate; copy, imitate; * adj fake, spurious, suppositious; false, feigned, hypocritical, mock, sham, spurious; copies, resembling; * n copy, fake, forgery, sham.

counterpart n copy, duplicate; complement, correlative, reverse; fellow, mate, match, tally, twin.

couple vb pair, unite; copulate; embrace; buckle, clasp, connect, join, link, pair, unite; * n brace, pair, twain, two; bond, coupling, link, tie.

courage n audaciousness, audacity, boldness, bravery, daring, dauntlessness, fearlessness, fortitude, gallantry, hardihood, heroism, manhood, mettle, nerve, pluck, resolution, spirit, spunk, valour.

courageous adj audacious, brave, bold, daring, dauntless, fearless, gallant, hardy, heroic, intrepid, mettlesome, plucky, resolute, reliant, staunch, undismayed, valiant, valorous.

course vb chase, follow, hunt,

pursue, race, run; * n circuit, race, run; road, route, way; bearing, direction, path, tremor, track; beat, orbit, round; process, progress, sequence; order, succession, turn; behaviour, conduct, deportment; series, system.

court vb coddle, flatter; address; seek, solicit, invite, solicit, woe; * n area, courtyard; addresses, civilities, homage; respects; retinue, palace, tribunal.

courteous adj affable, attentive, civil, complaisant, courtly, elegant, gracious, obliging, polished, refined, urbane, well-bred, well-mannered.

cover vb overlay, overspread; conceal, curtain, disguise; hide, mask, screen, shroud, veil; defend, guard, protect, shelter, shield; clothe, envelop, invest, jacket; comprehend, embody, embrace, include; * n capsule, case, covering, integument, top; cloak, screen, veil; guard, defence, protection, shelter, shield; shrubbery, thicket, underbrush, underwood, woods.

covetous adj acquisitive, avaricious, grasping, greedy, miserly, parsimonious, penurious.

cow vb abash, break, browbeat, daunt, discourage, frighten, intimidate, overawe.

coward adj cowardly, timid; * n caitiff, craven, milksop, poltroon, recreant, skulker, sneak.

cowardly adj base, coward, dastardly, faint-hearted, fearful, mean, pusillanimous, timid, white-livered, yellow.

cower vb bend, cringe, fawn, shrink, squat.

coy adj backward, bashful, diffident, distant, evasive, modest, reserved, retiring, self-effacing, shrinking, shy; affected, arch.

crabbed adj acrid, rough, sore, tart; acrimonious, captious, caustic, censorious, churlish, cross, harsh, ill-tempered, morose, petulant, snappish, snarling, splenetic, surly, touchy, waspish; difficult, perplexing, tough, trying, unmanageable.

crack vb break; chop, cleave, split; snap; craze: boast, brag, crow, vapour, vaunt; * adj capital, excellent, first-class, first-rate, tip-top; * n break, cleft, cranny, crevice, fissure, fracture, opening, rent, rift, split; clap, explosion, report.

craft n ability, aptitude, cleverness, dexterity, skill, tact, talent; artfulness, craftiness, deceitfulness, deception, guile, subtlety; art, avocation, business, calling, employment, handicraft, trade, vocation.

cram vb glut, gorge, satiate, stuff; compress, crowd, press, squeeze; grind.

cramp vb convulse; check, clog, confine, hamper, hinder, obstruct, restrain, restrict; * n convulsion, spasm; check, restraint, restrict.

crash vb break, shatter, shiver, smash; * adj emergency, fast, intensive, rushed, speeded-up; * n clang, clash, concussion, jar.

crave vb ask, beg, beseech, entreat, petition, supplicate; desire, hanker after, long for, need, want.

craven adj coward, dastard, milk-sop, poltroon.

craving n hankering, hungering, longing, yearning.

craze vb bewilder, confuse, derange, madden; disorder, impair, weaken; * n mania, mode, novelty.

crazy adj broken, crank, shaky; delirious, demented, deranged; idiotic, insane, mad, silly.

create vb originate, procreate; cause, fashion, form, invent, occasion, produce; make.

creator n architect, author,

designer, inventor, fashioner, maker; god.

creature *n* animal, beast, body, brute, man, person; dependant, minion, parasite, retainer, vassal; miscreant, wretch.

credit *vb* accept, believe, trust; loan, trust; * *n* belief, faith, reliance, trust; esteem, regard, reputation; influence, power; honour, merit.

creditable *adj* creditable, estimable, honourable, meritorious, reputable, respectable.

creed *n* belief, catechism, confession, doctrine, dogma, opinion, tenet.

creep *vb* crawl; steal upon; cringe, fawn, grovel; * *n* crawl, scrabble, scramble; groveller, toady.

crest *n* comb, plume, topknot; apex, head, ridge, summit, top; arms, badge.

crew *n* company, hands; company, corps, gang, mob, party, set, squad, team, throng.

crick *vb* jar, rick, wrench, wrick; * *n* convulsion, cramp, jarring, rick, wrench.

crime *n* felony, misdeed, misdemeanour, violation; delinquency, fault, guilt, iniquity, sin, wickedness, wrong.

criminal *adj* culpable, felonious, flagitious, guilty, immoral, iniquitous, unlawful, vicious, wicked, wrong; * *n* convict, culprit, delinquent, offender, sinner, transgressor.

cringe *vb* bend, bow, cower, fawn, grovel, kneel, stoop, truckle.

cripple *vb* cramp, disable, enfeeble, impair, lame, mutilate, ruin, weaken.

crisis *n* acme, climax; exigency, juncture, pass, push, strait, urgency.

criterion *n* canon, gauge, measure, principle, rule, standard, test.

critic *n* arbiter, caviller, connoisseur, judge, reviewer.

critical *adj* accurate, exact, nice; captious, carping, censorious; crucial, decisive, determining, important, timing: dangerous, exigent, hazardous, imminent.

criticise *vb* appraise, evaluate, examine, judge.

croak *vb* complain, groan, moan, repine; die.

crony *n* ally, associate, chum, friend, mate, pal.

crook *vb* bend, bow, incurvate, turn, wind; * *n* bend, flexion, turn; artifice, machination, trick; thief, villain

crooked *adj* angular, bent, bowed, curved, winding; askew, aslant, awry, disfigured, distorted, twisted, wry; crafty, deceitful, devious, dishonest, insidious, intriguing, knavish, tricky, unfair.

crop *vb* gather, mow, pluck, reap; browse, nibble; clip, lop, reduce; * *n* harvest, produce, yield.

cross *vb* intersect, pass over, traverse; hinder, obstruct, thwart; interbred, intermix; * *adj* transverse; captious, crabbed, churlish, crusty, fractious, fretful, grouchy, ill-natured, ill-tempered, irascible, morose, peevish, pettish, petulant, snappish, sour, spleeny, splenetic, sulky, sullen, testy, touchy, waspish; * *n* crucifix, gibbet, rood; misfortune, trial, trouble, vexation; crossbreeding, intermixture.

crouch *vb* cower, cringe, duck, truckle; stoop, squat.

crow *vb* bluster, boast, chuckle, exult, gasconade, triumph, vapour, vaunt.

crowd *vb* compress, cram, jam, press; collect, flock, herd, huddle, swarm; * *n* assembly, company, flock, herd, horde, host, jam, press; mob, pack, populace, rabble.

crown *vb* dignify, honour;

recompense, requite, reward; cap, complete, consummate, perfect; * n bays, chaplet, coronal, coronet, garland, diadem; monarchy, royalty, sovereignty; diadem; dignity, honour, reward; apex, crest, summit.

crucial adj intersecting, transverse; critical, decisive, severe, testing.

crude adj raw, uncooked, undressed, unworked; rough, unripe; crass, course, unrefined; immature, rude, uncouth, unpremeditated.

cruel adj barbarous, dire, fell, ferocious, hard-hearted, inhuman, merciless, relentless, ruthless, sanguinary, savage, uncompassionate, unfeeling, unmerciful; bitter, cold, hard, severe, sharp.

crumble vb bruise, crush, disintegrate, perish, pound, pulverise.

crumple vb rumple, wrinkle.

crush vb bruise, compress, contuse, squash, squeeze; comminute, disintegrate, mash; demolish, shatter; conquer, overcome, overpower, overwhelm, quell.

crusty adj churlish, crabbed, cynical, fretful, forward, morose, peevish, petulant, snappish, snarling, surly, testy, touchy; friable, hard, short.

cry vb call, clamour; blubber, snivel, sob, wail, weep, whimper; bawl, hoot, roar, shout, vociferate, scream, screech, squall, squeal, yell; announce, proclaim, publish; * n acclamation, clamour, exclamation, outcry; crying, lamentation, plaint; bawl, bellow, howl, roar, scream, screech, yell; announcement, proclamation.

cuddle vb nestle, snuggle, squat; caress, embrace, hug, pet; * n caress, embrace, hug.

cue vb intimate, prompt, sign, signal; * n catchword, hint, nod, sign, signal, suggestion.

cuff vb beat, box, buffet, knock, punch, slap, strike, thump; * n blow, box, punch, slap, strike, thump.

culmination n acme, apex, climax, consummation, crown, summit, top, zenith.

culprit n delinquent, criminal, evil-doer, felon, offender.

cultivate vb farm, fertilise, till, work; civilise, discipline, elevate, improve, meliorate, refine, train; prosecute, pursue, search; cherish, foster, nourish, patronise.

culture n agriculture, farming, tillage; cultivation, elevation, improvement.

cumbersome adj burdensome, clumsy, embarrassing, heavy, inconvenient, oppressive, unmanageable, unwieldy, vexatious.

cunning adj artful, astute, crafty, crooked, deceitful, designing, diplomatic, foxy, intriguing, machiavellian, sharp, sly, subtle, tricky; curious, ingenious; * n art, artfulness, artifice, craft, shrewdness, subtlety; deceit, deception, intrigue.

curb vb bridle, check, control, hinder, moderate, restrain; * n bridle, check, control, hindrance, rein.

cure vb alleviate, correct, heal, mend, restore; kipper, pickle, preserve; * n corrective, help, remedy, reparative, restorative; alleviation, healing.

curiosity n inquisitiveness; curio, marvel, novelty, oddity, rarity, sight, spectacle.

curious adj interested, inquiring, inquisitive, meddling, prying; extraordinary, marvellous, novel, queer, rare, singular, strange, unusual; cunning, elegant, fine, finished, neat, well-wrought.

curl vb coil, twist, wind; bend, buckle, wave; * n curlicue, ringlet; flexure, sinuosity,

undulation, wave, waving.
current *adj* common, general, popular, rife; passing; existing, instant, present, prevalent; * *n* course, progression, river, stream, tide, currently; * *adv* commonly, generally, popularly.
curse *vb* anathematise, damn, denounce, execrate, imprecate, invoke, maledict; blast, blight, destroy, doom; annoy, harass, injure, plague, scourge, torment, vex; blaspheme; * *n* anathema, ban, denunciation, execration, imprecation, malediction; affliction, annoyance, plague, scourge, torment, trouble, vexation; ban, condemnation, sentence.
cursory *adj* brief, desultory, hasty, passing, rapid, slight, superficial, transient, transitory.
curt *adj* brief, concise, laconic, short, terse; rude, tart.
curtail *vb* abridge, dock, retrench, trim; abbreviate, contract, decrease, diminish.
curve *vb* bend, crook, inflect, turn, twist, wind; * *n* bend, bending, crook, curve, flexure, incurvation.
cushion *vb* absorb, damp, deaden, dull, mute, soften, subdue; cradle, pillow, support; * *n* bolster, hassock, pad, pillow.
custodian *n* curator, guardian, keeper, superintendent.
custody *n* care, guardianship, keeping, protection, watch, ward; confinement, durance, imprisonment, prison.
custom *n* convention, fashion, habit, manner, mode, practice, usage, use, way; formality; duty, impost, tax, toll.
customary *adj* accustomed, common, conventional, familiar, fashionable, general, prescriptive, usual, wonted.
cut *vb* chop, cleave, divide, gash, lance, sever, slice, slit, wound; carve, chisel; hurt, move, touch, wound; ignore, slight; abbreviate, curtail, shorten; * *n* gash, groove, incision, nick, slit; channel, passage; piece; fling, taunt; fashion, form, shape, style.
cutting *adj* keen, sharp; acid, biting, caustic, piercing, sarcastic, sardonic, severe, trenchant.
cycle *n* age, circle, era, phase, revolution, round.
cynical *adj* captious, carping, censorious, churlish, crabbed, cross, crusty, fretful, morose, peevish, pettish, sarcastic, satirical, snappish, surly, testy, touchy, waspish; contemptuous, misanthropic, pessimistic, scornful.

D

dab *vb* box, slap, strike; * *adj* adept, expert; pat; * *n* lump, mass, pat.
dabble *vb* dip, moisten, spatter, splash, sprinkle, wet; meddle, trifle.
daft *adj* absurd, delirious, foolish, giddy, idiotic, insane, silly, stupid; frolicsome, merry, mirthful, sportive.
dainty *adj* delicate, delicious, luscious, nice, savoury, tender; beautiful, charming, choice, exquisite, fine, neat; fastidious, finicky, over-nice, particular, scrupulous, squeamish; * *n* delicacy, titbit.
damage *vb* harm, hurt, impair, injure; * *n* detriment, harm, hurt, injury, loss.
damn *vb* condemn, doom, kill, ruin; * *n* bean, curse, fig, hoot, rap, straw.
damnable *adj* abominable, accursed, atrocious, cursed, detestable, hateful, odious.
damp *vb* dampen; allay, abate, cheek, depress, discourage, hinder, moderate, restrain; chill, cool, deaden, deject, dispirit; * *adj* dank, humid, moist, wet; * *n* dampness, fog,

mist, moisture, vapour; chill, dejection.

danger *n* jeopardy, insecurity, hazard, peril, risk.

dangerous *adj* critical, hazardous, insecure, perilous, risky, ticklish.

dank *adj* damp, humid, moist, wet.

dare *vb* challenge, defy, hazard, provoke, risk; * *n* challenge, gage.

daring *adj* adventurous, bold, brave, courageous, dauntless, doughty, fearless, gallant, heroic, valiant, valorous; * *n* adventurousness, bravery, courage, dauntlessness, fearlessness, intrepidity, undauntedness.

dark *adj* black, cloudy, darksome, dim, dusky, inky, lurid, murky, opaque, overcast, pitchy, shady, shadowy, sunless, swart, tenebrous, unenlightened, unilluminated; abstruse, cabbalistic, incomprehensible, mysterious, mystical, obscure, opaque, transcendental, unintelligible; cheerless, despondent, discouraging, dismal, funereal, gloomy, joyless; benighted, darkened, ignorant, unlettered; atrocious, damnable, infamous, flagitious, foul, internal, vile, wicked; private, secret; * *n* darkness, dusk, murkiness, obscurity; concealment, secrecy; blindness, ignorance.

darken *vb* cloud, dim, obscure, shade, shadow; chill, depress, gloom, sadden; benight, stupefy; obscure, perplex; defile, dull, stain, sully.

dart *vb* ejaculate, hurl, launch, propel, sling; emit, shoot; dash, rush, scoot.

dash *vb* break, disappoint, frustrate, ruin, shatter, spoil, thwart; confound, disappoint; bolt, dart, fly, run, speed, rush; * *n* blow, stroke; onset, rush; infusion, smack, spice, tincture, tinge, touch; show.

date *n* age, day, generation, time; epoch, period; appointment, arrangement, assignation, interview, rendezvous, tryst; catch.

dawdle *vb* dally, delay, idle, lag, loaf, loiter, trifle.

dawn *vb* appear, begin, break, gleam, glimmer, open, rise; * *n* daybreak, dawning, sunrise, sun-up.

day *n* daylight, sunlight, sunshine; age, generation, time.

daze *vb* blind, dazzle; bewilder, confound, confuse, stun, stupefy; * *n* bewilderment, confusion, perturbation, pother; coma, stupor, swoon, trance.

dazzle *vb* blind, daze; astonish, confound, overpower; * *n* brightness, brilliance, splendour.

dead *adj* breathless, deceased, defunct, departed, gone, inanimate, lifeless; callous, cold, dull, frigid, inert, lukewarm, numb, obtuse, spiritless, unfeeling; flat, insipid, tasteless, vapid; barren, inactive, sterile, unemployed, useless; * *adv* absolutely, completely, downright, fundamentally; direct, due, exactly, just, right, squarely, straight; * *n* depth, midst; hush, peace, silence, stillness.

deaden *vb* abate, damp, dampen, dull, impair, muffle, mute, restrain, retard, weaken; blunt, hebetate, obtund, paralyse.

deadly *adj* destructive, fatal, lethal, malignant, murderous, pernicious, poisonous, venomous; mortal, sanguinary.

deal *vb* allot, apportion, assign, dispense, distribute, divide, give, share; bargain, trade, traffic, treat with; * *n* degree, extent, lot, portion, share; bargain, transaction.

dear *adj* costly, expensive; beloved, darling, precious,

DECORATION

treasured; * *n* beloved, darling, honey, love, precious, sweet.

dearth *n* deficiency, scarcity; famine, lack, need, shortage.

deathless *adj* eternal, everlasting, immortal, imperishable, undying; dull.

debase *vb* adulterate, alloy, depress, impair, injure, lower, pervert, reduce; abase, degrade, disgrace, dishonour, humble, mortify, shame; contaminate, corrupt, defile, foul, pollute, soil, taint.

debate *vb* argue, contest, discuss, dispute; contend, deliberate, wrangle; * *n* controversy, discussion; altercation, contention, contest, dispute.

debonair *adj* affable, civil, complaisant, courteous, easy, gracious, kind, polite, urbane, well-bred.

debris *n* detritus, dross, fragments, remains, rubbish, ruins, wreck, wreckage.

debt *n* arrears, debit, due, liability, obligation; fault, offence, sin, transgression.

decay *vb* decline, deteriorate, disintegrate, fail, perish, waste, wither; decompose, putrefy, rot; * *n* caducity, decadence, decomposition, degeneracy, degeneration, deterioration, disintegration, fading, failing, perishing, putrefaction, ruin, wasting.

deceit *n* artifice, cheating, chicanery, craftiness, deception, double-dealing, duplicity, fraud, guile, hypocrisy, imposition, imposture, sham, treachery, tricky, wile.

deceitful *adj* counterfeit, deceptive, delusive, hollow, illusive, illusory, misleading; cunning, designing, dodgy, double-dealing, false, guileful, insincere, tricky, wily.

deceive *vb* beguile, betray, cheat, chouse, circumvent, defraud, delude, disappoint, double-cross, ensnare, entrap, fool, gull, hoax, humbug, outwit, overreach, trick.

decent *adj* appropriate, befitting, comely, seemly, decorous, fit, proper; delicate, modest, pure; moderate, respectable, tolerable.

deception *n* cheating, chicanery, craftiness, deceitfulness, double-dealing, duplicity, fraud, guile, hoax, hypocrisy, imposition, pretence, sham, tricky, underhandedness, wile; cheat, chouse, ruse, stratagem.

decide *vb* close, conclude, determine, end, settle; resolve; adjudicate, award.

decided *adj* determined, firm, resolute, unhesitating, unwavering; absolute, positive, unequivocal; certain, clear, undeniable, unmistakable.

decision *n* determination, judgement, settlement; adjudication, award, pronouncement; firmness, resolution.

decisive *adj* conclusive, determinative, final.

declaration *n* affirmation, assertion, avowal, protestation, statement; announcement, proclamation, publication.

declare *vb* advertise, affirm, announce, assert, aver, certify, proclaim, promulgate, pronounce, publish, state, utter.

decline *vb* incline, lean, slope; decay, droop, fail, pine, sink; degenerate, depreciate, deteriorate; decrease, diminish, fade, ebb, lapse, lessen, wane; avoid, refuse, reject; inflect, vary; * *n* decadence, decay, declination, degeneracy, deterioration, diminution, wane; atrophy, consumption; declivity, hill, incline, slope.

decorate *vb* adorn, beautify, deck, embellish, enrich, garnish, grace.

decoration *n* adorning, decking, enriching, garnishing, ornamenting, adornment,

45

embellishment, ornament.
decorous *adj* appropriate, befitting, decent, fit, suitable; proper, sedate, seemly, staid.
decoy *vb* allure, deceive, ensnare, entice, entrap, lure, seduce, tempt; * *n* lure, enticement.
decrease *vb* abate, contract, decline, diminish, ebb, lessen, subside; curtail, diminish, lessen, lower, reduce, retrench; * *n* contraction, declension, decline, diminishing, ebb, ebbing, lessening, reduction, waning.
decree *vb* command, decide, determine, enact, enjoin, order; * *n* act, command, edict, enactment, fiat, law, order, ordinance, regulation, statute.
decrepit *adj* feeble, shattered, wasted, weak; aged, crippled.
dedicate *vb* consecrate, devote, sanctify; address.
deduce *vb* conclude, derive, draw, gather.
deduction *n* removal, subtraction, withdrawal; abatement, allowance, discount, rebate, reduction; conclusion, consequence, inference.
deed *n* act, action, derring-do, exploit, feat; fact, truth, reality; charter, contract, document, instrument, transfer.
deep *adj* abysmal, profound; abstruse, difficult, hard, intricate, knotty, mysterious, profound, unfathomable; astute, cunning, designing, discerning, intelligent, penetrating, sagacious, shrewd; absorbed, engrossed; bass, low; entire, great, thorough; * *n* main, ocean, sea; abyss, depth, profound; enigma, mystery; silence.
deeply *adv* profoundly; entirely, profoundly; affectingly, distressingly, feelingly.
defeat *vb* beat, checkmate, conquer, overcome, overpower, overthrow, repulse, rout, ruin, vanquish; balk, disappoint, disconcert, foil, frustrate, thwart; * *n* downfall, overthrow, repulse, rout; bafflement, checkmate, frustration.
defect *vb* abandon, desert, rebel, revolt; * *n* default, deficiency, destitution, lack, shortcoming, spot, want; blemish, error, flaw, imperfection, mistake; fault.
defence *n* defending, guarding, maintaining, maintenance, protection; bulwark, fortification, guard, rampart, resistance, shield; apology, justification, vindication.
defend *vb* cover, fortify, guard, preserve, protect, screen, shelter, shield; assert, espouse, justify, uphold, vindicate.
defer *vb* adjourn, delay, postpone, prorogue, protract, shelve, table; abide by, bow to, give way, submit, yield; admire, honour, regard, respect.
deference *n* esteem, homage, honour, regard, respect, reverence, veneration; consideration; obedience, submission.
deferential *adj* considerate, respectful, reverential.
defiance *n* challenge, daring; disobedience, disregard, opposition.
defiant *adj* resistant; bold, courageous, resistant.
deficiency *n* default, deficit, insufficiency, lack, meagreness, scarcity, shortage, shortness, want; defect, error, failing, falling, fault, frailty, imperfection, weakness.
define *vb* bound, circumscribe, delimit, determine, explain, limit, specify.
definite *adj* defined, determinate, determined, fixed; assured, certain, clear, exact, explicit, precise, specific, unequivocal.
definitive *adj* categorical, determinate, express, positive, conclusive, decisive, final.
deformity *n* crookedness, defect

disfigurement, distortion, irregularity, malformation, misproportion, monstrosity, ugliness.

defraud vb beguile, cheat, chouse, circumvent, deceive, delude, diddle, dupe, gull, outwit, pilfer, rob, swindle, trick.

deft adj adroit, apt, clever, dextrous, expert, handy, ready, skilful.

defy vb challenge, dare; brave, contemn, despise, disregard, provoke, scorn, slight.

degree n stage, step; class, grade, order, quality, rank, station; measure; division, interval, space.

dejected adj depressed, despondent, disheartened, dispirited, doleful, downcast, downhearted, gloomy, miserable, sad.

delay vb defer, postpone; arrest, detain, check, hinder, impede, stay, stop; protract; dawdle, linger, loiter, tarry; * n deferment, procrastination; check, detention, hindrance, impediment, stoppage; prolonging, protraction; dallying, lingering, stay, stop.

delegate vb appoint, authorise, mission, deputise, transfer; entrust; * n ambassador, commissioner, delegate, deputy, envoy.

delete vb cancel, edit, erase, expunge, obliterate, remove.

deliberate vb cogitate, consider, consult, meditate, reflect, ruminate, think, weigh; * adj careful, considerate, heedful, purposeful, thoughtful, wary; well-advised, well-considered; intentional, premeditated, purposed, studied.

deliberation n caution, coolness, prudence, reflection, thought, thoughtfulness; purpose.

delicacy n agreeableness, daintiness, deliciousness, relish, savouriness; bonne bouche, dainty, titbit; elegance, fitness, lightness, niceness, nicety, softness, tenderness; fragility, frailty, slightness, tenderness, weakness; carefulness, daintiness, fastidiousness, finesse, nicety, sensitivity, subtlety, tact; refinement, sensibility.

delicate adj agreeable, delicious, pleasant, pleasing; exquisite, fine, nice; careful, dainty, discriminating, fastidious, scrupulous; frail, slender, slight, tender, delicate; pure.

delicious adj dainty, delicate, luscious, nice, palatable; agreeable, choice, delightful, exquisite, grateful.

delight vb charm, enchant, gratify, please, ravish, rejoice, satisfy; * n charm, ecstasy, gladness, gratification, happiness, joy, pleasure, rapture, satisfaction.

delightful adj agreeable, captivating, charming, enchanting, enjoyable, enrapturing, ravishing, transporting.

delinquent adj negligent, offending; * n criminal, culprit, defaulter, malefactor, offender, wrong-doer.

deliver vb emancipate, free, liberate, release; redeem, rescue, save; give, impart, transfer; grant, relinquish, resign, yield; declare, emit, pronounce, speak, utter; deal.

deliverance n emancipation, escape, liberation, release.

delivery n surrender; giving, rendering, transference, transmission; elocution, enunciation, pronunciation, speech, utterance; childbirth, confinement, labour.

delusion n artifice, cheat, deceit, dodge, fetch, fraud, imposition, ruse, snare, trick; deception, error, fallacy, fancy, illusion, mistake.

demand vb challenge, exact, require; claim; ask, inquire; * n claim, draft, exaction; call, want; inquiry, question.

demolish vb annihilate, destroy, dismantle, level, overturn, raze, ruin.

demon n devil, fiend, goblin, troll.

demonstrate vb establish, exhibit, illustrate, manifest, prove, show.

demonstration n display, exhibition, show.

denial n controverting, negation; disavowal, disclaimer, disowning; disallowance, refusal.

dense adj close, compact, compressed, thick; slow, stupid.

dent vb depress, dint, indent; * n depression, dint, indentation.

deny vb contradict, oppose, refute, traverse; disavow, disown, renounce; refuse, reject, withhold.

depart vb absent, disappear, vanish; abandon, go, leave, migrate, quit, remove; decease, die; diverge, vary.

department n district, division, part, portion, province; office, sphere, station; branch, division, subdivision.

departure n exit, leaving, parting, removal, removal, retirement; abandonment, forsaking; death, decease, deviation.

depend vb hang, hinge, turn.

dependant n client, hanger-on, retainer, subordinate, vassal; attendant, circumstance, consequence, corollary.

dependent adj hanging, pendant; conditioned, immature, relying, subject, subordinate.

deplorable adj calamitous, distressful, lamentable, melancholy, miserable, mournful, regrettable.

depose vb break, degrade, dethrone, dismiss, displace, oust, reduce; declare, depone, testify.

deposit vb drop, dump; lay, put; bank, hoard, lodge, put, save, store; commit, entrust; * n diluvium, dregs, precipitate, precipitation, sediment, settlings, silt; money, pawn, pledge, security, stake.

depraved adj abandoned, corrupt, corrupted, debased, degenerate, dissolute, evil, hardened, immoral, lascivious, lewd, lost, perverted, reprobate, shameless, sinful, vicious, wicked.

depreciate vb underestimate, undervalue, underrate; belittle, censure, degrade, disparage, malign.

depress vb bow, drop, lower, reduce, sink; abash, degrade, debase, disgrace, humble; chill, damp, dampen, deject, discourage, dishearten, sadden; lower.

depression n cavity, concavity, dent, dint, excavation, hollow, indentation, pit; blues, cheerlessness, dejection, dejectedness, despondency, dispiritedness, dolefulness, dumps, gloom, gloominess, hypochondria, sadness, vapours; inactivity, lowness, stagnation; abasement, debasement, humiliation.

deprive vb denude, despoil, dispossess, rob, strip.

depth n abyss, deepness, drop, profundity; extent; midst; astuteness, penetration, perspicacity, profoundness, profundity, shrewdness.

deputation n commission, delegation; deputies, delegates, delegation, embassies, envoys.

deputy adj acting, assistant, subordinate, vice; * n agent, commissioner, delegate, factor, legate, lieutenant, representative, substitute.

derelict adj abandoned, left; delinquent, faithless, guilty, neglectful, unfaithful; * n outcast, tramp, vagrant, wreck, wretch.

derision n contempt, insult, laughter, mockery, ridicule, scorn.

derisive adj contemptuous,

mocking, ridiculing, scoffing, scornful.

derivation n descent, extraction; etymology; deriving, getting, obtaining; foundation, source.

derive vb draw, get, obtain; deduce, follow, infer, trace.

descend vb alight, drop, fall, pitch, plunge, sink, swoop; go, pass, proceed; devolve; derive, issue.

descendants npl offspring, issue, posterity.

descent n drop, fall; descending; decline, dip, pitch, slope; ancestry, derivation, genealogy, lineage, parentage, pedigree; assault, attack, foray, raid.

describe vb define, delineate, draw, sketch, specify, trace; detail; explain, narrate, portray, recount, relate, represent.

description n delineation, tracing; account, depiction, narration, narrative, portrayal, recital, relation, report; class, kind, sort, species.

desert n due, excellence, merit, worth; * vb abandon, forsake, leave, quit, renounce, resign, quit, vacate; * adj barren, desolate, lonely, solitary, uncultivated, uninhabited, unproductive, waste, wild.

deserve vb earn, gain, merit, win.

design vb brew, contrive, devise, intend, mean, plan, project, scheme; intend, mean, purpose; describe, draw, outline, sketch, trace; * n aim, device, drift, intent, intention, meaning, object, plan, proposal, project, purport, purpose, scheme, scope; drawing, outline, plan, sketch; adaptation, artifice, invention, inventiveness.

designing adj artful, astute, crafty, cunning, deceitful, insidious, intriguing, scheming, sly, subtle, treacherous, tricky, unscrupulous, wily.

desire vb covet, crave, fancy, hanker after, long for, lust after, want, wish; ask, entreat, request, solicit; * n eroticism, libidinousness, libido, lust, passion; eagerness, fancy, hope, inclination, mind, partiality, pleasure, volition, want, wish.

desolate vb depopulate, destroy, devastate, pillage, plunder, ruin, sack; * adj bare, barren, bleak, desert, forsaken, lonely, solitary, uninhabited, waste, wild; companionable, lonely, solitary; desolated, destroyed, devastated, ruined; cheerless, comfortless, disconsolate, dreary, forsaken, miserable, wretched.

desolation n destruction, devastation, ravage, ruin; barrenness, desolateness, dreariness, loneliness, solitude; gloominess, misery, sadness, unhappiness.

despair vb give up, lose hope; * n dejection, desperation, despondency, hopelessness.

desperate adj despairing, despondent, desponding, hopeless; forlorn, hopeless; extreme; audacious, daring, despairing, frantic, furious, headstrong, rash, violent, wild, wretched; extreme, great, monstrous, supreme.

desperation n anxiety, despair, hopelessness; fury, rage.

despicable adj abject, base, contemptible, low, mean, paltry, pitiful, shameful, vile, worthless.

despise vb disdain, disregard, neglect, scorn, slight, spurn.

despite n malevolence, malice, malignity, spite; contempt; * prep notwithstanding.

despondent adj blue, dejected, depressed, discouraged, low-spirited, melancholy, sad.

despotic adj absolute, arrogant, autocratic, imperious; oppressive, tyrannical, tyrannous.

destination n appointment, decree, destiny, doom, fate,

destitute *adj* distressed, moneyless, needy, penniless, pinched, poor, reduced, wanting.

destroy *vb* demolish, overthrow, overturn, subvert, ruin; dissolve, efface, quench; desolate, devastate, devour, ravage, waste; extinguish, kill, uproot, slay.

destruction *n* demolition, ruin, desolation, devastation, holocaust; annihilation, eradication, extirpation; death, massacre, murder, slaughter.

destructive *adj* baleful, baneful, deadly, deleterious, fatal, hurtful, injurious, lethal, mischievous, pernicious, ruinous; eradicative.

detach *vb* disengage, disconnect, disjoin, disunite, divide, part, separate, sever, unfix; detail, send.

detail *vb* delineate, depict, describe, particularise, portray, recount, rehearse, relate, specify; appoint, detach, send; * *n* account, narration, narrative, relation; appointment; item, part.

detain *vb* arrest, check, delay, hinder, hold, keep, retain, stay, stop.

detect *vb* ascertain, catch, disclose, discover, expose, reveal.

deter *vb* debar, discourage, hinder, restrain, stop.

deteriorate *vb* corrupt, debase, degrade, disgrace, impair, spoil; decline, degenerate, worsen.

determination *n* decision, deciding, determining, settlement; conclusion, decision, judgement, purpose, resolution, resolve, result; leaning, tendency; firmness, grit, persistence, stamina, resoluteness; definition, limitation, qualification.

determine *vb* adjust, conclude, decide, end, fix, resolve, settle; ascertain, certify; incline, induce, influence, lead, turn; decide, resolve; define, limit; compel.

detest *vb* abhor, abominate, despise, hate, loathe, recoil from.

detestable *adj* abominable, accursed, execrable, hateful; disgusting, loathsome, nauseating, offensive, repulsive, vile.

detract *vb* abuse, asperse, belittle, debase, decry, defame, disparage, slander, vilify; deprecate, diminish, lessen.

devastation *n* despoiling, destroying, plundering, ravaging, sacking, spoiling; desolation, destruction, havoc, pillage, rapine, ravage, ruin, waste.

develop *vb* disentangle, disclose, evolve, exhibit, uncover, unfold, unravel; grow, mature, progress.

development *n* disclosure, exhibition, unfolding; growth, maturation; evolution, progression; elaboration, expansion.

deviate *vb* alter, digress, diverge, sheer off, slew, tack, turn aside, wheel; err, go astray, stray, swerve; differ, diverge, vary.

device *n* contraption, gadget, invention; design, plan, project, resort, resource, scheme; artifice, evasion, fraud, ruse, stratagem, trick, wile; blazon, emblem, sign, symbol, type.

devious *adj* deviating, erratic, roundabout, wandering; confusing, crooked, obscure; crooked, misleading.

devise *vb* compass, concert, concoct, contrive, dream up, imagine, invent, plan, project,

devote vb appropriate, dedicate; set apart; addict, apply, give up, resign; consign, doom.
devoted adj affectionate, attached, caring, loving; ardent, earnest.
devotion n consecration, dedication; devotedness, godliness, holiness, piety, religion, religiousness; adoration, devoutness, prayer, worship; affection, love; ardour, devotedness, zeal.
devour vb gorge, gulp down, raven, swallow eagerly, wolf; consume, destroy, expend, spend, swallow up, waste.
devout adj devotional, godly, holy, pious, saintly; earnest, grave, serious, sincere.
dexterity n ability, address, adroitness, aptitude, aptness, art, expertness, knack, quickness, readiness, skill, tact.
diabolic, **diabolical** adj atrocious, barbarous, cruel, devilish, fiendish, hellish, infernal, malign, malignant, satanic, wicked.
dialogue n communication, conference, conversation, converse, interlocution; script, speech, text, words.
dictate vb bid, direct, command, decree, ordain, order, prescribe, require; * n command, decree, injunction, order; precept, rule.
dictator n autocrat, despot, oppressor, tyrant.
dictatorial adj absolute, unrestricted; authoritative, despotic, domineering, imperious, peremptory, tyrannical.
dictatorship n absolutism, authoritarianism, autocracy, despotism, tyranny.
die vb demise, depart, expire, pass on; decline, fade, fade out, wither; cease, disappear, vanish; faint, fall, sink.
differ vb deviate, diverge, vary; disagree, dissent; contend, dispute, quarrel.
difference n contrast, departure, deviation, disagreement, disparity, dissimilitude, divergence, diversity, nuance, opposition, unlikeness, variation; alienation, breach, contention, contest, debate, disagreement, disharmony, dispute, dissension, falling out, irreconcilability, jarring, misunderstanding, quarrel, schism, strife, variance, wrangle; discrimination.
different adj distinct, separate, unlike; contrary, contrasted, deviating, disagreeing, dissimilar, divergent, diverse, incompatible, unlike, variant, various; divers, manifold, many, sundry, various.
difficult adj arduous, exacting, hard, stiff, tough, uphill; abstruse, complex, intricate, knotty, perplexing; austere, rigid, uncompliant; dainty, fastidious.
difficulty n arduousness, laboriousness; bar, barrier, crux, deadlock, dilemma, emergency, fix, hindrance, impediment, knot, obstacle, obstruction, pickle, pinch, predicament, stand, thwart, trial, trouble; objection; complication, controversy, difference, embarrassment, embroilment.
diffident adj distrustful, hesitant, hesitating, reluctant; bashful, modest, sheepish, shy.
dig vb channel, delve, grub, quarry, scoop, tunnel; * n poke, punch.
dignified adj august, decorous, grave, imposing, noble, stately.
dignify vb advance, elevate, ennoble, exalt; adorn, grace, honour.
dignity n elevation, eminence, exaltation, glory, honour, place, rank, respectability, station; decorum, grandeur, majesty, nobleness, stateliness;

dilapidated *adj* decadent, decayed, ruined, run down.

dilemma *n* difficulty, fix, plight, predicament, quandary, strait.

diligent *adj* active, attentive, busy, careful, constant, earnest, hard-working, industriousness, laborious, painstaking, persevering, tireless.

dim *vb* blur, cloud, darken, dull, obscure, sully; * *adj* cloudy, dark, dusky, faint, ill-defined, indistinct, mysterious, obscure, shadowy; dull; clouded, confused, darkened, faint, obscured; blurred, dull, sullied, tarnished.

diminish *vb* abate, belittle, contract, decrease, lessen, reduce; contract, curtail, cut, decrease, dwindle, melt, narrow, shrink, taper off.

din *vb* beat, boom, clamour, hammer, pound, repeat, ring, thunder; * *n* clamour, clash, clatter, crash, crashing, noise, racket, row, shout, uproar.

dingy *adj* brown, dull, dusky; colourless, dimmed, dulled, faded, obscure, soiled.

dip *vb* douse, duck, immerse, plunge; bail, ladle; dive, duck, pitch, plunge; incline, slope; * *n* decline, declivity, descent, drop, fall; depression, hole, hollow, pit; bathe, dipping, ducking, swim.

diplomat *n* diplomatist, envoy, go-between, legate.

dire *adj* alarming, awful, calamitous, cruel, destructive, disastrous, dreadful, gloomy, horrible, horrid, implacable, inexorable, shocking, terrible, terrific, tremendous.

direct *vb* aim, cast, level, point, turn; advise, control, dispose, guide, govern, regulate, rule; command; bid, enjoin, order; guide, lead, point, show; address, superscribe; * *adj* straight, undeviating; absolute, categorical, express, plain, unambiguous; earnest, frank, ingenuous, open, plain, sincere, straightforward.

direction *n* aim; bearing, course; administration, conduct, control, management, oversight, superintendence; lead; command, order, prescription; address.

dirty *vb* befoul, defile, foul, pollute, soil; * *adj* begrimed, defiled, foul, mucky, nasty, soiled, unclean; clouded, cloudy, dark, dull, muddy, sullied; base, grovelling, low, mean, pitiful, shabby, sneaking, squalid; disagreeable, foul, muddy, nasty, rainy, sloppy, uncomfortable.

disability *n* disqualification, impotence, impotency, inability, incompetence, incompetency, weakness.

disable *vb* cripple, enfeeble, hamstring, impair, weaken; disqualify, incapacitate, unfit.

disaffected *adj* alienated, dissatisfied, estranged.

disaffection *n* alienation, disagreement, dislike, disloyalty, estrangement, repugnance, unfriendliness.

disagree *vb* deviate, differ, vary; argue, bicker, clash, debate, dispute, quarrel.

disagreeable *adj* displeasing, distasteful, nasty, offensive, unpleasant, unsuitable.

disagreement *n* deviation, difference, discrepancy, dissimilitude, divergence, diversity, unlikeness; disaccord, dissent; argument, bickering, conflict, contention, dispute, disunion, disunity, jarring, misunderstanding, quarrel, strife, wrangle.

disappear *vb* depart, ebb, fade, vanish; cease.

disappoint *vb* baffle, balk, deceive, defeat, delude, foil, frustrate, mortify, thwart, vex.

disappointment *n* baffling, balk, failure, foiling, miscarriage, unfulfilment.

disapprove vb blame, censure, condemn, dislike, displeasure; disallow, reject.

disarrange vb confuse, derange, disallow, dishevel, dislocate, disturb, jumble, reject, tumble.

disaster n accident, adversity, blow, casualty, catastrophe, misadventure, misfortune, mishap, ruin, stroke.

disastrous adj calamitous, destructive, hapless, ill-fated, ruinous, unfortunate, unlucky, untoward; disaster, gloomy, portentous, threatening.

discard vb abandon, cast off, lay aside, reject; banish, break, cashier, discharge, dismiss, remove.

discern vb differentiate, discriminate, judge; behold, descry, discover, espy, notice, observe, recognise, see.

discharge vb unburden, unload; eject, emit, expel; cash, liquidate, pay; absolve, acquit, clear, free, release, relieve; discard, sack; destroy, remove; execute, perform, fulfil, observe; annul, cancel, invalidate; * n unloading; dismissal, displacement, ejection, emission, excretion, expulsion, vent; blast, explosion, filing; execution, fulfilment, observance; annulment, clearance, payment, satisfaction, settlement; exemption, liberation; flow, flux.

disciple n leaner, pupil, scholar, student; adherent, follower, supporter.

discipline vb breed, drill, educate, exercise, form, teach, train; control, govern, regulate, school; chasten, punish; * n culture, drill, drilling, exercise, instruction, training; control, subjection; chastisement, correction.

disclose vb discover, expose, manifest, uncover; bare, betray, communicate, divulge, impart, reveal, show, tell, unfold, unveil.

discomfort n annoyance, disquiet, distress, malaise, uneasiness, unpleasantness.

discompose vb confuse, derange, disarrange, disorder, embroil, unsettle; agitate, annoy, chafe, displease, disquiet, fret, irritate, nettle, provoke, ruffle, trouble, upset, vex, worry; bewilder, embarrass, fluster, perplex.

disconcert vb baffle, balk, contravene, defeat, frustrate, thwart, undo, upset; abash, agitate, demoralise, disturb, perplex, perturb, unbalance, worry.

disconnect vb detach, disengage, disjoin, disunite, separate, sever.

disconsolate adj cheerless, comfortless, desolate, gloomy, heartbroken, inconsolable, melancholy, sad, sorrowful, unhappy, woeful.

discontent n discontentment, displeasure, inquietude, restlessness.

discount vb allow for, lower, rebate, reduce; disregard, ignore, overlook; * n abatement; allowance, deduction, rebate.

discourage vb abase, awe, damp, daunt, depress, deject, dismay, dishearten, frighten; deter, dissuade, hinder.

discouragement n disheartening; dissuasion; damper, hindrance, obstacle, wet blanket.

discover vb communicate, disclose, impart, show, reveal, tell; ascertain, discern, espy, see; detect, determine, discern; invent.

discredit vb disbelieve, doubt, question; disgrace, dishonour, disparage, reproach; * n disbelief, distrust; disgrace, dishonour, disrepute, notoriety, opprobrium, reproach.

discreet adj careful, circumspect, considerate, discerning, prudent, sagacious, wary.

discrepancy n contrariety,

DISCRIMINATION

difference, discordance, divergence, incongruity, variance.
discrimination n difference, distinction; acumen, acuteness, judgement, penetration.
discuss vb agitate, argue, confer, consider, debate, deliberate, examine, sift.
disdainful adj contemptuous, haughty, scornful.
disease n affection, ail, ailment, complaint, distemper, illness, indisposition, infirmity, malady.
disengage vb clear, deliver, discharge, disembarrass, disembroil, disentangle, liberate, release; detach, disjoin, disunite, divide, separate; withdraw.
disentangle vb loosen, separate, unfold, unravel; clear, detach, disconnect, disembroil, liberate, loose.
disfigurement n blemishing, deforming, injury, marring; blemish, defect, spot, stain.
disgrace vb degrade, humble, humiliate; abase, debase, discredit, dishonour, disparage, reproach, stain, sully, taint, tarnish; * n disrepute, infamy, mortification, shame.
disgraceful adj discreditable, dishonourable, disreputable, infamous, scandalous, shameful.
disguise vb cloak, conceal, cover, hide, mask, muffle, screen, secrete, veil; * n cover, mask, veil; blind, cloak, masquerade, pretence, pretext.
disgust vb nauseate; abominate, detest, displease, offend, repel, revolt; * n disrelish, distaste, loathing, nausea; antipathy, aversion, dislike, repugnance, revulsion.
dish vb deal out, ladle, serve; blight, dash, mar, ruin, spoil; * n bowl, plate, saucer, vessel.
dishearten vb cast down, damp, daunt, deject, deter, discourage.
dishevelled adj disarranged,
disordered, messed, tumbled, unkempt, untidy.
dishonest adj cheating, corrupt, crafty, crooked, deceiving, deceptive, faithless, false, fraudulent, slippery, unfair, unscrupulous.
dishonour vb abase, defame, degrade, discredit, disfavour, dishonour, disgrace, reproach, shame, taint; * n abasement, contempt, degradation, disesteem, disfavour, dishonour, disparagement, disrepute, ignominy, infamy, odium, reproach, scandal, shame.
dishonourable adj discreditable, disgraceful, ignominious, scandalous, shameful; base, false, false-hearted.
disinfect vb cleanse, fumigate, purify.
disintegrate vb crumble, decompose, dissolve, disunite, pulverise.
disinterested adj candid, fair, high-minded, impartial, unbiased, unselfish; liberal, unselfish.
disjointed adj desultory, disconnected, loose.
dislike vb abominate, detest, disapprove, disrelish, hate, loathe; * n antagonism, aversion, disapproval, disgust, displeasure, distaste, loathing, repugnance.
dislocate vb disarrange, disorder, displace, disturb; disjoint, slip.
dislodge vb dismount, displace, eject, expel, oust.
disloyal adj disaffected, faithless, false, traitorous, treacherous, unfaithful, unpatriotic.
dismal adj cheerless, dark, dull, gloomy; blue, calamitous, doleful, dolorous, funereal, melancholy, mournful, sad, sorrowful.
dismantle vb divest, strip.
dismay vb affright, alarm, appal, daunt, discourage, dishearten, frighten, horrify, scare, terrify; * n affright, alarm,

fear, fright, horror, terror.
dismiss *vb* banish, cashier, discharge, disperse, reject, release.
disobey *vb* contravene, infringe, transgress, violate.
disorder *vb* confound, confuse, derange, disorganise, disturb, upset; * *n* confusion, disarray, disorganisation, irregularity, jumble, mess, topsy-turvy; brawl, disturbance, fight, quarrel, riot; tumultuousness, turbulence; ail, aliment, illness, indisposition, malady, sickness.
disorderly *adj* chaotic, confused, intemperate, irregular, untidy; lawless, riotous, tumultuous, turbulent, ungovernable, unruly.
disown *vb* disavow, disclaim, reject, renounce; deny, disallow.
disparage *vb* belittle, decry, depreciate, doubt, question, ran down, underestimate, underpraise, underrate; defame, inveigh against, reflect on, reproach, slur, speak ill of.
dispassionate *adj* calm, collected, composed, imperturbable, moderate, quiet, serene, staid, undisturbed, unexcitable, unimpassioned, unruffled; disinterested, fair, neutral, unbiased.
dispatch, **despatch** *vb* assassinate, kill, murder, slay; accelerate, conclude, dismiss, expedite, finish, forward, hasten, hurry, speed; * *n* sending; expedition, haste, rapidity, speed; conduct, doing, transaction; document, instruction, letter, missive, report.
dispel *vb* banish, disperse, dissipate.
dispensation *n* allotment, apportioning, dispensing, distributing, distribution; stewardship; economy, plan, scheme; exemption, indulgence, licence.

dispirited *adj* dejected, depressed, disheartened, downcast, down-hearted.
display *vb* expand, open, spread, unfold; exhibit, show; parade; * *n* exhibition, manifestation, show; ostentation, parade, pomp.
displease *vb* disgruntle, disoblige, dissatisfy, offend; affront, anger, annoy, chafe, chagrin, fret, nettle, pique, vex.
disposal *n* arrangement, disposition; conduct, direction, government, management, ordering, regulation.
dispose *vb* arrange, distribute, marshal, group, range, rank, set; regulate, settle; incline, induce, lead, move, predispose; decide; rule, settle; arrange, bargain, compound; convey, sell, transfer.
disposed *adj* apt, inclined, prone, ready, tending.
disposition *n* arrangement, arranging, classification, grouping, placing; adjustment, control, direction, disposal, management, ordering; aptitude, bent, bias, nature, proneness, predisposition, proclivity, propensity, tendency; constitution, humour, native, nature, temper; inclination, willingness; bestowal, bestowment, dispensation, distribution.
disproportion *n* disparity, inadequacy, inequality, insufficiency; incommensurateness.
dispute *vb* altercate, argue, debate, litigate; bicker, brawl, jangle, quarrel, spar, spat, squabble, tiff; agitate, argue, debate; challenge, contradict, controvert, deny, contest, struggle for; * *n* controversy, discussion, disputation; altercation, argument, brawl, disagreement, dissension, squabble, rift.
disregard *vb* contemn, despise, disdain, disobey, ignore,

neglect, overlook, slight; * *n* contempt, inattention, neglect, oversight; disfavour.

disreputable *adj* discreditable, dishonourable, disgraceful, infamous, shameful; base, contemptible, low, mean, vile, vulgar.

disrespect *n* irreverence, neglect, slight; discourteousness, incivility, rudeness.

dissect *vb* analyse, examine, explore, scrutinise, sift.

dissemble *vb* cloak, conceal, cover, disguise, hide.

disseminate *vb* circulate, diffuse, proclaim, promulgate, propagate, scatter, spread.

dissent *vb* decline, differ, disagree, refuse; * *n* difference, disagreement, opposition, refusal.

disservice *n* disfavour, harm, hurt, ill-turn, injury.

dissidence *n* disagreement, dissent, sectarianism.

dissimilar *adj* different, diverse, heterogeneous, unlike, various.

dissimulation *n* concealment, deceit, dissembling, double-dealing, feigning, hypocrisy.

dissipate *vb* dispel, disperse, scatter; consume, expend, lavish, spend, waste; vanish.

dissolute *adj* abandoned, corrupt, debauched, disorderly, dissipated, graceless, lax, lewd, licentious, loose, shameless, vicious, wanton, wild.

dissolve *vb* liquefy, melt; divide, loose, separate, sever; ruin; disappear, fade, vanish; crumble, decompose, perish.

distance *vb* excel, outdo, outstrip, surpass; * *n* remoteness; aloofness, coldness, frigidity, reserve, stiffness; absence, space.

distant *adj* far, far-away, remote; aloof, cold, cool, frigid, haughty, reserved, stiff; faint, obscure, slight.

distasteful *adj* disgusting, loathsome, nauseating, unpalatable; disagreeable, offensive, repugnant, repulsive.

distinct *adj* definite, discrete, disjunct, individual, separate; clear, defined, definite, obvious, plain, unconfused, unmistakable.

distinction *n* discernment, discrimination, distinguishing; difference; account, credit, eminence, fame, name, note, rank, renown, reputation, repute.

distinctive *adj* characteristic, differentiating, discriminating, distinguishing.

distinguish *vb* characterise, mark; discern, discriminate, perceive, recognise, see, single out, tell; divide, separate; honour.

distinguished *adj* celebrated, eminent, famous, illustrious, noted; laureate, marked, shining, superior.

distort *vb* contort, deform, screw, twist, warp; falsify, misrepresent, pervert.

distract *vb* divert, draw away; bewilder, confound, confuse, derange, disconcert, disturb, embarrass, madden, mystify, perplex, puzzle.

distress *vb* afflict, annoy, grieve, pain, perplex, trouble; seize, take; * *n* affliction, disaster, misery, misfortune, hardship, perplexity, trial; agony, anguish, grief, suffering; gnawing, gripe, pain, torment, torture; poverty, privation, straits, want.

distribute *vb* allocate, allot, assign, deal, dispense, divide, dole out, give, partition, share; arrange, assort, class, classify, dispose.

distribution *n* allocation, allotment, assignment, assortment, dispensing; arrangement, disposal, classification, division, dole, grouping, partition, sharing.

district *n* circuit, department, neighbourhood, quarter,

distrust vb disbelieve, doubt, mistrust, question, suspect; * n doubt, mistrust, question, suspicion.

disturb vb shake, stir; confuse, disarrange, disorder, unsettle, upset; annoy, discompose, disconcert, disquiet, distract, fuss, molest, perturb, plague, trouble, ruffle, vex, worry; interrupt, hinder.

disturbance n agitation, commotion, confusion, derangement, disorder, perturbation; annoyance, discomposure, excitement, fuss; hindrance, interruption; brawl, commotion, disorder, excitement, riot, rising, tumult, turmoil, uproar.

disunite vb detach, disconnect, disjoin, dissociate, divide, part, rend, separate, segregate, sever.

disuse n discontinuance, neglect.

ditch vb dig, excavate, furrow, gouge, trench; abandon, discard, dump, scrap; * n channel, drain, fosse, moat, trench.

dive vb descend, explore, fathom, plunge, sound; * n drop, fall, header, plunge; bar, den, joint, saloon.

diverge vb divide, separate; deviate, differ, disagree, vary.

diverse adj different, differing, disagreement, dissimilar, divergent, multiform, separate, unlike, variant, various, varying.

divert vb deflect, distract, disturb; amuse, beguile, delight, entertain, gratify, recreate, refresh, solace.

divest vb disrobe, strip, unclothe, undress; dispossess, strip.

divide vb bisect, cleave, cut, dismember, disunite, open, part, rend, segregate, separate, sever, shear, split, sunder; allocate, allot, assign, dispense, distribute, dole, mete, portion, share; demarcate, partition; alienate, disunite, estrange.

divine vb foretell, predict, presage, vaticinate, prophesy; believe, conjecture, fancy, guess, suppose, surmise, suspect, think; * adj deiform, godlike, superhuman; angelic, celestial, heavenly, holy, sacred, spiritual; exalted, supreme, transcendent; * n churchman, minister, parson, priest.

division n compartmentalisation, disjunction, dismemberment, separation; category, class, compartment, head, parcel, section, segment; demarcation; alienation, allotment, apportionment, distribution; difference, disagreement, discord, estrangement, feud, rupture.

divorce vb disconnect, dissolve, disunite, part, separate, sever; split up, sunder; * n disjunction, dissolution, disunion, division, parting, severance.

divulge vb communicate, declare, disclose, discover, expose, impart, promulgate, publish, reveal, tell, uncover.

dizzy adj giddy, vertiginous; careless, heedless, reeling.

do vb accomplish, achieve, act, commit, effect, execute, perform; end, finish, settle, terminate; conduct, transact; observe, perform, practice; render; prepare; cheat, chouse, cozen, hoax, swindle; serve, suffice; * n act, action, deed, doing, exploit, feat, thing; banquet, event, function, party.

docile adj amenable, obedient, pliant, teachable, yielding.

dock vb clip, curtail, cut, truncate; lessen, shorten; anchor, moor; join, meet; * n anchorage, basin, berth, dockyard, dry dock, harbour,

doctor vb adulterate, alter, cook, falsify, manipulate, tamper with; attend, cure, heal, treat; fix, mend, overhaul, repair, service; * n general practitioner (GP), leech, medic, physician; adept.

doctrine n article, belief, creed, dogma, precept, principle, teaching.

dodge vb equivocate, evade, prevaricate, shuffle; * n artifice, cavil, quibble, subterfuge, trick.

dogma n article, belief, creed, doctrine, opinion, principle.

dogmatic adj categorical, settled; arrogant, confident, imperious, opinionated, oracular, peremptory, positive.

domain n authority, dominion, jurisdiction, sway; dominion, empire, realm, territory; branch, department, province, realm, region.

domestic n help, home help, maid, servant; * adj family, home, household, private; internal, intestine.

domesticate vb break, tame; adopt, naturalise.

domicile vb dwell, inhabit, live, reside; * n abode, dwelling, habitation, harbour, home, house.

dominant adj ascendant, ascending, chief, controlling, governing, outstanding, paramount, preeminent, preponderant, presiding, prevailing, ruling.

dominate vb control, rule, sway; command, overtop, surmount.

domineer vb rule, tyrannise; bluster, bully, menace, swagger, threaten.

dominion n authority, command, control, jurisdiction, mastery, rule, sovereignty, sway; country, kingdom, realm, territory.

donation n alms, benefaction, contribution, dole, gift, grant, offering, present.

done adj accomplished, achieved, effected, performed; completed, concluded, ended, finished; transacted; cooked; cheated, cozened, swindled; (with **for**) damned, hors de combat, ruined, spoiled, wound up.

double vb fold, plait; duplicate, increase, multiply, repeat; return; * adj binary, coupled, geminate, paired; dual, twice, twofold; dishonest, double-dealing, false, hollow, insincere, knavish, two-faced; * adv doubly, twice, twofold; * n doubling, fold; manoeuvre, ruse, shift, stratagem, trick; copy, counterpart, twin.

doubt vb demur, fluctuate, hesitate, waver; distrust, mistrust, query, question, suspect; * n dubiousness, hesitation, indecision, irresolution, question, suspense, uncertainty, distrust, misgiving, mistrust, suspicion.

doubtful adj dubious, hesitating, sceptical, undetermined, wavering; ambiguous, dubious, equivocal, hazardous, obscure, problematical, unsure; questionable, undecided, unquestioned.

dowdy adj awkward, dingy, drab, ill-dressed, shabby, slovenly; old-fashioned, unfashionable.

downcast adj crestfallen, depressed, despondent, discouraged, disheartened, downhearted, low-spirited, sad, unhappy.

downfall n descent, destruction, fall, ruin.

downhearted adj chapfallen, crestfallen, dejected, depressed, discouraged, disheartened, downcast, low-spirited, sad, unhappy.

downright adj absolute, clear, explicit, plain, positive, sheer, simple, undisguised; above-board, artless, blunt, direct, frank, honest, open, sincere,

DROOP

straightforward.
doze vb drowse, nap, sleep, slumber; * n drowse, forty-winks, nap.
dozy adj drowsy, heavy, sleepy, sluggish.
draft vb detach, select; conscript, impress; delineate, draw, outline, sketch; * n drawing, selection; outline, sketch; bill, cheque, order.
drag vb draw, haul, pull, tow, rug; trial; linger; * n favour, influence, pull; brake, check, curb, lag, resistance, skid, slackening, slack-off, slowing.
drain vb milk, sluice, tap; empty, evacuate, exhaust; dry; * n channel, ditch, sewer, sluice, trench, watercourse; exhaustion.
draw vb drag, haul, tow, tug, pull; attract; drain, suck, syphon; extract; breathe in, inhale, inspire; engage, induce, influence, lead, move, persuade; extend, protract, stretch; depict, sketch; deduce, derive, infer; compose, draft, frame, prepare; blister, write.
drawback n defect, deficiency, disadvantage, fault, flaw, imperfection, injury; discount, reduction.
dread vb apprehend, fear; * adj dreadful, frightful, horrible, terrible; awful, venerable; * n alarm, fear, terror; awe.
dreadful adj alarming, appalling, awesome, fearful, frightful, horrible, horrid, terrible, terrific, tremendous; awful.
dream vb fancy, imagine, think; * n conceit, day-dream, delusion, fancy, fantasy, illusion, imagination, reverie, vision.
dreamer n enthusiast, visionary.
dreamy adj absent, fanciful, ideal, misty, shadowy, unreal, visionary.
dreary adj cheerless, dark, depressing, dismal, drear, gloomy, lonely, sad, solitary, sorrowful; boring, dull, tedious, uninteresting, wearisome.
drench vb dowse, drown, saturate, soak, souse, wet; purge.
dress vb align, straighten; adjust, arrange, dispose; fit, prepare; accoutre, clothe, robe; deck, decorate, drape, trim; * n attire, clothes, clothing, costume, garb, guise, garments, habit, raiment, suit, toilet, vesture; bravery; frock, gown, robe.
dressy adj flashy, showy.
drift vb accumulate, drive, float, wander; * n bearing, course, direction; aim, design, intent, intention, mark, object, purpose, scope, tendency; deposit; passage, tunnel; current, rush, sweep; heap, pile.
drill vb bore, pierce; discipline, exercise, instruct, teach, train; * n borer; discipline, exercise, training.
drink vb sip, swill; indulge, revel; swallow; absorb; * n beverage, draught, liquid, potion; nip, sip, refreshment.
drip vb dribble, drop, leak, trickle; distil, filter; ooze, seep, weep; * n dribble, drop, leak, leaking, trickle; bore, nuisance, wet blanket.
drive vb hurl, impel, propel, send, shoot, thrust; incite, press, urge; compel, constrain, force, oblige, overburden, press, rush; go, guide, ride, travel; aim, intend; * n effort, energy, pressure; airing, ride; road.
drivel vb babble, dote, dribble, slaver, slobber; * n drivelling, fatuity, nonsense, rubbish, slaver, stuff.
drizzle vb mizzle, rain, shower, sprinkle; * n mist, rain, sprinkling.
drone vb dawdle, drawl, idle, loaf, lounge; * n idler, loafer, lounger.
droop vb fade, wither; decline, fail, faint, flag, sink, weaken; bend, hang.

drop vb distil, drip, shed; decline, depress, descend, dump, lower, sink; desert, forswear, leave, omit, quit; cease, discontinue, intermit, remit; fall, precipitate; * n bead, globule; earring, pendant.

drought n aridity, dryness, thirstiness.

drown vb deluge, flood, immerse, overflow, sink, submerge, swamp; overcome, overpower, overwhelm.

drowse vb doze, nap, sleep, slumber, snooze; * n doze, forty winks, nap, siesta, sleep, snooze.

drudge vb fag, grub, grind, plod, slave, toil, work; * n fag, grind, hack, hard worker, menial, plodder, slave, toiler, worker.

drug vb dose, medicate; disgust, surfeit; * n medicine, physic, remedy; poison.

drunk adj boozed, drunken, intoxicated, soaked, tipsy; ablaze, delirious, fervent, suffused; * n alcoholic, boozer, dipsomaniac, soak; bender, binge.

dry vb dehydrate, desiccate, drain, parch; * adj desiccated, dried, juiceless, sapless, unmoistened; arid, parched; drouthy, thirsty; barren, dull, insipid, plain, pointless, tame, tedious, tiresome, vapid; cutting, keen, sarcastic, severe, sharp, sly.

dub vb call, christen, designate, entitle, name, style, term.

dubious adj doubtful, fluctuating, hesitant, uncertain, undecided; ambiguous, equivocal.

duck vb dip, dive, immerse, plunge, submerge; bend, bow, dodge, stoop.

duct n canal, channel, conduit, funnel, pipe, tube.

due adj owed, owing; appropriate, becoming, befitting, fit, proper, suitable, right; * adv direct, directly, exactly, just, squarely, straight; * n claim, debt, desert, right.

dull vb blunt; benumb, besot, deaden, paralyse, stupefy; deject, depress, discourage, dishearten, dispirit; allay, alleviate, assuage, moderate, quiet, soften; deaden, dim, sully; * adj blockish, brutish, stolid, stupid, unintelligent; apathetic, callous, dead, insensible, passionless, unfeeling, unimpassioned, unresponsive; heavy, inactive, inert, lifeless, slow, sluggish; blunt, dulled, obtuse; cheerless, dreary, gloomy, sad, sombre; dim, lack-lustre, lustreless, obscure, opaque, tarnished; dry, flat, insipid, tedious, tiresome, uninteresting.

duly adv befittingly, fitly, properly, rightly; regularly.

dumb adj inarticulate, mute, silent, soundless, speechless, voiceless.

dumbfound vb amaze, astonish, astound, bewilder, confound, confuse, pose.

duplicate vb copy, double, repeat, replicate, reproduce; * adj doubled, twofold; * n copy, counterpart, replica.

duplicity n circumvention, deceit, deception, dishonesty, double-dealing, falseness, fraud, guile, perfidy.

durable adj abiding, constant, continuing, enduring, firm, permanent, stable.

duration n continuance, continuation, permanency; period, time.

duress n captivity, confinement, constraint, durance, hardship, restraint; compulsion.

dutiful adj duteous, obedient, submissive; respectful, reverential.

duty n allegiance, obligation, reverence; business, function, office, service; excise, tariff, tax, toll.

dwell vb inhabit, live, lodge, remain, reside, rest, stay, stop tenant.

dwindle vb decrease, diminish,

lessen, shrink; decay, decline, sink, waste away.
dye *vb* colour, stain; * *n* cast, colour, hue, shade, stain, tinge, tint.
dying *adj* mortal, perishable; * *n* death, decease, demise, departure, exit.
dynasty *n* dominion, government, rule.

E

eager *adj* avid, anxious, desirous, fain, greedy, impatient, keen, longing; enthusiastic, fervent, fervid, forward, glowing, hot, sanguine, vehement, zealous.
ear *n* attention, hearing, heed, regard.
early *adj* opportune, timely; forward, premature; dawning; * *adv* anon, beforehand, ere, seasonably, shortly, soon.
earn *vb* acquire, collect, gain, get, obtain, procure, reap, win; deserve, merit.
earnest *adj* animated, ardent, eager, cordial, fervid, glowing, hearty, importune, warm; fixed, intent, steady; sincere, true, truthful; important, serious, weighty; * *n* reality, seriousness, truth; foretaste, pledge, promise; payment.
earnings *npl* allowance, income, pay, proceeds, profits, reward, salary.
earth *n* globe, orb, planet, world; clay, dirt, ground, land, sod, soil, turf, mankind, world.
earthly *adj* terrestrial; base, low, gross, sensual, sordid, unspiritual, worldly; bodily, material, natural, secular, temporal.
earthy *adj* earth-like; earthly, terrestrial; coarse, gross, material, unrefined.
ease *vb* pacify, quiet, relieve, still; abate, allay, alleviate, assuage, diminish, mitigate, soothe; loosen, release; favour; * *n* leisure, quiescence, rest; calmness, content, enjoyment, happiness, peace, quiet, quietness, relief, repose, satisfaction, serenity, tranquillity; easiness, facility, readiness; flexibility, liberty, lightness, naturalness, unconcern; comfort.
easy *adj* light; comfortable, contented, effortless, painless, quiet, satisfied, tranquil, untroubled; complaisant, complying, facile, manageable, submissive, tractable, yielding; graceful, informal, natural; flowing, ready, smooth, unaffected; gentle, lenient, mild, moderate; comfortable, loose, unconcerned.
eat *vb* chew, consume, devour, ravage, swallow; consume, demolish, erode; breakfast, dine, feed, lunch, sup.
eatable *adj* edible, harmless, wholesome.
ebb *vb* abate, recede, retire, subside; decay, decline, decrease, deteriorate, sink, wane; * *n* refluence, regress, regression, retrocession, retrogression, return; decay, decline, degeneration, deterioration, wane; decrease, diminution.
eccentricity *n* flattening, flatness; aberration, oddity, peculiarity, singularity, strangeness.
echo *vb* resound, reverberate, ring; repeat; * *n* answer, repetition; imitation.
eclipse *vb* cloud, darken, dim, obscure, veil; annihilate, blot out, extinguish; * *n* clouding, concealment, darkening, dimming, disappearance, hiding, occultation, vanishing, veiling; blotting out, extinguishment.
economise *vb* manage, save; retrench.
economy *n* frugality, providence, retrenchment, saving, thrift; administration, arrangement,

method, order, plan, regulation; dispensation.

ecstasy n frenzy, madness, trance; delight, gladness, joy, rapture, ravishment, transport.

edge vb sharpen; border, fringe, rim; * n border, brim, brink, border, bound, fringe, hem, lip, margin, rim, verge; animation, interest, keenness, sharpness, zest; bitterness, sharpness, sting.

edible adj eatable, harmless, wholesome.

edict n act, command, decision, decree, law, mandate, notice, order, ordinance, proclamation, regulation, statute.

edify vb educate, enlightenment, improve, inform, instruct, teach, upbuild.

educate vb breed, cultivate, develop, discipline, drill, exercise, inform, instruct, mature, rear, school, teach, train.

education n breeding, cultivation, culture, discipline, drilling, instruction, nurture, schooling, teaching, training, tuition.

eerie adj awesome, creepy, frightening, strange, uncanny.

effect vb cause, create, effectuate, produce; accomplish, achieve, carry, compass, complete, conclude, contrive, do, execute, force, perform, realise, work; * n consequence, event, fruit, issue, outcome, result; fact, force, power, reality; weight; drift, intent, meaning, significance, tenor.

effective adj able, active, adequate, convincing, effectual, sufficient; efficacious, energetic, potent, powerful.

effects npl furniture, goods, movables, property.

efficient adj active, capable, effective, effectual, efficacious, operative; able, energetic, skilful.

effigy n figure, image, likeness, portrait, statue.

effort n attempt, endeavour, essay, exertion, spurt, strife, stretch, struggle, trial.

effrontery n assurance, audacity, boldness, disrespect, incivility, insolence, presumption, rudeness, shamelessness.

effusion n discharge, emission, gush, outpouring; shedding, waste; speech, talk, utterance.

egotistic, egotistical adj conceited, opinionated, self-asserting, self-centred, self-conceited, self-important, vain.

eject vb belch, discharge, evacuate, puke, spew, spit, spout, spurt, vomit; bounce, discharge, dismiss, disposes, evict, expel, fire; banish, reject, throw out.

elaborate vb develop, improve, mature, produce, ripen; * adj complicated, decorated, detailed, laboured, laborious, perfected, studied.

elbow vb crowd, force, hustle, jostle, nudge, push; * n angle, bend, corner, joining, turn.

elder adj older, senior; ancient, earlier; * n ancestor, senior; senator, senior.

elect vb appoint, choose, designate, pick, select; * adj choice, chosen, picked, selected; appointed, elected.

election n appointment, choice, preference, selection.

elector n chooser, selector, voter.

electrify vb charge; astonish, excite, rouse, startle, stir, thrill.

elegant adj beautiful, classical, dainty, graceful, handsome, neat, tasteful, well-made, well-proportioned; courtly, cultivated, fashionable, genteel, polite, refined.

element n basis, component, constituent, factor, ingredient, part, principle, unit; sphere.

elementary adj primordial, simple, uncompounded; basic, component, fundamental, primary, rudimentary.

elevate vb erect, lift, raise; advance, exalt, promote;

dignify, exalt, improve, refine; animate, cheer, elate, excite, rouse.

eligible *adj* desirable; qualified, suitable.

eliminate *vb* disengage, eradicate, exclude, expel, remove, separate; omit, reject.

elope *vb* bolt, decamp, disappear, leave.

eloquence *n* oratory, rhetoric.

else *adv* besides, differently, otherwise.

elucidate *vb* clarify, explain, expound, illuminate, illustrate, unfold.

elusive *adj* deceptive, deceitful, delusive, evasive, fraudulent, illusory; equivocatory.

emancipate *vb* deliver, discharge, enfranchise, free, liberate, release, unchain, unfetter.

embargo *vb* ban, bar, blockade, debar, exclude, prohibit, stop, withhold; * *n* ban, bar, blockade, prohibition, prohibitory, restraint, restriction, stoppage.

embark *vb* engage, enlist.

embarrass *vb* beset, entangle, perplex; annoy, distress, harass, involve, plague, trouble, vex; abash, confound, confuse, disconcert, mortify, pose, shame.

embellish *vb* beautify, deck, decorate, enhance, enrich, grace, ornament.

embezzle *vb* appropriate, misappropriate, peculate, pilfer, steal.

emblem *n* badge, crest, device, mark, sign, symbol, token, type.

embody *vb* combine, compact, concentrate; comprehend, contain, embrace, include; codify.

embrace *vb* clasp; accept, seize; comprehend, comprise, contain, embody, encircle, enclose, encompass, enfold, hold, include; * *n* clasp, fold, hug.

emerge *vb* rise; emanate, escape, issue; appear.

emergency *n* crisis, difficulty, dilemma, extremity, necessity, pass, pinch, push, strait, urgency; conjuncture, crisis, pass.

eminence *n* elevation, hill, projection, prominence; celebrity, conspicuousness, distinction, fame, loftiness, note, prominence, reputation, repute, renown.

eminent *adj* elevated, high, lofty; celebrated, conspicuous, distinguished, famous, illustrious, notable, prominent, remarkable.

emit *vb* breathe out, dart, discharge, eject, exhale, hurl, jet, outpour, shed, shoot, spurt, squirt.

emotion *n* agitation, excitement, feeling, passion, sentiment.

emphasis *n* accent, stress; force, importance, moment, weight.

emphatic *adj* decided, distinct, energetic, expressive, forcible, intensive, positive, significant, strong.

empire *n* domain, dominion, sovereignty; authority, command, control, rule, sway.

employ *vb* busy, devote, engage, exercise, occupy, retain; apply, use; * *n* employment, service.

employment *n* avocation, business, calling, employ, engagement, occupation, pursuit, trade, work.

empty *vb* deplete, drain, exhaust; discharge; flow; * *adj* blank, hollow, unoccupied, vacant, vacuous, void; devoid, hungry; unfilled, unfurnished; unsatisfactory, unsatisfying, useless, vain; clear, deserted, exhausted, free, unburdened, unloaded, waste; foolish, senseless, silly, stupid, weak.

enable *vb* authorise, empower, fit, permit, prepare, qualify, warrant.

enact *vb* authorise, command, decree, establish, ordain, order; act, perform, personate, play.

enchant *vb* beguile, charm,

ENCHANTMENT

delude, fascinate; captivate, catch, win; beatify, delight, rapture, transport.

enchantment *n* incantation, magic, necromancy, spell; bliss, delight, fascination, rapture, transport.

enclose *vb* circumscribe, coop, encompass, fence in, hedge, include, pen, shut in, surround; box, cover, envelop, wrap.

encounter *vb* confront, meet; attack, combat, contend, engage, strive, struggle; * *n* assault, attack, clash, meeting, onset; action, battle, brush, combat, conflict, contest, dispute.

encourage *vb* assure, cheer, comfort, console, embolden, fortify, hearten, incite, reassure, stimulate, strengthen; aid, advance, approve, countenance, favour, foster, help, promote, support.

encumbrance *n* burden, clog, deadweight, drag, hampering, hindrance, load; claim, debt.

end *vb* abolish, close, conclude, discontinue, dissolve, drop, finish, stop; annihilate, destroy, kill; cease; * *n* tip; cessation, close, ending, finale, finish, last, period, stoppage; completion, conclusion; annihilation, catastrophe, destruction, dissolution; bound, limit, termination; consequence, event, issue, result, settlement, upshot; fragment, remnant, tag, tail; aim, design, goal, intent, intention, object, purpose.

endanger *vb* commit, hazard, peril, risk.

endear *vb* attach, attract, bind, captivate, charm, win.

endearment *n* attachment, fondness, love, tenderness; caress.

endeavour *vb* aim, essay, labour, seek, strive, struggle, study, try; * *n* aim, attempt, effort, essay, trial, struggle, trial.

endless *adj* boundless, infinite, limitless, unlimited; eternal, everlasting, perpetual, unending; deathless, ever-enduring, eternal, ever-living, immortal, undying.

endorse *vb* approve, back, confirm, guarantee, sanction, superscribe, support, visa, vouch for, warrant;

endow *vb* bequeath, confer, dower, endue, enrich, gift, invest, supply.

endowment *n* bequest, boon, gift, grant, largesse, present; fund, property, revenue; ability, aptitude, capability, capacity, faculty, genius, gift, power, quality, talent.

endurance *n* abiding, bearing, sufferance, toleration; backbone, bottom, forbearance, guts, patience, resignation.

endure *vb* bear, support, sustain; experience, suffer, weather; permit, pocket, swallow, tolerate, stomach, submit, withstand; continue, last, remain, wear.

enemy *n* foe; antagonist, opponent, rival.

energetic *adj* active, effective, emphatic, enterprising, forceful, hearty, potent, powerful, strenuous, strong, vigorous.

energy *n* activity, drive, efficacy, efficiency, force, go, impetus, intensity, might, potency, power, strength, vim; life, spirit, spiritedness, zeal.

enforce *vb* compel, constrain, exact, force, oblige, require.

engage *vb* bind, commit, pledge, promise; affiance, plight, promise; book, brief, employ, enlist, hire, retain; arrest, attach, draw, entertain, gain, win; busy, employ, occupy; attack, encounter; combat, contend, contest, fight, struggle; embark, enlist; agree, bargain, promise, undertake, warrant.

engagement *n* appointment,

assurance, contract, obligation, pledge, promise; betrothal; avocation, business, calling, employment, enterprise, occupation; battle, combat, encounter, fight.
engine *n* invention, machine; agency, device, instrument, means, method, weapon.
engrave *vb* carve, chisel, cut, etch, grave, sculpture; grave, impress, imprint, inscribe.
engross *vb* absorb, engage, occupy, take up; buy up, forestall, monopolise.
enhance *vb* advance, aggravate, elevate, increase, intensify, raise.
enigma *n* conundrum, mystery, problem, puzzle.
enjoyment *n* delight, happiness, pleasure, satisfaction.
enlarge *vb* amplify, broaden, extend; distend, expand, increase, magnify, widen; ennoble, expand, greaten; descant; expand, extend, increase, swell.
enlighten *vb* illume, illuminate; counsel, civilise, instruct, teach.
enlist *vb* enrol, levy, recruit, register; list; embark, engage.
enliven *vb* animate, quicken, rouse, wake; cheer; brighten, delight, gladden, inspire, inspirit, rouse.
enmity *n* aversion, bitterness, hate, hatred, hostility, ill-will, malevolence.
enormous *adj* abnormal, exceptional, irregular; colossal, huge, immense, monstrous, vast; gigantic, prodigious, tremendous.
enough *adj* abundant, adequate, ample, plenty, sufficient; * *adv* sufficiently; * *n* abundance, plenty, sufficiency.
enrage *vb* anger, exasperate, incense, inflame, irritate, madden, provoke.
enrich *vb* endow; adorn, deck, decorate, grace, ornament.
enrol *vb* engage, engross, enlist, list, register; record.
enslave *vb* captivate, dominate, master, overpower, subjugate.
ensnare *vb* catch, entrap; inveigle, seduce; bewilder, confound, entangle.
entangle *vb* catch, ensnare, entrap; confuse, intertwine, intertwist, knot, mat, tangle; bewilder, embarrass, encumber, ensnare, involve, perplex, puzzle.
enterprise *n* adventure, attempt, cause, endeavour, essay, project, scheme, venture; activity, daring, dash, energy, readiness; push.
enterprising *adj* adventurous, audacious, bold, daring, venturesome; adventurous, alert, energetic, resourceful, smart, stirring, strenuous.
entertain *vb* fete, receive, treat; cherish, hold, lodge, shelter; consider; amuse, cheer, please, recreate.
entertainment *n* banquet, feast, reception, treat; amusement, diversion, pastime, recreation, sport.
enthusiasm *n* fanaticism; ardour, earnestness, devotion, eagerness, fervour, passion, warmth.
enthusiast *n* devotee, fan, fanatic; dreamer.
entice *vb* allure, attract, bait, cajole, decoy, lure, persuade, prevail on, seduce, tempt, wile.
entire *adj* complete, integrated, perfect, unbroken, undivided, unimpaired, whole; complete, full, thorough; mere, pure, sheer, unalloyed, unmingled, unmixed.
entitle *vb* call, characterise, christen, designate, dub, name style; enable, fit for, qualify for.
entrance *n* access, approach, avenue, incoming; adit, avenue, door, doorway, entry, gate, lobby, mouth, passage, portal, vestibule; beginning, commencement, debut, introduction; admission,

entrée; * *vb* bewitch, charm, delight, enchant, enrapture, fascinate, transport.

entreaty *n* appeal, importunity, petition, prayer, request, suit, supplication.

entrust *vb* assign, commit, confide, consign.

entwine *vb* entwist, interlace, intertwine, inweave, twine, twist, weave; embrace, encircle, encumber, surround.

enumerate *vb* calculate, cite, compute, count, detail, number, reckon, recount, specify.

envelop *vb* enfold, enwrap, fold, pack, wrap; cover, encompass, enfold, fold, hide, surround.

envelope *n* capsule, case, covering, shroud, skin, wrapper, veil, wrap.

envoy *n* ambassador, minister; courier, messenger.

envy *vb* hate; grudge; covet, desire; * *n* enviousness, hate, hatred, ill-will, jealousy, malice; grudge.

ephemeral *adj* brief, evanescent, fleeting, fugitive, momentary, occasional, short-lived, transient.

epidemic *adj* general, pandemic, prevailing, prevalent; * *n* outbreak, plague, spread, wave.

epigrammatic *adj* antithetic, concise, laconic, poignant, pointed, sharp, terse.

epitome *n* abbreviation, abridgement, abstract, breviary, brief, comment, condensation, digest, summary, syllabus.

epitomise *vb* abbreviate, abridge, abstract, condense, contract, cut, reduce, summarise.

equable *adj* calm, equal, even, regular, steady, uniform, serene, tranquil.

equal *vb* equalise, even, match; * *adj* alike, coordinate, equivalent, like; even, level; equable, regular; equitable, even-handed, fair, impartial, just, unbiased; commensurate, corresponding, parallel; adequate, competent, fit, sufficient; * *n* fellow, match, peer; rival.

equip *vb* arm, furnish, provide, supply; array, dress.

equipment *n* apparatus, baggage, equipage, furniture, gear, outfit.

equitable *adj* even-handed, honest, impartial, just, unbiased, upright; adequate, fair, proper, right.

equity *n* just, right; fair play, fairness, justice, rectitude, reasonableness, righteousness.

era *n* age, date, period, time.

eradicate *vb* root, uproot; abolish, destroy.

erase *vb* blot, cancel, delete, expunge, scrape out.

erasure *n* cancellation, effacing, obliteration.

erect *vb* build, construct, raise, rear; create, form, found; * *adj* standing, uplifted, upright; elevated, vertical, straight; bold, firm, undaunted, unshaken.

erode *vb* abrade, consume, corrode, destroy, eat away, rub.

erotic *adj* amorous, amatory, arousing, seductive, titillating.

err *vb* deviate, ramble, stray, wander; blunder, misjudge, mistake; fall, nod, sin, stumble, trip.

errand *n* charge, commission, mandate, message, purpose.

erratic *adj* nomadic, rambling, roving, wandering; moving, planetary; abnormal, deviating eccentric, odd, strange.

erroneous *adj* false, incorrect, inaccurate, mistaken, untrue, wrong.

error *n* blunder, fallacy, mistake, oversight; delinquency, fault, iniquity, misdoing, misstep, offence, shortcoming, sin, trespass, wrongdoing.

erudition *n* knowledge, learning, scholarship.

eruption *n* explosion, outbreak, outburst; rash.

EVENT

escape *vb* avoid, elude, evade, flee from; abscond, decamp, fly; slip; * *n* flight; release; passage, passing.

escort *vb* convey, guard, protect; accompany, attend, conduct; * *n* attendant, companion, convoy, guard; protection, safe conduct, safeguard; company.

especial *adj* chief, distinguished, marked, particular, principal, uncommon, unusual; discovery, notice, observation.

espouse *vb* plight, promise; marry, wed; adopt, champion, defend, maintain, support.

essay *vb* attempt, endeavour, try; * *n* aim, effort, endeavour, exertion, struggle; article, composition, paper, thesis.

essence *n* nature, quintessence, substance; part; odour, perfume; being, existence, nature.

essential *adj* fundamental, indispensable, important, inward, intrinsic, necessary, vital; pure, volatile.

establish *vb* fix, secure, set; decree, ordain; constitute, form, found, institute, organise, originate, pitch, plant, raise; ground, place, plant, root, secure; approve, confirm, ratify, sanction; prove, verify.

estate *n* condition, state; position, rank; order; effects, fortune, possessions, property.

esteem *vb* appreciate, estimate, rate, reckon, value; admire, appreciate, prize, respect, revere, value, venerate, worship; believe, consider, fancy, hold, imagine, suppose, regard, think; * *n* account, consideration, estimate, estimation, judgement, reckoning; credit, honour, regard, respect.

estimable *adj* appreciable, calculable; admirable, credible, deserving, excellent, good, precious, respectful, valuable.

estimate *vb* appreciate, esteem, prise, rate, value; calculate, count, judge, reckon; * *n* estimation, judgement, valuation; calculation.

estimation *n* appreciation, estimate, valuation; esteem, estimate, opinion; honour, regard, respect.

eternal *adj* absolute, necessary, self-existent; ceaseless, endless, ever-enduring, everlasting, interminable, never-ending, perennial, perpetual, unending; deathless, immortal, incorruptible, indestructible, never-dying, undying; unchangeable; ceaseless, continual, unbroken, uninterrupted.

eulogy *n* discourse, eulogium, panegyric, speech; applause, encomium, commendation, praise.

evacuate *vb* empty, discharge; clean out, clear out, eject, excrete, expel, void; abandon, desert, leave, quit, withdraw.

evade *vb* elude, escape; avoid, decline, dodge, shun; baffle, elude, foil; dodge, fence, quibble.

evaporate *vb* distil; dry, vaporise; dissolve, fade, vanish.

evasion *n* avoidance, bluffing, deceit, dodge, escape, excuse, prevarication, quibble, shift, subterfuge, sophistical.

evasive *adj* elusive, equivocating, shuffling, slippery, sophistical.

even *vb* balance, equalise, harmonise, symmetrise; flatten, flush, level, smooth; * *adj* flat, level, plane, smooth; calm, composed, equable, equal, placid, regular, steady, uniform, unruffled; direct, fair, impartial, just; * *adv* exactly, just, verily; likewise; * *n* eve, evening, eventide, vesper.

evening *n* dusk, eve, even, nightfall, sunset, twilight.

event *n* circumstance, fact, happening, occurrence;

conclusion, consequence, end, issue, result, sequel; affair.
eventful *adj* critical, important, momentous, remarkable, signal.
eventual *adj* final, last, ultimate; contingent, possible.
ever *adv* always, aye, constantly, continually, eternally, evermore, forever, incessantly, unceasingly.
everlasting *adj* ceaseless, constant, endless, eternal, ever-during, incessant, perpetual, unceasing, unending, uninterrupted; deathless, ever-living, immortal, imperishable, never-dying, undying.
evermore *adv* always, constantly, continually, ever, forever, to the end of time.
everyday *adj* accustomed, common, commonplace, customary, habitual, usual.
evict *vb* dispossess, eject, thrust out.
evidence *vb* evince, prove, show, testify, vouch; * *n* affirmation, confirmation, grounds, indication, proof, testimony, token, trace, witness.
evil *adj* bad, ill; bad, base, corrupt, malicious, malevolent, malign, sinful, vicious, vile, wicked, wrong; destructive, harmful, hurtful, injurious, mischievous; adverse, bad, calamitous, disastrous, unfortunate, unhappy; * *n* calamity, disaster, ill, misery, misfortune, pain, sorrow, suffering, woe; baseness, corruption, sin, viciousness, wickedness; harm, ill, injury, mischief, wrong.
evolve *vb* develop, educe, expand, open, unfold.
exact *vb* elicit, extort, require; ask, claim, compel, demand, enforce, requisition, take; * *adj* rigid, scrupulous, strict; diametric, express, precise, true; accurate, close, correct, faithful; accurate, critical, delicate, fine; careful, precise, punctual, regular.
exacting *adj* critical, difficult, exactive, rigid.
exaggerate *vb* enlarge, magnify, overstate, strain, stretch.
exalted *adj* august, elated, elevated, high, high-flown, magnificent.
examination *n* inspection, observation; exploration, inquisition, investigation, research, search, scrutiny, survey; review, test, trial.
examine *vb* inspect, observe; consider, explore, inquire, investigate, study, test; interrogate.
example *n* archetype, model, piece, representative, sample, specimen, standard; instance, precedent, warning.
exasperate *vb* affront, anger, enrage, irritate, offend, provoke; aggravate, exacerbate, rouse.
exasperation *n* annoyance, exacerbation, irritation; anger, fury, passion, rage, wrath; heightening, increase, worsening.
exceed *vb* surpass, transcend; excel, outdo, outstrip, pass.
excel *vb* beat, outdo, outrival, outstrip, surpass; cap, exceed, surpass.
excellent *adj* admirable, choice, crack, eminent, prime, superior, transcendent; deserving, praiseworthy, virtuous, worthy.
except *vb* exclude, leave out, omit, reject.* *conj* unless; * *prep* bar, but, excepting, excluding.
exceptional *adj* aberrant, abnormal, exceptive, irregular, peculiar, rare, special, strange, superior, uncommon, unusual.
excess *adj* excessive, unnecessary, redundant, spare, surplus; * *n* disproportion, fulsomeness, glut, redundance, redundancy, surfeit, superfluity; overplus,

remainder, surplus; dissipation, immoderation, overindulgence, unrestraint; immoderation, overdoing.

excessive *adj* exuberant, superabundant, superfluous, undue; extravagant, enormous, outrageous, unreasonable; extreme; vehement, violent.

exchange *vb* barter, change, commute, substitute, swap, trade. truck; interchange; * *n* barter, change, dealing, shuffle, substitution, trade; interchange, reciprocity; fair, market.

excise *n* customs, dues, duty, tariff, tax, taxes, toll; * *vb* cancel, cut, delete, edit, efface, erase, expunge, remove, strike out.

excitable *adj* impressible, nervous, sensitive, susceptible; hot-headed, hot-tempered, irritable, passionate.

excite *vb* animate, arouse, awaken, brew, evoke, incite, inflame, kindle, move, prompt, provoke, rouse, spur, stimulate; elicit, evoke, raise; agitate, disturb, irritate, provoke.

excitement *n* excitation, exciting; incitement, motive; activity, agitation, bustle, commotion, disturbance, flutter, sensation, stir, tension; heat, irritation, passion, violence, warmth.

exclaim *vb* call, cry, declare, shout, utter.

exclude *vb* ban, bar, debar, preclude, reject; hinder, prevent, restrain, withhold; except, omit; eject, eliminate, expel.

exclusive *adj* debarring; narrow, narrow-minded, selfish, uncharitable; aristocratic, choice, fastidious, fashionable, select; only, sole, special.

excursion *n* drive, expedition, jaunt, ride, tour, trip, voyage, walk; digression.

excusable *adj* allowable, forgivable, pardonable, warrantable.

excuse *vb* absolve, acquit, forgive, pardon, remit; justify; exempt, free; overlook.* *n* absolution, extenuation, justification, plea; colour, disguise, guise, pretence, semblance, subterfuge.

execute *vb* achieve, carry out, complete. consummate, do, effect, finish, perform; administer, enforce, seal, sign; behead, electrocute, hang.

executive *adj* administrative, commanding, directing, managing, officiating, presiding, ruling; * *n* director, manager.

exemplary *adj* close, exact, faithful, punctual, rigid, rigorous; commendable, correct, good; estimable, excellent, praiseworthy, virtuous; condign, monitory, warning.

exempt *vb* absolve, except, excuse, free, release, relieve; * *adj* absolved, excepted, excused, exempted, free, liberated, released.

exercise *vb* apply, busy, employ, exert, use; effect, produce, wield; break in, discipline, drill, school, train; practise, use; task, test, try; afflict, agitate, annoy, burden, pain, trouble, try; * *n* application, custom, operation, play, practice, usage, use, working; action, activity, effort, exertion, labour, toil, work; discipline, drill, schooling, training; lesson, praxis, study, task, test.

exert *vb* employ, endeavour, exercise, expend, strain, strive, struggle, toil, use, work.

exertion *n* action, exercise, exerting; use; attempt, effort, endeavour, strain, stretch, struggle.

exhaust *vb* drain, draw, empty; consume, destroy, expend, spend, squander, waste; cripple, deplete, disable,

enervate, overtire, weaken.
exhaustion n debilitation, fatigue, weariness.
exhibit vb demonstrate, disclose, display, expose, express, indicate, offer, present, reveal, show; offer, present.
exhilarate vb animate, cheer, elate, enliven, gladden, inspire.
exhilaration n animating, cheering, elating, gladdening, rejoicing; animation, cheer, cheerfulness, gaiety, gladness, good spirits, hilarity.
exile vb banish, expatriate, expel, ostracise, proscribe; * n banishment, expulsion, ostracism, separation; outcast, refugee.
exist vb be, breathe, live; continue, endure, last.
existence n being, subsisting, subsistence, subsisting; being, creature, essence, thing; animation, life.
exit vb depart, go, leave; * n departure; death, decrease, demise, end; outlet.
exorbitant adj enormous, excessive, extravagant, unreasonable.
exorcise vb cast out, drive away, expel; deliver, purify; address.
exotic adj extraneous, foreign; extravagant.
expand vb develop, open, spread, unfold; enlarge, extend, increase, stretch; enlarge.
expanse n area, expansion, extent, field, stretch.
expansion n expansion, opening, spreading; dilation, swelling; development, enlargement, increase; expanse, extent, stretch.
expect vb anticipate, assume, await, calculate, contemplate, foresee, hope, rely.
expectancy n expectance, expectation; prospect.
expectation n anticipation, expectance, hope, prospect; assurance, confidence, presumption, trust.

expedient adj advisable, appropriate, convenient, fit, proper, suitable; advantageous, useful; * n contrivance, device, means, method, resource, scheme, substitute.
expedite vb accelerate, advance, facilitate, forward, hasten, hurry, precipitate, quicken.
expedition n alertness, celerity, dispatch, haste, quickness, speed; enterprise, undertaking; campaign, journey, march, quest, voyage.
expel vb dislodge, eject, eliminate; discharge, eject, void; bounce, discharge, exclude, exscind, fire, oust, relegate, remove; banish, disown, exile, expatriate, proscribe.
expenditure n outlay, outlaying, spending; charge, cost, outlay.
experience vb endure, suffer; feel, know; encounter, suffer, undergo; * n endurance, trial; evidence, knowledge, proof, test.
experienced adj able, expert, instructed, knowing, old, practised, qualified, versed, wise.
experiment vb examine, test, try; * n examination, investigation, practice, proof, test, testimony, trial.
expert adj able, apt, clever, dextrous, proficient, quick, ready, skilful; * n adept, authority, crack, master, specialist.
expertise n adroitness, aptness, dexterity, promptness, skill.
expire vb cease, close, conclude, end, lapse, stop; emit, exhale; depart, die, perish.
explain vb demonstrate, elucidate, expound, interpret, solve, unfold; account for, justify, warrant.
explanation n clarification, description, elucidation, exposition, illustration, interpretation; account, answer, deduction, key,

meaning, secret, solution.
explicit *adj* absolute, clear, definite, exact, express, plain, positive, precise, unequivocal.
explode *vb* burst, discharge, displode, shatter; contemn, discard, repudiate, scorn.
exploit *vb* milk, use, utilise; * *n* achievement, act, deed, feat.
explore *vb* examine, fathom, inquire, inspect, investigate, seek.
explosion *n* blast, burst, clap, crack, detonation, discharge, pop.
exponent *n* example, illustration, index, specimen, type; commentator, demonstrator, expounder, illustrator.
expose *vb* bare, display, uncover; descry, detect, disclose, unearth; denounce; subject; endanger, risk.
exposé *n* exhibit, exposition, manifesto; divulgement, exposure, revelation.
expound *vb* develop, present, rehearse, unfold; clear, elucidate, explain.
express *vb* air, assert, declare, emit, enunciate, manifest, utter, vent; signify, speak, state, voice; denote, exhibit, indicate, intimate, present, represent, show, signify; * *adj* categorical, clear, definite, explicit, outspoken, plain, positive; accurate, close, exact, faithful, precise, true; special; fast, nonstop, quick, rapid, swift; * *n* dispatch, message.
expressive *adj* indicative, meaningful, significant; eloquent, energetic, forcible, lively, strong, vivid.
expulsion *n* discharge, eviction, expelling; evacuation, excretion; ejection, excision, extrusion, separation.
exquisite *adj* accurate, delicate, exact, fastidious, nice, refined; choice, elect, excellent, rare, valuable; complete, matchless, perfect; acute, keen, intense; * *n* beau.

extant *adj* existent, existing, present, surviving, visible.
extend *vb* reach, stretch; lengthen, prolong, protract, widen; dilate, distend, enlarge, expand, increase; spread; give, impart, offer; lie, range, reach, spread, stretch.
extensive *adj* broad, expanded, extended, far-reaching, large, wide, widespread.
extent *n* expanse, expansion; amount, bulk, degree, size; compass, length, proportions, reach, stretch; field, range, scope; breadth, depth, height, width.
exterior *adj* external, outlying, outside, outward, superficial, surface; extrinsic; * *n* outside, surface; appearance.
extinct *adj* extinguished, quenched; dead, ended, vanished.
extinction *n* death; abolition, annihilation, destruction, excision, extermination.
extinguish *vb* choke, douse, put out, quell, smother, stifle; destroy, subdue; eclipse, obscure.
extol *vb* celebrate, glorify, laud, magnify, praise; applaud, commend.
extort *vb* bully, exact, extract, force, squeeze, wrench, wrest, wring.
extortion *n* compulsion, demand, exaction, oppression, overcharge, tribute.
extortionate *adj* bloodsucking, exacting, harsh, rapacious, rigorous, severe; unreasonable.
extra *adj* accessory, additional; another, farther, fresh, further, more, new, other, plus; side, spare, supplemental, supplementary, surplus; extraordinary, extreme, unusual; * *adv* additionally, also, beyond, furthermore, more, moreover, plus; * *n* accessory, nonessential, special, supplement; bonus, premium; balance, leftover,

remainder, spare, surplus.
extract *vb* extort, pull out, remove, withdraw; derive, distil, draw, express; cite, determine, derive, quote, select; * *n* excerpt, passage, quotation, selection; distillation, infusion, juice.
extraction *n* drawing out, derivation, essence, pulling out; birth, descent, lineage, origin, parentage.
extraordinary *adj* abnormal, amazing, distinguished, exceptional, marvellous, monstrous, particular, peculiar, phenomenal, rare, remarkable, signal, special, strange, uncommon, unusual, wonderful.
extravagant *adj* excessive, exorbitant, inordinate, unreasonable; absurd, foolish, irregular, wild; lavish, spendthrift, useful.
extreme *adj* farthest, outermost, remotest, utmost; greatest, highest; final, last, ultimate; drastic, excessive, extravagant, immoderate, outrageous, unreasonable; * *n* extremity, limit; climax, degree, height; danger, distress.
extremity *n* border, edge, end, extreme, verge.
extricate *vb* clear, deliver, disentangle, liberate, release, relieve.
exult *vb* gloat, glory, rejoice, transport, triumph, vaunt.
eye *vb* contemplate, inspect, scrutinise, view, watch; * *n* estimate, judgement, look, sight, vision, view; notice, observation, scrutiny, sight, vigilance.

F

fable *n* allegory, legend, myth, parable, story, tale; fiction, figment, forgery, untruth.
fabric *n* building, edifice, pile, structure; make, texture; cloth, material, stuff, textile, tissue, web.
fabulous *adj* amazing, fabricated, fictitious, forged, imaginary, invented, legendary, mythical, unbelievable, unreal.
face *vb* confront; brave, dare, defy, front, oppose; dress, level, polish, smooth; cover, veneer; * *n* cover, facet, surface; escarpment, front; countenance, features, grimace, visage; appearance, expression, look, semblance; audacity, boldness, confidence, effrontery.
facile *adj* easy; complaisant, conversable, mild; compliant, flexible, fluent, manageable, pliable, pliant, tractable; dextrous, ready, skilful.
facilitate *vb* ease, expedite, help.
facility *n* ease, easiness; ability, dexterity, expertness, knack, quickness, readiness; pliancy; advantage, appliance, means, resource; complaisance, politeness.
facsimile *n* copy, duplicate, fax, reproduction.
fact *n* act, circumstance, event, incident, performance; actuality, existence, reality, truth.
faculty *n* ability, capability, capacity, power, property, quality; ableness, address, aptitude, aptness, capacity, clearness, competency, dexterity, efficiency, facility, forte, ingenuity, knack, power, quickness, skill, talent, turn; body, department, profession; authority, power; license, privilege, right.
fade *vb* disappear, die, fall, faint, perish, vanish; decay, decline, fall, wither; blanch, pale; dissolve.
fail *vb* break, collapse, decay, decline, fade, sink; cease, disappear; fall, miss; neglect, omit; bankrupt, break.
failing *adj* deficient, lacking,

FAMILIARITY

needing, wanting; declining, deteriorating, fading, sinking, waning, wilting; * *prep* lacking, needing, wanting; * *n* decay, decline; failure; defect, deficiency, fault, foible, frailty, shortcoming, vice, weakness; error, lapse, slip; insolvency.

failure *n* defectiveness; fail, negligent, neglect, nonperformance, omission, slip; botch, breakdown, collapse, fiasco; bankruptcy, crash, downfall, ruin; decay, decline, loss.

faint *vb* swoon; decline, fade, fail, languish, weaken; * *adj* swooning; exhausted, feeble, languid, listless, sickly, weak; gentle, little, slight, small, soft, thin; dim, dull, scarce, slight; cowardly, dastardly, faint-hearted, fearful, timid; dejected, depressed, discouraged, disheartened; * *n* blackout, swoon.

fair *adj* spotless, unspotted; blond, light, lily, white; beautiful, handsome, shapely; clear, cloudless, pleasant; favourable, prosperous, hopeful, propitious; clear, distinct, plain, unobstructed; candid, frank, honest, honourable, just, open, unbiased, upright; proper; equitable, just; average, decent, indifferent, ordinary, passable, reasonable, tolerable; * *n* bazaar, carnival, exposition, festival, fête.

faith *n* belief, confidence, credence, dependence, reliance, trust; creed, doctrines, religion, tenets; faithfulness; loyalty, truth, truthfulness.

faithful *adj* constant, devoted, loyal, staunch, true; honest, reliable, trustworthy, trusty; reliable, truthful; accurate, close, exact.

fall *vb* collapse, depend, descend, drop, sink, tumble; abate, decline, decrease, ebb, subside; err, sin, stumble, trespass, trip; die, perish; befall, chance, come, happen, occur, pass; become, get; come, pass; * *n* collapse, descent, downcome, downfall, dropping, falling, tumble; cascade, cataract, waterfall; death, destruction, overthrow, ruin, surrender; comeuppance, degradation; declension, failure, lapse, slip; decline, decrease, ebb, sinking, subsidence; close, sinking; declivity, slope.

fallible *adj* erring, frail, ignorant, imperfect, mortal, weak.

false *adj* lying, truthless, untrue; dishonest, disloyal, faithless, false-hearted, treacherous, two-faced, unfaithful; fictitious, forged, made-up, unreliable; artificial, bastard, bogus, counterfeit, forged, hollow, hypocritical, make-believe, pretended, pseudo, sham, suppositious; improper, incorrect, unfounded, wrong; deceiving, deceptive, disappointing, misleading.

falsify *vb* alter, adulterate, belie, counterfeit, doctor, fake, garble, misstate; violate.

falter *vb* halt, hesitate, lisp, quaver, stammer, stutter; fail, stumble, tremble; dodder, hesitate.

fame *n* hearsay, report, rumour; celebrity, credit, eminence, glory, greatness, honour, notoriety, renown, repute.

familiar *adj* acquainted, aware, conversant; amicable, close, cordial, fraternal, friendly, intimate, near; affable, conversable, courteous, civil, friendly, kindly, sociable, social; easy, free and easy; common, frequent, well-known; * *n* acquaintance, associate, companion, friend.

familiarity *n* acquaintance, knowledge, understanding; friendship; closeness; freedom; disrespect, presumption;

familiarise vb accustom, inure, train, use.
family n people; ancestors, breed, clan, dynasty, kindred, house, race, stock, tribe; class, genus, kind.
famine n destitution, hunger, scarcity, starvation.
famish vb distress, exhaust, pinch, starve, raven.
famous adj celebrated, eminent, excellent, famed, far-famed, glorious, great, heroic, honoured, immortal, notable, noted, remarkable, renowned, signal.
fan vb agitate, beat, winnow; blow, cool, refresh, ventilate; excite, rouse, stimulate; * n cooler, punkah, ventilator; admirer, enthusiast, follower, pursuer, supporter.
fanatic n bigot, enthusiast, visionary.
fancy vb apprehend, believe, conjecture, imagine, think; conceive, imagine; * adj elegant, fine, nice; extravagant, fanciful; * n imagination, conception, impression; idea, image, notion, thought; approval, fondness, liking, taste; caprice, fantasy, freak, humour, quirk, vagary, whimsy; apparition, daydream, delusion, hallucination, vision.
fantastic adj fanciful, imaginary, romantic, unreal, visionary; grotesque, odd, queer, strange, wild.
far adj distant, long, protracted, remote; farther, remoter; estranged, hostile; * adv considerably, greatly, very much; afar, far away, remotely.
farcical adj absurd, comic, derisory, funny, ludicrous, ridiculous.
fare vb go, journey, pass, travel; happen, prove; feed, live, manage, subsist; * n charge, price, ticket money; passenger, traveller; board, food, table, victuals; condition, experience, fortune, luck.
farewell n adieu, leave-taking, valediction; departure, leave, parting.
farther adj additional; remoter, ulterior; * adv beyond, further; besides, furthermore, moreover.
fascinate vb affect, overpower, spellbind, stupefy, transfix; captivate, catch, charm, delight, enchant, entrance.
fascination n absorption, charm, enchantment, magic, spell, witchcraft.
fashion vb contrive, create, design, forge, form, make, mould, pattern, shape; adjust, fit, suit; * n appearance, cast, cut, figure, form, make, model, mould, pattern, shape, stamp; manner, method, sort, wake; custom, fad, mode, style, usage, vogue; breeding; quality.
fashionable adj stylish; current, modem, prevailing, up-to-date; customary, usual; well-bred.
fast adj close, fastened, firm, fixed, immovable, tight; constant, faithful, resolute, steadfast, unwavering; fortified, strong; deep, profound, sound; fleet, quick, rapid, swift; dissolute, giddy, reckless, thoughtless, wild; * adv firmly, immovably, tightly; quickly, rapidly, swiftly; reckless, wildly; * vb abstain, go hungry, starve; * n diet, fasting, starvation.
fasten vb attach, bind, bolt, catch, fix, gird, lace, lock, pin, secure; belay, bend; connect, hold, join, unite.
fat adj fatty, greasy, oily, unctuous; corpulent, fleshy, gross, obese, portly, plump, pursy; coarse, dull, heavy, sluggish, stupid; profitable; fertile, fruitful, productive, rich; * n tissue, ester, grease, oil; best part, cream, flower; fatness, fleshiness, obesity, plumpness, stoutness.

FEELING

fatal *adj* deadly, lethal, mortal; catastrophic, destructive, mischievous, ruinous; destined, doomed, inevitable.

fate *n* destination, destiny, fate; cup, die, doom, experience, lot, fortune; death, destruction, ruin.

fatherly *adj* benign, kind, paternal, protecting, tender.

fathom *vb* comprehend, divine, reach; estimate, gauge, measure, plumb.

fatigue *vb* exhaust, fag, jade, tire, weaken, weary; * *n* exhaustion, lassitude, tiredness; hardship, labour, toil.

fault *n* blemish, defect, frailty, imperfection, infirmity, negligence, shortcoming, spot, weakness; error, indiscretion, lapse, misdeed, offence, slip, transgression, trespass, vice, wrong; blame.

favour *vb* befriend, countenance, encourage; approve; ease, facilitate; aid, assist, help, oblige, support; humour, indulge, spare; * *n* approval, countenance, esteem, goodwill, grace, kindness; benefaction, benefit, dispensation, kindness; patronage, popularity, support; gift; decoration; leave, pardon, permission; advantage, cover, indulgence, protection; bias, prejudice.

favourable *adj* auspicious, friendly, kind, well-disposed, willing; conductive; adapted, advantage, beneficial, benign, convenient, good, helpful, suitable.

favourite *adj* beloved, darling, dear; choice, fancied, pet, pick.

fear *vb* apprehend, dread; revere, reverence; * *n* affright, alarm, apprehension, dread, fright, horror, panic, phobia, scare, terror; perturbation, quaking, quivering, trembling, tremor, trepidation; concern, misdoubt, misgiving, qualm; awe, dread, reverence.

fearful *adj* afraid, apprehensive, haunted; chicken-livered, cowardly, faint-hearted, nervous; timid, timorous; dire, dreadful, frightful, horrible, shocking, terrible.

feast *vb* delight, rejoice; * *n* banquet, entertainment, repast, treat; celebration, festival, fête; delight, pleasure.

feat *n* accomplishment, achievement, act, deed, performance, trick.

feature *vb* envisage, envision, picture, imagine; specialise; appear in, headline, star; * *n* appearance, aspect; fashion; characteristic, particularity, peculiarity, trait; leader, lead item, special; article, film, motion picture, movie, story; highlight.

federation *n* alliance, allying, confederation, federation, leaguing, union, uniting; alliance, combination, compact, entente, federacy, league; copartnership.

fee *vb* pay, reward; * *n* account, bill, charge, compensation, remuneration, reward, tip; feud.

feeble *adj* anaemic, declining, drooping, exhausted, frail, infirm, languid; dim, faint, imperfect.

feed *vb* contribute, supply; cherish, eat, nourish, subsist; * *n* fodder, food, foodstuff, forage.

feel *vb* apprehend, intuit, perceive, sense; examine, handle, touch; experience, suffer; prove, sound, test, try; look, seem, sound; believe, conceive, infer, suppose, think; * *n* atmosphere, feeling, quality; finish, surface, texture.

feeling *n* consciousness, impression, notion, perception, sensation, sense, touch; affecting, emotion, passion, sensibility, sentiment; susceptibility; impression,

FELL

opinion.
fell vb beat, demolish, knock down, level, prostrate; cut.
fellow adj affiliated, associated, joint, like, mutual, similar, twin; * n associate, comrade; equal, peer; counterpart, mate, match, partner; member; boy, individual, man, person.
fellowship n brotherhood, companionship, comradeship, familiarity; participation; partnership; converse; affability, sociableness.
feminine adj affectionate, delicate, gentle, modest, soft, tender, womanish; effeminacy, softness, womanliness.
fence vb enclose, guard, protect, surround; circumscribe, evade, equivocate, hedge; guard; * n barrier, hedge, hoarding, palings, stockade, wall; defence, guard, security, shield; fencing, swordsmanship; receiver.
ferocious adj ferine, fierce, savage, untamed, wild; barbarous, bloody, brutal, cruel, inhuman, merciless, murderous, pitiless, ruthless, violent.
fertile adj bearing, breeding, fecund, prolific; fruitful, luxuriant, productive, rich; female, fruit-bearing.
fervent adj burning, hot, glowing, melting, seething; ardent, earnest, fervid, fierce, fiery, glowing, intense, passionate, vehement, warm, zealous.
festival n carnival, feast, fete, gala, holiday; banquet, celebration, entertainment, treat.
festivity n conviviality, festival, gaiety, jollity, joviality, joyfulness, mirth.
fetch vb bring, get; accomplish, achieve, effect, perform; reach; * n artifice, dodge, ruse, trick.
feud vb argue, bicker, clash, contend, dispute, quarrel; * n argument, broil, clashing, contest, discord, enmity, fray, grudge, hostility, quarrel, rupture, strife.
fever n agitation, excitement, ferment, fire, heat.
fibre n filament, pile, staple, strand, texture; stamina, strength.
fickle adj capricious, changeable, faithless, fitful, inconstant, mercurial, mutable, shifting, unsettled, unstable, vacillating, variable, violate, volatile, wavering.
fictitious adj assumed, fanciful, feigned, imaginary, invented, unreal; artificial, dummy, false, spurious, suppositious.
fiddle vb dawdle, fidget, tinker; cheat, swindle, tamper; * n fraud; fiddler, violin.
fidelity n constancy, devotedness, devotion, faithfulness, fealty, true-heartedness, truth; accuracy, faithfulness, precision.
fidget vb chafe, fret, jiggle, twitch, worry; * n fidgetiness, impatience, restlessness.
field n clearing, meadow; expanse, extent, opportunity, range, room, surface; province, realm, region.
fierce adj barbarous, brutal, cruel, fell, ferocious, furious, ravenous, savage; impetuous, murderous, passionate, tearing, truculent, turbulent, untamed, violent.
fiery adj fervent, fervid, heated, hot, glowing, lurid; ardent, fervent, glowing, impetuous, inflamed, passionate.
fight vb battle, combat, contend, war; contend, contest, oppose, strive, struggle; encounter, engage; handle, manage; * n affair, affray, action, battle, combat, contest, encounter, melée, quarrel, struggle, war; brawl, broil, riot, row; fighting, pluck, resistance, struggle, temper.
figure vb adorn, ornament;

delineate, depict, represent, signify, typify; conceive, image, imagine, picture, represent; calculate, cipher; act, appear; * n configuration, conformation, form, outline, shape; effigy, image; design, drawing, pattern; image, metaphor; emblem, symbol, type; character, number, numeral.

file vb order, record, tidy; burnish, polish, rasp, refine, smooth; * n data, dossier, folder; column, line, list, rank, row, series.

fill vb occupy, pervade; dilate, distend, trim; furnish, replenish, stock, store, supply; cloy, congest, content, cram, glut, pall, sate, satiate, satisfy, saturate, stuff, suffuse, swell; engage, hold, occupy, perform.

film vb becloud, cloud, coat, cover, darken, fog, mist, obscure, veil; shoot, take; * n cloud, coating, gauze, nebula, scum, skin, veil.

filter vb filtrate, strain; exude, ooze; * n diffuser, riddle, sieve, sifter, strainer.

filthy adj defiled, dirty, foul, licentious, nasty, unclean; corrupt, gross, unclean; miry, muddy.

final adj eventual, extreme, last. latest, terminal, ultimate; conclusive, decisive.

finale n conclusion, end, termination.

finances npl funds, resources, revenues, treasury; income.

find vb discover, fall upon; gain, get, obtain, procure; discover, notice, perceive, remark; catch; contribute, provide, supply; * n catch, discovery, finding, prize, strike.

fine vb filter, purify, refine; mulct, penalise, punish; * adj little, minute, small; delicate, small; choice, light; exact, keen, sharp; attenuated, subtle, tenuous, thin; exquisite, nice, refined, sensitive, subtle; superb, superior; beautiful, elegant, magnificent, splendid; clean, pure; * n forfeit, mulct, penalty, punishment.

finish vb accomplish, achieve, complete, execute, fulfil, perform; elaborate, perfect; close, conclude, end, terminate; * n elegance, perfection, polish; close, end; death, termination.

fire vb ignite, kindle, light; animate, excite, inflame, inspirit, rouse, stir up; discharge, expel, hurl; * n combustion; blaze; discharge; animation, ardour, enthusiasm, fervour, fervency, fever, force, heat, intensity, passion, spirit, violence; light, radiance, splendour; imagination, inspiration, vivacity; affliction, torture, trouble.

firm adj established, coherent, confirmed, consistent, fast, fixed, inflexible, rooted, secure, stable; compressed, dense, hard, solid; constant, resolute, steadfast, steady, unshaken; loyal, robust, stout, sturdy, strong; * n association, business, company, concern, conglomerate, corporation.

first adj capital, chief, highest, prime, principal; earliest, original; elementary, primary, rudimentary; primal, pristine; * adv chiefly, firstly, initially, mainly, principally; before, foremost, headmost; rather, rather than, sooner; * n alpha, prime.

fit vb adapt, adjust, suit; become, conform; equip, prepare, provide; * adj capacitated, fitted; appropriate, apt, becoming, befitting, consonant, convenient, fitting, meet, proper, suitable; * n convulsion, paroxysm, seizure, spasm, spell; fancy, humour; mood, pet; interval, period, spell.

fitful adj changeable, convulsive, fanciful, fantastic, fickle, impulsive, intermittent,

FIX

irregular, odd, spasmodic, unstable, variable, whimsical; eventful.

fix *vb* establish, fasten, place, plant, set; repair; bind, clinch, connect, fasten, lock, stay, tie; appoint, decide, define, limit, seal, settle; consolidate, harden; abide, remain, rest, settle; congeal, harden, stiffen; * *n* difficulty, plight, predicament.

flabby *adj* feeble, inelastic, limp, soft, yielding.

flag *vb* droop, hang, loose; decline, fail, faint, lag, languish, sink, weary; stale; indicate, mark, sign, signal; * *n* banner, colours, ensign, pennant, standard.

flagrant *adj* burning, flaming, glowing; crying, enormous, glaring, monstrous, notorious, outrageous, shameful, wicked.

flamboyant *adj* bright, gorgeous, ornate.

flame *vb* blaze, shine; burn, flash, glow, warm; * *n* blaze, brightness, fire, flare; affection, ardour, enthusiasm, fervency, fervour.

flap *vb* beat, flutter, shake, wave. * *n* fly, lap, lappet, tab; beating, flapping, flop, slap, shaking.

flare *vb* blaze, flicker, flutter, waver; dazzle, flame, glare; spread, widen; * *n* blaze, flame, glare.

flash *vb* blaze, glare, glisten, light, shimmer, sparkle, twinkle; * *n* instant, moment.

flashy *adj* flaunting, gaudy, loud, pretentious, showy, tinsel.

flat *adj* horizontal, level; even, plane, smooth, unbroken; low, overthrow; dull, frigid, lifeless, monotonous, prosaic, tame, uniform, uninteresting; dead, flashy, insipid, stale, tasteless; absolute, clear, direct, downright, positive; * *adv* flatly, flush, horizontally, level; * *n* bar, sandbank, shoal, strand; lowland, plain; apartment, floor, storey.

flatter *vb* compliment, gratify, praise; blandish, butter up, coax, court, entice, humour, inveigle, wheedle.

flattery *n* adulation, blandishment, blarney, fawning, obsequiousness, servility, sycophancy.

flavour *n* gust, gusto, relish, savour, seasoning, smack, taste, zest; lacing; aroma, essence, soul.

flaw *n* breach, break, crack, fracture, rent, rift; blemish, defect, fault, imperfection, spot.

fleck *vb* dapple, mottle, spot, streak; * *n* speckle, spot, streak.

flee *vb* abscond, avoid, depart, escape, fly, leave, run.

fleece *vb* shear; cheat, despoil, plunder, rifle, rob, steal.

fleeting *adj* brief, ephemeral, flitting, flying, fugitive, passing, short-lived, transient.

flesh *n* brawn, food, meat; desires; race, stock; man, mankind.

fleshly *adj* animal, bodily, carnal, lustful, lecherous, sensual.

fleshy *adj* corpulent, fat, obese, stout.

flexible *adj* flexible, lithe, pliable, pliant, supple; affable, complaisant, ductile, docile, gentle, pliant, tractable, yielding.

flight *n* flying, mounting, soaring; shower; steps, stairs; departure, fleeing, flying, retreat, stampede.

flighty *adj* deranged, fickle, giddy, light-headed, mercurial, unbalanced, volatile, wild.

flinch *vb* flee, recoil, retreat, shirk, shrink, wince, withdraw.

fling *vb* cast, dart, emit, heave, hurl, pitch, shy, throw, toss; wince; * *n* cast, throw, toss.

flippant *adj* fluent, glib, voluble; forward, glib, impertinent, inconsiderate, irreverent, pert, saucy.

flirt vb chuck, fling, hurl, pitch, shy, throw; flutter, twirl, whisk; dally, philander; * n jilt, philanderer; jerk.

flit vb flicker, flutter, hover; hasten, pass.

float vb drift, glide, ride, sail, soar, swim, waft; support.

flock vb collect, congregate, gather, group, herd, throng; * n collection, group; bevy, company, drove, flight, herd, pack, swarm, team.

flog vb beat, castigate, chastise, drub, flay, lash, thrash, whip.

flood vb deluge, overflow, submerge, swamp; * n deluge, inundation, overflow, tide; bore, flow, outburst, rush; abundance, excess.

floor vb deck, pave; beat, conquer, overthrow, prevail, puzzle; florid; * n storey; bottom, deck, pavement, stage.

flounder vb blunder, flop, plunge, struggle, toss, wallow.

flourish vb grow, thrive; boast, bluster, brag, show off, vaunt; brandish, flaunt, swing, wave; * n dash, display, parade, show; bombast; brandishing, shake, waving; blast, fanfare.

flout vb chaff, deride, gibe, insult, jeer, mock, ridicule, sneer, taunt; * n gibe, fling, insult, jeer, mock, mocking, scoff, taunt.

flow vb pour, run, stream; deliquesce, melt; arise, come, emanate, grow, issue, proceed, spring; glide; float, wave, waver; abound, run; * n current, flood, flux, gush, rush, stream, trickle; abundance.

flower vb bloom, blossom; develop; * n bloom, blossom; best, cream, essence, pick; freshness, vigour.

flowery adj florid; embellished, figurative, florid.

fluent adj current, flowing, gliding, liquid; smooth; copious, easy, facile, glib, voluble.

fluff vb bungle, forget, fumble, mess up, miscue, muddle; * n down, flue, fur, lint, nap; cobweb, feather; blunder, bungle, muff.

Flurry vb agitate, confuse, disconcert, disturb, excite, hurry, perturb; * n gust, flaw; agitation, bustle, commotion, confusion, excitement, flutter, haste, hurry, ruffle, scurry.

flush vb flow, rush, start; glow, mantle; animate, elate, elevate; cleanse, drench; disturb, eject, rouse, start, uncover; * adj bright, fresh, glowing, vigorous; affluent, exuberant, generous, lavish, liberal, prodigal, prolific, rich; even, flat, plane; * adv evenly, flat, level; full, point-blank, right, square, straight; * n bloom, blush, glow, rosiness, ruddiness; shock, thrill.

flutter vb flap, hover; flit; beat, palpitate, quiver, tremble; fluctuate, waver; * n agitation, tremor; agitation, hurry; commotion, confusion, excitement, fluster, quivering, tremble, tumult.

fly vb aviate, hover, soar; flap, float, flutter, sail, soar, vibrate, wave; explode; decamp, depart, flee, vanish; flit, glide, pass, slip; * adj alert, bright, sharp, smart; astute, cunning, sly; agile, fleet, nimble, quick.

foam vb cream, froth, lather, spume; boil, ferment, seethe, stew; * n bubbles, cream, froth, scum, spume, suds.

foe n adversary, antagonist, enemy, opponent.

fog vb bemist, blear, blur, cloud, dim, mist; addle, confuse, muddle; * n blear, blur, dimness, haze, mist, smog, vapour; confusion, fuddle, maze.

foggy adj cloudy, dim, dimmed, hazy, indistinct, obscure; bewildered, confused, dazed, muddled, stupid.

foible n defect, failing, fault, frailty, infirmity, weakness.

foil *vb* baffle, balk, check, checkmate, defeat, disappoint, frustrate; * *n* film, flake; background, contrast.

fold *vb* bend, cover, double, envelop; clasp, embrace, enfold, gather, interlace; collapse, fail; * *n* double, gather, plait; cot, enclosure, pen.

folk *n* kindred, nation, people.

follow *vb* ensue, succeed; chase, dog, hound, pursue, run after, trail; attend; conform, heed, obey, observe; cherish, cultivate, seek; pursue; copy, imitate; arise, come, flow, issue, proceed, result, spring.

follower *n* attendant, associate, companion, retainer, supporter; admirer, discipline, partisan, pupil; copier, imitator.

folly *n* dullness, fatuity, foolishness, imbecility, levity, shallowness; absurdity, extravagance, imprudence, indiscretion, ineptitude, nonsense, senseless; blunder, faux pas, indiscretion.

fond *adj* absurd, foolish, senseless, silly, vain, weak; affectionate, doting, loving, tender.

fondle *vb* blandish, caress, coddle, cosset, pet.

food *n* board, bread, cheer, commons, diet, fare, meat, nourishment, nutrition, provisions, subsistence, sustenance, viands; feed, fodder, forage.

fool *vb* jest, play, toy, trifle; cheat, deceive, delude, dupe, gull, hoodwink, trick; * *n* dolt, idiot, imbecile, simpleton; antic, buffoon, clown, droll, jester, punch; butt, dupe.

foolhardy *adj* adventurous, bold, desperate, headlong, rash, reckless, venturous.

foolish *adj* brainless, daft, idiotic, inane, inept, irrational, senseless, shallow, silly, simple, vain, weak, witless; absurd, ill-judged, imprudent, indiscreet, nonsensical, ridiculous, unreasonable, unwise; contemptible, idle, trifling, vain.

footing *n* foothold; basis, foundation, groundwork, installation; condition, rank, standing, status; settlement; establishment.

footman *n* footboy, menial, runner, servant.

footstep *n* footmark, footprint, trace, track; footfall, step; mark, token, trace.

forage *vb* feed, graze, provender, provision, victual; hunt for, range, search, seek; maraud, plunder, raid; * *n* feed, fodder, food, provender; hunt, search

foray *n* descent, invasion, inroad, raid.

forbid *vb* ban, debar, disallow, embargo, inhibit, interdict, prohibit, taboo, veto.

forbidding *adj* disagreeable, displeasing, odious, offensive, off-putting, threatening.

force *vb* coerce, compel, constrain, necessitate; drive, impel, overcome, press, urge; ravish, violate; * *n* energy, head, might, power, strength, stress, vim; agency, efficacy, efficiency, cogency, potency; coercion, compulsion, vehemence, violence; army, battalion, squadron, troop.

forcible *adj* irresistible, mighty, potent, powerful, strong, weighty; impetuous, violent; coerced, coercive; convincing, energetic, effective, efficacious, vigorous.

forecast *vb* anticipate, foresee, predict; contrive, devise, plan, project; * *n* anticipation, foresight, forethought, prevision, prophecy, provident.

foregoing *adj* antecedent, anterior, former, preceding, prior.

foregone *adj* bygone, former, past, previous.

foreign *adj* alien, distant, exotic, exterior, outlandish, remote, strange; exterior,

extraneous, inappropriate, irrelevant, outside, unnatural.
foremost *adj* first, front, highest, leading, main.
forerunner *n* foregoer, herald, precursor; omen, precursor, prelude, premonition, sign.
foresight *n* foreknowledge, prescience; anticipation, care, caution, forecast, forethought, precaution, providence.
foretaste *n* anticipation, forestalling.
foretell *vb* predict, prophesy; augur, forebode, forecast, foreshadow, portend, presage, prognosticate, prophesy.
forever *adv* always, constantly, continually, eternally, ever, evermore, everlastingly, perpetually.
forfeit *vb* alienate, lose; * *n* damages, fine, forfeiture, mulct, penalty.
forge *vb* beat, form, hammer; coin, devise, frame, invent; counterfeit, fabricate, falsify; * *n* furnace, ironworks, smithy.
forgery *n* counterfeit, fake, falsification, imitation, phony.
forgetful *adj* careless, heedless, inattentive, neglectful, negligent, oblivious.
forgive *vb* absolve, acquit, condone, excuse, pardon.
forgiving *adj* absolutory, acquitting, clearing, excusing, pardoning.
forlorn *adj* abandoned, deserted, helpless, lost, solitary; abject, comfortless, desolate, helpless, hopeless, pitiable, miserable, wretched.
form *vb* fashion, model, mould, shape; build, construct, create, make, produce; contrive, devise, invent; compose, develop, organise; discipline, educate, teach, train.* *n* body, build, cast, configuration, conformation, cut, figure, format, mould, pattern, shape; formula, formulary, method, mode, ritual; class, kind, order, sort, system, type; arrangement, order, shapeliness; ceremonial, conventionality, etiquette, formality, observance, rite; seat; class, rank; arrangement, combination.
formal *adj* explicit, express, official, strict; fixed, regular, stiff; affected, ceremonious, exact, prim, starch, starched; constitutive, essential; external, outward, perfunctory; innate.
former *adj* antecedent, anterior, earlier, previous, prior; late, old-time, quondam; by, bygone, foregone, gone.
forsake *vb* abandon, desert, leave, quit; drop, forswear, relinquish, surrender, yield.
fortify *vb* brace, encourage, entrench, garrison, reinforce, stiffen, strengthen; confirm.
fortitude *n* bravery, courage, determination, endurance, firmness, patience, resolution, strength, valour.
fortuitous *adj* accidental, casual, chance, incidental.
fortunate *adj* bright, favoured, happy, lucky, successful; advantageous, favourable, happy, lucky.
fortune *n* accident, casualty, chance, contingency, luck; estate, property, substance; affluence, felicity, prosperity, wealth; destination, destiny, doom, fate, lot; event, issue, result; success.
forward *vb* advance, aid, encourage, favour, foster, help, promote, support; dispatch, expedite, hasten, hurry, quicken, speed; dispatch, post, send, ship; * *adj* ahead, advanced, onward; anterior, front, fore, head; prompt, eager, earnest, hasty, quick, ready, willing; assuming, bold, brazen, confident, impertinent, pert, presuming; advanced, early, premature; * *adv* ahead, onward.
foster *vb* feed, nurse, nourish,

FOUL

support, sustain; aid, breed, cherish, cultivate, encourage, favour, forward, harbour, patronise, promote, rear.

foul *vb* defile, dirty, pollute, soil, stain; clog, collide, entangle, jam; * *adj* dirty, fetid, filthy, impure, nasty, polluted, soiled, stained, sullied, rank, unclean; disgusting, hateful, odious, offensive; underhand, unfair; sinister; base, dark, detestable, infamous, scandalous, shameful, wile, wicked; coarse, low, obscene, vulgar; abusive, foulmouthed; cloudy, rainy, rough, stormy, wet; muddy, thick.

found *vb* base, fix, ground, place. rest, set; build, construct, raise; establish, institute, plant; cast, mould.

foundation *n* base, basis, bed, bottom, footing, groundwork; endowment, establishment, settlement.

fountain *n* fount, spring, well; jet; cause, fountainhead, origin, source.

fracture *vb* break, crack; * *n* breaking; breach, break, cleft, crack, opening, rift, rent.

fragile *adj* breakable, brittle, delicate; feeble, frail, weak.

fragility *n* breakability, breakableness, brittleness; feebleness, infirmity, weakness.

fragment *vb* atomise, break, pulverise; * *n* bit, chip, fraction, fracture, morsel, part, remnant, scrap.

fragrant *adj* ambrosial, aromatic, balmy, odorous, perfumed, spicy, sweet, sweet-scented, sweet-smelling.

frail *adj* breakable, delicate, fragile, frangible, slight; feeble, infirm, weak.

frame *vb* build, compose, constitute, construct, form, make, mould, plan, shape; devise, fashion, invent, plan; * *n* body, carcass, framework, framing, shell, skeleton; fabric, form, structure, scheme, system; state, temper.

frank *adj* artless, candid, direct, downright, free, genuine, ingenuous, naïve, open, outspoken, outright, plain, sincere, straightforward, truthful, unreserved.

frantic *adj* crazy, distracted, distraught, frenzied, infuriate, mad, frenetic, rabid, raving, wild.

fraud *n* artifice, cheat, craft, deception, deceit, guile, hoax, imposition, sham, treachery, trick, wile.

fraudulent *adj* crafty, deceitful, deceptive, dishonest, false, treacherous, tricky, wily.

freak *adj* bizarre, freakish, grotesque, monstrous, odd, unexpected, unforeseen; * *n* caprice, crotchet, fancy, maggot, whim, whimsy; antic, caper; abnormality, abortion.

free *vb* deliver, discharge, enlarge, liberate, manumit, ransom, release, redeem, rescue, save; clear, disengage, rid, unbind, unchain, unfetter, unlock; exempt, privilege; * *adj* bondless, independent, loose, unattached, unentangled, unimpeded, unrestrained; autonomous, delivered, emancipated, freeborn, liberated, ransomed, released, self-governing; clear, exempt, immune, privileged; allowed, open, permitted; devoid, empty, open; affable, artless, candid, frank, sincere, unreserved; bountiful, charitable, generous, liberal, open-handed; lavish, prodigal; eager, prompt, ready, willing; available, gratuitous, willing; careless, lax, loose; bold, easy, familiar, unconstrained; * *adv* openly, outright, unreservedly, unrestrainedly; freely, gratis.

freedom *n* emancipation, independence, liberation, liberty, release; play, range, scope, swing; franchise, immunity, privilege; laxity, license.

freeze vb benumb, congeal, glaciate, harden, stiffen; chill.

frequent vb attend, haunt, visit; * adj oft-repeated; common, customary, everyday, familiar, habitual, persistent, usual; constant.

fresh adj new, novel, recent; new, renewed, revived; blooming, flourishing, green, unfaded, unwithered; sweet; blooming, delicate, fair, ruddy, rosy; hardy, healthy, strong, vigorous; active, energetic, unwearied, vigorous; keen, lively, unimpaired, vivid; further; uncured, undried, unsalted; bracing, invigorating, refreshing, sweet; brink, stiff, strong; raw, uncultivated, unpractised, unskilled, untrained, unused.

freshen vb quicken, refresh, revive.

friend adj chum, companion, comrade, confidant, intimate; ally, associate, partisan; adherent, advocate, favourer, supporter.

friendly adj affectionate, benevolent, favourable, kind, kindly, well-disposed; amicable, cordial, fraternal, neighbourly; peaceable.

friendship n affection, love, regard; fellowship, intimacy; amicableness, amity, cordiality, familiarity, fellowship, harmony.

fright n affright, alarm, dismay, funk, horror, panic, scare.

frighten vb affright, alarm, appal, daunt, dismay, scare, stampede.

frightful adj alarming, awful, dire, direful, dread, dreadful, horrid, terrible, terrific; ghastly, grim, grisly.

fringe vb border, bound, edge, hem, march, skirt, verge; * n border, edge, edging; * adj edging, extra, unofficial.

frisky adj lively, playful, sportive.

frivolous adj childish, empty, flighty, flimsy, flippant, foolish, idle, light, petty, silly, trifling, trivial, unimportant, vain.

frolic vb caper, frisk, gambol, lark, play, sport; * n escapade, lark, romp, spree, trick; fun, play, sport.

front vb confront, encounter, face, oppose; * adj anterior, forward; foremost, frontal; * n brow, face, forehead; boldness, brass, effrontery, face; breast, head, van, vanguard; anterior, face, forepart, facade.

frontier n border, boundary, coast, limits.

frosty adj chill, cold, icy, stinging, wintry; cold, cold-hearted, frigid, indifferent, unaffectionate, unimpassioned, unloving; cold, lifeless, spiritless, unanimated; frosted.

froth vb bubble, cream, lather, spume; * n bubbles, foam, lather, spume; nonsense, trash.

frown vb glower, lower, look daggers, scowl.

frugal adj abstemious, careful, choice, economical, provident, saving, sparing, temperate, thrifty.

fruit n crop, harvest, production; consequence, effect, good, product, profit, result; offspring, young.

fruitless adj barren, sterile, unfertile, unproductive; abortive, barren, futile, idle, ineffectual, profitless, unavailing, useless, vain.

frustrate vb baffle, baulk, block, circumvent, disappoint, foil, thwart; check.

fugitive adj escaping, fleeing; brief, fleeting, fugacious, short, short-lived, temporal, temporary, transient, unstable; * n émigré, escapee, evacuee, outlaw, refugee, runaway.

fulfil vb accomplish, complete, consummate, effect, effectuate, execute, realise; adhere, discharge, perform; answer,

satisfy.
full *adj* brimful, filled, flush, replete; replete, well-stocked; bagging, flowing, loose; crammed, glutted, gorged, packed, sated, satiated, saturated, soaked, swollen; adequate, complete, entire, mature, perfect; ample, copious, plentiful, sufficient; clear, deep, distinct, loud, rounded, strong; broad, large, comprehensive, extensive; circumstantial, detailed, exhaustive; * *adv* fully; directly, exactly, precisely.
fully *adv* abundantly, amply, completely, entirely, largely, plentifully.
fumble *vb* bungle, grope, mismanage; mumble, stammer, stutter.
fume *vb* reek, smoke, vaporise; * *n* reek, smell, smoke, steam, vapour; agitation, fret, passion, pet, rage, storm.
fun *adj* amusing, diverting, entertaining; * *n* amusement, diversion, frolic, gaiety, humour, jollity, joy, mirth, play, pranks, sport.
function *vb* act, discharge, go, operate, perform, run, serve, work; * *n* discharge, execution, exercise, operation, purpose, use; business, duty, occupation, office, part, role; rite.
fund *vb* afford, endow, finance, provide, support; gamer, hoard, stock, store; * *n* capital, endowment, reserve, stock; store, supply.
fundamental *adj* basic, bottom, cardinal, elementary, essential, indispensable, principal, primary, radical; * *n* essential, principal, rule.
funereal *adj* dark, dismal, gloomy, melancholy, mournful, sad, sombre.
funny *adj* amusing, comic, diverting, droll, farcical, humorous, jocular, laughable, sportive, witty; curious, odd, queer, strange; * *n* jest, joke; cartoon.
furious *adj* angry, fierce, frantic, frenzied, fuming, mad, raging, violent; boisterous, fierce, stormy, tumultuous, turbulent.
furnish *vb* appoint, endow, provide, supply; decorate, equip, fit; afford, give, offer, present, yield.
furniture *n* effects, household goods, movables; apparatus, appliances, equipment, fittings; decorations
further *vb* advance, aid, assist, encourage, help; forward, strengthen; * *adj* additional; * *adv* also, besides, farther, furthermore, moreover.
furtive *adj* clandestine, hidden, secret, sly, sneaking, sneaky, stolen.
fury *n* anger, frenzy, fit, furore, ire, madness, passion, rage; fierceness, turbulence, turbulency, vehemence; bacchant, bacchante, hag, shrew, vixen.
fuse *vb* dissolve, melt; liquefy, smelt; blend, coalesce, combine, intermingle, merge, unite; * *n* match.
fuss *vb* bustle, fidget, fret, worry; * *n* ado, agitation, bother, bustle, disturbance, excitement, fidget, flurry, fluster, fret, stir, worry.
futile *adj* frivolous, trifling; bootless, idle, ineffectual, profitless, unprofitable, vain, valueless, worthless.
future *adj* coming, eventual, forthcoming, prospective, subsequent; * *n* hereafter, outlook, prospect.

G

gag *n* jape, jest, joke, stunt, wisecrack; muzzle; * *vb* muffle, silence, stifle, throttle; retch, throw up, choke, gasp, pant.
gain *vb* achieve, acquire, obtain,

secure; enlist, persuade, prevail, win; arrive, attain, reach; clear, net, profit. * *n* addition, gainings, profits; acquisition, earnings, lucre; advantage, benefit, profit.

gainful *adj* advantageous, beneficial, lucrative, paying, productive.

galaxy *n* assemblage, collection, constellation, group.

gale *n* blast, hurricane, squall, storm, tempest.

gallant *adj* fine, magnificent, showy, splendid; bold, brave, courageous, daring, fearless, high-spirited, intrepid, valiant, valorous; fine, honourable, high-minded, lofty, magnanimous, noble; * *n* beau, spark; lover.

gallantry *n* boldness, bravery, chivalry, courage, heroism, intrepidity, prowess, valour; courtesy, elegance, politeness.

galling *adj* aggravating, chafing, irritating, vexing.

gamble *vb* bet, game, hazard, plunge, wager; * *n* chance, risk, speculation; bet, wager.

gambol *vb* caper, cut, frisk, frolic, hop, jump, leap, skip; * *n* frolic, hop, jump, skip.

game *vb* gamble, sport; * *n* amusement, contest, play, sport; adventure, enterprise, measure, plan, project, scheme, undertaking; prey, quarry, victim; * *adj* brave, courageous, dauntless, disabled, fearless, gallant, heroic, injured, intrepid, lame, unflinching, valorous; enduring, persevering, ready; eager, willing.

gang *n* band, clique, company, crew, horde, party, set, troop.

gap *n* breach, break, chasm, chink, cleft, crack, crevice, hollow, interval, interstice, opening, pass, ravine, rift, space.

gape *vb* burst open, open, stare, yawn.

garish *adj* bright, dazzling, flaunting, gaudy, glaring, loud, showy.

garment *n* apparel, clothes, clothing, dress, vestment.

gasp *vb* blow, pant, puff; * *n* blow, exclamation, gulp.

gather *vb* assemble, cluster, collect, convene, group, rally; accumulate, amass, board, huddle, lump; bunch, crop, pick, pluck, rake, reap, shock; acquire, gain, get, win; deduce, derive, infer; fold, plait; condense, grow, increase, thicken.

gathering *n* acquisition, earning, gain, heap, pile, procuring; assemblage, assembly, collection, company, meeting, muster; abscess, fester, pustule, sore, tumour, ulcer.

gaudy *adj* bespangled, brilliant, cheap, flashy, flaunting, garish, glittering, loud, ostentatious, over-decorated, sham, showy, spurious.

gauge *vb* calculate, check, determine, weigh; assess, estimate, reckon; * *n* example, measure, meter; bore, depth, height, magnitude, size, thickness.

gaunt *adj* angular, emaciated, haggard, lean, meagre, spare, thin.

gear *vb* adapt, equip, suit, tailor; * *n* clothes, clothing, dress, garb; appliances, appointments, array, harness, goods, movables; rigging, tackle, trappings; mechanics.

general *adj* broad, generic, popular, universal, widespread; common, current, ordinary, usual; indefinite, inexact, vague.

generate *vb* beget, breed, procreate, reproduce; cause, form, make, produce.

generation *n* creation, formation, production; age, era, period, time; breed, children, family, kind, offspring, race, stock.

generosity *n* disinterestedness, nobleness; bountifulness, charity, liberality.

generous *adj* high-minded, honourable, noble; bountiful, charitable, free, liberal; abundant, ample, plentiful

genius *n* aptitude, aptness, bent, capacity, faculty, flair, gift, talent, turn; brains, intellect, invention, parts, wit; master, master hand, character, disposition, nature; deity, spirit.

gentle *adj* amiable, bland, compassionate, humane, indulgent, kind, meek, merciful, mild, moderate, soft, tender, docile, pacific, peaceable, placid, quiet, tame; easy, gradual, light, mild, slight, soft; high-born, noble, well-born; courteous, polished, refined, well-bred.

genuine *adj* authentic, honest, proper, pure, real, right, true, uncorrupted; frank, native, sincere.

gesture *vb* indicate, motion, signal, wave; * *n* action, attitude, gesturing, posture, sign, signal.

get *vb* achieve, acquire, earn, gain, obtain, procure, receive, relieve, win; finish, prepare; beget, breed, engender.

ghastly *adj* corpse-like, deathly, ghostly, lurid, pale, wan; dismal, fearful, frightful, grim, grisly, gruesome, horrible, shocking, terrible.

ghost *n* soul, spirit; apparition, phantom, shade, spectre, sprite.

giant *adj* colossal, enormous, huge, large, monstrous, prodigious, vast; * *n* colossus, monster.

gibe, jibe *vb* deride, jeer, mock, ridicule, scoff, sneer, taunt; * *n* ridicule, sneer, taunt.

gift *n* allowance, benefaction, bequest, bonus, bounty, contribution, donation, dowry, endowment, favour, grant, legacy, offering, present, prize, subscription, subsidy, tip; faculty, talent.

gifted *adj* able, adroit, capable, clever, ingenious, intelligent, talented.

gild *vb* adorn, beautify, brighten, decorate, grace, illuminate.

gird *vb* belt, girdle; encircle, enclose, encompass, environ, surround; support; * *n* band, belt, girdle, girth, sash.

girl *n* lass, maiden, miss, virgin.

gist *n* basis, core, essence, force, ground, meaning, pith, point.

give *vb* accord, bequeath, bestow, confer, devise, present; afford, donate, grant, proffer, spare, supply; communicate, impart; deliver, exchange, pay; allow, permit; emit, render, utter; produce, yield; cause, occasion; addict, apply; surrender; bend, sink, retire, retreat, yield.

glad *adj* delighted, gratified, happy, pleased, rejoiced; animated, cheerful, gladsome, happy, joyful, joyous, light, light-hearted, merry, playful; bright, cheering, gladdening, gratifying, pleasing.

gladden *vb* bless, cheer, delight, elate, gratify, please, rejoice.

glamour *n* charm, enchantment, fascination, spell.

glance *vb* gleam, glisten, glitter, scintillate, shine; dart; gaze, glimpse, look, view; * *n* gleam, glitter; gleam, view.

glare *vb* dazzle, flame, flare, glitter, sparkle; frown, gaze, glower; * *n* flare, glitter.

gleam *vb* beam, flash, glance, glimmer, glitter, shine, sparkle; * *n* beam, flash, glance, glimmer, glimmering, glow, ray; brightness, flashing, glitter, glittering, lustre.

glee *n* exhilaration, fun, gaiety, hilarity, jollity, joviality, joy, liveliness, merriment, mirth.

glib *adj* slippery, smooth; artful, facile, fluent, talkative, voluble.

glide *vb* float, glissade, roll on, skate, skim, slide, slip; run, roll; * *n* gliding, lapse, sliding,

slip.
glimmer *vb* flash, flicker, gleam, glitter; * *n* beam, gleam, glimmering, ray; glance, glimpse.
glimpse *vb* look, spot, view; * *n* flash, glance, glint, look, sight.
glitter *vb* coruscate, flash, glance, glare, gleam, glister, shine, sparkle; * *n* beam, beaming, brightness, brilliancy, gleam, glister, lustre, radiance, shine, sparkle, splendour.
gloomy *adj* dark, dim, dusky, obscure; cheerless, dismal, lowering, lurid; dejected, depressed, despondent, disheartened, dispirited, downcast, glum, melancholy, morose, sad; dark, depressing, disheartening, dispiriting, heavy, melancholy, sad.
glorify *vb* adore, bless, celebrate, exalt, laud, magnify, worship; brighten, ennoble, exalt, make bright.
glorious *adj* celebrated, eminent, excellent, famous, illustrious, renowned; brilliant, bright, grand, magnificent, radiant splendid; exalted, excellent, high, lofty, noble, supreme.
glow *vb* radiate, shine; blush, flush, redden; * *n* blaze, brightness, brilliance, burning, incandescence, luminosity, reddening; ardour, bloom, fervour, flush, warmth.
glower *vb* frown, glare, scowl, stare; * *n* frown, glare, scowl.
glum *adj* churlish, crest-fallen, crusty, depressed, frowning, gloomy, glowering, moody, sour, spleenish, sulky, sullen.
glut *vb* block up, cloy, gorge, satiate, stuff; * *n* excess, superabundance, surfeit, surplus.
glutton *n* gobbler, gorger, greedy-guts, pig.
go *vb* advance, move, pass, proceed, repair; act, operate; be about, fare, journey, roam, travel, walk, wend; depart, disappear; extend, lead, reach, run; avail, contribute, tend, serve; fare, turn out; accept, approve, bear, endure; afford, bet, risk; * *n* action, case, chance, circumstance, doings, turn; custom, mode; energy, endurance, power; avaunt, begone, be off.
goal *n* bound, limit, mark, mete; end, object; aim, design.
gobble *vb* bolt, devour, gorge, gulp, swallow.
goblin *n* apparition, demon, hobgoblin, phantom, spectre, sprite.
god *n* almighty, creator, deity, divinity, idol, omnipotence.
godsend *n* fortune, gift, luck, present, windfall.
golden *adj* brilliant, bright, gilded, shining, splendid; excellent, precious; blessed, delightful, glorious, happy.
good *adj* beneficial, favourable, profitable, serviceable, useful; appropriate, becoming, fit, proper, suitable, well-adapted; dutiful, honest, just, pious, reliable, religious, upright, virtuous, well-behaved, worthy; admirable, excellent, genuine, healthy, precious, sincere, sound, sterling, valid, valuable; favourable, friendly, gracious, humane, kind, merciful, obliging; fair, honourable, immaculate, unimpeachable, unimpeached, unsullied; cheerful, lively, genial, social; able, dextrous, expert, qualified, ready, skilful, thorough; competent; agreeable, gratifying, pleasant; * *n* advantage, benefit, boon, favour, gain, profit, utility; interest, welfare, weal; excellence, virtue, worth.
goodness *n* excellence, quality, value, worth; honesty, virtue; benevolence, beneficence, humaneness, humanity, kindness.
goodwill *n* benevolence, good nature, kindness; earnestness, willingness, zeal; patronage.

gorgeous *adj* bright, brilliant, dazzling, grand, magnificent, rich, shining, showy, splendid.

gory *adj* bloody, sanguinary.

gospel *n* creed, doctrine, message, news, revelation.

gossip *vb* chat, cackle, clack, gabble, prate, tattle; * *n* babbler, busybody, chatterer, gadabout, gossipmonger, newsmonger, tell-tale; cackle, chat, chit-chat, prattle, tattle.

gourmet *n* connoisseur, epicure, epicurean.

govern *vb* administer, conduct, direct, manage, regulate, reign, rule, supervise; guide, pilot, steer; bridle, check, command, control, restrain, rule.

government *n* autonomy, command, control, direction, guidance, management, regulation, restraint, rule, sway; administration, cabinet, commonwealth, polity, sovereignty, state.

governor *n* director, head, manager, overseer, ruler, superintendent, supervisor; chief magistrate; guardian, instructor, tutor.

grab *vb* capture, clutch, latch on to, seize, snatch.

grace *vb* adorn, beautify, deck, decorate; dignify, honour; * *n* benignity, condescension, favour, good-will, kindness, love; devotion, holiness, love, piety, religion, virtue; forgiveness, mercy, pardon; accomplishment, charm, elegance, polish, refinement; beauty, ease, gracefulness, symmetry; blessing, thanks.

graceful *adj* beautiful, becoming, easy, elegant; flowing, natural; appropriate; happy, tactful.

grade *vb* arrange, group, order, rank, sort; * *n* brand, degree, intensity, stage, step, rank; gradient, slope.

gradual *adj* approximate, continuous, progressive, regular, slow.

graduate *vb* adapt, adjust, proportion, regulate; * *n* laureate, postgraduate.

grand *adj* august, elevated, eminent, exalted, great, illustrious, lordly, majestic, princely, stately; fine, gorgeous, magnificent, lofty, noble, splendid, sublime, superb; chief, leading, main, principal, superior.

grandeur *n* elevation, loftiness, vastness; dignity, glory, magnificence, majesty, nobility, pomp, splendour, state.

grant *vb* accord, admit, allow, cede, concede, give, impart; bestow, confer, deign, invest; transfer, yield; * *n* admission, allowance, benefaction, bounty, donation, endowment, gift, indulgence, present; cession.

graphic *adj* descriptive, figural, figurative, forcible, lively, picturesque, striking, telling, vivid, well-drawn.

grapple *vb* catch, clutch, grasp, grip, hold, hug, seize, wrestle.

grasp *vb* catch, clasp, clutch, grip, seize; comprehend understand; * *n* clasp, grip, hold; comprehension, reach, scope, understanding.

grasping *adj* acquisitive, avaricious, exacting, greedy, sordid, tight-fisted.

grate *vb* abrade, rub, scrape; rasp; creak, fret, grind, jar, rasp, vex; * *n* bars, grating, screen; basket, fire bed.

gratify *vb* delight, please; burnout, fulfil, grant, indulge, requite.

gratitude *n* goodwill, gratitude, indebtedness.

grave *adj* heavy, important, momentous, serious, weighty; dignified, serious, slow, thoughtful; dull, plain, quiet, sober, sombre; cruel, hard, harsh, severe; dire, dismal, gross, outrageous, scandalous, shameful, shocking; heavy, hollow, low.

gravity *n* heaviness, weight; demureness, seriousness, sobriety; importance, moment, seriousness, weightiness.

graze *vb* brush, glance, scrape, shave, skim; feed, pasture; * *n* bruise, scrape, scratch.

great *adj* ample, big, bulky, enormous, gigantic, huge, large, pregnant, vast; decided, excessive, high, much; chief, grand, important, leading, main, pre-eminent, principal, superior, weighty; eminent, exalted, excellent, famed, famous, illustrious, noted, prominent, renowned; elevated, exalted, grand, lofty, majestic, noble; chivalrous, generous, high-minded; fine, magnificent, rich.

greatness *n* bulk, dimensions, largeness, size; distinction, elevation, eminence, fame, importance, renown; dignity, majesty, loftiness, nobility, nobleness; disinterestedness, generosity, spirit.

greed, greediness *n* gluttony, hunger, omnivorousness; avidity, covetousness, desire, eagerness, greed, longing; graspingness, rapacity, selfishness.

greedy *adj* devouring, gluttonous, insatiable, insatiate, rapacious; desirous, eager; grasping, rapacious, selfish.

green *adj* emerald, olive, verdant, verdure, viridescent; blooming, flourishing, fresh, undecayed; fresh, new, recent; unfledged; callow, crude, ignorant, inexperienced, raw, untrained, verdant, young; raw, unseasoned; * *n* common, grass plot; lawn, sward, turf.

greet *vb* accost, complement, hail, receive, welcome.

greeting *n* compliment, hail, salutation, salute, welcome.

grief *n* agony, anguish, distress, heartbreak, misery, regret, sadness, sorrow, suffering, woe; distress, sorrow, trial, woe; disaster, failure, mishap.

grievance *n* burden, complaint, hardship, injury, oppression, wrong; affliction, distress, grief, sorrow, trial, woe.

grieve *vb* afflict, agonise, discomfort, distress, hurt, oppress, pain, wound; bewail, lament, mourn, regret, sorrow, suffer.

grievous *adj* afflicting, afflictive, deplorable, distressing, heavy, oppressive, painful, sad, sorrowful; calamitous, destructive, hurtful, injurious, mischievous, troublesome; aggravated, atrocious, dreadful, flagrant, gross, iniquitous, intense, severe, outrageous, wicked.

grim *adj* cruel, ferocious, fierce, harsh, relentless, ruthless, savage, unyielding; dire, dreadful, fearful, frightful, grisly, horrid, horrible, terrific.

grimace *vb, n* frown, scowl, smirk, sneer, wry face.

grimy *adj* defiled, dirty, filthy, foul, soiled, unclean.

grind *vb* bruise, crunch, crush, grate, grit, rub, triturate; sharpen; afflict, harass, oppress, plague, trouble; * *n* chore, drudgery, labour, toil.

grip *vb* clasp, clutch, grasp, hold, seize; * *n* clasp, clutch, domination, grasp, hold.

grit *vb* clench, grate, grind; * *n* bran, gravel, sand; courage, decision, determination, perseverance, pluck, spirit.

groan *vb* complain, lament, moan, whine; creak; * *n* cry, moan, whine; complaint; grumble.

gross *vb* accumulate, earn, make; * *adj* big, bulky, burly, fat, great, large; dense, dull, stupid; broad, coarse, crass, earthy, indelicate, licentious, low, obscene, unbecoming, unrefined, unseemly, vulgar; sensual; aggravated, brutal, enormous, flagrant, glaring, manifest, obvious, palpable, plain, shameful; aggregate, entire, total, whole; * n bulk, total, whole.

grotesque *adj* bizarre, extravagant, fanciful, fantastic, odd, strange, whimsical, wild; absurd, burlesque, ludicrous.

ground *vb* fell, place; base, establish, fix, found, set; instruct, train; * n area, distance, earth, loam, mould, sod, soil, turf; country, domain, land, region; estate, field, property; base, basis, foundation, groundwork, support; account, excuse, gist, motive, opinion, reason.

grounds *npl* deposit, dregs, grouts, lees, precipitate, settlings; accounts, arguments, reasons, support; gardens, lawns, premises, yard.

group *vb* arrange, assemble, dispose, order; * n aggregation, assemblage, assembly, body, combination, class, clump, collection, order.

grow *vb* enlarge, expand, extend, increase, swell; arise, develop, shoot, sprout; advance, improve, progress, swell, thrive, wax; produce, raise.

growl *vb* complain, croak, find fault, groan, grumble, lament, murmur, snarl; * n croak, grown, snarl.

growth *n* augmentation, development, expansion, growing, increase; excrescence, formation, germination, sprouting, vegetation; cultivation, produce, product, production; advance, progress; maturity

grudge *vb* begrudge, envy; complain, grieve; * n aversion, dislike, grievance, hate, hatred, malevolence, malice, rancour, spite, venom.

grumble *vb* croak, complain, murmur; growl, snarl; roar, rumble; * n growl, murmur, complaint, roar, rumble.

grumpy *adj* cross, glum, moody, morose, sour, surly.

guarantee *vb* assure, insure, pledge, secure, warrant; * n assurance, pledge, security, warrant.

guard *vb* defend, keep, patrol, protect, safeguard, save, secure, shelter, watch; * n bulwark, defence, palladium, protection, safeguard, security, shield; keeper, guardian, patrol, sentry, warden, watch, watchman; conduct, escort; attention, care, caution, circumspection, heed.

guarded *adj* careful, cautious, circumspect, reserved, reticent, wary.

guardian *n* custodian, defender, guard, keeper, protector, warden.

guess *vb* conjecture, divine, mistrust, suspect; find out, penetrate, solve; believe, fancy, imagine, reckon, suppose, think; * n conjecture, notion, supposition, surmise.

guide *vb* conduct, escort, lead, pilot; control, direct, govern, manage, regulate, rule, steer, superintend, supervise; * n conductor, director, monitor, pilot; adviser, counsellor, instructor, mentor; index, key, thread; guidebook, itinerary.

guilt *n* blame, culpability, guiltless; iniquity, wrong; crime, offence, sin, wrong.

guilty *adj* criminal, culpable, evil, sinful, wicked, wrong.

guise *n* appearance, aspect, costume, dress, fashion, figure, form, manner, mode, shape; air, behaviour; custom, habit, manner, mode, practice.

gusto *n* brio, gust, liking, pleasure, relish, zest.

gusty *adj* blustering, blustery, squally, stormy, unsteady, windy.

guy *vb* caricature, mimic; * n boy, man, person; eccentric, fright.

guzzle *vb* drink, gorge, quaff, swill, tipple, tope.

H

habit vb array, attire, clothe, dress, equip, robe; * n condition, temperament; addiction, custom, habitude, manner, practice, rule, usage, way; costume, dress, garb.

habitual adj accustomed, common, confirmed, everyday, familiar, ordinary, regular, routine, settled, usual, wonted.

hackneyed adj banal, common, overworked, pedestrian, stale, trite.

haggard adj intractable, unruly, untamed, wild; careworn, gaunt, ghastly, lank, lean, spare, thin.

haggle vb argue, bargain, chaffer, dispute, stickle; annoy, bait, fret, tease, worry.

hail vb acclaim, greet, salute, welcome; address, call, hallo, signal; bombard, rain, shower, storm, volley; * n greeting, salute; rain, shower, storm, volley.

hale adj hardy, healthy, hearty, robust, sound, strong.

halfwitted adj dull, dull-witted, feeble-minded, foolish, shallow, silly, simple, stupid, thick.

hallow vb consecrate, dedicate, devote, sanctify; enshrine, honour, respect, reverence.

hallowed adj blessed, holy, honoured, revered, sacred.

hallucination n blunder, error, mistake; aberration, delusion, fantasy, illusion, phantasm, vision.

halo n aura, aureole, glory.

halt vb cease, hold, rest, stand, stop; hesitate, pause, waver; falter, limp; * adj crippled, lame; * n end, pause, stop; hobble, limp.

hammer vb beat, forge, form, shape; contrive, invent.

hamper vb bind, confine, curb, embarrass, entangle, fetter, hinder, impede, prevent, restrain, restrict, shackle; * n basket, crate, picnic basket; embarrassment, fetter, handicap, obstruction, restraint, trammel.

hand vb deliver, give, present, transmit; guide, lead; * n direction, part, side; ability, dexterity, faculty, skill, talent; course, management, rum; agency, participation, share; control, possession, power; artisan, craftsman, employee, labourer, workman; indicator, pointer; handwriting.

handful n fistful, maniple, smattering, sprinkling.

handicap vb hamper, hinder, restrict; * n disadvantage, encumbrance, hindrance.

handle vb feel, finger, paw, touch; direct, manage, manipulate, use; discourse, discuss, treat; * n helve, hilt, stock.

handsome adj admirable, stately, well-formed, well-proportioned; appropriate, suitable; easy, graceful; generous, gracious, liberal, magnanimous, noble; large, plentiful, sufficient.

handy adj clever, dextrous, expert, ready, skilful, skilled; close, near.

hang vb attach, swing; execute, truss; drop, droop, incline; adorn; dangle, depend, impend, swing, suspend; rely; cling, loiter, rest, stick; float, pay

hanker vb covet, crave, desire, hunger, long, lust, want, yearn.

haphazard adj aimless, chance, random.

hapless adj ill-fated, luckless, miserable, unfortunate, unhappy, unlucky, wretched.

happen vb befall, betide, chance, come, occur.

happiness n cheerfulness, delight, gaiety, joy, pleasure; blessedness, bliss, felicity; enjoyment, welfare.

happy adj blessed, blest, cheerful, contented, joyful, joyous, merry; charmed, delighted, glad, gladdened, pleased, rejoiced; fortunate, lucky, prosperous, successful; able, apt, expert, ready, skilful; befitting, felicitous, pertinent, well-timed; bright, favourable.

harangue vb address, declaim, spout; * n address, declamation, rant, speech, tirade.

harass vb exhaust, fag, fatigue, jade, tire, weary; annoy, distress, gall; disturb, harry, plague, tantalise, tease, torment, trouble, vex, worry.

harbour vb protect, lodge; cherish, foster, indulge; * n asylum, cover, resting place, retreat, sanctuary, shelter; anchorage, haven, port.

hard adj compact, firm, flinty, marble, rigid, solid, resistant, stony, stubborn; difficult, intricate, knotty; arduous, exacting, fatiguing, laborious, toilsome, wearying; callous, cruel, exacting, hard-hearted, inflexible, insensible, rigorous, severe, unkind, unsympathetic, unyielding; calamitous, distressing, grievous, painful, unpleasant; acid, harsh, rough, sour; intemperate; * adv close, near; diligently, earnestly, incessantly, laboriously; painfully, rigorously, severely; forcibly, violently.

harden vb accustom, discipline, form, inure, train; fortify, nerve, steel, stiffen.

hardly adv barely, scarcely; harshly, rigorously, roughly, severely.

hardy adj enduring, firm, healthy, hearty, lusty, robust, rugged, stout, strong, tough; bold, brave, daring, heroic, manly, stout-hearted, valiant.

harm vb damage, hurt, injure, scathe; abuse, ill-use, molest; * n damage, detriment, hurt, injury, misfortune, prejudice, wrong.

harmful adj hurtful, injurious, mischievous, pernicious.

harmless adj beneficial, innocent, innocuous; inoffensive, safe, unoffending.

harmonious adj concordant, consonant, harmonic; musical; comfortable, consistent, correspondent, orderly; agreeable, amicable, brotherly, cordial, friendly, neighbourly.

harmonise vb adapt, reconcile, unite; agree, blend, chime, conform, correspond, tune.

harmony n melodiousness, melody; accord, accordance, agreement, concord, order; adaptation, congruence, congruity, correspondence, fairness, smoothness; amity, friendship, peace.

harry vb pillage, plunder, raid, ravage, rob; annoy, chafe, disturb, fret, gall, harrow, molest, pester, plague, molest, tease, trouble, vex.

harsh adj acid, acrid, biting, caustic, corrosive, crabbed, hard, rough, sharp, sour, tart; discordant, grating, metallic, raucous, unmelodious; abusive, austere, crabby, cruel, disagreeable, hard, ill-natured, morose, rigorous, severe, stem, unfeeling; bluff, brutal, gruff, rude, uncivil.

harvest vb gather, glean, reap; * n produce, yield; effect, outcome, produce, result.

haste n dispatch, expedition, nimbleness, promptitude, quickness, rapidity, speed, urgency, velocity; hurry, hustle, press, rashness, rush, vehemence.

hasten vb haste; dispatch, press, push, quicken, speed, urge.

hasty adj brisk, fast, fleet, quick, rapid, speedy, swift; hurried, passing, rapid, slight, superficial; rash, reckless; headlong, pell-mell; abrupt, choleric, excitable, fiery, fretful, hot-headed, passionate, peevish, testy, waspish.

hatch vb breed, brew, contrive, excogitate, design, devise,

plan, plot, project, scheme; incubate.
hate *vb* abhor, abominate, detest, dislike, execrate, loathe, nauseate; * *n* antipathy, detestation, dislike, enmity, hatred, hostility, loathing.
hatred *n* animosity, enmity, hate, hostility, ill-will, malevolence, malice, malignity, rancour; antipathy, aversion, detestation, disgust, horror, loathing, revulsion.
haughty *adj* arrogant, assuming, contemptuous, insolent, lofty, lordly, overbearing, proud, scornful, supercilious.
haul *vb* drag, draw, pull, tow, trail, tug; * *n* heaving, pull, tug; booty, takings, yield.
haunt *vb* frequent, resort; follow; hover, inhabit, obsess; * *n* resort, retreat.
have *vb* cherish, exercise, experience, hold, own, possess; gain, get, obtain; accept, take.
havoc *n* carnage, damage, desolation, destruction, ruin, waste, wreck.
hazard *vb* adventure, risk; endanger, imperil; * *n* accident, casualty, chance, event, fortuity, stake; danger, peril, risk, venture.
hazardous *adj* dangerous, insecure, perilous, precarious, uncertain.
hazy *adj* foggy, misty; cloudy, dim, obscure; confused, indefinite, indistinct, vague.
head *vb* command, control, direct, govern, lead, rule; aim, point, tend; beat, excel, outdo, precede; * *adj* chief, first, grand, highest, leading, main, principal; contrary; * *n* summit, top; beginning, origin, rise, source; chief, commander, director, leader, master, superintendent, superior; intellect, mind, thought; branch, class, department, division, section, topic; brain, intellect, mind, understanding; cape, point.

headlong *adj* dangerous, hasty, heady, impulsive, precipitate, reckless, ruinous, thoughtless; perpendicular, sheer, steep; * *adv* hastily, headfirst, hurriedly, precipitately, rashly.
headstrong *adj* dogged, forward, headless, heady, obstinate, stubborn, ungovernable, unruly, violent, wayward.
heady *adj* hasty, headlong, impetuous, impulsive, rash, reckless, rushing, stubborn, thoughtless; exciting, strong.
heal *vb* cure, remedy, repair, restore, harmonise, reconcile; soothe.
healthy *adj* active, hale, hearty, lusty, sound, vigorous, well; bracing, healthful, nourishing, wholesome.
heap *vb* accumulate, amass, collect, overfill, pile up, store; * *n* collection, huddle, lot, mass, mound, pile, stack.
hear *vb* hearken, heed, listen, overhear; discover, gather, learn, understand; judge.
heart *n* bosom; centre, core, essence, interior, marrow, meaning; affection, character, disposition, feeling, love, purpose, will; affections, emotion, feeling, love; boldness, courage, fortitude, spirit.
heartbroken *adj* cheerless, comfortless, desolate, forlorn, inconsolable, miserable, wretched.
hearten *vb* animate, assure, cheer, comfort, console, encourage, incite, inspire, reassure, stimulate.
heartless *adj* brutal, cold, cruel, hard, harsh, merciless, unfeeling; spiritless, timid, timorous.
hearty *adj* cordial, deep, earnest, heartfelt, profound, sincere, true; active, earnest, vigorous, warm; hale, hearty, robust, sound, strong, warm; full, heavy; nourishing, rich.
heat *vb* excite, flush, inflame;

animate, rouse, stimulate, stir; * n calorie, warmth; excitement, fever, flush, passion, vehemence, violence; earnestness, fervour, glow, intensity, zeal; frenzy, rage.

heath n field, moor, wasteland; plain, prairie.

heave vb elevate, hoist, lift, raise; breathe, raise; cast, hurl, send, throw, toss; breathe, dilate, pant, rise; retch, throw up; strive.

heaven n firmament, sky; bliss, ecstasy, felicity, happiness, paradise, rapture, transport.

heavenly adj celestial, ethereal; angelic, beatified, cherubic, divine, glorious, sainted, saintly, seraphic; blissful, celestial, delightful, divine, ecstatic, glorious, golden, rapturous, ravishing, seraphic.

heavy adj grave, ponderous, weighty; crushing, grievous, oppressive, severe, serious; dull, inactive, indolent, inert, lifeless, sleepy, slow, sluggish, stupid; crestfallen, crushed, dejected, despondent, gloomy, low-spirited, melancholy, sad, sobered, sorrowful; difficult, hard, laborious, tedious, tiresome, weary; burdened, encumbered; clammy, muddy, oppressive, soggy; deep, loud, severe, strong, violent; cloudy, dark, dense, gloomy, overcast.

hectic adj animated, excited, fevered, feverish, flushed, hot.

hedge vb block, encumber, obstruct, surround; enclose, fence, fortify, guard, protect; disappear, evade, hide, temporise; * n barrier, fence.

heed vb attend, mark, mind, note, notice, observe, regard; * n attention, care, carefulness, caution, consideration, heedfulness, notice, regard, vigilance, watchfulness.

heedful adj attentive, careful, cautious, mindful, observant, observing, watchful, wary.

heedless adj careless, inattentive, negligent, precipitate, rash, reckless, unmindful.

height n altitude, elevation, tallness; acme, apex, eminence, head, pinnacle, summit, top, zenith; eminence, hill, mountain; dignity, exaltation, grandeur, loftiness.

heighten vb elevate, raise; exalt, magnify, make greater; augment, improve, increase, strengthen; intensify.

help vb relieve, save; abet, aid, assist, back, second, serve, support, sustain, wait; better, cure, heal, improve, restore; control, hinder, prevent, repress, resist; avoid, forbear, control; * n aid, assistance, support; relief, remedy; assistant, helper, servant.

helper n aider, ally, assistant, colleague, helpmate, partner, supporter.

helpful adj advantageous, beneficial, favourable, kind, profitable, serviceable, useful.

helpless adj disabled, feeble, imbecile, impotent, powerless, prostrate, weak; abandoned, defenceless, exposed; desperate.

hem vb border, edge, skirt; beset, confine, enclose, surround, sew; hesitate; * n border, edge, trim.

herald vb announce, proclaim, publish; * n announcer; harbinger, proclaimer.

herd vb drive, gather, lead, tend; assemble, associate, flock; * n drover, shepherd; crowd, multitude, populace, rabble; assembly, collection, drove, flock.

heritage n bequest, estate, inheritance, legacy, patrimony.

hermit n anchoress, anchorite, ascetic, eremite, monk, recluse, solitaire.

heroic adj brave, courageous, daring, fearless, gallant, illustrious, magnanimous, noble, valiant; desperate.

heroism n boldness, bravery, courage, daring, endurance,

hesitate vb delay, demur, doubt, pause, scruple, waver; falter, stutter.

hesitation n halting, misgiving, reluctance; doubt, indecision, suspense, vacillation.

hidden adj blind, clandestine, cloaked, concealed, covered, covert, latent, masked, occult, private, secret, undiscovered, veiled; abstruse, cryptic, dark, hermetic, inward, mysterious, mystic, mystical, obscure, oracular.

hide vb bury, conceal, cover, secrete, withhold; cloak, disguise, eclipse, mask, screen, shelter, veil.

hideous adj appalling, awful, dreadful, ghastly, grim, grisly, horrible, horrid, repulsive, revolting, terrible, terrifying.

high adj elevated, lofty, soaring, tall, towering; distinguished, eminent, pre-eminent, superior; admirable, dignified, exalted, lofty, great, noble; arrogant, haughty, lofty, lordly, proud, supercilious; strong, turbulent, violent; costly, dear, pricey; acute, high-toned, piercing, sharp, shrill; * adv powerfully, profoundly; eminently, loftily, richly.

hilarious adj boisterous, cheerful, convivial, happy, jolly, joyful, mirthful, noisy.

hilarity n boisterousness, cheerfulness, conviviality, exhilarated, glee, jollity, joviality, merriment, mirth.

hinder vb bar, check, clog, delay, embarrass, impede, interrupt, oppose, prevent, restrain, stop, thwart.

hindrance n encumbrance, hitch, impediment, interruption, obstruction, restraint, stop.

hint vb allude, glance, imply, insinuate, intimate, suggest; * n allusion, implication, insinuation, intimation, mention, reminder, trace.

hire vb buy, rent, secure; employ, engage, lease, let; * n allowance, compensation, pay, remuneration, reward, stipend.

hiss vb shrill, sibilate, whistle, whir, whiz; condemn, ridicule; * n fizzle, hissing, sibilation, sizzle.

history n account, biography, chronicle, genealogy, memoirs, narrative, record, relation, story.

hit vb discomfit, hurt, knock, strike; achieve, attain, gain, reach, succeed, win; fit, suit; beat, clash, collide, smite; * n blow, strike, stroke; chance, fortune, success, venture.

hitch vb catch, impede, stick, stop; connect, harness, join, tether, tie, unite, * n catch, cheek, hindrance, impediment, obstacle; knot.

hoard vb amass, collect, deposit, hive, husband, save, store, treasure; * n accumulation, deposit, fund, mass, reserve, savings, store.

hoarse adj discordant, gruff, guttural, harsh, low, raucous, rough.

hoax vb deceive, dupe, fool, gammon, swindle, trick; * n cheat, deception, fraud, humbug, joke, trick, swindle.

hoist vb elevate, heave, lift, raise, rear; * n elevator, lift.

hold vb clasp, clinch, clutch, grasp, grip, seize; have, keep, possess, retain; bind, control, detain, restrain, restrict; fix, lock; cheek, stay, stop, withhold; continue, keep up, maintain, manage, prosecute, support, sustain; embrace, entertain; account, believe, consider, count, entertain, judge, reckon, regard, think; accommodate, admit, carry, contain, receive; assemble, conduct; continue, endure, last, persist, remain; adhere, cling, cohere, stick; * n anchor, bite, clasp, control, embrace, grasp, grip, possession, retention; prop, stay, support; claim; castle, fort, fortress, stronghold, tower; locker, storage.

hole *n* aperture, opening, perforation; abyss, bore, cavity, chasm, excavation, eye, hollow, pit, pore, void; cover, den, lair, retreat; den.

holiness *n* blessedness, devotion, godliness, piety, purity, religiousness, sacredness, saintliness, sanctity.

hollow *vb* dig, excavate, groove, scoop; * *adj* concave, depressed, empty, sunken, vacant, void; deceitful, false, false-hearted, hypocritical, insincere, treacherous, unfeeling; deep, low, muffled, reverberating, sepulchral; * *n* basin, bowl, depression; cave, cavity, concavity, dent, dimple, dint, depression, hole, pit; canal, channel, cup, dimple, dig.

holocaust *n* carnage, destruction, devastation, genocide, inferno.

holy *adj* blessed, dedicated, devoted, hallowed, sacred; devout, pious, pure, religious, righteous, saintly, spiritual.

homage *n* devotion, fealty, fidelity, loyalty; deference, duty, honour, respect, service; adoration, devotion.

home *adj* domestic, family; close, direct, effective, pointed; * *n* abode, dwelling, seat, quarters.

homely *adj* domestic, familiar, house-like; coarse, plain, simple, unpretentious.

honest *adj* equitable, fair, faithful, honourable, open, straightforward; fair, faithful, reliable, sound, square, true, trusty, uncorrupted, upright, virtuous; faithful, genuine, thorough, unadulterated; decent, honourable, proper, respectable, suitable; chaste, decent, virtuous; candid, direct, frank, open, sincere.

honesty *n* equity, fairness, faithfulness, fidelity, honour, integrity, justice, probity, trustiness, uprightness; truth, truthfulness, veracity; faithfulness, thoroughness; candour, openness, sincerity, truth, unreserve.

honorary *adj* formal, nominal, titular, unofficial, unpaid.

honour *vb* dignify, exalt, glorify, grace; respect, revere, venerate; adore, hallow, worship; celebrate, keep, observe; * *n* civility, deference, esteem, homage, respect, reverence; dignity, distinction, elevation, consideration, esteem, fame, glory; high-mindedness, honesty, integrity, , probity, uprightness; purity, virtue; boast, glory, ornament, pride.

honourable *adj* elevated, famous, great, noble; admirable, fair, honest, just, true, trustworthy, upright, virtuous, worshipful; esteemed, estimable, proper, respected, reputable, right.

hoodwink *vb* blind; cloak, conceal, cover, hide; cheat, circumvent, deceive, delete, fool, overreach, trick.

hoot *vb* boo, cry, jeer, shout, yell; condemn, denounce, hiss; * *n* boo, cry, jeer, shout, yell.

hop *vb* bound, frisk, jump, leap, spring; dance, trip; halt, limp, * *n* bound, caper, dance, jump, leap, skip.

hope *vb* anticipate, desire, expect, long; believe, trust; * *n* confidence, belief, faith, reliance, sanguinity, trust; anticipation, desire.

hopeful *adj* confident, expectant, fond, optimistic; cheerful, encouraging.

hopeless *adj* abject, crushed, depressed, despondent, despairing, downcast, helpless incurable, remediless; impossible, impracticable.

horde *n* clan, crew, gang, troop; crowd, pack, throng.

horrid *adj* alarming, awful, bristling, dreadful, fearful, frightful, hideous, horrible,

horrific, rough, terrible; abominable, disgusting, offensive, repulsive, revolting, shocking.
horrify vb affright, alarm, frighten, petrify, terrify, terrorise.
horror n alarm, consternation, dismay, fear, fright, panic; abhorrence, abomination, antipathy, disgust, hatred, repugnance, revulsion.
hospitable adj attentive, kind; bountiful, cordial, generous, liberal, open; sociable, unreserved.
host n entertainer, landlord, master of ceremonies, owner, presenter, receptionist; array, army, legion; assemblage, assembly, horde; altar bread, bread, consecrated bread, loaf.
hostile adj inimical, warlike; adverse, antagonistic, contrary, opposed, opposite.
hot adj burning, fiery; boiling, flaming, heated, incandescent, roasting, torrid; heated, sweltering, warm; angry, excitable, furious, hasty, impatient, impetuous, lustful, passionate, touchy, urgent, violent; animated, eager, fervent, fervid, glowing; acrid, biting, highly flavoured, highly seasoned, pungent, sharp, stinging.
house vb harbour, lodge, protect, shelter; * n domicile, dwelling, habitation, home, mansion, residence; building; family, household; kindred, race, tribe; company, concern, firm, partnership; hotel, inn.
however adv but, however, nevertheless, still, though, yet.
howl vb bawl, cry, lament, weep, yell; * n cry, yell, ululation.
huddle vb cluster, crowd, gather; crouch, curl up; * n confusion, crowd, disorder, disturbance, jumble.
hue n cast, colour, dye, shade, tinge, tint, tone.
huff vb blow, breathe, exhale, puff; * n anger, fume, passion, pet, quarrel, rage, temper, tiff.
hug vb clasp, cling, embrace, grasp, grip; cherish, retain; * n clasp, cuddle, embrace, grasp, squeeze.
huge adj bulky, colossal, enormous, gigantic, immense, stupendous, vast.
hum vb buzz, drone, murmur; croon.
humane adj benevolent, benign, clement, compassionate, gentle, good-hearted, kind, kind-hearted, merciful, tender, sympathetic.
humanity n benignity, charity, fellow-feeling, humaneness, kind-heartedness, kindness, sympathy, tenderness; humankind, mankind.
humanise vb civilise, cultivate, educate, enlighten, improve, polish, refine.
humble vb abase, abash, break, crush, debase, degrade, lower, reduce, sink, subdue; * adj meek, modest, lowly, simple, submissive, unobtrusive; low, meek, obscure, mean, plain, poor, small, undistinguished.
humdrum adj boring, dreary, dry, dull, monotonous, stupid, tedious.
humid adj damp, dank, moist, wet.
humiliate vb abase, debase, degrade, depress, mortify, shame.
humility n diffidence, lowliness, meekness, modesty.
humorous adj comic, comical, droll, funny, humorous, jocose, laughable, ludicrous, merry, playful, pleasant, sportive, witty.
humour vb favour, gratify, indulge; * n bent, bias, disposition, predilection, temper, vein; mood, state, temper; caprice, crotchet, fancy, freak, vagary, whim, wrinkle; drollery, fun, wit; fluid, moisture, vapour.
hunch vb arch, nudge, punch,

HUNGRY

push, shove; * n bunch, hump, knob, nudge, punch, push, shove; feeling, idea, intuition.
hungry adj craving, desirous, greedy; famished, starved, starving; barren, poor.
hunt vb chase, drive, follow, hound, pursue, trap, trail; shoot; search, seek; * n chase, field-sport, hunting.
hurl vb cast, fling, pitch, project, sling, throw, toss.
hurricane n gale, storm, tempest, tornado, typhoon.
hurried adj breakneck, cursory, hasty, slight, superficial.
hurry vb drive; dispatch, hasten, quicken, speed; haste, scurry; * n agitation, bustle, confusion, flutter, precipitation; celerity, haste; dispatch, expedition, promptness, quickness.
hurt vb damage, disadvantage, harm, impair, injure; afflict, grieve, offend; ache, pain; * n detriment, disadvantage, harm, injury; ache, bruise, pain, suffering, wound.
hush vb quiet, repress, silence, still, suppress; calm, quiet, still; * n quiet, quietness, silence, stillness.
hypocrite n deceiver, dissembler, pretender.
hypocritical adj deceiving, false, insincere, two-faced.
hysterical adj frantic, frenzied, uncontrollable; comical.

I

icy adj glacial; chilling, cold, frosty; indifferent.
idea n archetype, essence, exemplar, ideal, model, pattern, plan, model; image, imagination; apprehension, conceit, conception, illusion, impression, thought; notion, opinion, sentiment.
ideal adj intellectual, mental; fanciful, fantastic, imaginary, unreal, visionary; complete, consummate, excellent; impractical, unattainable, utopian; * n example, model, standard.
identical adj equivalent, same, selfsame.
idiot n dunce, fool, ignoramus, imbecile, simpleton.
idiotic adj foolish, imbecile, senseless, sottish, stupid.
idle adj unemployed, unoccupied, vacant; inert, lazy, slothful; abortive, fruitless, futile, groundless, unavailing, useless, vain; foolish, frivolous, trifling, trivial, unimportant; * vb dally, laze, loiter, waste; drift, shirk, slack.
idol n deity, god, icon, image, pagan, symbol; delusion, pretender; beloved, darling, pet.
idolise vb canonise, deify; adore, admire, honour, love, reverence.
ignoble adj low-born, mean, peasant, vulgar; degraded, insignificant, mean, worthless; dishonourable, low, unworthy.
ignominious adj discreditable, disgraceful, dishonourable, disreputable, infamous, scandalous, shameful; base.
ignorance n darkness, illiteracy; blindness, unawareness.
ignorant adj blind, unaware, uneducated, unenlightened, uninformed, unlearned, unread, untaught.
ignore vb disregard, neglect, overlook, reject.
ill adj bad, evil, harmful, iniquitous, unfavourable, unfortunate, unjust, wicked; diseased, indisposed, sick, wrong; cross, hateful, surly, unkind; ill-bred; ill-favoured, ugly; * adv badly, poorly, unfortunately; * n badness, evil, mischief, misfortune; affliction, ailment, harm, misery, pain, trouble.
illegal adj contraband, forbidden, illegitimate, prohibited, unauthorised, unlicensed.
illegible adj indecipherable, obscure, unreadable.

illegitimate *adj* bastard, misbegotten, natural.
illiberal *adj* close, close-fisted, covetous, mean, narrow, niggardly, penurious, selfish, sordid, stingy, ungenerous; narrow, narrow-minded, vulgar.
illicit *adj* illegal, illegitimate, unauthorised, unlicensed; criminal, guilty, improper, wrong.
illiterate *adj* uneducated, unlearned, unlettered, unstructured, untaught.
illness *n* ailing, ailment, complaint, disease, distemper, malady, sickness.
illogical *adj* absurd, fallacious, inconsistent, inconsequent, incorrect, unreasonable.
illusion *n* deception, delusion, error, fallacy, false appearance, fantasy, hallucination.
illusive, illusory *adj* deceitful, deceptive, delusive, fallacious, imaginary, make-believe, mock, sham, unsatisfying, unreal, visionary.
illustrate *vb* demonstrate, elucidate, enlighten, explain; depict, draw.
illustrative *adj* elucidative, elucidatory, exemplifying.
illustrious *adj* bright, brilliant, glorious, radiant, splendid; celebrated, distinguished, eminent, famous, noble, noted.
image *n* idol; copy, effigy, figure, form, likeness, picture, resemblance, representation, shape, statue, symbol; conception, embodiment, idea, reflection.
imagery *n* dream, hallucination, phantasm, phantom, vision.
imaginable *adj* assumable, conjecturable, plausible, possible, thinkable.
imaginary *adj* dreamy, fancied, fanciful, fantastic, fictitious, ideal, illusory, invented, shadowy, unreal, visionary, wild; assumed, conceivable, supposed.

imagination *n* conception, fancy, fantasy, invention, unreality; device, scheme.
imaginative *adj* creative, fanciful, inventive, poetical, visionary.
imagine *vb* conceive, dream, fancy, imagine, pretend; contrive, create, devise, invent, mould, project; assume, suppose; apprehend, assume, believe, deem, guess, suppose, think.
imbecile *adj* feeble-minded, foolish, helpless, idiotic, imbecilic, infirm; * *n* driveller.
imitate *vb* copy, counterfeit, duplicate, echo, follow, mirror, reproduce, simulate; ape, mimic, mock, personate; travesty.
imitation *adj* artificial, fake, man-made, reproduction, synthetic; * *n* aping, copying, imitation, mimicking; copy, duplicate, likeness; mimicry, mocking; burlesque.
immaculate *adj* clean, pure, spotless, stainless, undefiled, unpolluted, unspotted, untainted; faultless, guiltless, holy, innocent, pure, stainless.
immaterial *adj* bodiless, ethereal, incorporeal, mental, metaphysical, spiritual, unbodied, unsubstantial; inconsequential, insignificant, unimportant.
immature *adj* crude, green, imperfect, raw, rudimentary, unfinished, unprepared, unripe, youthful; hasty, premature, untimely.
immediate *adj* close, near, next, proximate; intuitive, primary; direct, instant, present, pressing, prompt.
immediately *adv* closely; directly, instantly, presently, pronto.
immense *adj* boundless, infinite, interminable, unbounded, unlimited; enormous, gigantic, huge, large, monstrous, prodigious, stupendous,

tremendous, vast.
immerse *vb* baptise, bathe, dip, douse, duck, plunge, sink, souse; absorb, engage, sink.
imminent *adj* close, impending, near, threatening; alarming, dangerous.
immobile *adj* fixed, immovable, inflexible, motionless, stable, static, stationary, steadfast; dull, impassive, rigid, stiff.
immoderate *adj* excessive, exorbitant, extravagant, extreme, inordinate.
immoral *adj* antisocial, corrupt, loose, sinful, vicious, wicked, wrong; dissolute, unprincipled, vicious; depraved, dissolute, indecent, licentious.
immortal *adj* deathless, undying; ceaseless, continuing, endless, everlasting, never-ending, perpetual; enduring, lasting, permanent; * *n* god, goddess; genius, hero.
immunity *n* exemption, freedom, release; franchise, liberty, prerogative, right.
immutable *adj* constant, fixed, inflexible, permanent, stable, unchangeable.
impact *vb* collide, crash, strike; * *n* brunt, impression, shock, touch; collision, contact, striking.
impair *vb* blemish, damage, deteriorate, injure, ruin, spoil; decrease, diminish, lessen, reduce; enfeeble.
impale *vb* hole, pierce, puncture, spike, stab.
impart *vb* confer, give, grant; communicate, disclose, discover, relate, reveal.
impartial *adj* candid, equal, even-handed, just, unbiased, unprejudiced, unwarped.
impassable *adj* blocked, closed, impermeable, inaccessible, pathless, unattainable, unreachable.
impassioned *adj* animated, ardent, burning, excited, fervent, fiery, glowing, intense, passionate, warm.

impassive *adj* calm, passionless; apathetic, indifferent, insensible, unfeeling, unsusceptible.
impatience *n* disquietude, restlessness, uneasiness; eagerness, haste; heat, irritableness, violence.
impatient *adj* restless, uneasy; eager, hasty, impetuous, vehement; abrupt, hot, intolerant, irritable, sudden, vehement, violent.
impeach *vb* accuse, charge, indict; censure, denounce, disparage, discredit, impair, lessen.
impeccable *adj* faultless, incorrupt, innocent, perfect, pure, uncorrupted.
impede *vb* bar, block, check, clog, curb, delay, hinder, interrupt, obstruct, stop.
impediment *n* bar, barrier, block, check, curb, hindrance, obstacle, obstruction.
impel *vb* drive, push, send, urge; actuate, animate, compel, constrain, incite, influence, move, persuade, stimulate.
impend *vb* approach, gather, menace, near, threaten.
impenitent *adj* hardened, hard-hearted, irreclaimable, obdurate, relentless, stubborn, uncontrite, unrepentant.
imperative *adj* authoritative, commanding, domineering, imperious, overbearing; urgent.
imperceptible *adj* inaudible, indistinguishable, invisible; fine, gradual, minute.
imperfect *adj* abortive, crude, deficient, poor; defective, faulty.
imperfection *n* defectiveness, deficiency, incompleteness; defect, fault, flaw, lack, stain, taint; failing, frailty, vice, weakness.
imperial *adj* kingly, regal, royal, sovereign; august, grand, great, kingly, majestic, noble, regal, royal, sovereign,

supreme, consummate.
imperil *vb* endanger, hazard, jeopardise, risk.
imperious *adj* authoritative, commanding, despotic, domineering, haughty, lordly, magisterial, overbearing, tyrannical, urgent.
impersonate *vb* act, enact, imitate, mimic, personate; embody, incarnate, typify.
impersonation *n* incarnation, personification; enacting, imitation, impersonating, personating, representation.
impertinence *n* irrelevance, irrelevancy, unfitness; impropriety; assurance, boldness, face, impudence, insolence, intrusiveness, presumption, rudeness; pertness, presumption.
impertinent *adj* inapplicable, inapposite, irrelevant; bold, forward, impudent, insolent, intrusive, pert, rude.
imperturbable *adj* calm, collected, composed, cool, placid, serene, unmoved, undisturbed, unmoved.
impetuous *adj* ardent, boisterous, brash, fierce, fiery, furious, hasty, hot, hot-headed, impulsive, precipitate, vehement, violent.
impetus *n* energy, force, goad, momentum, propulsion.
implacable *adj* deadly, merciless, pitiless, relentless, unappeasable, unforgiving, unrelenting.
implement *vb* effect, execute, fulfil; * *n* instrument, tool.
implication *n* entanglement, involvement; connotation, hint; conclusion, meaning, significance.
implicit *adj* implied, inferred, understood; absolute, constant, firm, steadfast.
imply *vb* include, infer, insinuate, involve, mean, signify.
impolite *adj* discourteous, disrespectful, ill-bred, insolent, rough, rude, uncivil, ungentle, ungracious.
impolitic *adj* ill-advised, imprudent, indiscreet, injudicious, unwise.
import *vb* bring in, introduce, transport; denote, imply, mean, purport, signify; * *n* goods, importation, merchandise; intention, interpretation, matter, meaning, purpose, sense, signification.
importance *n* concern, gravity, import, moment, significance, weight; consequence.
important *adj* considerable, grave, material, momentous, notable, pompous, serious, significant; influential, prominent; consequential.
importune *vb* ask, beg, beset, ply, press, solicit, urge.
impose *vb* lay, place, put, set; appoint, charge, dictate, enjoin, force, obtrude, tax; (with **on, upon**) abuse, cheat, circumvent, deceive, delude, dupe, exploit, victimise.
imposing *adj* commanding, dignified, grand, grandiose, lofty, magnificent, majestic, noble, striking.
impossible *adj* impracticable, infeasible, unattainable; inconceivable, unthinkable.
impostor *n* cheat, counterfeiter, deceiver, double-dealer, humbug, hypocrite, knave, pretender, rogue.
impotent *adj* disabled, enfeebled, frail, helpless, incompetent, inefficient, powerless, unable, weak, sterile.
impoverish *vb* beggar, ruin; deplete, exhaust.
impracticable *adj* impossible, infeasible; recalcitrant, unmanageable; impassable, insurmountable.
impracticality *n* impossibility, impracticableness, impractibility, infeasibility; irrationality, unpracticalness, unreality.
imprecatory *adj* appealing, beseeching, entreating,

imploring, imprecatory, pleading; cursing, damnatory.

impregnable *adj* immovable, invincible, inviolable, secure, unconquerable, unassailable.

impregnate *vb* fecundate, fertilise, fructify; dye, fill, pervade, saturate, tincture, tinge.

impress *vb* engrave, imprint, print, stamp; affect, move; fix; draft, enlist, levy, press, requisition; * *n* impression, mark, print, seal, stamp; device, emblem, motto, symbol.

impressible *adj* excitable, impressionable, receptive, sensitive, soft, susceptible.

impression *n* edition, printing, stamping; dent, impress, mark, stamp; effect, influence; fancy, idea, instinct, notion, recollection.

impressive *adj* affecting, effective, emphatic, exciting, forcible, moving, powerful, solemn, speaking, splendid, stirring, telling, touching.

imprison *vb* confine, immure, jail, shut up.

imprisonment *n* captivity, commitment, confinement, constraint, durance, restraint.

improbable *adj* doubtful, uncertain, unlikely.

impromptu *adj* extempore, improvised, spontaneous, unpremeditated, unprepared; * *adv* extemporaneously, extemporarily, extempore, offhand; ad-lib.

improper *adj* immodest, inapposite, inappropriate, unadapted, unfit, unsuitable, unsuited; indecent, unseemly; inaccurate, incorrect, wrong.

improve *vb* amend, better, correct, edify, meliorate, mend, reform; correct; cultivate; gain, mend, progress; increase, rise.

improvement *n* amelioration, amendment, improving, melioration; advancement, amendment, betterment, melioration, proficiency, progress.

improvisation *n* ad-libbing, contrivance, extemporariness, extemporisation, invention; (music) extempore, impromptu.

imprudent *adj* careless, heedless, ill-judged, improvident, incautious, indiscreet, rash, unwise.

impudence *n* assurance, boldness, brashness, brass, cheek, cheekiness, face, flippancy, forwardness, front, gall, impertinence, insolence, nerve, pertness, rudeness, shamelessness.

impudent *adj* bold, brazen, cool, flippant, forward, immodest, impertinent, insolent, insulting, pert, rude, saucy.

impulse *n* force, impetus, momentum, push, thrust; appetite, instinct, passion; incitement, influence, instigation, motive.

impulsive *adj* impelling, moving, propulsive; emotional, hasty, heedless, hot, impetuous, passionate, rash, vehement, violent.

impure *adj* defiled, dirty, filthy, foul, polluted, unclean; bawdy, coarse, gross, immoral, indecent, lewd, licentious, loose, obscene, ribald, unchaste, unclean; corrupt, mixed.

impute *vb* ascribe, attribute, charge, consider, insinuate, refer.

inability *n* impotence, incapacity, incompetence, inefficiency; disability.

inaccuracy *n* impropriety, incorrectness, inexactness; defect, error, fault, mistake.

inaccurate *adj* defective, faulty, incorrect, inexact, mistaken.

inactive *adj* inactive; dormant, inert, peaceful, quiescent; drowsy, dull, idle, inanimate, indolent, inert, lazy, lifeless, passive, sleepy, stagnant, supine.

inactivity *n* dilatoriness,

idleness, inaction, indolence, laziness, sloth, supineness, torpor.
inadequate adj incapable, insufficient, unequal; defective, inapt, incompetent.
inadmissible adj improper, incompetent, unacceptable, unqualified.
inadvertently adv accidentally, inconsiderately, negligently, thoughtlessly, unintentionally.
inane adj empty, vacuous, void; foolish, idiotic, puerile, senseless, stupid, trifling, vain.
inanimate adj breathless, dead, extinct; dead, dull, lifeless, soulless.
inanity n emptiness, foolishness, inanition; folly, frivolousness, vanity.
inapplicable adj inapposite, inappropriate, inapt, unfit, unsuitable.
inappropriate adj inapposite, unadapted, unbecoming, unsuitable.
inarticulate adj indistinct, thick; dumb, mute.
inattentive adj careless, heedless, inadvertent, neglectful, thoughtless, unmindful.
inaudible adj muffled; mute, noiseless, silent, still.
inaugurate vb install, introduce, invest; begin, commence, institute.
incalculable adj countless, enormous, incalculable, innumerable, unknown.
incapable adj incompetent, insufficient, unable, unfit, unfitted, weak.
incapacitate vb cripple, disable; disqualify, immobilise, make unfit.
incautious adj impolitic, imprudent, indiscreet, unwary; careless, heedless, negligent, rash, reckless.
incense vb anger, enkindle, exasperate, excite, heat, irritate, madden, provoke; * n aroma, fragrance, perfume; admiration, adulation, applause.
incentive n encouragement, goad, incitement, inducement, instigation, mainspring, motive, provocation, spur.
incessant adj ceaseless, constant, continual, continuous, eternal, everlasting, perpetual, unceasing, unending.
incident n circumstance, event, fact, happening, occurrence; * adj happening; belonging; appertaining, accessory, relating, natural; falling.
incidental adj accidental, casual, chance, contingent, fortuitous, subordinate; extraneous, occasional.
incision n cut, gash, notch, opening, slash.
incisive adj cutting; acute, biting, sarcastic, sharp; acute, clear, distinct, sharp-cut.
incite vb actuate, animate, drive, encourage, excite, goad, impel, instigate, prod, prompt, provoke, push, rouse, spur, urge.
inclement adj boisterous, rigorous, rough, stormy; cruel, harsh, severe.
inclination n inclining, leaning, slant, slope; aptitude, bent, bias, penchant, predisposition, propensity, tendency, turn, twist; desire, fondness, liking, taste, predilection, wish; bow, nod.
incline vb lean, slant, slope; nod, verge; tend; bias, turn; bend, bow; * n ascent, descent, grade, rise, slope.
include vb contain, hold; comprehend, contain, cover, embody, embrace, involve, take in.
incognito, **incognita** adj disguised, unknown; * n camouflage, concealment.
incoherent adj detached, loose, nonadhesive; disconnected, inconsequential, inconsistent, uncoordinated; confused, rambling, unintelligible, wild.
income n earnings, gains, interest, pay, proceeds, profits,

rents, return, revenue, wages.

incommode *vb* annoy, disquiet, disturb, embarrass, hinder, trouble, upset, vex.

incommunicative *adj* exclusive, unsociable, unsocial; reserved.

incomparable *adj* matchless, inimitable, surpassing, transcendent, unequalled, unparalleled.

incompatible *adj* contradictory, incongruous, inharmonious, irreconcilable, unadapted.

incompetent *adj* incapable; inadequate, insufficient; disqualified, unconstitutional, unfit.

incomplete *adj* defective, deficient, partial; unexecuted, unfinished.

incomprehensible *adj* inconceivable, inexhaustible, unfathomable, unimaginable; unintelligible, unthinkable.

inconclusive *adj* inconsequent, inconsequential, indecisive; unconvincing, unproved.

incongruous *adj* contradictory, discrepant, inappropriate, incoherent, inconsistent, inharmonious, unfit.

inconsequent *adj* disconnected, illogical, inconclusive, inconsistent, loose.

inconsiderable *adj* immaterial, insignificant, petty, slight, small, trifling.

inconsiderate *adj* intolerant, uncharitable; careless, hasty, imprudent, inadvertent, inattentive, indifferent, rash, thoughtless.

inconsistent *adj* different, discrepant, incompatible, incongruous, inconsequent, irreconcilable; contradictory, contrary; fickle, inconstant, unstable, unsteady, variable.

inconstant *adj* capricious, changeable, faithless, fickle, mutable, unsettled, unsteady, variable, varying, volatile; mutable, uncertain, variable.

incontestable *adj* certain, incontrovertible, indisputable, indubitable, sure, undeniable.

incontrovertible *adj* certain, incontestable, indisputable, indubitable, sure, undeniable, unquestionable.

inconvenience *vb* annoy, disturb, trouble, vex; * *n* annoyance, disadvantage, disturbance, trouble, vexation; unfitness, unsuitableness.

inconvenient *adj* awkward, cumbrous, disadvantageous, incommodious, troublesome, uncomfortable, unfit, unhandy, unseasonable, unsuitable, untimely.

incorporate *vb* amalgamate, associate, blend, combine, consolidate, include, merge, mix, unite; incarnate; * *adj* incorporeal; immaterial, spiritual; blended, united.

incorrect *adj* erroneous, false, inaccurate, untrue, wrong; faulty, improper, unbecoming, unsound.

incorrigible *adj* abandoned, graceless, hardened, lost, recreant, reprobate, shameless; hopeless, irremediable, irreparable, irretrievable, irreversible.

incorruptible *adj* honest, unbribable; imperishable, indestructible; immortal, undying, deathless.

increase *vb* advance, augment, enlarge, extend, grow, mount; multiply; enhance, heighten, raise, reinforce; extend, prolong; aggravate, prolong; * *n* accretion, accumulation, addition, crescendo, expansion, extension, growth, heightening, intensification; gain, produce, product, profit; issue, offspring, progeny.

incredulous *adj* distrustful, dubious, sceptical, unbelieving.

increment *n* addition, accrual, augmentation, enlargement, increase.

incriminate *vb* blame, charge, criminate, impeach.

inculcate *vb* enforce, implant,

impress, infuse, inspire, instil.
incumbent *adj* binding, devolved, devolving, obligatory; leaning, prone, reclining; * *n* holder, occupant.
incur *vb* acquire, bring, contract.
incurable *adj* cureless, hopeless, irrecoverable; helpless, incorrigible, irreparable.
incursion *n* descent, foray, raid; inroad.
indebted *adj* beholden, obliged, owing.
indecent *adj* bold, improper, indecorous, outrageous, unbecoming; coarse, dirty, filthy, gross, immodest, impure, lewd, nasty, obscene, salacious.
indecipherable *adj* illegible, undecipherable, undiscoverable, inexplicable, unintelligible.
indecision *n* changeableness, fickleness, hesitation, irresolution.
indecisive *adj* dubious, hesitating, inconclusive, undecided, unsettled, wavering.
indeed *adv* absolutely, actually, certainly, in truth, in reality, positively, really, strictly, truly; * *interj* really! you don't say! is it possible!
indefatigable *adj* assiduous, never-tiring, persevering, persistent, sedulous, tireless, unflagging, untiring, unwearied.
indefeasible *adj* immutable, inalienable, irreversible, irrevocable.
indefensible *adj* censurable, defenceless, unpardonable, untenable; insupportable, unjustifiable, unwarrantable.
indefinite *adj* confused, doubtful, equivocal, general, indecisive, indefinable, indeterminate, inexplicit, loose, nondescript, uncertain, undefined, unfixed, unsettled, vague.
indelicate *adj* broad, coarse, gross, rude, unbecoming; broad, foul, gross, immodest, indecent, lewd, vulgar.
indemnify *vb* compensate, endorse, reimburse, secure.
indent *vb* bruise, jag, notch, pink, scallop; bind.
independence *n* freedom, liberty; distinctness, nondependence, separation.
independent *adj* absolute, autonomous, free, unrestricted; (person) self-reliant.
indescribable *adj* ineffable, inexpressible, unutterable.
indestructible *adj* abiding, endless, enduring, everlasting, imperishable, undecaying.
indeterminate *adj* indefinite, uncertain, undetermined, unfixed.
index *vb* alphabetise, catalogue, codify, file, list, mark, tabulate; * *n* catalogue, list, register, tally; lead, mark, pointer, sip, signal, token; contents, table of contents; forefinger.
indicate *vb* betoken, denote, designate, evince, manifest, mark, point out, prefigure, register, show, signify, specify, tell; hint, intimate, sketch.
indication *n* hint, index, manifestation, note, sign, suggestion, token.
indicative *adj* significant, suggestive, symptomatic.
indictment *n* (law) indicting, presentment; accusation, arraignment, charge.
indifference *n* carelessness, coolness, heedlessness, inattention, insignificance, negligence, unconcern, uninterestedness; impartiality.
indifferent *adj* cold, cool, dead, distant, dull, easy-going, frigid, inattentive, incurious, insensible, listless, nonchalant, regardless, unconcerned, uninterested, unmindful, unmoved; equal; fair, middling, moderate, ordinary, tolerable; mediocre, so-so; immaterial; disinterested, impartial, unbiased.

indignant adj angry, exasperated, incensed, provoked, roused, wrathful.
indignation n anger, displeasure, exasperation, rage, resentment, wrath.
indignity n abuse, contumely, disrespect, ignominy, insult, outrage, slight.
indirect adj circumlocutory, devious, oblique, tortuous; deceitful, dishonest, unfair; remote, secondary, subordinate.
indiscreet adj foolish, hasty, imprudent, incautious, inconsiderate, injudicious, rash.
indiscretion n folly, imprudence, inconsiderateness; blunder, lapse, misstep.
indiscriminate adj confused, heterogeneous, indistinct, mingled, miscellaneous, promiscuous, undiscriminating.
indispensable adj crucial, essential, expedient, necessary, needful.
indisposed adj ill, sick, unwell; averse, backward, disinclined, loath, unfriendly.
indisputable adj certain, evident, incontestable, obvious, undeniable, indubitable.
indissoluble adj enduring, firm, incorruptible, indestructible, lasting, stable.
indistinct adj ambiguous, doubtful, uncertain; dim, dull, faint, misty, nebulous, obscure, vague; confused, inarticulate, indefinite, indistinguishable, undefined.
individual adj characteristic, distinct, identical, marked, one, particular, personal, separate, single, special, unique; peculiar, personal, proper, singular; decided, definite, independent, positive, unconventional, unique; * n being, character, party, person, personage, someone; type, unit.
individuality n definiteness, personality; characterfulness, originality, self-determination, singularity, uniqueness.
indivisible adj indissoluble, inseparable, unbreakable.
indoctrinate vb brainwash, ground, initiate, instruct, teach.
indolent adj easy, easy-going, inactive, inert, lazy, listless, lumpish, sluggish.
indomitable adj invincible, unconquerable.
indubitable adj certain, evident, incontestable, unquestionable.
induce vb allure, bring, draw, drive, entice, incite, influence, instigate, move, persuade, spur, urge; bring on, cause, effect, motivate, lead, produce.
inducement n draw, enticement, instigation, persuasion; cause, impulse, incentive, influence, motive, spur.
induct vb inaugurate, initiate, instal, institute, introduce.
indulge vb gratify, license, revel, satisfy, yield to; favour, humour, pet, spoil; allow, foster, permit.
indulgent adj easy, favouring, gentle, humouring, kind, lenient, mild, tender.
industrious adj diligent, laborious, notable, operose; brisk, busy, persistent.
industry n activity, application, assiduity, diligence; vigour; effort, labour, toil.
ineffectual adj abortive, fruitless, futile, inadequate, inoperative, useless, vain; feeble, inefficient, powerless, weak.
inefficient adj feeble, incapable, ineffectual, ineffective, weak.
ineligible adj disqualified, unqualified; inexpedient.
inept adj awkward, improper, inapposite, unapt, unfit; null, useless, void, worthless; foolish, nonsensical, pointless, silly.
ineptitude n inappropriateness, unfitness, unsuitableness; nullity, uselessness; folly, foolishness, nonsense, silliness,

stupidity.
inequality *n* disproportion, inequitableness, injustice; disparity, disproportion, diversity, imparity, roughness, unevenness; incompetency.
inequitable *adj* unfair, unjust.
inert *adj* comatose, dead, inactive, lifeless, motionless, passive; dull, idle, indolent, lazy, lethargic, lumpish, sluggish, torpid.
inertia *n* apathy, inertness, lethargy, slothfulness.
inevitable *adj* certain, necessary, unavoidable, undoubted.
inexcusable *adj* indefensible, irremissible, unjustifiable.
inexhaustible *adj* boundless, exhaustless, unfailing, unlimited.
inexorable *adj* cruel, firm, hard, immovable, inflexible, relentless, severe, steadfast, unbending, unmerciful, unyielding.
inexperienced *adj* green, raw, strange, undisciplined, uninitiated, unskilled, untrained, untried, young.
inexpert *adj* bungling, clumsy, inapt, unhandy, unskilful.
inexplicable *adj* enigmatical, incomprehensible, inscrutable, mysterious, unaccountable.
inexpressible *adj* indescribable, ineffable, unutterable; infinite, surpassing.
inexpressive *adj* bland, blank, characterless, dull, unexpressive.
inextricable *adj* entangled, intricate, unsolvable.
infallible *adj* certain, indubitable, oracular, sure, unfailing.
infamous *adj* atrocious, base, dark, detestable, discreditable, disgraceful, dishonourable, disreputable, heinous, odious, outrageous, shameful, shameless, vile, villainous, wicked.
infancy *n* beginning; childhood, minority, pupillage.
infant *n* babe, baby, brat, minor, nursling, papoose, suckling.
infantile *adj* childish, infantine, newborn, tender, young; childish, weak; childlike.
infatuate *vb* befool, captivate, delude, stultify.
infect *vb* affect, corrupt, defile, poison, pollute, taint.
infection *n* affection, contagion, contamination, corruption, poison, pollution, taint.
infelicitous *adj* miserable, unfortunate, unhappy, wretched; inauspicious, unfavourable; inappropriate, unfitting.
infer *vb* collect, conclude, deduce, draw, gather, guess, reason.
inferior *adj* lower; junior, minor, secondary; bad, deficient, imperfect, indifferent, mean, mediocre, poor, second-rate, shabby.
inferiority *n* subordination; deficiency, imperfection, inadequacy.
infernal *adj* atrocious, damnable, dark, demoniacal, devilish, fiendish, fiendlike, hellish, malicious, satanic.
infertility *n* barrenness, infecundity, sterility, unfruitfulness.
infidel *n* agnostic, atheist, disbeliever, heathen, sceptic, unbeliever.
infidelity *n* adultery, disloyalty, faithlessness, unfaithfulness; scepticism, unbelief.
infiltrate *vb* absorb, pervade, soak.
infinite *adj* boundless, endless, illimitable, immeasurable, inexhaustible, interminable, limitless, perfect, unbounded, unlimited; enormous, vast; absolute, self-determined, unconditioned.
infinitesimal *adj* atomic, infinitely small.
infinity *n* boundlessness, endlessness, immensity, infiniteness, infinitude, self-determination, vastness.

infirm *adj* ailing, enfeebled, feeble, frail, weak, weakened; irresolute, vacillating; insecure, precarious, unsound.

inflame *vb* arouse, excite, fire, heat, incite, inspirit, intensify, rouse, stimulate; anger, embitter, exasperate, incense, infuriate, madden, provoke.

inflammable *adj* combustible, ignitible; excitable.

inflammatory *adj* fiery, inflaming; incendiary, seditious.

inflate *vb* bloat, blow up, distend, expand; elate, puff up; enlarge, increase.

inflated *adj* bloated, distended, puffed-up; bombastic, declamatory, grandiloquent, magniloquent, overblown, rhetorical, tumid, turgid.

inflation *n* enlargement, increase, over-enlargement; bloatedness, distension, expansion; bombast, conceit, conceitedness, self-conceit, self-importance, vainglory.

inflection *n* bend, bending, curvature, flexure; (gram) conjugation, declension; (music) modulation.

inflexible *adj* rigid, rigorous, stiff, unbending; headstrong, heady, inexorable, intractable, obdurate, pertinacious, stubborn, unyielding; firm, immovable, resolute, steadfast.

inflict *vb* bring, impose, lay on.

infliction *n* inflicting; judgment, punishment.

influence *vb* affect, bias, control, direct, lead, modify, prepossess, sway; arouse, impel, induce, instigate, move, persuade, prevail upon, rouse; * *n* ascendancy, authority, mastery, predominance, rule, sway; credit, reputation, weight; inflow; magnetism, power, spell.

influential *adj* controlling, effective, effectual, powerful, strong; authoritative, weighty.

inform *vb* animate, inspire, quicken; advise, apprise, enlighten, notify, teach, tell, warn.

informal *adj* unceremonious, unconventional; easy, familiar, natural, simple; irregular, unusual.

informality *n* unceremoniousness; ease, familiarity; naturalness, simplicity; nonconformity.

informant *n* advertiser, adviser, informer, notifier, relator; accuser, complainant, informer.

information *n* advice, knowledge, notice; advice, enlightenment, instruction, tip, word, warning; accusation, complaint.

informer *n* accuser, betrayer, complainant, informant.

infrequent *adj* rare, uncommon, unusual; occasional, rare, scarce.

infringe *vb* break, contravene, disobey, intrude, invade, violate.

infringement *n* breach, breaking, disobedience, nonobservance, violation.

infuriated *adj* angry, furious, incensed, maddened, raging.

infuse *vb* breathe into, implant, inculcate, ingraft, inspire, instil; steep.

ingenious *adj* able, artful, bright, clever, fertile, gifted, inventive, ready, witty.

ingenuity *n* ability, acuteness, aptitude, capacity, capableness, cleverness, faculty, genius, gift, inventiveness, skill, turn.

ingenuous *adj* candid, childlike, downright, frank, generous, honest, innocent, naïve, open, plain, sincere, single-minded, straightforward, transparent, truthful, unreserved.

inglorious *adj* humble, mean, obscure, undistinguished, unknown, unmarked, unnoted; disgraceful, humiliating, ignominious, shameful.

ingratitude *n* thanklessness, ungratefulness.

ingredient *n* component,

constituent, element.
inhabit *vb* abide, dwell, live, occupy, people, reside.
inhabitant *n* citizen, denizen, dweller, resident.
inhale *vb* breathe in, draw in, inbreathe, inspire.
inherent *adj* essential, inborn, inbred, indwelling, ingrained, innate, intrinsic, natural, proper; adhering.
inherit *vb* get, receive.
inheritance *n* heritage, legacy, patrimony.
inhibit *vb* bar, check, hinder, obstruct, prevent, restrain, stop; forbid, prohibit.
inhibition *n* check, hindrance, obstruction, restraint; embargo, interdiction.
inhospitable *adj* cool, forbidding, unfriendly; illiberal, narrow, prejudiced, ungenerous, unreceptive.
inhuman *adj* barbarous, brutal, cruel, ferocious, merciless, pitiless, ruthless, savage, unfeeling.
inhumanity *n* barbarity, brutality, cruelty, ferocity.
inimical *adj* hostile, unfriendly; adverse, contrary, harmful, hurtful, noxious, opposed, repugnant.
inimitable *adj* incomparable, matchless, unequalled, unexampled, unmatched, unrivalled.
iniquitous *adj* atrocious, criminal, inequitable, sinful, wrong, unfair, unjust, unrighteous.
initial *adj* first; beginning, incipient, introductory, original; elementary.
initiate *vb* begin, commence, enter upon, introduce, open; ground, instruct, prime.
initiative *n* beginning; energy, enterprise.
inject *vb* force in, interject, insert, introduce.
injudicious *adj* foolish, hasty, ill-advised, ill-judged, imprudent, indiscreet, rash, unwise.
injunction *n* admonition, bidding, command, exhortation, order, precept.
injure *vb* damage, disfigure, harm, hurt, impair, spoil, wound; abuse, wrong; affront, dishonour, insult.
injurious *adj* baneful, damaging, deadly, destructive, evil, fatal, hurtful, mischievous, noxious, pernicious, prejudicial, ruinous; iniquitous, unjust, wrongful; detractory.
injury *n* evil, ill, injustice, wrong; damage, harm, hurt, impairment, loss, prejudice.
injustice *n* inequity, unfairness; grievance, iniquity, injury, wrong.
inkling *n* hint, suggestion, whisper.
innate *adj* constitutional, inborn, inbred, indigenous, inherited, instinctive, native, natural.
inner *adj* interior, internal.
innermost *adj* deepest, inmost.
innocence *n* blamelessness, guilelessness, guiltlessness, purity, simplicity.
innocent *adj* blameless, clean, clear, faultless, guiltless, pure, sinless, unfallen, upright; harmless, innoxious; lawful, legitimate, permitted; artless, ignorant, ingenuous, simple; * *n* babe, child, naïf, naïve.
innocuous *adj* harmless, innocent, inoffensive, safe.
innovation *n* change; departure, novelty.
innuendo *n* allusion, hint, insinuation, intimation.
innumerable *adj* countless, numberless.
inoffensive *adj* harmless, innocent, innocuous, unobjectionable.
inoperative *adj* inactive, ineffectual, inefficacious, not in force.
inopportune *adj* ill-timed, mistimed, unfortunate, unhappy, untimely.

inordinate *adj* excessive, extravagant, immoderate, intemperate, irregular.

inquest *n* inquiry, inquisition, investigation, quest.

inquire *vb* ask, catechise, interpellate, interrogate, investigate, question, quiz.

inquiry *n* examination, research, study; query, question.

inquisition *n* examination, inquest, inquiry, investigation.

inquisitive *adj* curious, inquiring, scrutinising; curious, peering, prying.

inroad *n* encroachment, foray, incursion, invasion, raid.

insane *adj* abnormal, crazed, crazy, deranged, distracted, lunatic, mad, maniacal.

insanity *n* craziness, dementia, lunacy, madness, mania, mental; aberration.

insatiable *adj* greedy, rapacious; unappeasable.

inscribe *vb* emblaze, engrave, impress, imprint, letter, mark, write.

insecure *adj* risky, uncertain, unconfident, unsure; exposed, unprotected; dangerous, perilous; infirm, shaky, tottering, unstable.

insecurity *n* uncertainty; danger, peril; instability, weakness.

insensible *adj* imperceivable, imperceptible; blunted, brutish, deaf, dull, insensate, numb, senseless, sluggish, stolid, stupid, torpid; callous, phlegmatic, impassive, indifferent, insensitive, unfeeling, unsusceptible.

inseparable *adj* close, friendly, intimate, together; indivisible.

insert *vb* inject, intercalate, introduce, parenthesise, place, put, set.

inside *adj* inner, interior, internal, intimate; * *prep* in, in the interior of, within; * *n* inner part, interior; nature.

insidious *adj* creeping, gradual, secretive; artful, crafty, crooked, cunning, deceitful, diplomatic, guileful, sly, sneaky, subtle, treacherous, tricky, wily.

insignificant *adj* contemptible, empty, inconsequential, inferior, meaningless, petty, small, sorry, unessential, unimportant.

insincere *adj* deceitful, dishonest, disingenuous, dissimulating, double-faced, empty, faithless, false, hollow, hypocritical, truthless, untrue.

insinuate *vb* hint, inculcate, infuse, instil, intimate, introduce, suggest.

insipid *adj* dead, dull, flat, heavy, inanimate, lifeless, monotonous, pointless, spiritless, stupid, tame, unentertaining, uninteresting; flat, savourless, stale, tasteless.

insist *vb* demand, maintain, persist, urge.

insistence *n* importunity, solicitousness, urging, urgency.

insolence *n* impertinence, impudence, pertness, rudeness; contempt, contumacy, disrespect, insubordination.

insolent *adj* contemptuous, disrespectful, domineering, insulting, offensive, rude, supercilious; cheeky, impudent, pert, saucy; disobedient.

insoluble *adj* indissoluble; inexplicable.

insolvable *adj* inexplicable.

insolvent *adj* bankrupt, failed, ruined.

inspect *vb* examine, investigate, look into, pry into; oversee, supervise.

inspector *n* critic, examiner, visitor; boss, superintendent.

inspire *vb* breathe, inhale; infuse, instil; cheer; elevate, exalt, stimulate; animate, fill imbue, impart, inform.

instability *n* changeableness, fickleness, inconstancy, insecurity.

install *vb* introduce; establish,

INTANGIBLE

place, set up.
installation *n* inauguration, induction, instalment.
instalment *n* earnest, payment, portion.
instance *vb* mention, specify; * *n* case, example, exemplification, occasion; impulse, incitement, instigation, motive, request.
instant *adj* direct, immediate, instantaneous, prompt, quick; current, present; fast, pressing, urgent; ready cooked; * *n* flash, moment, second; hour, time.
instantaneous *adj* abrupt, immediate, instant, quick.
instead *adv* in lieu, in place, rather.
instigate *vb* agitate, encourage, impel, influence, initiate, move, prevail upon, prompt, provoke, rouse, set on, spur on, stir up, urge.
instigation *n* encouragement, incitement, influence, instance, prompting, solicitation, urgency.
instil *vb* enforce, implant, ingraft; impart, infuse, insinuate.
instinct *n* aptitude, natural impulse.
instinctive *adj* automatic, inherent, intuitive, natural, spontaneous; impulsive.
institute *n* academy, college, foundation, guild, institution, school; custom, dogma, law, precedent, principle, rule; * *vb* begin, commence, constitute, initial, install, introduce, originate, start.
institution *n* enactment, establishment, foundation, institute, society; law, practice.
instruct *vb* discipline, educate, enlighten, exercise, guide, inform, school, teach, train; bid, command, direct, order, prescribe to.
instruction *n* breeding, discipline, education, information, schooling, teaching, training, tuition; advice, precept; command, direction, order.
instructor *n* educator, master, schoolteacher, teacher, tutor.
instrument *n* appliance, musical instrument, tool, utensil; agent, means; charter, deed, indenture, writing.
instrumental *adj* assisting, conducive, contributory, helpful, helping, ministerial, serviceable, subservient.
insubordinate *adj* disobedient, disorderly, riotous, turbulent, ungovernable, unruly.
insufferable *adj* intolerable, unbearable, unendurable, insupportable; detestable, disgusting, outrageous.
insufficient *adj* deficient, inadequate, incompetent, scanty; unqualified, unsuited.
insular *adj* contracted, limited, narrow, petty, prejudiced, restricted; remote.
insulate *vb* detach, disconnect, disengage, disunite, isolate, separate.
insult *vb* abuse, injure, offend, outrage, slander, slight; * *n* abuse, cheek, indignity, offence, outrage, slight.
insuperable *adj* impassable, insurmountable.
insupportable *adj* insufferable, intolerable, unbearable, unendurable.
insuppressible *adj* irrepressible, mercurial, uncontrollable.
insure *vb* assure, guarantee, indemnify, secure, underwrite.
insurgent *adj* disobedient, insubordinate, rebellious, revolting, revolutionary; * *n* mutineer, rebel, revolutionary.
insurmountable *adj* impassable, insuperable.
insurrection *n* insurgence, mutiny, rebellion, revolt, revolution, rising, uprising.
intact *adj* unharmed, unhurt, uninjured, untouched; complete, entire, integral, sound, undiminished, whole.
intangible *adj* dim, impalpable,

imperceptible, indefinite, insubstantial, vague; aerial, phantom.

integrity *n* goodness, honesty, principle, purity, soundness, virtue; completeness, entirety.

intellect *n* brain, brain power, brains, intelligence, mind, rational, reason, sense, thinker, understanding.

intellectual *adj* cerebral, intelligent, mental, scholarly; * *n* academic, highbrow, scholar.

intelligence *n* brightness, imagination, quickness, understanding, wits; advice, news, notice, tidings; brains, intellect, mentality, spirit.

intelligent *adj* acute, alert, apt, astute, brainy, bright, clever, discerning, keen-sighted, knowing, long-headed, quick, sagacious, sensible, sharp-witted, shrewd, understanding.

intemperate *adj* drunken; extravagant, extreme, immoderate, inordinate, uncontrolled, unrestrained.

intend *vb* aim at, contemplate, design, drive at, mean, meditate, propose, think of.

intense *adj* ardent, fervid, passionate, close, intent, severe, strained, stretched, strict; energetic, forcible, keen, potent, sharp, strong, vigorous, violent; acute, deep, exquisite, poignant.

intensify *vb* aggravate, enhance, heighten, strengthen, whet.

intensive *adj* demanding, emphatic, intensifying.

intent *adj* absorbed, attentive, close, eager, earnest, engrossed, occupied, pre-occupied; bent, decided, resolved, set; * *n* aim, design, drift, end, intention, mark, meaning, object, plan, purport, purpose, scope, view.

intention *n* aim, design, drift, end, import, intent, mark, object, plan, purpose, scope, view.

intentional *adj* contemplated, deliberate, designed, intended, premeditated, purposed, studied, voluntary.

intercede *vb* arbitrate, mediate; entreat, plead, supplicate.

intercept *vb* cut off, interrupt, obstruct.

intercession *n* interposition, intervention, mediation; pleading, prayer.

interchange *vb* alternate, change, exchange, vary; * *n* alternation.

intercourse *n* commerce, communication, communion, converse, correspondence, dealings; acquaintance, intimacy.

interest *vb* affect, concern, touch; absorb, attract, enlist, excite, grip, hold; * *n* advantage, benefit, good, profit, weal; concern, regard, sympathy; part, portion, share, stake; discount, premium, profit.

interested *adj* concerned, involved, occupied; partial; self-seeking.

interesting *adj* attractive, engaging, entertaining, pleasing.

interfere *vb* intermeddle, interpose, meddle; clash, conflict.

interim *n* intermediate time, interval, meantime.

interior *adj* inner, internal, inward; inland; domestic, home; * *n* inner part; inland, inside.

interject *vb* comment, inject, insert, interpose.

intermediary *n* go-between, mediator.

intermediate *adj* interposed, intervening, mean, median, mid, middle.

interminable *adj* boundless, endless, immeasurable, limitless, unlimited; tedious.

intermingle *vb* blend, commingle, commix, mingle, mix.

intermission *n* cessation, interruption, lull, remission, respite, rest, stop, stoppage.

intermittent *adj* broken, capricious, discontinuous,

INTROSPECTION

fitful, intermitting, periodic, recurrent.
internal *adj* inner, inside, interior, inward; mental, spiritual; deeper, emblematic, hidden, higher, secret, spiritual, under; genuine, intrinsic, real, true; domestic, home, inland, interior.
international *adj* cosmopolitan, universal.
interpolate *vb* add, insert, interpose; (maths) intercalate, introduce.
interpret *vb* decipher, decode, define, elucidate, explain, expound, solve, unfold, unravel; render.
interpretation *n* meaning, sense, signification; elucidation, explanation, exposition; construction, rendition, version.
interrogate *vb* ask, catechise, examine, inquire of, question.
interrogation *n* catechising, examination, examining, interrogating, questioning; inquiry, interrogatory, query, question.
interrupt *vb* break, check, disturb, hinder, interfere with, obstruct, stop; break, cut, disconnect, dissever, dissolve, divide, separate, sunder; break off, cease, intermit, leave off.
interruption *n* hindrance, impediment, obstacle, obstruction, stop, stoppage; discontinuance, intermission, pause; break, breaking, disconnecting, disconnection, dissolution, disunion, division, separation, severing.
intersect *vb* cross, cut, divide, interrupt.
intersperse *vb* intermingle, sprinkle; diversify, mix.
interval *n* interlude, pause, period, recess, season, space, term; interstice, space.
intervene *vb* come between, interfere, mediate.
intervention *n* interference, interposition; agency.

intimacy *n* close acquaintance, familiarity, fellowship, friendship; closeness.
intimate *adj* close, near; familiar, friendly; close, dear, special; confidential, private, secret; first-hand, immediate, penetrating, profound; cosy, warm; * *n* chum, companion, friend; * *vb* express, hint, impart, insinuate, suggest, tell.
intimation *n* allusion, innuendo, insinuation, suggestion.
intimidate *vb* affright, alarm, appal, bully, cow, daunt, dismay, frighten, scare, subdue, terrify, terrorise.
intolerable *adj* insufferable, insupportable, unendurable.
intonation *n* accentuation, cadence, modulation, tone; musical recitation.
intoxication *n* drunkenness, inebriation, inebriety; excitement, infatuation.
intrepid *adj* bold, brave, daring, fearless, heroic, unawed, undaunted, valiant, valorous.
intricate *adj* complicated, difficult, entangled, involved, mazy, obscure, perplexed.
intrigue *vb* connive, machinate, plot, scheme; bewitch, charm, fascinate; * *n* conspiracy, deception, finesse, manoeuvre, plot, ruse, scheme, wile; love affair.
intriguing *adj* arch, artful, crafty, crooked, cunning, deceitful, designing, politic, sly, sneaky, subtle, trickish, tricky.
intrinsic *adj* essential, genuine, real, true; inbred, inherent, internal, inward, native.
introduce *vb* bring in, import, inject, lead in, usher in; begin, broach, commence, initiate, start.
introduction *n* preface, prelude; introducing, ushering in; presentation.
introductory *adj* precursory, prefatory, preliminary.
introspection *n* introversion,

self-contemplation.
intrude *vb* encroach, impose, infringe, interfere, obtrude, trespass.
intrusion *n* infringement, intruding, obtrusion.
intuition *n* apprehension, cognition, insight, instinct.
intuitive *adj* instinctive, intuitional, natural; distinct.
inundate *vb* deluge, drown, flood, overflow, overwhelm, submerge.
inundation *n* cataclysm, deluge, flood, glut, overflow.
inure *vb* accustom, discipline, habituate, train, use.
invade *vb* encroach upon, infringe, violate; attack, enter in, march into.
invalid *adj* baseless, false, inoperative, unfounded, unsound, worthless; (law) null, void; ailing, feeble, frail, ill, infirm, sick, sickly, weak, weakly; * *n* patient.
invalidate *vb* annul, cancel, nullify, overthrow, quash, repeal, reverse, undo.
invalidity *n* baselessness, fallacy, falsity, unsoundness.
invaluable *adj* inestimable, precious, priceless.
invariable *adj* changeless, constant, unchanging, unvarying; changeless, unchangeable.
invasion *n* encroachment, incursion, infringement; aggression, assault, foray, raid.
invective *n* abuse, censure, railing, reproach, sarcasm, satire.
inveigle *vb* contrive, devise; conceive, create, design, frame, imagine, originate; coin, forge, spin.
invent *vb* design, devise, discover, find out, frame, originate.
invention *n* creation, discovery, ingenuity, inventing; design, device; coinage, fiction, forgery.
inventive *adj* creative, fertile, ingenious.
inventor *n* author, contriver, creator.
inversion *n* inverting, reversing, transposal.
invert *vb* capsize, overturn; reverse, transpose, upset.
invest *vb* put at interest; confer, endue; (military) beset, besiege, enclose; array, clothe, dress.
investigate *vb* consider, dissect, explore, follow up, inquire into, look into, overhaul, probe, research, scrutinise, search into, search out.
investigation *n* examination, exploration, inquiry, research, scrutiny, search.
investiture *n* habilitation, induction, installation.
investment *n* money invested; endowment; (military) siege; clothes, dress, garments, robe.
inveterate *adj* besetting, confirmed, deep-seated, habitual, hardened, ingrained, obstinate.
invidious *adj* disagreeable, envious, hateful, offensive.
invigorate *vb* animate, energise, fortify, harden, quicken, refresh, vivify.
invincible *adj* impregnable, indomitable, ineradicable, insurmountable, irrepressible, unconquerable.
inviolable *adj* hallowed, holy, inviolate, sacred, sacrosanct.
inviolate *adj* unbroken; pure, stainless, undefiled, unhurt, unpolluted, unstained; inviolable, sacred.
invisible *adj* impalpable, imperceptible, intangible, unapparent, unseen.
invitation *n* bidding, call, challenge, summons.
invite *vb* ask, bid, call, request, solicit; allure, attract, draw on, lead, persuade, prevail upon.
inviting *adj* alluring, attractive, bewitching, engaging, pleasing, winning; promising.
invoke *vb* appeal to, beg, beseech, call upon, conjure,

implore, pray, pray to, solicit.
involuntary *adj* blind, instinctive, reflex; reluctant, unwilling.
involve *vb* comprise, contain, embrace, imply, lead to; complicate, compromise, embarrass, entangle; cover, envelop, surround, wrap; blend, connect, join, mingle; entwine, intertwine, inweave.
invulnerable *adj* incontrovertible, invincible.
inward *adj* inner, interior, internal; hidden, mental; private, secret.
inwards *adv* inwardly, towards the inside.
iota *n* atom, bit, glimmer, grain, jot, scintilla, scrap, spark, trace.
irascible *adj* hasty, impatient, irritable, peevish, petulant, quick, snappish, testy, touchy.
irate *adj* angry, incensed, ireful, irritated.
ironic, **ironical** *adj* cutting, mocking, sarcastic.
irony *n* mockery, ridicule, sarcasm, satire.
irradiate *vb* brighten, illume, illuminate, light up, shine upon.
irrational *adj* absurd, foolish, preposterous, ridiculous, silly; unreasonable; brute, brutish; aberrant, crazy, fantastic, idiotic, imbecilic, insane, lunatic.
irreclaimable *adj* hopeless, incurable, irrecoverable, irreparable, irretrievable, irreversible; abandoned, graceless, incorrigible, lost, shameless, unrepentant.
irreconcilable *adj* inexorable, inexpiable, unappeasable; incongruous.
irrecoverable *adj* hopeless, incurable, irremediable, irreparable, irretrievable.
irrefutable *adj* impregnable, incontestable, incontrovertible, indisputable, invincible, irresistible, unassailable.
irregular *adj* abnormal, anomalistic, anomalous, crooked, devious, eccentric, erratic, exceptional, raged, unconformable, unusual; capricious, changeable, fitful, uncertain, unpunctual, unsettled, variable; disordered, disorderly, improper, unsystematic; asymmetric, uneven; disorderly, dissolute, immoral, loose, wild; * *n* casual, hireling, mercenary.
irrelevant *adj* foreign, illogical, impertinent, inapplicable, inappropriate, inconsequent, unrelated.
irreligious *adj* godless, ungodly, undevout; disrespectful, irreverent, profane, wicked.
irremediable *adj* hopeless, incurable, irrecoverable, irreparable.
irreparable *adj* irrecoverable, irremediable, remediless.
irrepressible *adj* insuppressible, uncontrollable, unsmotherable.
irreproachable *adj* blameless, faultless, innocent, irreprovable, unblamable.
irresistible *adj* irrefragable, irrepressible, overpowering, overwhelming.
irresolute *adj* changeable, faltering, hesitant, mutable, undecided, undetermined, unsettled, unstable, unsteady, wavering.
irrespective *adj* independent, regardless.
irresponsible *adj* unaccountable; untrustworthy.
irretrievable *adj* incurable, irrecoverable, irreparable.
irreverent *adj* blasphemous, impious, profane; disrespectful.
irreversible *adj* irrepealable, irrevocable, unchangeable; changeless, immutable.
irrevocable *adj* irrepealable, irreversible, unalterable.
irritable *adj* captious, excitable, fiery, hasty, hot, irascible, passionate, peevish, petulant, snappish, susceptible, testy,

touchy.
irritate *vb* anger, annoy, enrage, exacerbate, fret, incense, nettle, offend, provoke, rile, ruffle, vex; gall, tease; (medical) excite, inflame, stimulate.
isolate *vb* detach, insulate, quarantine, segregate, separate.
issue *vb* come out, flow out, flow forth, run, rush out, spout, spring, well; arise, come, emanate, flow, follow, originate, proceed, spring; end, eventuate, result; appear, come out, deliver, depart, debouch, emerge, emit, put forth, send out; distribute, give out; utter; * *n* conclusion, end, effect, event, finale, outcome, result, upshot; contest, controversy; delivering, delivery, discharge, emergence, emission, issuance; flux, outpouring, stream; copy, number; egress, exit, outlet, passage out, way out; escape, sally; children, offspring, posterity.
itch *vb* tingle; * *n* itching; burning, importunate craving, teasing desire.
item *adv* also, in like manner; * *n* article, detail.
itinerant *adj* nomadic, roaming, travelling, unsettled.

J

jabber *vb* chatter, prattle.
jaded *adj* dull, exhausted, fatigued, satiated, tired.
jagged *adj* cleft, divided, notched, ragged, uneven.
jam *vb* block, cram, crowd, crush, press; * *n* block, crowd, mass, pack.
jangle *vb* bicker, chatter, jar, quarrel, spar, spat, rift, wrangle; * *n* clang, clangour, clash, din.
jar *vb* clash, grate, interfere, shake; jangle, quarrel, spar, spat, tiff, wrangle; agitate, jolt, jounce, shake; * *n* clash, conflict, disaccord, jangle, dissonance; jolt, jostle, shake, shaking, shock, start; can, cruse, ewer.
jargon *n* gabble, gibberish, nonsense; cant, lingo, slang: chaos, confusion, disarray, jumble.
jaundiced *adj* biased, envious, prejudiced.
jaunty *adj* airy, cheery, garish, gay, fine, showy, unconcerned.
jealous *adj* distrustful, envious, suspicious; apprehensive, intolerant.
jeer *vb* deride, despise, gibe, jape, jest, mock, sneer, spurn, rail, taunt; * *n* abuse, derision, sneer, ridicule, taunt.
jeopardise *vb* endanger, hazard, imperil, risk.
jeopardy *n* danger, hazard, peril, risk.
jerk *vb*, *n* flip, hitch, pluck, twitch.
jest *vb* banter, joke, quiz; * *n* fun, joke, sport.
jingle *vb* chink, clink, rattle, tinkle; * *n* chink, clink, jangle, rattle, tinkle; ditty, melody, song.
join *vb* add, annex, append, attach; cement, conjoin, connect, couple, link, unite, yoke; assemble, associate, consolidate, meagre, unite.
joint *vb* fit, join, unite; * *adj* combined, concerted, conjoint; * *n* junction, juncture, hinge.
joke *vb* banter, jest, frolic, rally; * *n* crank, jest, witticism.
jolly *adj* airy, blithe, cheerful, frolicsome, funny, gay, jovial, joyous, merry, mirthful, jocular, playful, sportive, sprightly; bouncing, lusty, plump, stout.
jolt *vb* jar, jolt, shake, shock; * *n* jar, jolting, shaking.
jostle *vb* collide, elbow, joggle, shake, shove.
jot *n* ace, atom, bit, grain, mite, scrap, whit.

journey *vb* ramble, roam, rove, travel: fare, go; * *n* excursion, jaunt, passage, tour, travel, trip, voyage.

jovial *adj* airy, animated, convivial, festive, jolly, joyous, merry.

joy *n* beatification, beatitude, delight, ecstasy, gladness, glee, pleasure, rapture, transport, beatification; bliss, felicity, happiness.

joyful *adj* blithe, buoyant, delighted, elate, exultant, glad, happy, jolly, joyous.

jubilant *adj* exultant, exulting, rejoicing, triumphant.

judge *vb* conclude, decide, determine; adjudicate, arbitrate, doom, sentence, try; account, believe, consider, decide, deem, esteem, guess, hold, imagine, reckon, regard, suppose, think; estimate; * *n* adjudicator, arbiter, arbitrator, justice, magistrate, referee, umpire, critic.

judgment, **judgement** *n* brains, ballast, depth, discernment, discrimination, intelligence, judiciousness, prudence, sagacity, sense, sensibility, taste, wisdom, wit; conclusion, decision, determination, notion, thought; adjudication, arbitration, award, censure, condemnation, decree, doom.

judicious *adj* considerate, cool, critical, discreet, enlightened, politic, prudent, rational, reasonable, sensible, sober, solid, sound, staid, wise.

juicy *adj* lush, moist, succulent; entertaining, exciting, lively, racy, spicy.

jump *vb* bound, caper, hop, leap, skip, vault; * *n* bound, leak, skip, spring, vault; hurdle, obstacle; break, gap, space; advance, increase, rise; jolt, shock, start, twitch.

junction *n* combination, connection, joining, linking, seam, union; conjunction, joint.

just *adj* lawful, legitimate, reasonable, right; candid, fair, fair-minded, impartial; good, honest, honourable, pure, straightforward, virtuous; accurate, exact, normal, proper, regular, true; deserved, due, merited.

justice *n* accuracy, equity, honesty, impartiality, right; judge, justiciary.

justifiable *adj* defensible, fit, proper, right, warrantable.

justify *vb* approve, defend, exculpate, excuse, maintain, vindicate; support, warrant.

justness *n* accuracy, fitness, justice, propriety.

juvenile *adj* childish, immature, young, youthful; * *n* boy, child, girl, youth.

juxtaposition *n* adjacency, contiguity, proximity.

K

keen *adj* eager, earnest, fervid, intense, vivid; acute, sharp; acrimonious, bitter, caustic, poignant, sarcastic, severe; discerning, intelligent, quick, sharp-sighted, shrewd; * *vb* bemoan, bewail, lament, mourn, sorrow, weep; * *n* dirge, elegy, lament, lamentation, plaint, requiem.

keep *vb* detain, hold; continue, preserve; confine, detain, reserve, withhold; attend, guard, preserve; adhere to; celebrate, commemorate, honour, perform; maintain, support; husband, save, store; abide, dwell, remain, stay; endure, last; * *n* board, maintenance, support; donjon, dungeon, stronghold.

keeping *n* care, charge, guard; feed, maintenance, support; conformity, consistency, harmony.

key *adj* basic, crucial, essential, important, major; * *n* clue,

elucidation, explanation, solution; (music) keynote, tonic; clamp, lever.
kick *vb* boot, punt; oppose, rebel, resist, spurn; * *n* force, power, punch; excitement, pleasure.
kidnap *vb* abduct, capture, carry off, hijack, steal away.
kill *vb* assassinate, destroy, dispatch, massacre, murder, slay.
kin *adj* akin, allied, kindred, related; * *n* consanguinity, relationship; connections, kindred, relations, relatives.
kind *adj* accommodating, amiable, beneficent, benign, bland, brotherly, gentle, good, good-natured; friendly, gracious, humane, indulgent, mild, obliging, tender-hearted; * *n* breed, class, family, genus, race, set, type; brand, form, make, nature, persuasion, sort, strain, style.
kindle *vb* fire, ignite, light; animate, awaken, exasperate, excite, incite, provoke, stimulate, stir, thrill.
kindness *n* benefaction, favour; beneficence, benevolence, charity, clemency, goodness, grace, humanity, kindliness, mildness, sympathy.
kindred *adj* akin, allied, connected, related; * *n* consanguinity, flesh; kin, kinsfolk, relations, relatives.
king *n* majesty, monarch, sovereign.
kingdom *n* dominion, empire, monarchy, rule, supremacy; tract; division, department, domain, realm.
kingly *adj* monarchical, regal, royal, sovereign; august, grand, imperial, magnificent, noble, regal, royal.
kink *n* curl, entanglement, loop, twist; whim, wrinkle.
knack *n* ability, address, adroitness, aptness, dexterity, dextrousness, expertness, facility, skill.

knell *vb* peal, ring, toll; * *n* chime, peal, ring, toll.
knife *vb* cut, slash, stab; * *n* blade, lance.
knit *vb* ally, connect, interlace, join, unite, weave.
knob *n* boss, bunch, hunch, protuberance, stud.
knock *vb* clap, hit, rap, rattle, slap, strike; beat, blow, box, rap, slap; * *n* blow, slap, smack; blame, rejection, setback.
knot *vb* complicate, gnarl, kink, tie, weave; * *n* complication; connection; joint; bunch; band, cluster, clique, crew, gang, group, pack, set, squad.
knotty *adj* gnarled, hard, knurled, rough, rugged; complex, difficult, harassing, intricate, involved, perplexing.
know *vb* apprehend, cognise, comprehend, recognise, see, understand; discriminate.
knowing *adj* accomplished, competent, intelligent, qualified, well-informed; aware, intelligent, sensible; cunning, expressive, significant.
knowingly *adv* consciously, intentionally, purposely, wittingly.
knowledge *n* apprehension, discernment, perception, understanding, wit; erudition, information, learning, mastery, scholarship, science; cognition, consciousness, ken, notice, recognition.
knowledgeable *adj* aware, conscious, well-informed; educated, learned, scholarly.

L

laborious *adj* assiduous, diligent, hard-working, industrious, painstaking, sedulous, toiling; difficult, fatiguing, hard, irksome, onerous, tiresome, toilsome, wearisome.
labour *vb* drudge, exert, strive, toil, travail, work; * *n* effort,

industry, pains, toil, work; delivery, parturition.

lace *vb* attach, bind, intertwine, tie; * *n* filigree, lattice, mesh, net, network, web.

lack *vb* need, want; * *n* dearth, default, deficiency, deficit, destitution, insufficiency, need, scarcity, want.

laconic *adj* brief, compact, concise, pithy, short, succinct, terse.

lad *n* boy, schoolboy, youngster, youth.

log *vb* dawdle, delay, idle, loiter, tarry.

lair *n* burrow, couch, den, earth, resting place.

lame *vb* cripple, disable, hobble; * *adj* defective, disabled, halt, hobbling; feeble, insufficient, unsatisfactory.

lament *vb* complain, keen, moan, mourn, sorrow, wail, weep; bewail, deplore, regret; * *n* lamentation, moan, moaning, plaint, wailing; dirge, elegy, keen, requiem, threnody.

lamentable *adj* grievous, lamented, melancholy, woeful; miserable, pitiful, poor, wretched.

land *vb* debark, disembark; * *n* earth, soil; country, district, province, reservation, tract, weald.

language *n* dialect, speech, tongue, vernacular; speech; expression, jargon, parlance, phraseology, slang, style; expression, utterance, voice.

languid *adj* drooping, exhausted, faint, feeble, languishing, pining, weak; dull, heartless, heavy, inactive, listless, lukewarm, slow, spiritless, torpid.

languish *vb* decline, droop, fade, fail, faint, sicken, sink, wither.

languor *n* debility, faintness, feebleness, languishment, weakness; ennui, heartlessness, heaviness, lethargy, torpor, weariness.

lank *adj* attenuated, gaunt, lean, meagre, slender, slim, starveling, thin.

lap *vb* drink, lick, mouth, tongue; ripple, splash, wash; quaff, sip, sup, swizzle, tipple; cover, enfold, fold, turn, twist, wrap; distance, pass; overlap; * *n* draught, drain, drench, drink, gulp, lick, sip, sup, suck; splash, wash; fold, flap, lapel, plait; ambit, circle, circuit, cycle, loop, orbit, round, tour, rum, walk.

lapse *vb* glide, sink, slide, slip; err, fail, fall; * *n* course, flow; declension, decline, fall; fault, indiscretion, misstep, slip.

large *adj* big, broad, bulky, colossal, enormous, heroic, great, huge, immense, vast; broad, expanded, extensive, spacious, wide; abundant, ample, full, liberal, plentiful; capacious, comprehensive.

lash *vb* bind, strap, tie; fasten, join, moor, secure; beat, castigate, chastise, flagellate, flail, flay, goad, scourge, swinge, whip; assail, castigate, censure, excoriate, satirise, trounce; * *n* scourge, strap, thong, whip; cut, slap, stroke, stripe.

last *vb* abide, carry on, continue, dwell, endure, persist, remain, stand, stay, survive; * *adj* hindermost, latest; conclusive, final, terminal, ultimate; endmost, eventual, extreme, ultimate; greatest, highest, maximal, maximum, most, supreme, utmost; latest, newest; foregoing, latter, preceding; departing, farewell, final, leaving, parting, valedictory; * *n* conclusion, consummation, end, ending, finale, finish, termination; cast, form, matrix, mould; shape.

lasting *adj* durable, enduring, fixed, perennial, permanent, perpetual.

late *adj* behindhand, delayed, overdue, slow; deceased,

latent *adj* concealed, hidden, invisible, occult, secret, unseen, veiled.

latitude *n* amplitude, breadth, compass, range, scope; freedom, indulgence, liberty.

latter *adj* last, latest, modern, new, recent.

laugh *vb* cackle, chortle, chuckle, giggle, guffaw, snigger, titter; * *n* chuckle, giggle, laughter, titter.

laughter *n* cackle, chortle, chuckle, glee, giggle, laugh, laughing.

launch *vb* cast, dart, dispatch, hurl, lance, project, throw; enlarge; begin, commence, open, start.

lavish *vb* dissipate, expend, spend, squander, waste; * *adj* excessive, extravagant, generous, immoderate, prodigal, profuse, thriftless, unstinted, unthrifty, wasteful.

law *n* act, canon, command, commandment, decree, edict, order, precept, principle, statute; regulation, rule; litigation, process, suit.

lawful *adj* constitutional, constituted, legal, legitimate; allowable, authorised; just, rightful, proper.

lawless *adj* anarchical, chaotic, disorderly, insubordinate, rebellious, reckless, wild.

lay *vb* deposit, establish, leave, place, plant, put, set, settle, spread; arrange, dispose, locate, position; bear, deposit, produce; advance, offer, submit; allot, ascribe, assign, attribute, charge, impute; contrive, design, plan, plot, prepare; apply, burden, encumber, impose, saddle, tax; bet, hazard, risk, stake, wager; allay, alleviate, assuage, calm, relieve, soothe, still, suppress; disclose, divulge, explain, reveal, show; grab, grasp, seize; assault, attack, beat up; discover, find; bless, confirm, consecrate, ordain; * *n* array, form, formation; attitude, aspect, direction, lie, pose, position, set; ballad, carol, ditty, lyric, ode, poem, song; * *adj* amateur, inexpert, nonprofessional; civil, laic, laical, non-ecclesiastical, secular, temporal.

layer *n* bed, course, seam, stratum.

lazy *adj* idle, inactive, indolent, inert, slack, slow, sluggish.

lead *vb* conduct, deliver, direct, draw, guide; front, head, precede; advance, outstrip, pass; entice, induce, persuade, prevail; conduce, serve, tend; * *adj* chief, first, foremost, main, primary, prime; * *n* direction, guidance; advance; precedence.

leadership *n* conduct, direction, guidance, lead; headship, predominance, primacy.

leading *adj* governing, ruling; capital, chief, first, foremost, highest, principal, superior.

league *vb* ally, associate, band, combine, confederate, unite; * *n* alliance, combination, combine, confederacy, union.

leak *vb* drip, exude, ooze, pass, percolate; * *n* chink, crack, crevice, hole; leakage, leaking.

lean *adj* bony, gaunt, lank, meagre, poor, skinny, thin; dull, barren, meagre, tame; inadequate, scanty, slender; bare, barren, infertile; * *vb* incline, slope; recline, repose, rest; depend, rely, trust.

leaning *n* aptitude, bent, bias, disposition, inclination, liking, propensity, tendency.

leap *vb* bound, spring, vault; caper, frisk, gambol, hop, skip; * *n* bound, jump, spring, vault; caper, hop, skip.

learn *vb* acquire, attain, collect, gain, gather, hear, memorise.

learned *adj* erudite, lettered, literate, scholarly, well-read; expert, knowing, versed.

learning n acquirements, culture, education, knowledge, scholarship, tuition.

least adj meanest, minutest, smallest.

leave vb abandon, go, quit, vacate, withdraw; desert, forsake, renounce; commit, consign, refer; cease, desist from, refrain, stop; allow, cease, let, let alone, permit; demise, desist, will; * n allowance, liberty, permission, licence; departure, withdrawal; adieu, farewell, goodbye.

lecture vb censure, chide, reprimand, reprove, scold; address, teach; * n censure, lecturing, lesson, reprimand, reproof; address, discourse.

legacy n bequest, gift; heritage, inheritance, tradition.

legal adj allowable, authorised, constitutional, lawful, legalised, legitimate.

legend n fable, fiction, myth, romance, story.

legible adj clear, decipherable, fair, distinct, plain, readable; apparent.

legion n army, body, column, corps, detail, division, maniple, phalanx; squad; army, horde, host, number, swarm, throng; * adj many, multitudinous, myriad.

legislate vb enact, ordain.

legitimate adj authorised, lawful, legal; genuine, valid; justifiable, reasonable, warrantable, warranted.

leisure n convenience, freedom, opportunity, recreation, retirement.

lend vb advance, afford, confer, give, grant, impart, loan.

lengthen vb elongate, extend, produce, prolong, stretch; protract.

lengthy adj diffuse, lengthened, long, prolonged, protracted.

lenient adj assuasive, lenitive, mitigating, mitigative, softening, soothing; easy, forbearing, gentle, indulgent, merciful, mild, tolerant.

less adj baser, inferior, lower, smaller; fewer, lesser, reduced, smaller; * adv barely, below, least, under; decreasingly; * prep excepting, lacking, sans, short of, without.

lessen vb abate, contract, curtail, decrease, narrow, reduce, shrink; lower; weaken.

lesson n exercise; instruction; censure, chiding, lecture, lecturing, reproof, scolding.

let vb admit, allow, authorise, permit, suffer; hire, lease, rent; hinder, impede, instruct, prevent; * n hindrance, impediment, obstacle, obstruction.

lethal adj deadly, destructive, fatal, mortal, murderous.

lethargic adj apathetic, drowsy, dull, heavy, inactive, inert, sleepy, stupid, torpid.

letter n epistle, line, missive, note.

lettered adj bookish, educated, erudite, learned, literary.

level vb equalise, smooth; demolish, destroy; aim, direct, point; * adj equal, even, flush, horizontal, plain, plane, smooth; * n degree, equality, evenness, plain, plane, smoothness; deck, floor, stage, tier.

levity n buoyancy, fickleness, flightiness, frivolity, giddiness, inconstancy, volatility.

levy vb collect, exact, gather, tax; call, muster, raise, summon; * n duty, tax.

liability n accountability, duty, obligation, responsibility, tendency; exposedness; debt, obligation.

libel vb defame, lampoon, slander, vilify; * n calumny, defamation, satire, slander, vituperation.

liberal adj beneficent, charitable, disinterested, free, generous, munificent, open-hearted, unselfish; catholic, chivalrous, high-minded, honourable,

LIBERATE

magnanimous, tolerant, unbiased, unbigoted; ample, bounteous, full, unstinted; liberalising, refined.
liberate *vb* deliver, discharge, disenthral, free, release.
liberty *n* emancipation, freedom, independence, liberation, self-direction; franchise; licence, permission.
licence *n* authorisation, leave, permission, privilege, right; certificate, charter, permit; anarchy, disorder, freedom, lawlessness, liberty.
license *vb* allow, authorise, grant, permit, warrant; suffer.
lie *vb* recline, remain, repose, rest; consist; equivocate, falsify, fib, prevaricate; * *n* equivocation, falsehood, falsification, fib; delusion, illusion.
life *n* activity, alertness, animation, briskness, energy, spirit, verve, vigour; behaviour, conduct; being, duration, existence, lifetime.
lifeless *adj* dead, deceased, extinct, inanimate; cold, dull, flat, inert, passive, slow, sluggish, tame, torpid.
lift *vb* elevate, exalt, hoist, raise, uplift; * *n* aid, assistance, help; elevator.
light *vb* alight, land, perch, settle; fire, ignite, inflame, kindle; brighten, illume, illuminate, luminate, lighten; * *adj* sandy, well-leavened; loose, sandy; free, portable, unburdened; inconsiderable, moderate, negligible, small, trifling, trivial, unimportant; feathery, gossamer, insubstantial, weightless; easy, facile; fickle, frivolous, unsettled; unsteady; airy, carefree; unaccented, unstressed, weak; bright, clear, fair, lightsome, luminous, pale, pearly; * *n* dawn, day, daybreak, sunrise; blaze, effulgence, gleam, illumination, radiance, ray; candle, lamp, lighthouse,

torch; comprehension, enlightenment, information, instruction, knowledge; explanation, illustration; attitude, construction, interpretation, observation, regard, respect, view.
lighten *vb* allay, alleviate, ease, mitigate; disburden, relieve, unburden, unload; brighten, shine; light, illume, illuminate, illumine; enlighten, inform; emit, flash.
like *vb* approve, please; enjoy, love; fancy, regard; choose, desire, elect, list, prefer, wish; * *n* liking, partiality; equal, match, twin; * *adj* alike, allied, corresponding, parallel; equal, same; likely, probable; * *adv* likely, probably.
likelihood *n* probability, verisimilitude.
likely *adj* credible, liable, possible, probable; agreeable, convenient, likable, pleasing, suitable, well-suited; * *adv* doubtlessly, presumably, probably.
likeness *n* appearance, form, resemblance, semblance, similarity; copy, counterpart, effigy, image, picture, portrait, representation.
liking *n* desire, fondness, partiality, wish; appearance, bent, bias, inclination, leaning, penchant, proneness, tendency, turn.
limit *vb* bound, define; check, condition, hinder, restrain, restrict; * *n* bound, boundary, confine, frontier, march, term, termination, terminus; check, restraint, restriction.
limp *vb* halt, hitch, hobble, totter; * *n* hitch, hobble, shamble, shuffle, totter; * *adj* drooping, droopy, floppy, weak; flabby, flexible, limber, slack, soft.
limpid *adj* bright, clear, crystal, crystalline, lucid, pure, translucent, transparent.
line *vb* align, line up, range,

rank; border, bound, edge, fringe, hem, march, rim, verge; seam, stripe, streak, striate, trace; carve, chisel, crease, cut; define, delineate, describe; * *n* mark, streak, stripe; cord, rope, string; rank, row; ancestry, family, lineage, race, succession; course, method; business, calling, job, occupation, post, pursuit.

linger *vb* dally, delay, idle, lag, loiter, remain, stay, wait.

link *vb* bind, conjoin, connect, fasten, join, tie, unite; * *n* connection, connective, copula, coupler, joint, juncture; division, part.

liquefy *vb* dissolve, fuse, melt, thaw.

liquid *adj* fluid; clear, dulcet, flowing, mellifluous, soft; * *n* fluid, liquor.

list *vb* alphabetise, catalogue, chronicle, enumerate, file, index, record, register, tabulate, tally; enlist, enroll; desire, elect, like, please, prefer, wish; cant, heel, keel, lean, pitch, tip; * *n* catalogue, index, invoice, roll, schedule, scroll, table, tally; border, bound, limit; border, edge, strip, stripe; fillet; cant, inclination, incline, pitch, slope, tilt.

listen *vb* attend, hear, hearken, heed, obey, observe.

literally *adv* actually, really; exactly, precisely, strictly.

literary *adj* bookish, erudite, instructed, learned, lettered, scholarly, well-read.

lithe *adj* flexible, limber, pliable, pliant, supple.

litter *vb* derange, disarrange, disorder, scatter, strew; bear; * *n* bedding, sedan, stretcher; confusion, disarray, mess; fragments, rubbish, shreds.

little *adj* diminutive, minute, small, tiny, wee; brief, short, small; feeble, inconsiderable, insignificant, petty, slender, slight, trivial, unimportant, weak; contemptible, mean, narrow, selfish, stingy; * *n* handful, modicum, pinch, pittance, whit.

live *vb* be, exist; continue, endure, last, remain; abide, dwell, reside; feed, subsist, support; continue, lead; * *adj* alive, animate, living, quick; burning, hot; bright, brilliant, glowing, lively, vivid; active, earnest, glowing.

livelihood *n* employment, living, maintenance, subsistence, support, sustenance.

lively *adj* active, agile, alert, brisk, energetic, quick, smart, stirring, supple, vigorous, vivacious; animated, blithe, blithesome, buoyant, gleeful, jolly, merry, spirited, spry; bright, brilliant, clear, fresh, glowing, vivid; energetic, impassioned, keen, nervous, racy, strong, vigorous.

living *adj* alive, breathing, existing, live; active, lively, quickening; * *n* livelihood, maintenance, subsistence, support; estate.

load *vb* freight; burden, cumber, encumber, oppress, weigh; * *n* burden, pack, weight; cargo, freight, lading; clog, deadweight, oppression, pressure.

loathe *vb* abhor, abominate, detest, dislike, hate.

loathsome *adj* disgusting, nauseating, nauseous, offensive, repulsive, revolting, sickening; abominable, detestable, execrable, hateful, shocking.

local *adj* limited, neighbouring, provincial, regional, sectional, territorial.

lock *vb* bolt, fasten, padlock, seal; confine; clog, restrain, stop; clasp, embrace, encircle, enclose, hug, join, press; * *n* bolt, padlock; embrace, hug; curl, ringlet, tress.

lodge *vb* deposit, fix, settle; fix, place, plant; accommodate, cover, entertain, quarter, shelter; abide, inhabit, live, reside, rest; remain, rest, stay, stop; * n cabin, cot, cottage, hovel, hut; cave, den, haunt, lair; assembly, association club, group.

lofty adj elevated, high, tall, towering; arrogant, proud; elevated, exalted, sublime; dignified, imposing, majestic, stately.

logical adj close, coherent, consistent, dialectical, sound, valid; rational, reasoned.

lonely adj apart, dreary, isolated, lonesome, remote, retired, secluded, solitary; alone, lone, friendless, solitary, unaccompanied; deserted, desolate, forlorn.

long vb anticipate, await, expect; aspire, covet, crave, desire, hanker, wish, yearn; * adj drawn-out, extended, extensive, far-reaching, prolonged, protracted, stretched; diffuse, lengthy, wearisome; backward, lingering, slack, slow, tardy.

longing n aspiration, coveting, craving, desire, hunger, pining, yearning.

look vb behold, examine, notice, see, search; consider, examine, inspect, observe, study; contemplate, gaze, regard, scan, view; await; consider, heed, mind, watch; face, front; seem; * n gaze, glance, peep, search; appearance, aspect; air, aspect, manner.

loose vb free, liberate, release, unbind, undo, unfasten, unlock; ease, loosen, relax; detach, disengage; * adj unbound, unconfined, unfastened, unsewn, untied; disengaged, free, unattached; relaxed, slack; diffuse, diffusive, unconnected; indefinite, indistinct, vague; careless, negligent, lax; debauched, licentious, unchaste.

loosen vb liberate, relax, release, separate, slacken, unloose, untie.

loot vb despoil, pillage, plunder, ransack, rifle, rob, sack; * n booty, plunder, spoil.

lordly adj aristocratic, exalted, grand, lofty, majestic, noble; arrogant, domineering, haughty, insolent, proud, tyrannical; large, liberal.

lose vb deprive, dispossess, forfeit, miss; dislodge, displace, mislay, squander, waste; fall, yield.

loss n deprivation, failure, forfeiture, privation; damage, defeat, destruction, detriment, injury, overthrow, ruin; waste.

lost adj astray, missing; missed; dissipated, misspent, wasted; bewildered, distracted, perplexed, puzzled; absent, absentminded, abstracted, dreamy, preoccupied; corrupt, depraved, dissolute, graceless, hardened, irreclaimable, licentious, profligate, wanton.

lot n allotment, destiny, doom, fate; accident, chance, fate, hap, haphazard; division, part, portion.

loud adj noisy, resounding, sonorous; deafening, strong; boisterous, clamorous, noisy, tumultuous, uproarious, vociferous; impressive, positive; flashy, glaring, ostentatious, showy, vulgar.

love vb adore, like, worship; * n affection, courtship, delight, fondness, friendship, kindness tenderness, warmth; adoration, amour, attachment; devotion, fondness; benevolence, charity, goodwill.

lovely adj beautiful, charming, delectable, enchanting, exquisite, graceful, pleasing, sweet, winning; adorable, amiable.

low vb bellow, moo; * adj depressed, profound; gentle, grave, soft, subdued; cheap, mean, plebeian, vulgar; base, base-minded, dirty, ignoble,

low-minded, menial, servile, shabby, slavish; disgraceful, dishonourable, disreputable, undignified, unmanly; exhausted, feeble, weak; frugal, plain, poor, spare; humble, lowly, submissive; dejected, depressed, dispirited.
lower vb depress, drop, sink, subside; debase, disgrace, humiliate, reduce; abate, decrease, diminish, lessen; * adj baser, inferior, less, lesser, shorter, smaller; under.
lowly adj gentle, humble, meek, mild, modest, plain, poor, simple; low-born, mean, servile.
loyal adj attacked, constant, devoted, faithful, patriotic, true.
loyalty n allegiance, devotion, faithfulness, fidelity, patriotism.
luck n accident, casualty, chance, fate, fortune, hap, hazard, success.
lucrative adj advantageous, gainful, paying, profitable.
ludicrous adj absurd, burlesque, comic, farcical, funny, laughable, ridiculous.
lukewarm adj blood-warm, tepid; apathetic, cold, dull, indifferent, unconcerned.
lull vb calm, compose, hush, quiet, still, tranquillise; abate, cease, decrease, diminish, subside; * n calm, cessation.
luminous adj incandescent, radiant, refulgent, resplendent, shining; bright, brilliant, clear; clear, lucid, lucent, plain.
lunacy n craziness, derangement, insanity, madness, mania.
lunatic adj crazy, deranged, insane, mad; * n madman, maniac, psychopath.
lurch vb appropriate, filch, steal; deceit, defeat, disappoint, evade; lurk, skulk; contrive, shift, trick.
lure vb allure, attract, entice, inveigle, tempt; * n allurement, attraction, bait, decoy, enticement, temptation.
lurid adj dismal, ghastly, gloomy, lowering, pale, wan; glaring, sensational.
lurk vb crouch, hide, prowl, skulk, sneak, snoop.
luscious adj delicious, delightful, grateful, palatable, pleasing, savoury; sugary; fulsome, nauseous, unctuous.
lust vb covet, crave, desire, hanker, need, want, yearn; * n cupidity, desire, longing; concupiscence, lechery, salaciousness, salacity.
lustre n brightness, brilliance, brilliancy, splendour.
lusty adj healthful, lively, robust, stout, strong, sturdy; burly, corpulent, large, stout.
luxuriate vb abound, delight, enjoy, flourish, revel.
luxurious adj opulent, pampered, self-indulgent, sensual, voluptuous.
luxury n epicureanism, opulence, sensuality; delight, enjoyment, gratification, indulgence, pleasure; delicacy, treat.
lyrical adj ecstatic, enthusiastic, expressive; dulcet, lyric, mellifluous, melodic, musical, poetic.

M

macabre adj deathlike, deathly, dreadful, frightening, frightful, grim, grisly, gruesome, hideous, horrid, morbid, weird.
machine n instrument, tool; machinery, system; engine.
mad adj crazed, crazy, delirious, deranged, distracted, insane, irrational, lunatic, maniac, maniacal; furious, rabid, raging, violent; angry, enraged, furious, incensed, provoked; distracted, wild; frantic, frenzied, raving.
madden vb annoy, craze, exasperate, inflame, infuriate, irritate.

madness n craziness, insanity, lunacy, mania; frenzy, fury, rage.

magic adj bewitching, charming, enchanting, fascinating, magical, miraculous; * n conjuring, enchantment, sorcery, witchcraft.

magician n conjurer, enchanter, magus, necromancer, sorcerer, wizard.

magisterial adj august, dignified, majestic; authoritative, dictatorial, imperious.

magnanimity n chivalry, generosity, high-mindedness, nobility.

magnificent adj elegant, grand, majestic, splendid, superb; brilliant, imposing, luxurious, showy, stately, superb.

magnify vb amplify, enlarge; bless, celebrate, elevate, exalt, glorify, praise.

magnitude n bulk, extent, mass, size, volume; consequence, greatness; grandeur, sublimity.

maim vb cripple, disfigure, mangle, mutilate; * n crippling, mutilation; harm, hurt, injury.

main adj capital, cardinal, chief, leading, paramount, principal; essential, important, necessary, vital; huge, mighty, vast; pure, sheer; absolute, direct, entire; * n channel; force, might, power, strength; ocean; continent, mainland.

maintain vb keep, preserve, support, sustain, uphold; hold, possess; defend, justify; carry on, keep up; feed, provide, supply; assert, declare; affirm, allege, contend, hold, say.

maintenance n justification, preservation, support, sustenance, vindication; bread, food, provisions, subsistence, sustenance.

majestic adj august, imperial, imposing, lofty, noble, stately, regal, royal; grand, splendid.

majority n bulk, greater, mass, most, preponderance.

make vb create; fashion, figure, form, mould, shape; cause, construct, establish; do, execute, perform; acquire, gain, get, raise, secure; cause, compel, force, occasion; compose, constitute, form; go, move, proceed, tend, travel; contribute, effect, favour, operate; estimate, judge, reckon, suppose, think; * n brand, build, construction, form, shape, structure.

maker n creator, god; framer, manufacturer; composer, poet, writer.

malady n affliction, complaint, disease, illness, indisposition.

malevolent adj evil-minded, hateful, hostile, malicious, malignant, mischievous, spiteful.

malice n bitterness, enmity, grudge, hate, ill will, pique, rancour, spite, spitefulness, vindictiveness.

malicious adj bitter, envious, evil-minded, ill-natured, malevolent, malignant, rancorous, spiteful, vicious.

malign vb abuse, blacken, calumniate, disparage, revile, scandalise, slander, vilify; * adj malevolent, malicious, malignant, ill-disposed; injurious, unfavourable.

malignant adj bitter, envious, hostile, malevolent, malicious, malign, spiteful, rancorous, resentful; virulent; dangerous, fatal, virulent.

man vb crew, garrison; fortify, strengthen; * n adult, body, individual, one, person, personage, soul; humanity, humankind, mankind; attendant, dependant, servant, subject, valet, vassal; workman.

manage vb administer, conduct, direct, handle, order, regulate, superintend, supervise, treat; control, guide, rule; handle, manipulate, train; contrive, economise, save.

manageable adj controllable,

docile, easy, governable, tractable.

management *n* administration, care, charge, conduct, control, direction, superintendence, supervision, treatment.

manager *n* conductor, director, executive, governor, impresario, superintendent.

mandate *n* charge, command, commission, edict, injunction, order, precept.

mangle *vb* hack, mutilate, rend, tear; crush, destroy, maim, mutilate, spoil; calender, polish, press, smooth.

mania *n* craziness, delirium, derangement, frenzy, insanity, lunacy, madness; craze, desire, fad, fanaticism.

manifest *vb* declare, demonstrate, disclose, discover, evidence, express, reveal, show; * *adj* apparent, clear, conspicuous, evident, glaring, obvious, open, patent, plain, visible.

manifold *adj* complex, diverse, many, multiplied, numerous, several, varied.

manipulate *vb* handle, operate, ply, work.

manner *n* fashion, form, mode, style, way; habit; degree, extent, measure; kind, kinds, sorts; air, appearance, aspect, behaviour, deportment, look; mannerism, peculiarity, style; conduct, habits; civility, deportment.

manners *npl* conduct, habits, morals; air, behaviour, breeding, comportment, etiquette.

manoeuvre *vb* contrive, intrigue, manage, plan, plot, scheme; * *n* exercise, movement, operation; finesse, intrigue, plan, plot, ruse, scheme, trick.

manufacture *vb* build, compose, construct, fabricate, forge, form, mould, produce, shape; * *n* constructing, making.

many *adj* abundant, frequent, innumerable, manifold, multifold, numerous, sundry, varied, various; * *n* crowd, people.

map *vb* chart, draw up, plan, plot, sketch; * *n* chart, diagram, outline, plot.

mar *vb* blot, damage, hurt, impair, ruin, spoil, stain; deface, deform, disfigure, mutilate.

march *vb* go, pace, step, tramp, walk; * *n* hike, walk; parade, procession; step, stride; advance, progress.

margin *n* border, brim, brink, confine, edge, rim, verge; latitude, room, surplus.

marital *adj* connubial, conjugal, matrimonial, nuptial.

mark *vb* distinguish, earmark, label; brand, characterise, denote, designate, engrave, impress, imprint, print, stamp; heed, note, notice, observe, regard, show, spot; * *n* brand, characteristic, impress, line, note, print, sign, stamp, symbol, race; evidence, proof, symptom, token, track, vestige; badge, sign; footprint, trace, track; butt, object; consequence, distinction, fame, importance, position.

marked *adj* conspicuous, distinguished, eminent, noted, prominent, remarkable.

marriage *n* nuptials, wedding; matrimony, wedlock; union; alliance, association.

marshal *vb* arrange, array, dispose, gather, range; order, rank; guide, lead; * *n* conductor, master of ceremonies; harbinger, herald.

martial *adj* brave, heroic, military, soldier-like, warlike.

marvel *vb* gape, gaze, wonder; * *n* miracle, wonder; admiration, astonishment, surprise.

marvellous *adj* amazing, astonishing, extraordinary, strange, stupendous, wonderful, wondrous; improbable, surprising, unbelievable.

masculine *adj* hardy, manful, manlike, manly, virile;

MASK

powerful, strong; bold, coarse.
mask vb cloak, conceal, disguise, hide, screen, veil; * n blind, cloak, screen, veil; evasion, pretext, ruse, shift, subterfuge, trick; bustle, masquerade.
mass vb accumulate, assemble, collect, gather, throng; * adj large-scale, widespread; * n cake, lump; assemblage, collection, combination, heap; bulk, magnitude, size; body, sum, total, whole.
massacre vb annihilate, kill, murder, slaughter, slay; * n carnage, extermination, murder, slaughter.
massive adj big, bulky, colossal, enormous, heavy, huge, immense, solid, substantial, vast.
master vb conquer, defeat, direct, govern, overcome, overpower, rule, subdue, vanquish; acquire, learn; * adj cardinal, chief, grand, great, main, leading, prime; expert, proficient; * n director, governor, lord, manager, superintendent, ruler; captain, commander; preceptor, schoolteacher, teacher; owner, possessor, proprietor; chief, head, leader.
masterly adj clever, dextrous, excellent, expert, finished, skilful, skilled; despotic, domineering, imperious.
mastery n command, mastership, rule, supremacy, sway; leadership, superiority, supremacy, upper-hand; acquisition, acquirement; ability, cleverness, proficiency, skill.
match vb equal, rival; fit, harmonise, suit; marry, mate; combine, join, sort; pit; correspond, suit, tally; * n equal; competition, contest, game, trial; union.
matchless adj consummate, excellent, exquisite, inimitable, perfect, surpassing, unequalled, unmatched, unrivalled.

mate vb marry, match, wed; compete, equal, vie; confound, crush, subdue; * n companion, compeer, consort, friend, fellow, intimate; companion, equal, match; husband, wife.
material adj bodily, corporeal, nonspiritual, temporal; important, momentous, relevant, vital; * n body, stuff, substance.
matrimonial adj conjugal, connubial, marital, nuptial.
matter vb import, signify; * n body, content, sense, substance; difficulty, trouble; material, stuff; question, subject, topic; affair, business, concern, event; consequence, moment, significance; discharge, pus.
mature vb develop, mellow, perfect, ripen; * adj complete, fit, perfect; completed, prepared, ready.
meagre adj emaciated, gaunt, lank, lean, poor, spare, starved, thin; barren, poor, sterile, unproductive; bald, dry, dull, mean, poor; feeble, insignificant, scanty, small, uninteresting, vapid.
mean vb contemplate, design, intend, purpose; denote, imply, import, indicate, purport, symbolise; * adj average, medium, middle; intermediate; coarse, common, humble, ignoble, low, ordinary, vulgar; abject, contemptible, dirty, dishonourable, pitiful, scurvy, servile, shabby, sorry, spiritless, vile; illiberal, miserly, narrow, niggardly, penurious, selfish, sordid, stingy, ungenerous; diminutive, insignificant, petty, poor, small; * n measure, medium, moderation; average; agency, instrument, means, mode, way.
meaning n acceptation, drift, import, intention, purpose, sense.
means npl instrument, method, mode, way; expedient, measure, resource, step; estate, income,

resources, revenue, wealth.
measure *vb* mete; adjust, proportion; appreciate, estimate, gauge, value; * *n* gauge, meter, rule; degree, extent, limit; degree; means, step; metre, rhythm, verse.
meddle *vb* butt in, interfere, interpose, intrude.
meddlesome *adj* interfering, intermeddling, intrusive, officious.
mediation *n* arbitration, intercession, intervention.
meditate *vb* contrive, design, devise, intend, purpose, scheme; contemplate, study; muse, ponder, think.
meditation *n* contemplation, musing, pondering, reflection, study, thought.
meditative *adj* contemplative, pensive, reflective, studious, thoughtful.
medium *adj* average, mean, mediocre, middle; * *n* agency, instrument, instrumentality, means, organ; conditions, influences; average, means.
meek *adj* gentle, humble, lowly, mild, modest, soft, submissive, unassuming.
meet *vb* cross, intersect, transact; confront, encounter, engage; answer, comply, fulfil, satisfy; join, unite; assemble, collect, convene, congregate, forgather, rally; * *adj* adapted, appropriate, befitting, fit, fitting, proper, suitable, suited.
meeting *n* encounter, interview; assembly, company, conference, congregation, convention, gathering; encounter, conflux, joining, junction, union; collision.
melancholy *adj* blue, depressed, despondent, desponding, dismal, dispirited, doleful, downhearted, gloomy, glum, hypochondriac, lugubrious, moody, mopish, sad, sombre, unhappy; dark, grave, quiet, sad; * *n* blues, dejection, despondency, dumps, gloom, gloominess, sadness, vapours.
mellow *vb* mature, ripen; smooth, soften, tone; perfect; * *adj* ripe; dulcet, mellifluous, silver-toned; rich, smooth, soft; delicate, rich, soft; jolly, matured; rich, softened; perfected, well-prepared; disguised, tipsy.
melt *vb* dissolve, fuse, liquefy, thaw; mollify, relax, soften, subdue; dissipate; pass, shade.
member *n* arm, leg, organ; constituent, element, part; branch, clause, division.
memorable *adj* celebrated, distinguished, extraordinary, famous, great, important, notable, remarkable, signal.
memorandum *n* minute, note, record.
memorial *adj* commemorative, monumental; * *n* memento, monument, souvenir; record, remembrance.
menace *vb* alarm, frighten, threaten; * *n* danger, hazard, threat, warning; nuisance, pest.
mend *vb* dam, patch, rectify, refit, repair, restore; amend, better, correct, improve, rectify, reform; advance, help, improve; increase.
mendacious *adj* deceptive, false, lying, untrue, untruthful.
menial *adj* base, low, mean, servile, vile; * *n* attendant, domestic, footman, serf, servant, slave, underling, waiter.
mental *adj* ideal, immaterial, intellectual, subjective.
mention *vb* acquaint, cite, communicate, declare, disclose, divulge, impart, name, reveal, state, tell; * *n* allusion, designation, notice, noting.
mentor *n* adviser, counsellor, instructor, monitor.
mercantile *adj* commercial, marketable, trading.
mercenary *adj* hired, paid, purchased, venal; covetous,

grasping, mean, parsimonious, sordid, stingy; * n hireling, soldier.

merchandise n commodities, goods, stock, wares.

merchant n dealer, retailer, shopkeeper, trader, tradesman.

merciful adj clement, forgiving, lenient, pitiful; benignant, gentle, gracious, humane, kind, mild, tender.

merciless adj barbarous, callous, cruel, hard-hearted, inexorable, relentless, remorseless, ruthless, severe, uncompassionate, unfeeling, unrelenting, unrepenting.

mercurial adj active, lively, nimble, prompt, quick; cheerful, lighthearted, lively; changeable, fickle, mobile, volatile.

mercy n compassion, gentleness, kindness, lenience, lenity, pity, tenderness; blessing, favour, grace; disposal; forgiveness, pardon.

mere adj bald, bare, plain, sole, simple; entire, pure, unmixed; * n lake, pond, pool.

merge vb bury, dip, involve, lose, sink, submerge.

merit vb deserve, earn; acquire, desert, gain, value; * n claim, right; credit, desert, excellence, worth, worthiness.

merry adj agreeable, brisk, delightful, lively, pleasant, stirring; airy, blithesome, cheerful, comical, droll, gleeful, hilarious, jocund, jolly, joyous, light-hearted, lively, mirthful, sportive, sprightly.

mess n company, set; jumble, mass, miscellany, mixture; confusion, muddle, perplexity, plight, predicament.

message n communication, dispatch, letter, missive, notice, wire, word.

metaphorical adj allegorical, emblematic, figurative, symbolic, symbolical.

method n course, manner, means, mode, procedure, process, rule, way; order, plan, regularity, scheme, system.

methodical adj exact, orderly, regular, systematic, systematical.

mettle n constitution, material, stuff; character, disposition, spirit; ardour, courage, fire, life, nerve, pluck, spirit, vigour.

microscopic adj infinitesimal, minute, tiny.

middle adj central, halfway, mean, median, mid; * n centre, halfway, mean, midst.

might n ability, capacity, efficacy, force, main, prowess, strength.

mighty adj able, bold, potent, powerful, robust, strong, sturdy, valorous, vigorous; bulky, enormous, huge, monstrous, stupendous, vast.

mild adj amiable, compassionate, gentle, kind, merciful, pacific, tender; bland, gentle, soft, suave; calm, gentle, kind, pleasant, soft, tranquil; assuasive, demulcent, lenitive, soothing.

militant adj belligerent, combative, contending, fighting.

military adj martial, soldier, soldierly; * n army, militia, soldiers.

mill vb comminute, crush, grind, powder, pulverise; * n factory; grinder; crowd, throng.

mimic vb ape, counterfeit, impersonate, mock, parody; * adj imitative, simulated; * n imitator, impersonator, mime, mocker.

mince vb chop, cut, hash, shatter; attenuate, diminish, extenuate, mitigate, palliate, soften; pose, smirk; * n hash, mash, mincemeat.

mind vb attend, heed, note, notice, regard, tend, watch; obey, observe; design, intend, mean; recall, remember; beware, look out, watch out; balk, begrudge, grudge, object

resent; * n soul, spirit; common sense, intellect, reason, sense, understanding; consideration, contemplation, judgement, reflection, sentiment, thought; recollection, remembrance; desire, inclination, intention, leaning, will.
mindful adj attentive, careful, heedful, observant, thoughtful.
mindless adj dull, insensible, senseless, stupid, unthinking; careless, heedless, neglectful, negligent, regardless.
mine vb dig, excavate, quarry, unearth; sap; destroy, ruin; * n colliery, deposit, pit.
mingle vb blend, combine, commingle, compound, intermix, join, mix, unite.
miniature adj diminutive, little, small, tiny.
minister vb afford, furnish, give, supply; aid, assist, contribute, help; * n agent, servant, subordinate; administrator, executive; ambassador, delegate, envoy; chaplain, churchman, clergyman, divine, ecclesiastic, parson, priest, vicar.
ministry n agency, aid, help, instrumentality, intervention, ministration, support; administration, cabinet, council.
minor adj less, smaller; junior, secondary, subordinate, younger; petty, unimportant; small.
mint vb coin, stamp; fashion, forge, new, invent, produce; * adj fresh, new, perfect, undamaged; * n die, seal, stamp; (slang) heap, million, pile, wad.
minute adj diminutive, fine, little, microscopic, slight, tiny; circumstantial, critical, exact, fussy, nice, particular, precise; * n account, entry, item, note, proceedings, record; instant, moment, second, trice.
miracle n marvel, phenomenon, prodigy, wonder.

miraculous adj supernatural, thaumaturgic; amazing, extraordinary, incredible, supernatural, unaccountable, unbelievable, wondrous.
mirror vb copy, echo, emulate, reflect, show; * n reflector, speculum; archetype, exemplar, example, paragon, pattern.
mirth n cheerfulness, festivity, frolic, fun, gladness, glee, hilarity; festivity, joviality, laughter, merriment, rejoicing, sport.
misadventure n calamity, catastrophe, cross, disaster, failure, ill-luck, mischance, misfortune, reverse.
miscellaneous adj confused, diverse, heterogeneous, indiscriminate, jumbled, many, mingled, mixed, various.
mischievous adj destructive, detrimental, harmful, hurtful, injurious; malicious, sinful, vicious, wicked; annoying, naughty, troublesome.
miser n churl, niggard, screw, skinflint.
miserable adj broken-hearted, comfortless, disconsolate, distressed, heartbroken, unhappy, wretched; calamitous, hapless, unfortunate, unhappy, unlucky, wretched; poor, valueless; abject, contemptible, low, mean, worthless.
miserly adj avaricious, beggarly, close, close-fisted, grasping, mean, parsimonious, sordid, stingy, tight-fisted.
misery n affliction, agony, anguish, calamity, desolation, distress, grief, heavy-heartedness, misfortune, sorrow, suffering, torture, tribulation, unhappiness, woe, wretchedness.
misfortune n adversity, affliction, bad luck, blow, calamity, casualty, disaster, distress, harm, ill, infliction, mischance, mishap, reverse, stroke, trial, trouble.
misgiving n apprehension,

distrust, doubt, hesitation, suspicion, uncertainty.
mishap n accident, disaster, ill luck, mischance, misfortune.
mislead vb beguile, bluff, deceive, delude, misdirect, misguide.
misrepresent vb caricature, distort, falsify, misstate.
miss vb blunder, err, fail, fall short, forgo, lack, lose, mistake, omit; look, trip; escape, evade, skip; feel the loss of, need, want, wish; * n blunder, error, fault, mistake, oversight, slip, trip; loss, want; damsel, girl, lass, maid, maiden.
mission n commission; business, charge, duty, errand, office, trust; delegation.
mist vb cloud, drizzle, mizzle, smog; * n cloud, fog, haze; bewilderment, obscurity.
mistake vb misapprehend, miscalculate, misconceive, misjudge; confound, take; blunder, err; * n miscalculation, misconception, misunderstanding; blunder, error, fault, oversight, slip, trip.
mistaken adj erroneous, inaccurate, incorrect, wrong.
mistrust vb distrust, doubt, suspect; apprehend, fear, suspect; * n doubt, misgiving, suspicion.
misty adj clouded, dark, dim, foggy, obscure, overcast.
misunderstanding n error, misapprehension, mistake; difference, difficulty, discord.
misuse vb misapply, misemploy, pervert, profane; ill-treat, maltreat, ill-use; fritter, waste; * n abuse, perversion, prostitution; ill-treatment, ill-use, misusage; misapplication, solecism.
mitigate vb abate, alleviate, assuage, lessen, moderate, palliate, relieve; allay, appease, calm, pacify, quell, quiet, soothe; moderate, temper; diminish, lessen.
mix vb alloy, blend, commingle, combine, compound, interlard, mingle; associate, join, unite; * n alloy, amalgam, blend, compound, mixture.
mixture n jumble, melange, mishmash; miscellany, variety.
moan vb bewail, grieve, groan, lament, sigh, weep; * n groan, lament, sigh, wail.
mob vb crowd, surround, swarm; pack, throng; * n assemblage, crowd, rabble, throng, tumult; populace, scum.
mobile adj changeable, fickle; expressive, inconstant, variable.
mock vb ape, counterfeit, imitate, mimic, take off; deride, gibe, insult, jeer, taunt; balk, cheat, deceive, defeat, dupe, illude, mislead; * adj assumed, false, feigned, make-believe, spurious; * n fake, imitation, sham; insult, jeer, taunt.
mockery n counterfeit, derision, imitation, jeering, ridicule, scoffing, scorn, sham, travesty.
model vb design, fashion, form, mould, plan, shape; * adj admirable, exemplary, ideal, worthy; * n archetype, design, mould, original, pattern, protoplast, type; dummy, example; copy, imitation, representation.
moderate vb appease, assuage, blunt, dull, lessen, soothe; mitigate, pacify, quell, quiet, reduce, repress, soften, still; diminish, qualify, slacken; control, govern; * adj frugal, sparing, temperate; limited; abstemious, sober; calm, cool, reasonable, steady; gentle, mild.
moderation n abstemiousness, forbearance, frugality, restraint, sobriety; composure, coolness, deliberateness, sedateness.
modern adj fresh, late, latest, new, new-fangled, novel, present, recent, up-to-date.
modest adj bashful, diffident, humble, meek, reserved,

retiring, shy, unobtrusive, unpretending, unpretentious; proper, pure, virtuous; becoming, decent.

modify vb alter, change, reform, shape, vary; lower, moderate, soften.

modish adj fashionable, stylish; ceremonious, conventional, courtly.

modulate vb attune, harmonise; inflict; adjust, proportion.

molest vb annoy, bore, bother, disquiet, disturb, harry, fret, inconvenience, pester, tease, torment, trouble, vex, worry.

mollify vb soften; appease, calm, compose, pacify, quiet, soothe; abate, assuage, blunt, dull, ease, lessen, mitigate, relieve, temper; qualify, tone down.

moment n flash, instant, second, wink; avail, consequence, consideration, force, gravity, significance, value, weight; drive, force, impetus.

momentous adj grave, important, serious, significant, weighty.

monarch n autocrat despot; chief, dictator, emperor, king, potentate, ruler, sovereign.

monastic adj coenobitic, convenual, monkish, secluded.

moneyed, **monied** adj affluent, opulent, rich, well-off, well-to-do, well-heeled.

monitor vb check, observe, oversee, supervise, watch; * n admonisher, admonitor, adviser, counsellor, instructor, overseer.

monopolise vb control, dominate, engross, forestall.

monotonous adj boring, dull, tedious, tiresome, uniform, unvarying, wearisome.

monster adj enormous, gigantic, huge, immense, monstrous; * n marvel, prodigy, wonder; brute, demon, fiend, ruffian, villain, wretch.

monstrous adj abnormal, unnatural; colossal, enormous, extraordinary, huge, immense, stupendous, vast; marvellous, wonderful; dreadful, flagrant, frightful, hideous, horrible, terrible.

monument n memorial, record, remembrance, testimonial; gravestone, mausoleum, memorial, tomb, tombstone.

mood n disposition, humour, temper, vein

moody adj capricious, humoursome; angry, crusty, fretful, ill-tempered, irritable, passionate, peevish, petulant, snappish, snarling, sour; dogged, glowering, glum, perverse, stubborn, sulky, sullen; abstracted, gloomy, melancholy, pensive, sad.

moral adj ethical, good, honest, honourable, just, virtuous; ideal, intellectual, mental; * n intent, meaning.

morals npl ethics, morality; behaviour, conduct, habits.

morbid adj ailing, corrupted, diseased, sick, tainted, unhealthy, unsound; depressed, gloomy, pessimistic, sensitive.

morning n aurora, daybreak, dawn, morn, sunrise.

morose adj austere, crabbed, dejected, downcast, gloomy, melancholy, moody, sad, sullen, surly.

morsel n bite, mouthful; bit, fragment, part, piece, scrap.

mortal adj deadly, destructive, fatal, final, human, perishable, vital; * n being, human, man, person, woman.

mortality n corruption, death, destruction, fatality.

mortify vb annoy, depress, disappoint, displease, disquiet, harass, plague, vex, worry; abase, abash, confound, restrain, shame; corrupt, fester, gangrene.

motherly adj affectionate, kind, maternal, paternal, tender.

motion vb beckon, direct, gesture, signal; * n action, change, drift, flux, movement, stir, transit; air, port; gesture, impulse, prompting; proposal,

proposition.
motive *adj* activating, driving, moving, operative; * *n* cause, consideration, ground, incentive, inducement, influence, occasion, prompting, purpose, reason, spur.
mould *vb* cast, fashion, form, make, model, shape; * *n* cast, character, form, matrix, pattern, shape; material, matter; matrix, pattern; blight, mildew, mouldiness, must, mustiness, rot; fungus, mushroom, rust, smut; earth, loam, soil.
mouldy *adj* decaying, fusty, mildewed, musty.
mount *n* eminence, mountain, peak; charger, horse, ride, steed; * *vb* ascend, climb, rise, soar, tower; ascend, climb, escalate, scale; get upon.
mountain *n* height, hill, mount peak; abundance, heap, stack.
mourn *vb* bewail, deplore, grieve, lament, sorrow, wail.
mouth *vb* clamour, declaim, rant, roar, vociferate; * *n* jaws; aperture, opening; entrance, inlet; mouthpiece, speaker.
move *vb* dislodge, drive, propel, push, shift, stir; actuate, incite, rouse; determine, induce, influence, persuade; affect, impress, touch, trouble; agitate, awaken, excite, irritate; propose; go, march, proceed, walk; act, live; flit, remove; * *n* action, movement.
movement *n* change, move, motion, passage; emotion, motion; crusade, drive.
moving *adj* impelling, persuasive; affecting, pathetic, touching.
muddle *vb* confuse, disarrange, disorder; stupefy; muff, spoil; * *n* confusion, disorder, mess.
muddy *vb* dirty, foul, soil; confuse, obscure; * *adj* dirty, foul, impure, slimy, turbid; confused, dull, heavy, stupid; confused, obscure, vague.
muffle *vb* cover, envelop, shroud, wrap; conceal, disguise, involve; deaden, stifle.
multiply *vb* augment, extend, increase, spread.
multitude *n* host, legion; army, assemblage, assembly, collection, crowd, horde, mob, swarm, throng; herd, mass, pack, populace, rabble.
mundane *adj* earthly, secular, temporal, terrestrial.
murder *vb* assassinate, butcher, destroy, kill, massacre, slaughter; abuse, mar, spoil; * *n* assassination, butchery, killing, manslaughter.
murderer *n* assassin, butcher, cut-throat, killer, slaughterer, slayer.
murderous *adj* barbarous, bloodthirsty, bloody, cruel, sanguinary, savage.
murky *adj* cheerless, cloudy, dark, dim, dusky, hazy, lowering, obscure.
murmur *vb* grumble, mumble, mutter; hum, whisper; * *n* complaint, grumble, mutter, plaint; hum, undertone, whisper.
muscular *adj* sinewy; athletic, brawny, powerful, stout, strong, sturdy, vigorous.
muse *vb* brood, consider, contemplate, dream, meditate, ponder, reflect, ruminate, speculate, think.
musical *adj* dulcet, harmonious, melodious, sweet-sounding, symphonious.
muster *vb* assemble, collect, congregate, convene, convoke, gather, meet, rally, summon; * *n* assemblage, assembly, collection, convocation, gathering, meeting, rally.
musty *adj* foul, mouldy, rank, sour; hackneyed, old, stale; ill-favoured, stale, vapid; dull, heavy.
mute *vb* dampen, moderate, soften; * *adj* dumb, voiceless; silent, still, taciturn.
mutilate *vb* cripple, damage, disable, disfigure, injure, mangle, mar.

mutinous *adj* insubordinate, rebellious, riotous, turbulent, unruly; insurgent.

mutiny *vb* rebel, revolt, resist; * *n* insubordination, revolt, revolution, riot, uprising.

mutter *vb* growl, grumble, mumble, murmur.

mutual *adj* common, correlative, interchangeable, interchanged, reciprocal.

mysterious *adj* abstruse, cabbalistic, concealed, cryptic, dark, dim, enigmatic, hidden, incomprehensible, inexplicable, mystic, mystical, obscure, puzzling, recondite, secret, unfathomable, unintelligible.

mystery *n* enigma, puzzle, riddle, secret; art, calling, trade.

mystical *adj* abstruse, dark, enigmatical, esoteric, hidden, inscrutable, obscure, occult, transcendental; emblematic, symbolic.

mystify *vb* confound, confuse, embarrass, obfuscate, puzzle.

myth *n* fable, legend; allegory, fiction, parable, story; falsehood, figment, lie.

mythical *adj* fabled, fabulous, fictitious, imaginary.

N

nab *vb* catch, clutch, grasp, seize.

nag *vb* carp, fuss, hector, henpeck, pester, torment, worry; * *n* scold; crock, hack, horse, pony, scrag.

nail *vb* attach, fasten, hammer, join, pin, secure, tack.

naïve *adj* artless, ingenuous, natural, plain, simple, unaffected, unsophisticated.

naked *adj* bare, nude, uncovered; denuded, unclad, unclothed, undressed; defenceless, exposed, open, unarmed, unguarded, unprotected; evident, manifest, open, plain, unconcealed, undisguised; bare, simple; bare, unfurnished, unprovided; plain, uncoloured, unvarnished.

name *vb* call, christen, denounce, dub, entitle, phrase, style, term; mention; denominate, designate, indicate, nominate, specify; * *n* appellation, denomination, designation, epithet, title; character, credit, reputation, repute; celebrity, distinction, honour, note, renown.

narrate *vb* chronicle, describe, detail, recite, recount, rehearse, relate, tell.

narrow *vb* confine, contract, cramp, limit, restrict; * *adj* circumscribed, confined, contracted, cramped, limited, pinched, scanty; bigoted, illiberal, ungenerous; close, near.

nasty *adj* dirty, filthy, foul, impure, loathsome, polluted, squalid, unclean; gross, indecent, indelicate, lewd, obscene, vile; disagreeable, disgusting, nauseous, odious, offensive, repulsive, sickening; aggravating, annoying.

nation *n* commonwealth, realm, state; community, people, population, tribe.

native *adj* aboriginal, autochthonal, indigenous; vernacular; intrinsic, natural; inherent, innate, natal; * *n* aborigine, autochthon, inhabitant, national, resident.

natural *adj* indigenous, native; essential, native; normal, regular; artless, genuine, spontaneous, unaffected; bastard, illegitimate.

nature *n* universe, world; character, constitution, essence; kind, species, sort; disposition, humour, mood, temper.

naughty *adj* bad, corrupt, mischievous, perverse.

nauseous *adj* disgusting, distasteful, loathsome, offensive, repulsive, revolting, sickening.

naval *adj* marine, maritime, nautical.

navigate *vb* cruise, direct, guide, pilot, steer.

near *vb* approach, draw close; * *adj* adjacent, contiguous, neighbouring; approaching, forthcoming; imminent, impending; familiar, intimate; close, immediate, short; accurate, close; close, narrow.

neat *adj* clean, orderly, tidy, trim; nice, smart, spruce, trim; pure, unadulterated, undiluted; adroit, clever, exact, finished; dainty.

nebulous *adj* cloudy, hazy, misty, obscure.

necessary *adj* inevitable, unavoidable; essential, expedient, indispensable, requisite; * *n* essential, necessity, requirement, requisite.

necessitate *vb* compel, constrain, force, impel, oblige.

necessitous *adj* distressed, indigent, moneyless, needy, penniless, poor; destitute.

necessity *n* inevitability, unavoidability; emergency, urgency; exigency, indigence, indispensability; need, poverty, want; essentiality, requirement, requisite; compulsion, destiny, fate.

necromancy *n* black art, black magic, demonology, magic, sorcery, voodoo, witchcraft.

need *vb* demand, lack, require, want; * *n* emergency, exigency, extremity, necessity, strait, urgency, want; destitution, distress, indigence, neediness, penury, poverty, privation.

needy *adj* destitute, indigent, necessitous, poor.

negation *n* denial, disclaimer, rejection, renunciation.

neglect *vb* disregard, forget, ignore, omit, overlook; * *n* carelessness, default, failure, heedlessness, inattention, omission, remissness.

negligence *n* carelessness, disregard, heedlessness, inattention, indifference, neglect, remissness, slackness, thoughtlessness.

negligent *adj* careless, heedless, inattentive, neglectful, regardless, thoughtless.

negotiate *vb* arrange, bargain, deal, sell, settle, transact.

neighbourhood *n* district, environs, locality, vicinage, vicinity; adjacency, nearness, propinquity, proximity.

neighbourly *adj* civil, friendly, kind, obliging, social.

nerve *vb* fortify, invigorate, strengthen; * *n* coolness, courage, endurance, firmness, fortitude, pluck, resolution, steadiness.

nervous *adj* irritable, fearful, shaky, timid, timorous, weak, weakly.

nestle *vb* cuddle, harbour, lodge, nuzzle, snuggle.

nettle *vb* exasperate, harass, incense, irritate, provoke, ruffle, sting, tease, vex.

neutral *adj* impartial, indifferent; colourless, mediocre.

nevertheless *adv* however, nonetheless, notwithstanding, yet.

new *adj* fresh, latest, modern, novel, recent, unused; reinvigorated, renovated, repaired.

nice *adj* accurate, correct, definite, delicate, exact, exquisite, precise; difficult; discerning, discriminating, particular, precise, scrupulous; neat, tidy, trim; fine, minute, refined, subtle; dainty, delicate, delicious, luscious, palatable, savoury, soft, tender; agreeable, delightful, good, pleasant.

nicety *n* accuracy, exactness, precision, truth; daintiness, fastidiousness; discrimination, subtlety.

nimble *adj* agile, alert, brisk, lively, prompt, quick, speedy, sprightly, spry, swift.

nipple *n* breast, mamilla, teat, tit, udder.

noble *adj* dignified, eminent, exalted, generous, great, honourable, illustrious, magnanimous, superior, worthy; aristocratic, patrician; grand, lordly, magnificent, splendid, stately; * *n* aristocrat, grandee, lord, peer.

noise *vb* report, rumour; * *n* ado, blare, clamour, clatter, cry, din, fuss, hubbub, outcry, pandemonium, racket, row, sound, tumult, uproar.

noisy *adj* blustering, boisterous, clamorous; loud, uproarious, tumultuous, vociferous.

nomadic *adj* migratory, pastoral, vagrant, wandering.

nominal *adj* inconsiderable, minimal, ostensible, professed, so-called, titular.

nominate *vb* appoint, choose, designate, name, present, propose.

nonchalant *adj* apathetic, careless, cool, indifferent, unconcerned.

nondescript *adj* amorphous, characterless, commonplace, dull, ordinary, uninteresting, unremarkable.

nonplus *vb* astonish, bewilder, confound, confuse, discomfit, disconcert, floor, perplex, puzzle.

nonsensical *adj* absurd, foolish, irrational, senseless, silly, stupid.

norm *n* pattern, rule, standard.

normal *adj* natural, ordinary, regular, usual.

notable *adj* distinguished, extraordinary, memorable, remarkable, signal; evident, plain, prominent, striking; notorious, rare, well-known; * *n* celebrity, dignitary, worthy.

note *vb* heed, mark, notice, observe, regard, remark; record, register; * *n* minute, record; comment, remark; indication, mark, sign, symbol, token; account, bill, catalogue, reckoning; epistle, letter; consideration, heed, observation; celebrity, consequence, credit, eminence, fame, renown, reputation, respectability; bill.

noted *adj* celebrated, eminent, famed, famous, illustrious, renowned, well-known.

notice *vb* mark, observe, perceive, regard, see; mention, remark; attend to, heed; * *n* cognisance, heed, observation, regard; advice, announcement, information, intelligence, mention, news; intimation, premonition, warning; comments, remarks.

notify *vb* advertise, announce, declare, publish; acquaint, apprise, inform.

notion *n* concept, conception, idea; apprehension, belief, conviction, impression, judgement, opinion, sentiment, view.

notoriety *n* celebrity, fame, figure, name, note, publicity, reputation, repute.

notorious *adj* apparent, evident, notable, obvious; manifest, patent, well-known; famed, famous, flagrant, infamous, noted, remarkable, renowned.

nourish *vb* feed, nurture; maintain, supply, support; educate, instruct, train; cherish, encourage, foment, foster, succour.

nourishment *n* food, nutriment, nutrition, sustenance.

novel *adj* fresh, modern, new, recent, unusual; * *n* fiction, romance, story, tale.

novice *n* initiate, neophyte, novitiate, probationer; apprentice, beginner, learner, tyro.

nucleus *n* basis, centre, core, focus, heart, kernel, nub.

nude *adj* bare, exposed, naked, unclothed, undressed.

nuisance *n* annoyance, bother, infliction, offence, pest, plague, trouble.

nullify vb abolish, annul, cancel, invalidate, negate, quash, repeal, revoke.

numb vb deaden, stupefy; * adj deadened, dulled, insensible, paralysed.

number vb calculate, compute, count, enumerate, reckon; account, reckon; * n digit, figure, numeral; multitude, throng; aggregate, collection, sum, total.

numerous adj abundant, many, numberless.

nuptial adj bridal, conjugal, connubial, matrimonial.

nuptials npl espousal, marriage, wedding.

nurse vb nourish, nurture; rear, suckle; cherish, encourage, feed, pamper, promote, succour; manage; * n auxiliary, orderly, sister; au pair, baby-sitter, nanny, nursemaid.

nurture vb feed, nourish, nurse, tend; educate, instruct, rear, school, train; * n diet, food, nourishment; education, instruction, schooling, training, tuition; attention, nourishing.

nutritious adj invigorating, nourishing, strengthening, supporting, sustaining.

O

oaf n blockhead, dolt, dunce, fool, idiot, simpleton.

oath n blasphemy, curse, expletive, imprecation, malediction; affirmation, pledge, promise, vow.

obdurate adj hard, rugged; cantankerous, dogged, firm, hardened, inflexible, insensible, obstinate, pigheaded, stubborn, unbending, unyielding.

obedience n acquiescence, agreement, compliance.

obese adj corpulent, fat, fleshy, gross, plump, podgy, portly, stout.

obey vb comply, conform, heed, mind, observe.

obfuscate vb cloud, darken, obscure; bewilder, confuse, muddle.

object vb demur, deprecate, disapprove of, except to, oppose, protest, refuse; * n particular, phenomenon, precept, reality, thing; aim, destination, end, mark, recipient, target; design, drift, goal, intention, motive, purpose.

objection n censure, difficulty, doubt, exception, protest, remonstrance, scruple.

obligation n responsibility; agreement, bond, contract, covenant, engagement, stipulation; debt, indebtedness, liability.

oblige vb bind, coerce, compel, constrain, force, necessitate, require; accommodate, benefit, convenience, favour, gratify, please; bind, obligate.

obliging adj accommodating, civil, considerate, kind, friendly, polite.

oblique adj aslant, inclined, sidelong, slanting; indirect, obscure.

obliterate vb delete, destroy, efface, eradicate, erase, expunge.

oblivious adj careless, heedless, inattentive, negligent.

obnoxious adj censurable, reprehensible; hateful, objectionable, obscene, odious, offensive, repellent, repugnant, repulsive, unpleasant.

obscene adj broad, coarse, filthy, gross, immodest, indecent, indelicate, ribald, unchaste, lewd, licentious, offensive, pornographic; disgusting, dirty, foul.

obscure vb becloud, befog, cloud, darken, eclipse, dim, obfuscate, shade; conceal, cover, hide; * adj dark, dim, dusky, gloomy, murky, shadowy, sombre, unenlightened, unilluminated; abstruse, difficult, doubtful, enigmatic, incomprehensible, indefinite, indistinct, intricate, involved, mysterious, mystic, undefined, unintelligible, vague; remote, secluded; humble, inglorious, nameless, undistinguished, unhonoured, unknown, unnoted, unnoticed.

obsequious *adj* cringing, deferential, fawning, flattering, servile, slavish, subservient, sycophantic.

observant *adj* attentive, heedful, mindful, perceptive, vigilant, watchful.

observation *n* notice; annotation, note, remark; experience, knowledge, note.

observe *vb* eye, mark, notice, remark, watch; behold, detect, discover, perceive, see; express, mention, remark, say; comply, follow, fulfil, obey; regard.

obsess *vb* bedevil, consume, engross, grip, haunt, possess.

obsolete *adj* ancient, antiquated, antique, archaic, disused, neglected, old, old-fashioned, out-of-date, passé.

obstacle *n* barrier, difficulty, hindrance, impediment, interruption, obstruction, snag, stumbling block.

obstinate *adj* dogged, firm, headstrong, inflexible, immovable, intractable, mulish, obdurate, persistent, pertinacious, resolute, stubborn, unyielding, wilful.

obstruct *vb* bar, barricade, block, blockade, up, choke, clog, close, jam, obturate, stop; hinder, impede, oppose, prevent, stop; arrest, check, retard.

obstruction *n* bar, barrier, block, check, difficulty, hindrance, impediment, obstacle, stoppage; clog, hindrance, obturation.

obtain *vb* acquire, attain, earn, elicit, get, procure, secure.

obtrusive *adj* interfering, intrusive, meddling, officious.

obtuse *adj* boneheaded, dense, dopey, dull, insensitive, retarded, slow, stupid, thick, uncomprehending, unintelligent; blunt, rounded.

obvious *adj* exposed, open; apparent, clear, distinct, evident, manifest, patent, perceptible, plain, self-evident, unmistakable, visible.

occasion *vb* cause, create, originate, produce; induce, influence, move, persuade; * *n* event, incident, occurrence; conjuncture, convenience, juncture, opening, opportunity; necessity, need; exigency, requirement, want; cause, ground, reason; inducement, influence; circumstance, exigency.

occasional *adj* accidental, casual, incidental, infrequent, irregular, uncommon.

occupation *n* holding, occupancy, possession, tenure, use; business, calling, craft, employment, job, post, profession, trade, vocation.

occupy *vb* capture, hold, keep, possess; fill, inhabit, take up, tenant; engage, employ.

occur *vb* appear, arise; befall, chance, eventuate, happen, result.

odd *adj* additional, redundant, remaining; casual, incidental; inappropriate, unsuitable; eccentric, erratic, grotesque, irregular, peculiar, quaint, singular, strange, uncommon, unique, unusual, whimsical.

odds *npl* difference, inequality; advantage, superiority; probability.

odious *adj* detestable, hateful; hated, obnoxious, unpopular; disagreeable, forbidding, loathsome, offensive.

odorous *adj* aromatic, balmy, fragrant, perfumed, redolent, scented.

odour *n* aroma, fragrance, perfume, redolence, scent, smell.

offence *n* assault, attack; anger, displeasure, indignation, resentment, umbrage, wrath; affront, harm, injury, insult, outrage, wrong; crime, misdeed, misdemeanour, sin, transgression, trespass.

offend *vb* affront, annoy, chafe, displease, gall, irritate, mortify, nettle, provoke, vex; molest, shock, wound; sin, transgress.

offender *n* convict, criminal, culprit, felon, malefactor, sinner, transgressor, trespasser.

offensive *adj* attacking, invading; disgusting, loathsome, nauseating, sickening; abominable, detestable, displeasing, hateful, obnoxious, repugnant, revolting, shocking, unpalatable, unpleasant; repugnant; impertinent, insolent, insulting, irritating, rude, unpleasant; * *n* attack, onslaught.

offer *vb* present, proffer, tender; propose, propound, show; volunteer; endeavour; * *n* overture, proffering, proposal, proposition, tender; overture; attempt, bid, endeavour.

offhand *adj* abrupt, brusque, casual, curt, unpremeditated, unstudied; * *adv* carelessly, casually, clumsily, haphazardly, slapdash; ad-lib, extemporarily.

officer *n* agent, bureaucrat, dignitary, executive, official, representative.

officiate *vb* act, perform, preside, serve.

officious *adj* busy, dictatorial, forward, interfering, meddling, obtrusive, pushing, pushy.

offset *vb* balance, counteract, counterbalance, counterpoise; * *n* branch, offshoot, scion, shoot, sprout; counterbalance, counterpoise, set-off.

offspring *n* brood, children, descendants, issue, progeny; cadet, child, scion.

often *adv* frequently, generally, repeatedly.

ogre *n* demon, devil, goblin, hobgoblin, monster, spectre.

old *adj* aged, ancient, antiquated, antique, archaic, elderly, obsolete, superannuated; decayed, worn-out; former, preceding, pre-existing.

omen *n* augury, auspice, foreboding, portent, presage, sign, warning.

ominous *adj* inauspicious, monitory, portentous, premonitory, threatening.

omission *n* default, forgetfulness, neglect, oversight.

omit *vb* disregard, drop, exclude, miss, neglect, overlook, skip.

omnipotent *adj* all-powerful, almighty.

onerous *adj* burdensome, difficult, hard, heavy, laborious, oppressive, weighty.

one-sided *adj* partial, prejudiced, unfair, unilateral, unjust.

only *adj* alone, single, sole, solitary; * *adv* barely, merely.

onset *n* assault, attack, charge, onslaught, storm.

ooze *vb* shed; drain, exude, leak, percolate, transude; * *n* mire, mud, slime.

opaque *adj* dark, dim, hazy, muddy; abstruse, cryptic, enigmatic, enigmatical, obscure, unclear.

open *vb* expand, spread; begin, commence, initiate; disclose, reveal, show; unbar, unclose, unlock; * *adj* expanded, extended, unclosed; aboveboard, artless, candid, cordial, fair, frank, guileless, hearty, honest, sincere, undisguised, unreserved; free, generous, liberal; ajar, unclosed, uncovered; exposed; clear, unobstructed; accessible, public, unenclosed; apparent, debatable, evident, obvious, patent, plain, undetermined.

opening *adj* commencing, first, inaugural, introductory; * *n* aperture, breach, chasm, cleft, fissure, gap, gulf, hole, loophole, orifice, rent;

beginning, commencement, dawn; chance, opportunity, vacancy.
openly *adv* candidly, frankly, honestly, plainly, publicly.
operate *vb* act, function, work; cause, produce; manipulate, use; run, work.
operation *n* manipulation, performance, procedure, proceeding, process; action, affair.
operative *adj* active, effective, effectual, serviceable, vigorous; important, indicative, influential, significant; * *n* artisan, employee, labourer, mechanic, worker, workman.
opinion *n* conception, judgment, sentiment, view; belief, persuasion; estimation, favourable judgment.
opinionated *adj* biased, cocksure, conceited, dogmatic, stubborn.
opponent *adj* antagonistic, contrary, opposing, opposite; * *n* adversary, antagonist, competitor, contestant, counter-agent, enemy, foe, opposite, party, rival.
opportune *adj* appropriate, auspicious, convenient, favourable, fortunate, lucky, propitious, seasonable, suitable, timely.
oppose *vb* combat, contravene, counteract, dispute, obstruct, resist; check, prevent; obstruct; confront, counterpoise.
opposite *adj* facing, fronting; conflicting, contradictory, contrary; adverse, hostile, inimical, repugnant; * *n* contrary, converse, reverse.
opposition *n* antagonism, antimony, contrariety; counteraction, hostility, resistance; hindrance, obstacle, obstruction.
oppress *vb* burden, crush, harass, load, maltreat, overburden, overpower, overwhelm, persecute, subdue, suppress, tyrannise.
oppression *n* abuse, cruelty, injury, injustice, misery, persecution, severity, tyranny; depression, dullness, heaviness.
oppressive *adj* close, muggy, stifling, suffocating, sultry.
option *n* choice, discretion, election, preference, selection.
optional *adj* discretionary, elective, nonobligatory, voluntary.
opulent *adj* affluent, luxurious, moneyed, plentiful, rich, sumptuous, wealthy.
opus *n* brainchild, composition, creation, piece, production, works.
oral *adj* spoken, verbal, vocal.
oration *n* address, declamation, discourse, speech.
orbit *vb* circle, encircle, revolve around; * *n* course, path, revolution, track.
ordain *vb* appoint, call, elect, establish, institute; decree, enjoin, enact, order, prescribe.
order *vb* adjust, arrange, regulate, systematise; conduct, manage; bid, command, direct, instruct, require; * *n* arrangement, regularity, symmetry, system; law, regulation, rule; discipline, peace, quiet; command, commission, direction, injunction, instruction, mandate, prescription; class, degree, grade, kind, rank; brotherhood, class, fraternity; sequence, succession.
orderly *adj* methodical, regular, systematic; peaceable, quiet, well-behaved; neat, shipshape, tidy.
ordinary *adj* accustomed, customary, established, everyday, normal, regular, settled; common, frequent, habitual, usual; average, commonplace, indifferent, inferior, mediocre, second-rate, undistinguished; homely, plain.
organ *n* device, implement, instrument, tool; element, member, part, structure, unit; agency, channel, forum,

journal, medium, mouthpiece, newspaper, publication, voice.

organise *vb* constitute, form, shape; arrange, correlate, establish, systematise.

orgy *n* debauch, debauchery, revel, saturnalia.

origin *n* beginning, birth, commencement, cradle, derivation, foundation, fountain, root, source, spring, starting point; cause, occasion; birth, heritage, lineage, parentage.

original *adj* aboriginal, first, primary, primeval, primordial; fresh, inventive, novel; eccentric, odd, peculiar; * *n* archetype, exemplar, model, pattern, prototype, protoplast, type.

originate *vb* arise, begin, emanate, flow, proceed, rise, spring; create, form, invent, produce.

ornament *vb* adorn, beautify, bedeck, decorate, deck, emblazon, garnish, grace; * *n* adornment, bedizenment, decoration, design, garnish.

ornate *adj* beautiful, decorated, elaborate, elegant, florid, flowery, ornamented.

orthodox *adj* conventional, correct, sound.

ostensible *adj* apparent, assigned, avowed, declared, exhibited, manifest, presented, visible; professed.

ostentatious *adj* boastful, dashing, flaunting, pompous, pretentious, showy, vain; gaudy.

ostracise *vb* banish, exclude, excommunicate, exile, expatriate, expel.

oust *vb* dislodge, dispossess, eject, evict, expel.

outbreak *n* eruption, explosion, outburst; affray, conflict, commotion, riot, row; flare-up, manifestation.

outcast *n* exile, expatriate; castaway, pariah, vagabond.

outcome *n* conclusion, result, upshot.

outcry *n* scream, screech, yell; clamour, noise, tumult.

outdo *vb* beat, exceed, excel, outstrip, outvie, surpass.

outlandish *adj* alien, exotic, foreign, strange; bizarre, strange.

outlaw *vb* ban, banish, condemn, forbid, make illegal, prohibit; * *n* bandit, brigand, crook, highwayman, lawbreaker, robber, thief.

outline *vb* draft, draw, plan, silhouette, sketch; * *n* contour, profile; draft, drawing, plan, silhouette, sketch.

outlive *vb* last, live longer, survive.

outlook *n* future, prospect, sight, view; lookout, watch-tower.

outrage *vb* injure, insult, offend, shock; * *n* abuse, affront, indignity, insult, offence.

outrageous *adj* atrocious, enormous, flagrant, heinous, monstrous, villainous; excessive, extravagant, unwarrantable.

outskirts *n* borders, boundary, edge, periphery, suburbs, vicinity.

outstanding *adj* due, owing, uncollected, ungathered, unpaid, unsettled; conspicuous, eminent, prominent, striking.

outward *adj* exterior, external, outer, outside.

outwit *vb* cheat, circumvent, deceive, defraud, diddle, dupe, gull, outmanoeuvre, overreach, swindle.

overawe *vb* browbeat, cow, daunt, frighten, intimidate, scare, terrify.

overbalance *vb* capsize, overset, overturn, tumble, upset; outweigh, preponderate.

overbearing *adj* oppressive, overpowering; arrogant, dictatorial, dogmatic, domineering, haughty, imperious, supercilious.

overcast *vb* cloud, overcloud, overshadow, shade, shadow; * *adj* cloudy, hazy, murky,

obscure.
overcome *vb* beat, conquer, crush, defeat, overpower, overthrow, overturn, overwhelm, rout, subdue, subjugate, vanquish; conquer, prevail.
overhaul *vb* overtake; check, examine, inspect, repair, survey; * *n* check, examination, inspection.
overlook *vb* inspect, oversee, superintend, supervise; disregard, miss, neglect, slight; condone, excuse, forgive, pardon, pass over.
override *vb* outweigh, pass, quash, supersede, surpass.
overrule *vb* annul, cancel, nullify, recall, reject, repeal, repudiate, rescind, revoke, reject, set aside, supersede, suppress.
oversight *n* charge, control, direction, management, superintendence, supervision; error, fault, lapse, mistake, neglect, omission, slip.
overt *adj* apparent, glaring, open; manifest, patent, public, unconcealed.
overthrow *vb* overturn, upset; demolish, destroy, level; beat, conquer, crush, defeat, master, overpower, overwhelm, rout, subjugate, vanquish, worst; * *n* downfall; destruction, demolition, ruin; defeat, dispersion, rout.
overturn *vb* invert, overthrow, reverse, upset.
overture *n* invitation, offer, proposal, proposition.
overwhelm *vb* drown, engulf, inundate, submerge, swallow up, swamp; conquer, crush, defeat, overcome, overpower, subdue, vanquish.
overwrought *adj* overdone, overelaborate; agitated, excited, overexcited.
own *vb* have, hold, possess; acknowledge, admit, allow, avow, concede, confess; * *adj* particular, personal, private.
owner *n* landlord, master, mistress, proprietor.

P

pace *vb* go, hurry, move, step, walk; * *n* amble, step, walk.
pacify *vb* appease, conciliate, tranquillise; allay, appease, assuage, calm; compose, mollify, quell, quiet, smooth, soften, soothe, still.
pack *vb* compress, crowd, fill; bundle, load, stow; * *n* bale, bundle, packet, parcel; burden, load; assembly, assortment, collection, set; band, clan, company, crew, gang, knot, lot, set, squad.
pact *n* agreement, alliance, bargain, bond, contract, convention, covenant, league, stipulation.
pagan *adj* heathen, idolatrous, irreligious; * *n* gentile, heathen, idolater.
pain *vb* agonise, distress, hurt, rack, sting, torment, torture; afflict, aggrieve, annoy, bore, chafe, displease, grieve, harass, trouble, vex, worry; smart, sting, twinge; * *n* ache, agony, anguish, discomfort, distress, hurt, pang, smart, soreness, sting, suffering, torment, torture, twinge; affliction, anguish, anxiety, care, disquiet, distress, grief, heartache, misery, sorrow, vexation.
painful *adj* agonising, racking, tormenting, torturing; afflicting, disagreeable, displeasing, disquieting, distressing, dolorous, grievous, provoking, troublesome, unpleasant, vexatious; arduous, careful, difficult, hard, severe, sore.
pains *npl* care, effort, labour, task; childbirth, labour, travail.
painstaking *adj* assiduous, careful, conscientious, diligent, hard-working, industrious, persevering, plodding, strenuous.

paint *vb* depict, draw, figure, pencil, portray, represent, sketch; adorn, embellish, ornament; * *n* colouring, dye, pigment, stain; cosmetics, greasepaint, make-up.

pair *vb* couple, marry, match; * *n* brace, couple, double, duo, match, twosome.

pale *vb* blanch, lose colour, whiten; * *adj* ashen, ashy, blanched, bloodless, pallid, sickly, wan, white; dim, obscure, spectral; * *n* picket, stake; circuit, enclosure; district, region, territory; boundary, confine, fence, limit.

pall *n* cloak, cover, curtain, mantle, shield, shroud, veil; * *vb* cloy, glut, gorge, satiate, surfeit; deject, depress, discourage, dishearten, dispirit; cloak, cover, drape, overspread, shroud.

pallid *adj* ashen, cadaverous, colourless, pale, sallow, wan, whitish.

palpable *adj* corporeal, material, tangible; evident, glaring, gross, intelligible, manifest, obvious, patent, plain, unmistakable.

palpitate *vb* flutter, pulsate, throb; shiver, tremble.

paltry *adj* diminutive, feeble, inconsiderable, insignificant, miserable, petty, slight, sorry; trifling, trivial, unimportant, wretched.

pan *n* pot, saucepan, vessel; * *vb* look for, search for, separate; censure, criticise, knock, lambast, put down, slam.

pang *n* agony, anguish, distress, pain, throe, twinge.

panic *vb* alarm, scare, startle, terrify; become terrified, overreact; * *n* alarm, fear, fright, terror.

pant *vb* blow, gasp, puff; heave, palpitate; gasp, languish; desire, hunger, long, thirst, yearn; * *n* blow, gasp, puff.

parable *n* allegory, fable, story.

parade *vb* display, flaunt, show; * *n* ceremony, display, flaunting, ostentation, pomp; array, pageant, spectacle; mall, promenade.

parallel *vb* compare, conform, correlate, match; * *adj* abreast, concurrent; allied, analogous, correspondent, equal, like, similar; * *n* conformity, likeness; analogue, counterpart.

paramount *adj* chief, dominant, pre-eminent, principal, superior, supreme.

paraphernalia *n* accoutrements, appendages, baggage, effects, equipment, ornaments, trappings.

parasite *n* bloodsucker, flunky, hanger-on, leech, spaniel, sycophant, toady, wheedler.

pardon *vb* condone, forgive, overlook, remit; absolve, acquit, excuse, release; * *n* absolution, amnesty, condonation, discharge, excuse, forgiveness, grace, mercy, overlook, release.

parentage *n* ancestry, birth, descent, family, lineage, origin, pedigree, stock.

parity *n* correspondence, equality, sameness, similarity.

parody *vb* caricature, imitate, lampoon, mock, ridicule, satirise; * *n* caricature, imitation, ridicule, satire.

part *vb* dismember, divide, sever, subdivide, sunder; detach, disconnect, disjoin, dissociate, separate; allot, apportion, distribute, divide, mete, share; * *n* division, fraction, fragment, piece, portion, remnant, scrap, section, segment, subdivision; component, constituent, element, ingredient, organ; lot, share; concern, interest; allotment, apportionment, dividend; business, charge, duty, function, office, work; concern, faction, interest, side; character, cue, lines, role; clause, paragraph,

passage.
partial *adj* fractional, limited; biassed, interested, prejudiced, prepossessed, unfair, unjust; fond, indulgent.
participate *vb* engage in, partake, share.
particle *n* atom, bit, corpuscle, crumb, drop, glimmer, grain, granule, iota, mite, molecule, morsel, mote, scrap, shred, speck.
particular *adj* special, specific; distinct, individual, separate, special; characteristic, distinctive; individual, own, peculiar, personal, private; notable, special; definite, detailed, exact, narrow, precise; careful, close, critical, nice, scrupulous, strict; marked, notable, odd, peculiar, strange, uncommon: * *n* circumstance, detail, feature, instance, item, regard, respect.
parting *adj* dividing, separating; final, last, valedictory; declining; * *n* breaking, disruption, rupture, severing; detachment; departure, farewell.
partisan *adj* biased, factional, interested, partial, prejudiced; * *n* adherent, backer, disciple, follower, supporter.
partner *n* associate, colleague, partaker, participant; accomplice, ally, confederate; companion, consort, spouse.
partnership *n* association, company, firm, society; connection, interest, union.
parts *npl* accomplishments, endowments, faculties, genius, gifts, intellect, mind, qualities, powers, talents; districts, regions.
party *n* alliance, association, circle, clique, confederacy, faction, group, junta, league, ring, set; body, company, detachment, squad, troop; assembly, company, gathering; participant, sharer; defendant, litigant, plaintiff, individual, somebody; cause, division, interest, side.
pass *vb* devolve, fall, proceed; change, lapse; cease, die, expire, fade, vanish; happen, occur; convey, deliver, send, transmit, transfer; disregard, ignore, neglect; exceed, excel, surpass; ratify, sanction; answer, do, succeed, suffice, suit; deliver, pronounce, utter; beguile, wile; * *n* avenue, road, route, way; gorge, passage, ravine; authorisation, licence, passport, permission, ticket; condition, conjecture, situation, state; push, thrust; transfer, trick.
passable *adj* allowable, mediocre, moderate, ordinary, so-so, tolerable; acceptable, current, receivable; navigable.
passage *n* going, progress, transit; evacuation, journey, migration, transit, voyage; avenue, channel, course, pass, path, road, route, thoroughfare, way; access, entry, reception; act, deed, event, feat, incidence, occurrence; corridor, gallery, gate, hall; clause, paragraph, text; course, death, decease, departure, lapse; affair, change, combat, conflict, contest, encounter, exchange, pass.
passenger *n* fare, itinerant, tourist, traveller, voyager.
passionate *adj* animated, ardent, burning, earnest, enthusiastic, excited, fervent, fiery, furious, hot-blooded, impassioned, impulsive, intense, vehement, zealous; hot-headed, irascible, quick-tempered, tempestuous.
passive *adj* inactive, inert, receptive; apathetic, enduring, patient, stoical, submissive, suffering, unresisting.
past *adj* accomplished, elapsed, ended, gone, spent; ancient, bygone, former, obsolete; * *adv* above, extra, beyond, over; * *prep* above, after, beyond, exceeding; * *n* antiquity, history.

paste *n* adhesive, cement, glue, gum; * *vb* cement, fasten, fix.

pastime *n* amusement, diversion, entertainment, hobby, recreation, sport.

pat *vb* hit, rap, tap; caress, fondle, pet; * *n* dab, hit, rap, tap; caress; * *adj* appropriate, apt, pertinent, suitable; * *adv* aptly, conveniently, opportunely, seasonably.

patch *vb* mend, repair; * *n* repair; parcel, plot, tract.

patent *adj* open; apparent, clear, conspicuous, evident, glaring, indisputable, manifest, obvious, open, palpable, plain, unconcealed, unmistakable; * *n* copyright, privilege, right.

path *n* avenue, course, footway, passage, road, route, track, trail, way.

pathetic *adj* moving, pitiable, plaintive, sad, tender, touching.

patience *n* endurance, fortitude; calmness, composure, leniency; assiduity, constancy, diligence, indefatigability, perseverance, persistence.

patient *adj* uncomplaining; calm, composed, contented, quiet; indulgent, lenient; assiduous, constant, diligent, indefatigable, persevering, persistent; * *n* case, invalid, subject, sufferer.

patron *n* advocate, defender, favourer, guardian, protector, supporter.

pattern *vb* copy, follow, imitate; * *n* archetype, exemplar, model, original, paradigm, plan, prototype; example, guide, sample, specimen; paragon; design, shape, style.

pause *vb* cease, delay, desist, rest, stay, stop, wait; delay, forbear, intermit, stay, stop, tarry, wait; deliberate, demur, hesitate; * *n* cessation, halt, intermission, interruption, interval, remission, rest, stoppage, suspension; break, paragraph.

pawn *n* dupe, plaything, puppet, tool, toy; * *vb* hazard, lay, pledge, risk, stake, wager; * *n* assurance, bond, guarantee, pledge, security.

pay *vb* discharge, foot, honour, quit, settle; compensate, recompense, reimburse, reward; punish, revenge; give, offer, render; * *n* allowance, commission, compensation, hire, reimbursement, reward, salary, wages.

peace *n* calm, quiet, stillness; accord, friendliness, harmony; composure, equanimity, imperturbability, placidity, quietude, tranquillity; accord, agreement, armistice.

peaceable *adj* pacific; amiable, friendly, gentle, inoffensive, mild; placid, quiet, serene, still, tranquil, undisturbed.

peaceful *adj* quiet, undisturbed; amicable, friendly, gentle, harmonious, pacific; calm, composed, placid, serene, still.

peak *vb* climax, top; dwindle, thin; * *n* apex, crest, crown, pinnacle, summit, top, zenith.

peculiar *adj* idiosyncratic, individual; eccentric, odd, queer, rare, singular, strange, uncommon, unusual; especial, particular, select, specific.

peculiarity *n* distinctiveness, individuality; characteristic, idiosyncrasy, individuality, peculiarity, singularity, speciality.

pedigree *adj* thoroughbred; * *n* ancestry, breed, descent, extraction, family, genealogy, house, line, lineage, race, stock, strain.

peel *vb* decorticate, flake off, pare, skin, strip off; * *n* epicarp, peeling, rind, skin.

peer *vb* gaze, look, peek, peep, pry, squint; appear, emerge; * *n* associate, co-equal, companion, equal, equivalent, fellow, like, match; aristocrat, baron, count, duke, earl, grandee, lord, marquis, noble, nobleman, viscount.

pelt vb assail, batter, beat, belabour, bombard, pepper, stone, strike; cast, hurl, throw; hurry, rush, speed, tear; * n coat, hide, skin.

pen vb compose, draft, inscribe, write; coop, enclose, impound, imprison, incarcerate; * n cage, coop, crib, hutch, enclosure, paddock, pound, stall, sty.

penalty n chastisement, fine, forfeiture, punishment, retribution.

penetrate vb bore, burrow, enter, invade, pervade, pierce, soak; affect, sensitise, touch; comprehend, discern, perceive, understand.

penetrating adj piercing, sharp, subtle; acute, clear-sighted, discerning, intelligent, keen, quick, sharp-witted, shrewd.

penitent adj conscious-stricken, contrite, regretful, remorseful, repentant, sorrowful; * n penitentiary, repentant.

penniless adj impecunious, moneyless, poor; necessitous, needy, poverty-stricken.

pensive adj contemplative, dreamy, meditative, reflective, sober, thoughtful; grave, melancholic, mournful, sad, serious, solemn.

people vb colonise, inhabit, populate; * n clan, country, family, nation, race, state, tribe; folk, population, public; populace, proletariat; mob, multitude, rabble.

perceive vb behold, detect, discern, discover, discriminate, distinguish, notice, observe, recognise, remark, spot; appreciate, comprehend, know, understand.

perception n apprehension, cognition, recognition, seeing; comprehension, consciousness, discernment, perceptiveness, perceptivity, understanding; feeling.

peremptory adj absolute, authoritative, commanding, decisive, express, imperious, positive; determined, resolute, resolved; incontrovertible.

perennial adj ceaseless, constant, continual, deathless, enduring, imperishable, permanent, perpetual, unceasing, unfailing, uninterrupted.

perfect vb complete, elaborate, finish; * adj completed, finished; complete, full, whole; capital, consummate, excellent, exquisite, faultless, ideal; accomplished, expert, skilled; blameless, faultless, immaculate, pure, spotless, unblemished.

perfection n completion, consummation, correctness, excellence, faultlessness, finish, perfectness, wholeness; beauty, quality.

perfectionist n formalist, precisionist, purist, stickler.

perform vb accomplish, do, effect, transact; complete, discharge, execute, meet, observe, satisfy; act, play, represent.

performance n achievement, consummation, discharge, execution, fulfilment; act, deed, exploit; composition, production; entertainment, exhibition, play; hold; execution, playing.

perfume n aroma, bouquet, fragrance, incense, odour, redolence, scent, smell.

perfunctory adj careless, formal, indifferent, mechanical, negligent, reckless, slight, thoughtless, unmindful.

perhaps adv perchance, possibly.

peril vb endanger, jeopardise, risk; * n danger, hazard, jeopardy, pitfall, risk, snare, uncertainty.

period n aeon, age, epoch, season, span, spell, stage, term, time; continuance, duration; bound, conclusion, end, limit, termination; clause, phrase, proposition, sentence.

periodical adj intermittent, recurrent, regular, seasonal;

* *n* magazine, paper, review, serial, weekly.

perish *vb* decay, shrivel, waste, wither; decease, die, expire.

perishable *adj* decomposable, destructible; dying, mortal, temporary.

permanent *adj* abiding, constant, durable, enduring, fixed, immutable, lasting, perpetual, persistent, stable, standing, unchanging, unfading, unmovable.

permissible *adj* admissible, allowable, lawful, legal, legitimate, unprohibited.

permission *n* allowance, authorisation, consent, dispensation, leave, licence, sufferance, toleration, warrant.

permit *vb* allow, endure, tolerate; authorise, consent, empower, license, warrant; * *n* leave, liberty, licence, passport, permission, sanction, warrant.

permutation *n* alteration, change, shift, transposition.

perpetrate *vb* commit, do, execute, perform.

perpetual *adj* ceaseless, constant, endless, eternal, everlasting, incessant, interminable, never-ending, perennial, permanent, unceasing, unending, unfailing.

perplex *vb* complicate, encumber, entangle, involve, snarl, tangle; beset, bewilder, confound, confuse, distract, mystify, nonplus, pother, puzzle, set; annoy, bother, harass, pester, tease, trouble, vex, worry.

persecute *vb* afflict, distress, harass, molest, oppress, worry; annoy, beset, pester, tease.

persevere *vb* continue, determine, endure, persist, remain, resolve, stick.

persist *vb* continue, endure, last, remain; insist.

personable *adj* good-looking, graceful, seemly, well turned-out.

personal *adj* individual, peculiar, private, special; bodily, corporeal, material, physical.

perspective *n* panorama, view, vista; proportion, relation.

perspire *vb* glow, sweat, swelter.

persuade *vb* allure, entice, impel, incite, induce, lead, move, urge; advise, counsel; convince, satisfy; inculcate, teach.

persuasion *n* incitement, inducement, influence; belief, conviction, creed, doctrine, dogma, opinion, kind, sort.

pert *adj* brisk, dapper, lively, nimble, smart, sprightly; bold, flippant, forward, free, impertinent, impudent, presuming, saucy.

pertinent *adj* applicable, apposite, appropriate, apropos, apt, fit, germane, proper, relevant, suitable; belonging, concerning, pertaining, regarding.

perturb *vb* agitate, disquiet, disturb, trouble, unsettle, upset, vex, worry; confuse, disturb.

pervade *vb* affect, extend, fill, imbue, impregnate, infiltrate, penetrate, permeate.

perverse *adj* bad, disturbed, oblique; contrary, dogged, headstrong, obstinate, stubborn, ungovernable; intractable, unyielding, wayward, wilful; cantankerous, churlish, cross, crusty, cussed, petulant, snarling, spiteful, surly, testy, touchy, wicked, wrong-headed; inconvenient, troublesome, untoward, vexatious.

perversion *n* abasement, corruption, debasement, impairment, injury.

perverted *adj* corrupt, debased, distorted, evil, impaired, misguiding, wicked.

pessimistic *adj* cynical, dejected, depressed, despondent, downhearted, gloomy, glum, melancholy, morose, sad.

pest *n* disease, epidemic, pestilence, plague; annoyance, bane, curse, nuisance, scourge, trouble.

pestilent *adj* contagious, infectious, malignant, pestilential; deadly, evil, injurious, malign, mischievous, noxious, poisonous; annoying, corrupt, pernicious, vexatious.

petition *vb* ask, crave, entreat, pray, sue, supplicate; * *n* address, appeal, application, entreaty, request, supplication, suit.

petrify *vb* calcify, fossilise, lapidify; deaden; astonish, astound, confound, paralyse, stun, stupefy.

petty *adj* frivolous, inferior, insignificant, slight, small, trifling, trivial, unimportant.

petulant *adj* acrimonious, choleric, crabbed, cross, fretful, hasty, ill-humoured, ill-tempered, irascible, irritable, peevish, perverse, pettish, querulous, testy, touchy, waspish.

phantom *n* apparition, ghost, illusion, spectre, vision, wraith.

phase *n* aspect, chapter, condition, development, juncture, period, point, stage, state, time.

phenomenal *adj* marvellous, miraculous, prodigious, wondrous.

philanthropy *n* altruism, benevolence, charity, grace, humanitarianism, humanity, kindness.

philosophical, philosophic *adj* rational, reasonable, sound, wise; composed, cool, serene, stoical, tranquil, unruffled.

phlegmatic *adj* apathetic, calm, dull, heavy, impassive, indifferent, inert, sluggish, stoical, tame, unfeeling.

phobia *n* aversion, detestation, dislike, dread, fear, hatred.

phrase *vb* call, denominate, designate, dub, name, style; * *n* diction, expression, phraseology, style.

physical *adj* material, natural; bodily, corporeal, external, substantial, tangible.

pick *vb* peck, strike; detach, gather, pluck; choose, cull, select; acquire, collect, get; pilfer, steal; * *n* pickaxe, toothpick.

picture *vb* draw, imagine, paint, represent; * *n* drawing, engraving, painting, print; copy, illustration, image, likeness, portrayal, semblance, representation, resemblance, similitude; description, representation.

picturesque *adj* beautiful, charming, colourful, graphic, scenic, striking.

piece *vb* mend, patch; enlarge, increase; join, unite; * *n* amount, bit, chunk, cut, fragment, part, scrap, shred, slice; portion; article, item, object; composition, work, writing.

pierce *vb* gore, impale, pink, prick, stab; bore, drill, penetrate, perforate, puncture; affect, strike, touch.

piety *n* devotion, devoutness, holiness, godliness, grace, sanctity.

pile *vb* accumulate, amass; collect, gather, heap; * *n* accumulation, collection, heap, mass, stack; building, edifice, erection, fabric, structure, tower; reactor, nuclear reactor; beam, column, pillar, pole, post; down, feel, finish, fur, fluff, fuzz, grain, shag, surface, texture.

pilgrim *n* traveller, wanderer, wayfarer; crusader, devotee, palmer.

pill *n* capsule, pellet, pilule, tablet; oral contraceptive.

pillar *n* column, pier, post, shaft, stanchion; maintainer, prop, support, upholder.

pilot *vb* direct, guide, navigate, steer; * *adj* experimental, model, trial; * *n* helmsman, navigator, steersman; airman, aviator, director.

pinch vb compress, contract, cramp, nip, squeeze; afflict, famish, oppress, stint; frost; apprehend, arrest; economise, spare, stint; * n pang, throe; crisis, difficulty, emergency, exigency, oppression, pressure, push, strait, stress.

pine vb decay, droop, fade, flag, languish, wilt, wither; desire, long, yearn.

pinnacle n minaret, turret; apex, peak, summit, top, zenith.

pious adj devout, godly, holy, reverential, righteous, saintly.

pirate vb copy, crib, plagiarise, reproduce, steal; * n buccaneer, marauder, privateer, seadog, sea-robber, sea-rover, sea wolf.

pit vb match, oppose; gouge, hole, mark, notch, scar; * n cavity, hole, hollow; crater, dent, depression, excavation; abyss, chasm; pitfall, snare, trap: auditorium, orchestra.

pitch vb fall, lurch, plunge, reel; settle, rest; cast, fling, heave, hurl, launch, plunge, send, toss, throw; erect, establish, fix, place, set, settle, station; * n degree, extent, height, intensity, modulation, rate; declivity, descent, inclination, slope; cast, plunge, throw, toss; place, position, spot; field, ground; line, patter.

piteous adj affecting, distressing, grievous, mournful, pathetic, sorrowful, woeful; deplorable, lamentable, miserable, wretched; compassionate, tender.

pithy adj cogent, energetic, forcible, powerful; compact, concise, brief, laconic, pointed, substantial, terse; corky, porous.

pitiful adj compassionate, kind, lenient, merciful, sympathetic, tender, tenderhearted; deplorable, lamentable, miserable, pathetic, wretched; contemptible, despicable, disreputable, insignificant, mean, paltry, rascally, sorry, vile, worthless.

pitiless adj cruel, hardhearted, implacable, inexorable, merciless, relentless, unfeeling, unrelenting, unsympathetic.

pity vb commiserate, condole, sympathise; * n clemency, commiseration, compassion, condolence, humanity, leniency, mercy, quarter, sympathy.

place vb arrange, commit, deposit, dispose, install, locate, orientate, pitch, plant, pose, put, seat, set, settle, situate, stand, rest; allocate, arrange, classify, identify, order; appoint, assign, commission, establish, induct; * n area, square; bounds, district, division, locality, location, part, position, premises, region, scene, site, spot, tract; calling, charge, employment, function, occupation, office, post; calling, condition, grade, precedence, rank, sphere, stakes, standing; abode, building, dwelling, mansion, residence, seat; city, town, village; fortress, stronghold; part, passage, portion; ground, occasion, opportunity, reason, room; lieu, stead.

placid adj calm, composed, cool, equable, gentle, quiet, serene, tranquil, undisturbed, unexcitable, unruffled; halcyon, mild, serene.

plagiarise vb appropriate, borrow, crib, infringe, lift, pirate, steal, thieve.

plague vb afflict, annoy, bore, bother, chafe, disquiet, distress, disturb, embarrass, harass, gall, harry, hector, irritate, molest, tease, torment, trouble, vex, worry; * n disease, pestilence, pest; affliction, annoyance, curse, molestation, nuisance, torment, trouble, vexation.

plain adj even, flat, smooth, uniform; open, unencumbered;

apparent, certain, clear, conspicuous, evident, distinct, glaring, manifest, notable, obvious, open, palpable, patent, unmistakable; transparent, visible; explicit, unambiguous, unequivocal; homely, ugly; aboveboard, blunt, crude, candid, direct, frank, honest, open, sincere, straightforward, undesigning, unreserved, unsophisticated: artless, common, natural, simple, unsophisticated; absolute, mere, unmistakable; clear, direct, easy; frugal, homely, simple; artless, natural, simple, unaffected; unadorned, unornamented, * n grassland, plateau, prairie, steppe.

plan vb arrange, devise, diagram, figure, premeditate, project, represent, study; concoct, conspire, contrive, design, hatch, invent, manoeuvre, plot, prepare, project, scheme; * n chart, diagram, draught, drawing, layout, map, plot, sketch; design, idea, method, programme, project, proposal, proposition, scheme, system; cabal, conspiracy, intrigue, machination; custom, process, way.

plane vb flatten, even, level, smooth; float, fly, glide, skim; * adj even, flat, horizontal, level, smooth; * n evenness, level, levelness, smoothness; aeroplane, aircraft; scraper.

plant vb bed, sow; breed, engender; direct, set; furnish, inhabit; establish, introduce; fix, found, hide; * n organism, vegetable; establishment, equipment, factory, works.

plaque n badge, medal, panel, plate, slab, tablet.

plaster vb bedaub, coat, cover, smear; * n cement, gypsum, mortar.

plastic adj ductile, flexible, formative, mouldable, pliable, pliant.

platitude n dullness, flatness, insipidity, mawkishness; banality, commonplace, truism; chatter, fudge, jargon, palaver, stull, trash, twaddle.

play vb caper, frolic, gambol, revel, sport; flirt, toy, trifle; flutter, wave; act, impersonate, perform, personate, represent; bet, gamble, stake, wager; * n amusement, frolic, game, jest, pastime, prank, romp, sport; gambling, gaming; act, comedy, drama, farce, performance, tragedy; action, motion, movement; elbowroom, freedom, latitude, movement, opportunity, range, scope, sweep, swing, use.

playful adj frisky, frolicsome, kittenish, merry, rollicking, sportive; amusing, humorous, jolly, lively, mirthful, roguish, sprightly, vivacious.

plead vb appeal, argue, reason; argue, defend, reason; appeal, beg, beseech, entreat, implore, petition, supplicate.

pleasant adj agreeable, nice, pleasing, pleasurable, seemly, welcome; cheerful, enlivening, gracious, likable, lively, merry, sportive, sprightly, vivacious; amusing, humorous, jocular, witty.

please vb charm, delight, elate, gladden, gratify, rejoice; content, oblige, satisfy; choose, like.

pleasure n comfort, delight, delectation, elation, joy, gladness, gratification, gratifying, satisfaction, amusement, diversion, entertainment, indulgence, refreshment; gratification, luxury, sensuality; choice, desire, preference, purpose, will, wish; favour, kindness.

pledge vb mortgage, pawn, plight; bind, contract, engage, promise; * n collateral, deposit, pawn; guarantee, security; hostage, security.

plentiful adj abundant, ample,

copious, full; enough, fruitful, luxuriant, plenteous.

plenty *n* abundance, affluence, copiousness, enough, fertility, fruitfulness, fullness, overflow, plenteousness, plentifulness, plethora, profusion.

plethora *n* repletion; excess, redundance, redundancy, superabundance, superfluity, surfeit.

pliable *adj* flexible, limber, lithe, lithesome, supple; adaptable, ductile, facile, manageable, obsequious, tractable, yielding.

plight *n* condition, dilemma, imbroglio, mess, muddle, pass, predicament, scrape, situation, state, strait; * *vb* contract, covenant, engage, pledge, promise, propose, swear, vow; * *n* avowal, contract, covenant, oath, pledge, promise, vow, word; betrothal, engagement.

plot *vb* connive, conspire, intrigue, scheme; concoct, contrive, devise, hatch, plan, project; chart, map; * *n* blueprint, chart, diagram, outline, plan; combination, complicity, connivance, conspiracy, intrigue, plan, project, scheme, stratagem; script, story, theme, thread, topic; field, lot, parcel, patch, piece, plat, tract.

pluck *vb* cull, gather, pick; jerk, pull, snatch, tear, tug; * *n* backbone, bravery, courage, daring, determination, force, grit, hardiness, heroism, indomitability, mettle, nerve, resolution, spirit, valour.

plum *n* bonus, cream, find, pick, prize, treasure; * *adj* best, choice, first-class, prize.

plump *adj* bonny, bouncing, buxom, chubby, corpulent, fat, fleshy, full-figured, obese, portly, rotund, round, sleek, stout, well-rounded; distended, full, swollen, tumid; blunt, complete, direct, full; * *vb* dive, drop, plunge, plunk, put; choose, favour, support.

plunder *vb* despoil, devastate, fleece, harry, loot, maraud, pillage, raid, ransack, ravage, rifle, rob, sack, spoil; * *n* marauding, rapine, robbery, sack; booty, pillage, prey, spoil.

ply *vb* employ, exert, manipulate, wield; exercise, practise; assail, beset, press; importune, urge; offer, present; * *n* fold, layer, twist; bent, bias, direction, turn.

pocket *vb* appropriate, steal; endure, suffer, tolerate; * *n* cavity, hollow, pouch.

poignant *adj* intense, pierce, sharp; acrid, biting, piquant, pungent, sharp, stinging; irritating, keen, mordant, pointed, satirical, severe.

point *vb* sharpen; aim, direct, level; indicate, show; * *n* needle, nib, pin, spike, stylus, tip; cape, headland, projection, promontory; instant, moment, period, verge; place, site, spot, station; condition, degree, state; aim, design, intent, limit, object, purpose; nicety, pique, trifle; position, question, text, theme, thesis; aspect, matter, respect; characteristic, peculiarity; character, mark, stop; dot, speck; epigram, quip, witticism; poignancy, sting.

point-blank *adj* categorical, direct, explicit, express, plain; * *adv* categorically, directly, flush, fall, right, straight.

pointless *adj* blunt, obtuse; aimless, dull, fruitless, futile, meaningless, vague, stupid.

poise *vb* balance, float, hang, hover, support, suspend; * *n* aplomb, balance, composure, dignity, equilibrium.

poison *vb* contaminate, corrupt, defile, embitter, envenom, infect, intoxicate, pollute, taint; * *adj* deadly, lethal, toxic; * *n* bane, contagion, pest, taint, toxin, venom, virulence, virus.

poisonous *adj* corruptive, deadly,

fatal, noxious, pestilential, toxic, venomous.
poke *vb* jab, push, shove, thrust; interfere, meddle, pry, snoop; * *n* jab, push, shove, thrust; bag, pocket, pouch, sack.
polar *adj* Antarctic, Arctic, cold, extreme, freezing, glacial, terminal; antagonistic, antipodal, antithetical, contradictory, contrary, diametric, opposed, opposite.
policy *n* administration, government, management; plan, platform, role; art, address, prudence, shrewdness, skill, stratagem, strategy, tactics; acumen, astuteness, shrewdness, wisdom, wit.
polish *vb* brighten, buff, glaze, gloss, shine, smooth; civilise, refine; * *n* brightness, lustre; accomplishment, elegance, finish, grace, refinement.
polite *adj* attentive, affable, chivalrous, civil, courtly, courteous, cultivated, elegant, gallant, genteel, gentle, gracious, mannerly, obliging, polished, refined, suave, urbane, well-bred, well-mannered.
politic *adj* civic, political; astute, discreet, judicious, provident, prudent, prudential, wary, wise; artful, crafty, cunning, diplomatic, expedient, foxy, ingenious, intriguing, shrewd, skilful, sly, strategic, subtle, unscrupulous, wily; well-adapted, well-devised.
political *adj* civic, national, politic, public.
pollute *vb* defile, foul, soil, taint; contaminate, corrupt, debase, deprave, impair, infect, poison, stain, tarnish; desecrate, profane; abuse, defile, deflower, ravish, violate.
pollution *n* contamination, corruption, defilement, impurity, pollutedness, taint, uncleanness, vitiation.
pomp *n* display, grandeur, magnificence, ostentation, pageant, pageantry, parade, pride, show, splendour, state, style.
pompous *adj* boastful, bombastic, dignified, grand, inflated, lofty, magisterial, ostentatious, pretentious, showy.
ponder *vb* cogitate, consider, contemplate, deliberate, examine, meditate, muse, reflect, study, weigh.
poor *adj* necessitous; destitute, impecunious, insolvent, penniless, poverty-stricken, seedy; emaciated, gaunt, lean, lank, skinny, spare, thin; barren, fruitless, sterile, unfertile, unproductive; flimsy, inadequate, insignificant, insufficient, slight, trivial, unimportant, worthless; delicate, feeble, frail, infirm, unsound, weak; inferior, seedy, shabby, valueless, worthless; contemptible, despicable, humble, inferior, low, paltry, pitiful, shabby; barren, cold, dry, dull, feeble, frigid, languid, mean, tame, week; ill-fated, ill-starred, luckless, miserable, pitiable, unhappy, wretched; deficient, imperfect, inadequate, insufficient, meagre, scant, small; faulty, unsatisfactory; scanty.
popular *adj* plebeian, public; comprehensible, easy, plain; acceptable, accredited, admired, approved, favoured, liked, praised, received; current, prevailing, prevalent: cheap, inexpensive.
porous *adj* absorbent, absorptive, penetrable, permeable, pervious, spongy.
port *n* anchorage, harbour, haven, shelter; door, entrance, gate, passageway; * *n* air, appearance, bearing, behaviour, demeanour, deportment, presence.
portent *n* augury, omen, sign, warning; marvel, phenomenon, wonder.
portion *vb* allot, distribute,

divide, parcel; endow, supply;
* *n* bit, fragment, piece, scrap,
section; allotment, dividend,
division, quantity, quota,
ration, share; inheritance.

portray *vb* act, draw, depict,
describe, represent; paint,
picture, sketch; position.

pose *vb* arrange, bewilder,
confound, dumbfound,
perplex, place, puzzle, set;
affect; * *n* attitude, posture;
affectation, air, facade,
mannerism, pretence, role.

position *vb* arrange, fix, locate,
place, set, site, stand; * *n*
locality, place, post, site,
situation, station; relation;
attitude, bearing, posture;
affirmation, principle,
proposition, thesis; dignity,
honour, rank, standing, status;
circumstance, condition, phase,
place, state; berth, billet, post.

positive *adj* categorical, defined,
definite, determinate, explicit,
express, expressed, precise,
unequivocal, unmistakable;
actual, real, substantial, true,
veritable; assured, certain,
confident, convinced, sure;
decisive, indisputable,
inescapable; imperative,
unconditional, undeniable;
decided, emphatic, obstinate,
overbearing, stubborn,
tenacious.

possess *vb* control, have, hold,
keep, obsess, obtain, occupy,
own.

possession *n* ownership; control,
occupancy, tenancy, tenure;
bedevilment, lunacy, madness,
obsession; (*pl*) assets, estate,
property, wealth.

possible *adj* conceivable,
contingent, imaginable;
accessible, feasible, likely,
practical, workable.

post *vb* advertise, announce,
inform, publish; brand,
disgrace, vilify; enter, slate,
register; establish, fix, place,
put, station; drop, dispatch,
mail; * *n* column, picket, pillar,
stake, support; employment,
office, place, position, seat,
situation, station; courier,
express, mercury, messenger;
dispatch, haste, hurry, speed.

posterity *n* descendants,
offspring, progeny; brood,
children, family, heirs, issue.

postpone *vb* adjourn, defer,
delay, procrastinate, retard.

posture *vb* pose; * *n* attitude,
pose, position; condition,
disposition, mood, state.

potent *adj* forceful, intense,
powerful, strong; able,
capable, mighty, powerful,
puissant, strong; cogent,
influential, powerful.

pottery *n* ceramics, earthenware, stone ware, terra cotta.

pound *vb* beat, strike, thump;
bray, crush, levigate, pulverise;
confound, enclose, impound;
* *n* enclosure, fold, pen.

pour *vb* cascade, flood, flow,
issue, rain, shower, stream.

poverty *n* impecuniosity,
indigence, need, neediness,
penury, privation, straits,
want; beggary, mendicancy,
pauperism, pennilessness;
dearth, jejuneness, lack,
scantiness; meagreness;
exiguity, paucity, poorness;
humbleness, inferiority,
lowliness; barrenness,
sterility, unproductiveness.

power *n* ability, capability,
competency, faculty, might,
potency, talent; energy, force,
strength; capacity; faculty,
gift, talent; ascendancy,
authority, command, control,
domination, dominion,
government, influence,
pressure, proxy, puissance,
rule, sovereignty, sway,
warrant; governor, monarch,
potentate, ruler, sovereign;
army, troop.

powerful *adj* mighty, potent,
puissant; muscular, robust,
strong, sturdy, vigorous; able,
commanding, dominating,
forceful, forcible, overpowering;

effective, effectual, efficacious, efficient, energetic, influential, operative, valid.

practical *adj* matter-of-fact, pragmatic, pragmatical; practised, proficient, qualified, trained; skilled, thoroughbred, versed; effective, useful, virtual, workable.

practice *n* custom, habit, method, repetition; procedure, use; application, exercise, pursuit; action, acts, behaviour, dealing, proceeding.

practise *vb* apply, do, exercise, perform, perpetrate, pursue.

practised *adj* able, accomplished, experienced, practical, proficient, qualified, skilled, thoroughbred, trained, versed.

praise *vb* approbate, acclaim, applaud, commend; celebrate, compliment, eulogise, extol, flatter; adore, bless, exalt, glorify, magnify, worship; * *n* acclaim, approval; encomium, glorification, laud, laudation; exaltation, extolling, homage, tribute, worship; celebrity, distinction, fame, glory, honour, renown; desert, merit, praiseworthiness.

pray *vb* ask, beg, beseech, entreat, implore, importune, invoke, petition, request, solicit, supplicate.

prayer *n* beseeching, entreaty, imploration, petition, request, suit, supplication; devotion(s), litany, invocation, praise, suffrage.

preach *vb* declare, deliver, proclaim, publish; inculcate, press, teach, urge; exhort, lecture, moralise.

precarious *adj* doubtful, dubious, hazardous, insecure, perilous, risky, uncertain, unsettled, unstable, unsteady.

precaution *n* care, caution, foresight, providence, prudence, safeguard; anticipation, premonition, provision.

precede *vb* antedate, forerun, head, herald, lead, utter.

precedent *n* antecedent, authority, custom, model, pattern, procedure, standard, usage.

precept *n* bidding, charge, command, decree, edict, injunction, instruction, law, mandate, ordinance, order, regulation; direction, doctrine, maxim, principle, teaching, rubric, rule.

precinct *n* border, bound, boundary, confine, environs, enclosure, limit, list, march, neighbourhood; area, district.

precious *adj* costly, invaluable, priceless, prized, valuable; adored, beloved, cherished, dear, idolised, treasured; fastidious, precise.

precipitate *vb* advance, dispatch, expedite, forward, further, hurry, press, quicken, speed; * *adj* hasty, hurried, headlong, impetuous, overhasty, rash, reckless; abrupt, sudden.

precipitous *adj* cliffy, craggy, perpendicular, uphill; sheer, steep.

precise *adj* accurate, correct, definite, exact, explicit, express, nice, severe, strict, unequivocal, well-defined; careful, exact, scrupulous, strict; ceremonious, formal, punctilious, rigid, stiff.

precision *n* accuracy, correctness, definiteness, exactitude, exactness, nicety.

precocious *adj* advanced, forward, premature.

precondition *n* essential, must, necessity, prerequisite, requirement.

precursor *n* antecedent, forerunner, predecessor; harbinger, messenger, pioneer; omen, presage, sign.

predatory *adj* greedy, pillaging, plundering, predacious, rapacious, ravenous, voracious.

predicament *n* attitude, case, condition, plight, situation, state; conjecture, corner, dilemma, emergency, fix, hole,

impasse, mess, pass, pinch, quandary, scrape.
predict vb augur, divine, forebode, forecast, foresee, forespeak, foretell, forewarn, portend, prognosticate, prophesy, read, signify, soothsay.
predominant adj ascendant, controlling, dominant, prevailing, prevalent, ruling, sovereign, supreme.
pre-eminent adj chief, excellent, peerless, predominant, renowned, superior, supreme, surpassing, transcendent, unequalled.
pre-empt vb acquire, anticipate, appropriate, arrogate, assume, seize, take over, usurp.
preface vb begin, introduce, launch, open, precede; * n foreword, introduction, preamble, preliminary, prelude, prelusion, premise, prologue, prolusion.
prefer vb offer, present, tender; advance, elevate, promote, raise; adopt, elect, fancy, pick, select, wish.
preference n advancement, choice, election, estimation, priority, selection.
preferment n advancement, dignity, elevation, exaltation, promotion.
pregnant adj big, parturient; fraught, full, important, replete, weighty; fecund, fertile, fruitful, impregnating, potential, procreative, productive, prolific.
prejudice vb bias, influence, turn; damage, diminish, hurt, impair, injure; * n bias, intolerance, partiality, preconception, predilection, pre-judgment, unfairness; damage, detriment, harm, hurt, impairment, injury, loss.
preliminary adj antecedent, initiatory, introductory, precedent, precursory, preparatory, previous, prior; * n beginning, initiation, introduction, opening, preamble, preface, prelude, start.
prelude n introduction, opening, overture; preamble, preface, preliminary.
premature adj hasty, precipitate, unmatured, unprepared, unripe, untimely.
premeditation n deliberation, design, forethought, intention, predetermination, purpose.
premise vb introduce, preamble, preface, prefix; * n argument, assertion, assumption, basis, foundation, ground, hypothesis, presupposition, proposition, support, thesis, theorem.
premium n bonus, bounty, encouragement, fee, gift, meed, payment, prize, recompense, remuneration, reward; appreciation, enhancement.
premonition n forewarning, indication, omen, portent, presage, presentiment, sign, warning.
preoccupied adj absentminded, abstracted, engrossed, inattentive, lost, musing, unobservant.
prepare vb adjust, fit, qualify; arrange, concoct, fabricate, make, order, plan, provide.
prepossessing adj alluring, attractive, bewitching, captivating, charming, engaging, fascinating, inviting, winning.
preposterous adj absurd, exorbitant, foolish, improper, irrational, monstrous, nonsensical, ridiculous, unfit, unreasonable, wrong.
prescribe vb advocate, command, decree, dictate, direct, establish, institute, ordain, order.
presence n attendance, nearness, occupancy, propinquity, proximity, residence, ubiquity, vicinity; air, appearance, carriage, demeanour.
present adj near; current, happening, immediate, instant; available, quick, ready;

attentive, favourable; * n now, time being, today; benefaction, boon, donation, gift, grant, gratuity, offering; * vb exhibit, offer; bestow, give, grant; deliver, hand; advance, prefer, tender.

presently adv anon, directly, forthwith, immediately, soon.

preservation n conservation, maintenance, protection, support; safety, salvation, security; integrity, keeping, soundness.

preserve vb defend, guard, keep, protect, rescue, save, secure, shield; maintain, sustain, support, uphold; conserve, economise, husband, retain; * n compote, confection, jam, jelly, marmalade; enclosure.

preside vb control, direct, govern, officiate.

press vb crowd, crush, squeeze; flatten, iron, smooth; clasp, hug; force, compel, constrain; enforce, enjoin, urge; hasten, push, rush; crowd, throng; entreat, importune; * n crowd, crush, multitude, throng; hurry, pressure, urgency; case, closet, repository.

pressure n compressing, crushing, squeezing; influence; force; compulsion, hurry, persuasion, press, stress, urgency; affliction, calamity, embarrassment, grievance, oppression; impression, stamp.

prestige n credit, distinction, influence, reputation, weight.

presume vb anticipate, assume, believe, conjecture, expect, suppose, think; consider, presuppose, suppose; dare, undertake, venture.

presumption n anticipation, assumption, belief, concession, conjecture, guess, hypothesis, supposition; arrogance, assurance, audacity, boldness, brass, effrontery, forwardness, haughtiness.

presumptuous adj arrogant, assuming, audacious, bold, brash, forward, irreverent, insolent; overconfident, rash.

pretence n affectation, cloak, disguise, mask, semblance, show, veil, window dressing; excuse, evasion, fabrication, feigning, pretext, sham, subterfuge; claim.

pretend vb affect, counterfeit, dissemble, fake, falsify, feign, sham, simulate; act, imagine, lie, profess; aspire, claim.

pretext n affectation, cover, device, excuse, guise, ploy, pretence, ruse, semblance, show, veil.

pretty adj attractive, beautiful, bonny, comely, elegant, fair, handsome, neat, trim; * adv fairly, moderately, quite, rather, somewhat.

prevailing adj controlling, dominant, effectual, general, influential, overruling, persuading, predominant, ruling, successful.

prevalent adj ascendant, compelling, governing, predominant, successful, superior; extensive, general, rife, widespread.

prevaricate vb cavil, deviate, dodge, equivocate, evade, palter, quibble, shift, shuffle.

prevent vb bar, check, debar, deter, forestall, hinder, impede, inhibit, intercept, interrupt, obstruct, prohibit, restrain, save, stop.

prevention n anticipation, deterrent, frustration, hindrance, interception, interruption, obstruction, preclusion, prohibition, restriction.

previous adj antecedent, earlier, foregoing, foregone, former, preceding, prior.

previously adv at one time, before, beforehand, earlier, formerly, heretofore, hitherto, in advance, in the past, once, then, until now.

prey vb devour, feed on, live off; exploit, intimidate, terrorise;

burden, haunt, oppress, worry; * *n* booty, loot, plunder, rapine, spoil; food, game, kill, quarry, victim; depredation, ravage.

price *vb* assess, estimate, evaluate, rate, value; * *n* amount, cost, expense, outlay, value; charge, estimation, figure, quotation, rate, valuation, value, worth; compensation, return, reward.

priceless *adj* dear, expensive, invaluable, precious, valuable; amusing, comic, droll, funny, humorous, rich.

prick *vb* perforate, pierce, puncture; drive, impel, incite, spur; cut, hurt, pain, sting, wound; hasten, ride, spur; * *n* mark, perforation, point, puncture; sting, wound.

pride *vb* boast, brag, preen, revel in; * *n* conceit, self-esteem, self-importance, vanity; arrogance, haughtiness, hauteur, loftiness, lordliness, pomposity, presumption, superciliousness, vainglory; decorum, dignity, elevation, loftiness, self-respect; decoration, glory, ornament, show, splendour.

priest *n* churchman, clergyman, ecclesiastic, minister, pastor, presbyter.

prim *adj* demure, formal, precise, prudish, stiff, strait-laced.

primary *adj* aboriginal, earliest, first, initial, original, primeval, primordial; chief, main, principal; basic, elementary, fundamental; radical.

prime *adj* aboriginal, first, initial, original, primeval, primordial; chief, foremost, highest, leading, main, paramount, principal; blooming, early; capital, cardinal, dominant; excellent, first-class, optimal, optimum, quintessential; beginning, initial, opening; * *n* beginning, dawn, morning, opening; spring, springtime, youth; bloom, flower, height, heyday, optimum, quintessence, zenith; * *vb* charge, load, prepare; coach, groom, train, tutor.

primitive *adj* aboriginal, first, original, primal, primary, prime, primordial; antiquated, crude, quaint, simple; formal, grave, prim.

princely *adj* regal, royal; august, grand, magnanimous, magnificent, majestic, noble, pompous, splendid, superb, royal, titled; dignified, elevated, lofty, noble, stately.

principal *adj* capital, cardinal, chief, first, foremost, highest, leading, main; * *n* chief, head, leader; head teacher, master.

principle *n* cause, fountain, groundwork, nature, origin, source, spring; basis, essence; assumption, axiom, law, postulation; doctrine, dogma, impulse, maxim, opinion, precept, rule, theory; motive, reason; equity, goodness, honesty; honour, integrity, justice, rectitude, truth, uprightness, virtue, worth; faculty, power.

print *vb* engrave, impress, mark, stamp; issue, publish; * *n* book, publication; copy, engraving, photograph, picture; font, lettering, type, typeface.

pristine *adj* ancient, earliest, first, former, old, original, primary, primitive.

privacy *n* concealment, secrecy, retirement, seclusion, solitude.

private *adj* retired, secluded, solitary; individual, own, personal, special, unofficial; confidential, privy; concealed, hidden, secret; * *n* GI, soldier, tommy.

privilege *n* advantage, claim, favour, franchise, immunity, leave, liberty, licence, right.

prize *vb* appreciate, esteem, treasure, value; * *adj* champion, first-rate, outstanding, winning; * *n* honours, meed, premium, reward; cup,

decoration, laurels, medal, trophy; booty, capture, plunder, spoil; advantage, gain, privilege.

probable *adj* apparent, credible, likely, reasonable.

probably *adv* apparently, likely, maybe, perhaps, presumably, possibly.

probation *n* examination, ordeal, proof, test, trial; novitiate.

probe *vb* examine, explore, fathom, investigate, scrutinise, search, test, verify; * *n* examination, exploration, inquiry, investigation, scrutiny, study.

probity *n* candour, equity, fairness, faith, honesty, honour, incorruptibility, integrity, justice, loyalty, morality, principle, sincerity, truthfulness, uprightness, veracity, virtue, worth.

problem *adj* difficult, intractable, uncontrollable; * *n* dilemma, doubt, enigma, exercise, proposition, puzzle, riddle.

problematic *adj* debatable, disputable, enigmatic, puzzling, questionable, suspicious, uncertain.

procedure *n* conduct, course, custom, method, operation, policy, practice, process; act, action, deed, performance, proceeding, step.

proceed *vb* advance, continue, go, pass, progress; arise, come, ensue, flow, follow, issue, result, spring.

proceeds *npl* balance, earnings, effects, gain, income, produce, profits, returns.

process *vb* advance, deal with, fulfil, handle, progress; alter, convert, refine; * *n* advance, course, progress, train; action, conduct, measure, mode, performance, practice, procedure, proceeding, step, way; action, case, suit, trial; outgrowth, protuberance.

procession *n* cavalcade, cortege, file, march, parade.

proclaim *vb* advertise, announce, broach, broadcast, cry, declare, herald, publish, trumpet; ban.

procrastinate *vb* adjourn, defer, delay, postpone, retard; neglect, omit; lag, loiter.

procure *vb* acquire, gain, get, obtain; cause, contrive, effect.

prodigal *adj* abundant, excessive, extravagant, generous, lavish, profuse, reckless, thriftless, wasteful; * *n* spendthrift, waster.

produce *vb* show; bear, beget, breed, engender, furnish, generate, procreate, yield; achieve, cause, create, effect, make, occasion, originate; afford, give, impart, make; extend, protract; fabricate, manufacture; * *n* crop, fruit, harvest, vegetables, yield.

product *n* crops, fruits, outcome, proceeds, production, returns, yield; consequence, effect, fruit, issue, performance, production.

production *n* fruit, produce, product; construction, creation, erection, making, performance; fruition; birth, breeding, development, growth; opus, work; extension, lengthening.

productive *adj* copious, fertile, fruitful, luxuriant, plenteous, prolific, teeming; constructive, creative, life-giving, producing.

productivity *adv* abundance, output, productive capacity, work rate, yield.

profane *vb* defile, desecrate, pollute, violate; abuse; * *adj* godless, heathen, pagan, temporal, unconsecrated, unhallowed, unholy, worldly; impure, polluted, unconsecrated, unhallowed, unholy; secular, temporal, worldly.

profess *vb* acknowledge, affirm, allege, avow, confess, declare, own, proclaim, state; affect, feign.

profession *n* acknowledgement,

assertion, avowal, claim, declaration; avocation, evasion, pretence, pretension, protestation, representation; business, calling, employment, occupation, trade, vocation.

proficiency n advancement, forwardness; accomplishment, competency, dexterity, skill.

proficient adj able, accomplished, adept, competent, conversant, dextrous, expert, masterly, practised, skilful, trained, qualified; * n adept, expert, master.

profit vb advance, benefit, gain, improve; * n aid, earnings, fruit, gain, lucre, produce; advancement, advantage, interest, service, use, utility, weal.

profound adj deep, fathomless; heavy, undisturbed; erudite, learned, sagacious, skilled; heartfelt, intense, lively, strong, touching; submissive; abstruse, obscure, occult, subtle, recondite; complete.

profuse adj abundant, excessive, extravagant, exuberant, generous, improvident, lavish, plentiful, prodigal.

progress vb advance, proceed; better, gain, increase; * n advance, advancement, progression; course, headway, ongoing; betterment, increase, reform: circuit.

prohibit vb debar, hinder, preclude, prevent; ban, forbid, inhabit.

prohibitive adj forbidding, prohibiting, refraining, restrictive.

project vb cast, eject, fling, hurl, propel, shoot, throw; brew, design, devise, intend, plan, plot, purpose, scheme; draw, exhibit; bulge, extend, protrude; * n contrivance, design, device, intention, plan, purpose, scheme.

projectile n bullet, missile, rocket, shell.

projection n delivery, ejection, emission, throwing; contriving, designing, planning, scheming; bulge, outshoot, prominence, protuberance, salience, salient, spur; map, plan.

prolific adj abundant, fertile, fruitful, productive, teeming.

prolong vb continue, extend, protract, sustain; defer.

prominent adj convex, jutting, projecting, raised, relieved; conspicuous, eminent, famous, foremost, influential, leading, main; conspicuous, distinctly, important, manifest, marked, principal.

promiscuous adj confused, indiscriminate, intermingled, miscellaneous, mixed; abandoned, dissipated, immoral, licentious, loose, wanton.

promise vb pledge, subscribe, swear, underwrite, vow; attest, guarantee, warrant; agree, bargain, engage, undertake; * n agreement, assurance, contract, engagement, oath, pledge, profession, vow, word.

promising adj auspicious, encouraging, hopeful, likely.

promote vb advance, aid, assist, cultivate, further, help; dignify, exalt, graduate, pass, prefer, raise.

promotion n advancement, encouragement; elevation, exaltation.

prompt vb dispose, impel, incite, incline, instigate, stimulate, urge; dictate, hint, influence, suggest; * adj active, apt, quick, ready; forward, hasty; inclined; exact, immediate, instant, precise, seasonable, timely; * adv directly, forthwith, immediately, promptly; * n cue, hint, reminder.

prone adj flat, horizontal, prostrate; inclined, inclining, apt, bent, predisposed, tending; eager, ready.

pronounce vb articulate, frame, say, speak, utter; announce, assert, declare, deliver.

proof *adj* firm, fixed, stable, steadfast; * *n* examination, ordeal, test, trial; attestation, conclusion, confirmation, corroboration, demonstration, evidence, substantiation, testimony, verification.

prop *vb* bolster, brace, buttress, shore, stay, support, sustain, truss, uphold; * *n* brace, support, stay; brace, fulcrum, pin.

propaganda *n* advertising, agitprop, brainwashing, disinformation, promotion, publicity.

propel *vb* drive, force, impel, urge; cast, fling, hurl, throw.

proper *adj* individual, inherent, natural, original, particular, peculiar, special; adapted, appropriate, becoming, befitting, decent, decorous, demure, fit, fitting, legitimate, meet, respectable, right, seemly, suitable; accurate, exact, fastidious, formal, just; actual, real.

property *n* attribute, quality, trait, virtue; belongings, circumstances, effects, estate, goods, resources, wealth; ownership, possession, tenure; copyright, participation, right, title.

prophecy *n* augury, divination, forecast, portent, prediction, presage, prognostication; exhortation, preaching.

prophesy *vb* augur, divine, foretell, predict, prognosticate.

proportion *vb* adjust, graduate, regulate; form, shape; * *n* arrangement, relation; adjustment, dimension, distribution, symmetry; extent, lot, part, ratio, share.

proposal *n* design, motion, offer, overture, proposition, tender.

propose *vb* move, offer, pose, present, propound, put, state, suggest, tender; design, intend, mean.

proposition *vb* accost, proffer, solicit; * *n* offer, overture, project, proposal, tender, undertaking; affirmation, assertion, declaration, dictum, doctrine, position, postulation, statement, theorem, thesis.

propound *vb* advance, advocate, contend, lay down, postulate, present, propose, put forward, set forth, submit, suggest.

propriety *n* accuracy, adaptation, appropriation, correctness, fitness, reasonableness, rightness, seemliness; conventionality, decency, decorum, fastidiousness, formality, modesty, properness.

prosaic *adj* commonplace, dull, flat, humdrum, matter-of-fact, pedestrian, plain, prosing, sober, tame, tedious, tiresome, unimaginative, unromantic, vapid.

proscribe *vb* banish, expel, ostracise, outlaw; exclude, forbid, prohibit; censure, condemn, curse, reject.

prosecute *vb* conduct, continue, exercise, follow, persist; indict, sue.

prospect *vb* explore, search, seek, survey; * *n* display, landscape, outlook, scene, show, sight, survey, view, vista; picture, scenery; anticipation, calculation, expectance, expectancy, expectation, foreseeing, hope, presumption, trust; likelihood.

prosper *vb* favour, forward, help; flourish, grow rich, thrive, succeed; increase.

prosperity *n* blessings, happiness, good luck, success, thrift, welfare, well-being.

prosperous *adj* blooming, flourishing, fortunate, rich, successful, thriving; booming, bright, fortunate, good, golden, lucky, promising, propitious, providential.

prostrate *vb* demolish, destroy, fell, level, overturn, ruin; depress, exhaust, overcome, reduce; * *adj* fallen, prostrated,

PROTECT

prone; helpless, powerless.
protect *vb* cover, defend, guard, shield; harbour, house, preserve, save, screen, secure, shelter; countenance, foster.
protector *n* champion, defender, guardian, patron, warden.
protest *vb* assert, asseverate, attest, aver, declare, profess, testify; expostulate, object, remonstrate, repudiate; * *n* complaint, declaration, objection, protestation.
prototype *n* archetype, copy, exemplar, example, ideal, model, original, precedent, type.
protract *vb* continue, lengthen, prolong; delay, postpone.
protrude *vb* bulge, extend, jut, project.
proud *adj* conceited, contended, overweening, self-conscious, self-satisfied, vain; arrogant, boastful, haughty, highly strung, imperious, lofty, lordly, supercilious.
prove *vb* ascertain, conform, demonstrate, establish, evidence, evince, justify, manifest, show, substantiate; assay, check, examine, test, try.
proverb *n* adage, aphorism, byword, dictum, maxim, precept, saying.
proverbial *adj* acknowledged, current, notorious.
provide *vb* arrange, collect, plan, prepare, procure; keep, store; contribute, feed, furnish, produce, stock, supply, yield; agree, bargain, condition, contract, covenant, engage.
provident *adj* careful, cautious, considerate, discreet, prudent.
province *n* district, domain, section, territory; tract; colony, dependency; calling, capacity, charge, duty, function, office, part, post; department, division.
provision *n* anticipation, providing; preparation, readiness; equipment, fund, hoard, reserve, resources, store, supplies, supply; clause, condition, prerequisite, proviso.
provocation *n* incitement, stimulant; affront, indignity, insult; angering, vexation.
provoke *vb* animate, awaken, excite, incite, induce, inflame, instigate, move, stimulate; affront, aggravate, anger, annoy, enrage, exasperate, incense, infuriate, irritate, nettle, offend, vex; cause, evoke, instigate, occasion, produce, promote.
prudent *adj* careful, cautious, circumspect, considerate, discreet, foreseeing, judicious, provident, wary, wise.
prudish *adj* coy, modest, precise, prim, reserved, strait-laced.
prune *vb* abbreviate, clip, cut, dock, lop, thin; dress, trim.
pry *vb* examine, ferret, inspect, investigate, peep, peer, scrutinise, search; force, prise.
public *adj* civil, countrywide, general, national, political, state; known, notorious, open, popular, well-known; * *n* citizens, community, country, masses, nation, people, population; audience, buyers, supporters.
publication *n* announcement, disclosure, divulgement, divulgence, proclamation, promulgation, report; edition, issue, printing.
publicity *n* currency, daylight, limelight, notoriety; outlet, vent.
publish *vb* advertise, air, announce, blaze, blazon, communicate, declare, diffuse, disclose, impart, placard, post, promulgate, reveal, tell, vent, ventilate.
pull *vb* drag, draw, haul, row, tow, tug; cull, gather, pick, pluck; detach, rend, tear, wrest; * *n* pluck, tug, wrench; contest, struggle; attraction; graft, power.

pulsate vb beat, palpitate, throb, thump, vibrate.
punctual adj exact, nice, precise, punctilious; early, ready, regular, timely.
puncture vb bore, penetrate, perforate, pierce, prick; * n hole, sting, wound.
pungent adj acid, acrid, biting, burning, caustic, piercing, piquant, prickling, racy, salty, seasoned, sharp, smart, sour, spicy, stinging; acute, cutting, distressing, irritating, keen, painful, poignant, pointed, satirical, severe, smart, tart, trenchant.
punish vb beat, castigate, chastise, correct, discipline, flog, lash, whip.
punishment n castigation, chastening, chastisement, correction, discipline, retribution, trial; judgment, nemesis, penalty.
puny adj feeble, inferior, weak; dwarfish, insignificant, little, petty, small, stunted, tiny, underdeveloped.
purchase vb buy, gain, get, obtain, pay for; achieve, attain, earn, win; * n acquisition, buy, gain, property; advantage, foothold, grasp, hold, influence.
pure adj clean, immaculate, spotless, unadulterated, unblemished, undefiled, unspotted, unstained, untainted, untarnished; continent, guileless, holy, honest, incorrupt, innocent, modest, true, uncorrupted, upright, white; clear, genuine, real, simple, true; absolute, mere, sheer; classic, classical.
purge vb cleanse, clear, purify; clarify, evacuate; scour; pardon; * n elimination, eradication, expulsion, removal, suppression.
purify vb clean, cleanse, clear, depurate, purge, refine, wash; clarify, fine.
puritanical adj ascetic, prim, prudish, severe, strait-laced.

purity n clearness, fineness; cleanness, correctness, faultlessness, immaculateness; guiltlessness, honesty, innocence, integrity, piety, simplicity, truth, uprightness, virtue; excellence, integrity; simpleness; chastity, modesty, virginity.
purpose vb contemplate, design, intend, mean; determine, resolve; * n aim, design, drift, end, intention, object, resolve, view; plan, project; meaning, purport, sense; effect, end.
pursue vb chase, dog, follow, bound, hunt, track; conduct, continue, cultivate, practise; seek, strive; accompany, attend, follow.
pursuit n chase, hunt, race; conduct, cultivation, practice, prosecution; calling, business, employment, fad, hobby, vocation.
push vb elbow, crowd, hustle, impel, jostle, shoulder, shove, thrust; advance, drive, hurry, propel, urge; persuade, tease; * n pressure, thrust; emergency, pinch, strait, test, trial; assault, attack, charge, endeavour, onset.
put vb bring, deposit, impose, lay, place, set; enjoin, impose, levy; offer, present, propose, state; compel, force, oblige; entice, induce, urge; express.
puzzle vb bewilder, confound, confuse, embarrass, mystify, nonplus, pose, stagger; complicate, entangle.* n conundrum, labyrinth, maze, paradox, problem, riddle; bewilderment, confusion, dilemma, mystification, point, quandary.

Q

quail vb blench, cower, faint, flinch, shrink, tremble.
quaint adj antiquated, antique,

archaic, curious, extraordinary, fanciful, odd, old-fashioned, singular, uncommon, unique, unusual; fantastic, odd, singular, whimsical.

qualification *n* ability, capability, competency, eligibility; fitness, suitability; condition, exception, limitation, proviso, restriction, stipulation.

qualify *vb* adapt, empower, entitle, equip, fit; limit, modify, narrow, restrain, restrict; abate, moderate, reduce, soften; diminish, modulate, regulate, vary.

quality *n* affection, attribute, characteristic, distinction, feature, nature, peculiarity, property, timbre, trait; character, characteristic, condition; calibre, class, condition, grade, kind, rank, sort, stamp, standing, station, status; aristocracy, gentry, nobility.

qualm *n* agony, pang; nausea, queasiness, sickness; remorse, uneasiness, twinge.

quandary *n* difficulty; dilemma, perplexity, pickle, plight, predicament, problem, puzzle, strait.

quantity *n* extent, greatness, measure, number, portion, share, size; aggregate, batch; amount, bulk, lot, mass, sum, volume; duration, length.

quantum mechanics *n* matrix mechanics, wave mechanics.

quarrel *vb* altercate, bicker, contend, differ, dispute, fight, jar, scuffle, spar, spat, squabble, wrangle; * *n* altercation, bickering, brawl, breeze, clash, contention, controversy, difference, disagreement, discord, dispute, dissension, disturbance, feud, fight, fray, quarrelling, row, spat, squabble, strife, tumult, variance, wrangle.

quarrelsome *adj* argumentative, combative, contentious, discordant, disputatious, dissentious, fiery, irascible, irritable, petulant, pugnacious.

quarter *vb* billet, lodge, post, station; share; * *n* abode, billet, dwelling, habitation, lodgings, posts, stations; district, locality, location, lodge, position, region, territory; clemency, mercy, mildness.

quell *vb* conquer, crush, overcome, overpower, subdue; bridle, check, curb, extinguish, quench, repress, restrain, stifle; calm, compose, pacify, quiet, subdue, tranquillise; alleviate, appease, blunt, deaden, dull, mitigate, mollify, soothe.

quench *vb* extinguish, put out; destroy, repress, satiate, still, suppress; allay, dampen, extinguish, slake.

query *vb* ask, enquire, inquire, question; dispute, doubt; * *n* enquiry, inquiry, question.

quest *n* expedition, journey, search, voyage; pursuit, suit; desire.

question *vb* ask, enquire, examine, inquire, interrogate, quiz, sound out; doubt, query; dispute; * *n* examination, enquiry, inquiry, interrogation, enquiry, inquiry, query; examination, investigation, issue, trial; controversy, dispute, doubt; motion, mystery, point, poser, problem, proposition, puzzle, topic.

questionable *adj* ambiguous, controversial, debatable, doubtful, disputable, equivocal, problematic, problematical, suspicious, uncertain.

queue *n* chain, file, line, order, progression, sequence, series, string, succession, train.

quick *adj* agile, alert, animated, brisk, lively, nimble, prompt, ready, smart, sprightly; expeditious, fast, fleet, flying, hasty, hurried, rapid, speedy, swift; clever, dextrous, expert, skilful; hasty, impetuous, irascible, passionate, peppery, petulant, precipitate, sharp, unceremonious, testy, touchy, waspish; alive, animate, live, living.

quicken vb animate, energise, resuscitate, vivify; enliven, invigorate, reinvigorate, revive, whet; accelerate, dispatch, expedite, hasten, hurry, speed; incite, kindle, refresh, sharpen, stimulate; accelerate, live, take effect.

quiet adj hushed, motionless, still; calm, contented, gentle, meek, mild, modest, peaceable, peaceful, placid, silent, tranquil, undemonstrative, unobtrusive; contented, patient; secluded; * n calmness, peace, repose, rest, silence, stillness.

quieten vb still; allay, appease, calm, compose, lull, pacify, sober, soothe, tranquillise; hush, silence, still; alleviate, assuage, blunt, dull, mitigate, moderate, mollify, soften.

quite adv completely, entirely, exactly, perfectly, positively, precisely, totally, wholly.

quiz vb examine, question; peer at; banter, hoax, puzzle, ridicule; * n enigma, hoax, jest, joke, puzzle; jester, joker, hoax.

quotation n citation, extract, excerpt, reference, selection; estimate, rate, tender.

quote vb cite, excerpt, extract, repeat, take; estimate, tender.

R

rabble n crowd, horde, mob, swarm, throng; (*derogatory*) hoi polloi, lower classes, masses, riff-raff, the great unwashed.

race n ancestry, breed, family, house, kindred, line, lineage, pedigree, stock, strain; clan, family, folk, nation, people, tribe; breed, children, descendants, issue, offspring, progeny, stock; chase, contest, course, dash, heat, match, pursuit, run, sprint; flavour, quality, smack, strength, taste; * vb compete, contest, course, hasten, hurry, run, speed.

rack vb agonise, distress, torment, torture; exhaust, force, harass, oppress, strain, stretch, wrest; * n agony, anguish, torment, torture; crib, manger; crag; dampness, mist, moisture, vapour.

racket n clamour, clatter, din, disturbance, fracas, noise, outcry, tumult, uproar; game, scheme, understanding.

radiant adj beaming, brilliant, glittering, glorious, luminous, lustrous, resplendent, shining; ecstatic, happy, pleased.

radiate vb beam, gleam, glitter, shine; emanate, emit; diffuse, spread.

radical adj fundamental, inherent, innate, native, natural, organic, original, uncompromising; original, primitive, simple; complete, entire, extreme, fanatic, fundamental, insurgent, rebellious, total; * n radix, root; fanatic, revolutionary.

rage vb bluster, boil, fret, fume, rave; * n frenzy, fury, madness, passion, rampage, raving, wrath; craze, fashion, mania, mode, style, vogue.

raid vb assault, invade, pillage, plunder; * n attack, foray, invasion, plunder.

rain vb drizzle, drop, pour, shower, sprinkle; bestow, lavish; * n cloudburst, downpour, drizzle, shower, sprinkling.

raise vb boost, construct, erect, hoist, lift, upraise, rear; advance, elevate, ennoble, exalt, promote; advance, amplify, enhance, heighten, increase, invigorate; arouse, awake, cause, excite, rouse, stir up, start; assemble, collect, get, levy, obtain; breed, cultivate, grow, propagate, rear; ferment,

leaven.
ramble *vb* digress, meander, range, roam, rove, stray, stroll, wander; * *n* excursion, roving, tour, trip, stroll, wandering.
rancid *adj* bad, fetid, foul, musty, offensive, rank, sour, stinking, tainted.
random *adj* accidental, casual, chance, fortuitous, haphazard, irregular, wandering.
range *vb* course, extend, ramble, roam, rove, stroll, wander; bend, lie, run; arrange, class, rank; * *n* file, line, row, rank, tier; class, kind, order, sort; excursion, expedition, ramble, wandering; amplitude, bound, command, compass, distance, extent, reach, scope, sweep, view; compass.
rank *vb* arrange, class, classify; * *n* file, line, order, row, tier; class, division, group, order, series; birth, blood, caste, degree, grade, position, quality, standing; dignity, eminence, nobility; * *adj* dense, exuberant, luxuriant, overabundant, overgrown, vigorous, wild; excessive, extreme, extravagant, gross, rampant, sheer, unmitigated, utter; fetid, foul, musty, offensive, rancid; fertile, rich; coarse, foul, disgusting.
ransom *vb* deliver, free, redeem, rescue, unfetter; * *n* liberation, redemption, release.
rapid *adj* fast, fleet, quick, swift; brisk, expeditious, hasty, hurried, quick, speedy.
rapture *vb* ravish, transport; * *n* exultation, enthusiasm, rhapsody; beatitude, bliss, ecstasy, felicity, happiness, joy, spell, transport.
rare *adj* sparse; extraordinary, infrequent, scarce, strange, uncommon, unique, unusual; choice, excellent, exquisite, fine, incomparable; bloody, underdone.
rarity *n* attenuation, ethereality, etherealness, tenuousness, thinness; infrequency, scarcity, singularity, sparseness, uncommonness, unwontedness.
rascal *n* blackguard, knave, miscreant, rogue, reprobate, scallywag, scamp, scoundrel, vagabond, villain.
rash *adj* adventurous, careless, foolhardy, hasty, incautious, inconsiderate, indiscreet, injudicious; impetuous, impulsive, incautious, precipitate, quick, rapid, reckless, thoughtless, unwary, venturesome; * *n* breaking-out, eruption; epidemic, outbreak, plague, spate.
rate *vb* appraise, estimate, value; abuse, censure, chide, criticise, reprimand, reprove, scold; * *n* cost, price; degree, estimate, rank, value, worth; proportion, ration; assessment, charge, tax.
ratify *vb* confirm, corroborate, endorse, establish, seal, substantiate; approve, consent, sanction.
ration *vb* apportion, deal, distribute, restrict; * *n* allowance, portion, quota, share.
rational *adj* intellectual, reasoning; equitable, fair, just, moderate, proper, reasonable, right; discreet, enlightened, intelligent, judicious, sensible, sound, wise.
raucous *adj* harsh, hoarse, husky, rough.
ravenous *adj* devouring, ferocious, gluttonous, greedy, insatiable, rapacious, voracious.
raving *adj* delirious, deranged, frantic, frenzied, mad, frenetic, raging; * *n* delirium, frenzy, fury, madness, rage.
raw *adj* inexperienced, untried, unskilled; crude, green, immature, unfinished, unripe; bare, chaffed, sensitive, sore; bleak, cold, cutting, piercing, windswept; uncooked.
ray *n* beam, moonbeam, radiance, shaft, streak, sunbeam.

reach *vb* extend, stretch; grasp, hit, strike, touch; arrive at, attain, gain, get, obtain, win; * *n* capability, capacity, grasp.

readily *adv* easily, promptly, quickly; cheerfully, willingly.

ready *vb* arrange, equip, organise, prepare; * *adj* alert, prompt, quick; adroit, apt, dextrous, expert, handy, keen, nimble, prepared, prompt, ripe, sharp, skilful, smart; cheerful, eager, inclined, willing; accommodating, available, convenient, handy, near; easy, offhand, opportune, short, spontaneous.

real *adj* actual, certain, literal, positive, practical, substantial, substantive, veritable; authentic, genuine, true.

realise *vb* accomplish, achieve, discharge, effect, perform; apprehend, comprehend, recognise, understand; externalise, substantiate; acquire, earn, gain, obtain, produce.

reality *n* actuality, certainty, fact, truth, verity.

really *adv* absolutely, certainly, indeed, truly, verily, veritably.

rear *adj* aft, back, following, hind, last; * *n* background, reverse, heel, posterior, rump, tail; trail, train, wake; * *vb* elevate, erect, hoist, lift, raise; educate, foster, instruct, nourish, nurse, nurture, train; breed, grow; rouse, stir up.

reason *vb* argue, conclude, debate, deduce, infer, syllogise, think; * *n* faculty, intellect, intelligence, judgement, mind, principle, sanity, sense, thinking, understanding; account, argument, basis, cause, consideration, excuse, explanation, ground, motive; aim, purpose; argument; common sense, wisdom; equity, fairness, justice, right; exposition, rationale, theory.

reasonable *adj* equitable, fair, just, rational; enlightened, intelligent, judicious, sensible, wise; considerable, fair, moderate; credible, plausible, well-founded; sane, sober, sound; cheap, inexpensive, low-priced.

rebel *vb* mutiny, resist, revolt, strike; * *adj* insurgent, mutinous, rebellious; * *n* insurgent, mutineer, traitor.

rebellion *n* insurrection, mutiny, resistance, revolt, revolution, uprising.

rebellious *adj* defiant, disloyal, disobedient, insubordinate, obstinate, mutinous, rebel, seditious.

recall *vb* cancel, countermand, deny, nullify, overrule, recant, repeal, repudiate, rescind, retract, revoke, withdraw; commemorate, recollect, remember, review, revive; * *n* annulment, cancellation, nullification, recantation, repeal, repudiation, retraction, withdrawal; recollection, reminiscence.

recapitulate *vb* rehearse, reiterate, repeat, restate, review, summarise.

receive *vb* accept, acquire, gain, get, obtain; admit, shelter, take in; entertain, greet, welcome; allow, permit, tolerate; adopt, approve, embrace, learn, understand; accommodate, admit, contain, hold, include; bear, encounter, endure, meet, suffer, sustain.

recent *adj* new, novel; latter, modern, young; foregoing, late, preceding.

reception *n* acceptance, receipt, receiving; entertainment, greeting, welcome; soiree, party; acceptance, admission; belief, credence, recognition.

reckless *adj* breakneck, careless, desperate, devil-may-care, flighty, foolhardy, harebrained, headlong, heedless, inattentive, improvident, imprudent, indiscreet, mindless, negligent, rash, regardless, remiss, thoughtless, uncircumspect, volatile, wild.

reckon vb calculate, compute, consider, count, enumerate, guess; account, class, esteem, estimate, repute, value.

reckoning n calculation, computation, consideration; account, bill, charge, estimate, score; arrangement.

reclaim vb correct, reform; recover, redeem, regenerate, regain, reinstate, restore; civilise, tame.

reciprocal adj complementary, corresponding, equivalent, interdependent, multilateral, mutual.

reclusive adj recluse, retired, secluded, sequestered, solitary.

recognise vb apprehend, identify, perceive, remember; admit; allow, concede, grant; greet, salute.

recoil vb rebound, reverberate; retire, retreat, withdraw; fail, falter, shrink; * n backstroke, boomerang, elasticity, kick, rebound, repercussion, revulsion, ricochet, shrinking.

recollect vb recall, remember, reminisce.

recommend vb approve, endorse, praise, sanction; commit; advise, counsel, prescribe, suggest.

recommendation n advocacy, approval, commendation, credential, praise, testimonial.

reconcile vb appease, conciliate, pacify, placate, reunite; content, harmonise; adjust, compose, heal, settle.

record vb chronicle, note, register; * n account, annals, archive, chronicle, diary, entry, file, list, minute, memoir, memorial, note, register, registry, report, score; mark, memorial, relic, trace, vestige; memory, remembrance; achievement, career, history.

recover vb recapture, reclaim, regain; rally, repair, retrieve; cure, heal, restore, revive; rescue, salvage; convalesce, rally, recuperate.

recreation n amusement, diversion, entertainment, game, leisure, pastime, play, relaxation, sport.

recreational adj amusing, diverting, entertaining, refreshing, relaxing.

recruit vb repair, replenish; recover, refresh, reinvigorate, restore, strengthen, supply; * n auxiliary, beginner, helper, learner, novice.

rectify vb adjust, amend, correct, improve, mend, redress, reform, regulate, straighten.

rectitude n conscientiousness, equity, goodness, honesty, integrity, justice, probity, righteousness, uprightness, virtue.

recur vb reappear, resort, return, revert.

redemption n compensation, recovery, retrieval; deliverance, liberation, release, rescue, salvation.

redress vb compensate for, make amends, put right; amend, balance, correct, even up, rectify, reform, remedy, repair; * n aid, assistance, care, correction, help, justice, remedy; amends, atonement, compensation, payment, recompense, reparation, restitution.

reduce vb bring; remodel, render, resolve; abate, abbreviate, abridge, attenuate, contract, curtail, decimate, decrease, diminish, lessen, minimise, shorten, thin; abase, debase, degrade, depress, impair, lower, weaken; capture, conquer, master, overpower, overthrow, subject, subdue, subjugate, vanquish; impoverish, ruin.

redundant adj excessive, inordinate, lavish, needless, overflowing, overmuch, plentiful, superabundant, superfluous, unnecessary, useless; periphrastic, verbose, wordy.

reel *n* capstan, winch, windlass; bobbin, spool; pirouette, spin, turn, twirl, wheel, whirl; * *vb* falter, flounder, lurch, pitch, plunge, rear, roll, stagger, sway, toss, totter, tumble, vacillate; swing, turn, twirl, wheel, whirl.

refer *vb* commit, consign, direct, leave, relegate, submit; assign, impute; appertain, belong, concern, pertain, point, relate, respect; appeal, apply, consult; allude, cite, quote.

referee *vb* arbitrate, judge, umpire; * *n* arbiter, arbitrator, judge, umpire.

reference *n* concern, connection, regard, respect; allusion, ascription, citation, hint, intimation.

refine *vb* clarify, cleanse, purify; cultivate, improve, polish, rarefy, spiritualise.

refined *adj* courtly, cultured, genteel, polished, polite; discerning, discriminating, sensitive; filtered, processed, purified.

reflect *vb* imitate, mirror; consider, contemplate, deliberate, meditate, muse, ponder, ruminate, think.

reflection *n* echo, shadow; cogitation, consideration, contemplation, deliberation, idea, meditation, musing, thinking, thought; aspersion, censure, criticism, reproach, slur.

reform *vb* amend, ameliorate, better, improve, mend, meliorate, rectify, redeem, regenerate, repair, restore; reconstruct, remodel, reshape; * *n* amendment, correction, reconstruction, rectification.

refrain *vb* abstain, cease, desist, forbear, stop; * *n* chorus, song, undersong.

refresh *vb* air, brace, cool, enliven, exhilarate, invigorate, reanimate, recreate, recruit, reinvigorate, revive, slake.

refuge *n* asylum, harbour, haven, protection, retreat, safety, security, shelter.

refund *vb* reimburse, repay, return; * *n* reimbursement, repayment.

refuse *n* chaff, discard, dross, dregs, garbage, junk, leavings, lumber, offal, remains, rubbish, scum, sediment, slag, sweepings, trash, waste; * *vb* decline, deny, withhold; disallow, exclude, rebuff, reject, repudiate, revoke, veto.

regal *adj* imposing, imperial, kingly, noble, royal, sovereign.

regard *vb* behold, gaze, look, notice, observe, see, view, watch; consider, heed, mind, respect; esteem, honour, respect, revere, reverence, value; consider, estimate, imagine, reckon, suppose, think; * *n* gaze, look, view; attention, care, concern, consideration, heed, notice; reference, relation, respect, view; affection, attachment, concern, consideration, deference, esteem, honour, interest, liking, love, respect, reverence; note, reputation, repute; consideration, matter, point.

regardless *adj* careless, heedless, inattentive, indifferent, neglectful, unconcerned, unmindful, unobservant; * *adv* irrespectively, nevertheless, none the less, notwithstanding.

region *n* climate, country, district, division, locale, locality, province, quarter, territory; area, neighbourhood, place, spot, space, sphere, terrain, vicinity.

régime *n* administration, government, leadership, reign, rule, system.

register *vb* delineate, record, show; * *n* annals, archive, catalogue, chronicle, list, record, schedule; compass,

range.
regret *vb* bewail, deplore, grieve, lament, sorrow; bemoan, repent, mourn, rue; * *n* disappointment, grief, lamentation, rue, sorrow; contrition, penitence, remorse, repentance, repining.
regular *adj* conventional, natural, normal, ordinary, typical; correct, customary, cyclic, established, fixed, habitual, periodic, periodical, usual; recurring, rhythmic, seasonal, stated; constant, even, steady, uniform; orderly, systematic, uniform; complete, genuine, perfect, thorough; consistent, symmetrical.
regulate *vb* adjust, arrange, order, organise, settle, standardise, systematise; conduct, control, direct, govern, manage, order, rule.
regulation *adj* official, required, standard; * *n* adjustment, arrangement, control, law, management, order, ordering, precept, rule, settlement.
reign *vb* administer, command, govern, influence, prevail, rule; * *n* control, dominion, empire, influence, royalty, sovereignty, rule, sway.
rein *vb* bridle, check, control, curb, harness, restrain, restrict; * *n* bridle, check, curb, harness, restraint, restriction.
reject *vb* discard, dismiss, eject, exclude, decline, disallow, disapprove, disbelieve, rebuff, refuse, renounce, repudiate, slight, spurn, veto; * *n* cast-off, discard, failure, refusal, repudiation.
rejoice *vb* cheer, delight, enrapture, exhilarate, gladden, gratify, please; exult, delight, glory, jubilate, triumph, vaunt.
rejoin *vb* answer, rebut, respond, retort.
relate *vb* describe, detail, mention, narrate, recite, recount, tell; apply, connect, correlate.
relation *n* account, chronicle, description, detail, history, narration, narrative, recital, rehearsal, report, story, tale; affinity, connection; concern, reference, regard, respect; alliance, connection, nearness, rapport; affinity, blood, cousinship, kin, kindred, kinship; relative.
relax *vb* loose, loosen, slacken, unbrace; debilitate, enfeeble, unbrace, unstring, weaken; diminish, lessen, mitigate, reduce, remit; divert, ease, entertain, unbend.
release *vb* deliver, discharge, disengage, exempt, extricate, free, liberate, unloose; acquit, discharge, remit; * *n* discharge, freedom, liberation; absolution, exemption, exoneration; acquaintance, clearance.
relentless *adj* cruel, hard, implacable, inexorable, merciless, obdurate, pitiless, rancorous, remorseless, ruthless, unappeasable, unforgiving, unmerciful, unpitying, unyielding.
relevant *adj* applicable, apposite, apt, germane, pertinent, proper, suitable.
reliable *adj* certain, constant, dependable, sure, trustworthy, trusty, unfailing.
reliance *n* assurance, confidence, credence, dependence, trust.
relief *n* aid, alleviation, amelioration, assistance, comfort, deliverance, easement, help, mitigation, reinforcement, respite, rest, succour, softening, support; indemnification, redress; embossment, projection; distinction, perspective.
relieve *vb* aid, comfort, free, help, succour, support, sustain; abate, allay, alleviate, cure, lighten, mitigate, remedy, soothe; indemnify, redress, repair; free, release, remedy, rescue.

religious *adj* devotional, devout, god-fearing, godly, holy, pious, prayerful, spiritual; rigid, strict; canonical, divine, theological.

relinquish *vb* abandon, forsake, forswear, quit, renounce, resign, vacate; abdicate, cede, forbear, forego, surrender, yield.

relish *vb* appreciate, enjoy; season, flavour; * *n* appetite, appreciation, enjoyment, fondness, gusto, inclination, liking, partiality, predilection, taste, zest; flavour, quality, savour, seasoning, sort, touch, twang; appetiser, condiment; flavour, taste.

reluctant *adj* averse, disinclined, hesitant, indisposed, loath, unwilling.

rely *vb* confide, count, depend, hope, reckon, trust.

remain *vb* continue, endure, last, stay; survive; continue, dwell, halt, rest, sojourn, stay, stop, tarry, wait.

remainder *n* balance, excess, leavings, remnant, residue, rest, surplus.

remark *vb* notice, observe; comment, express, mention, observe, say, state, utter; * *n* consideration, notice, regard; annotation, comment, note; assertion, comment, saying, statement, utterance.

remarkable *adj* conspicuous, distinguished, eminent, extraordinary, famous, noteworthy, noticeable, strange, striking, uncommon, unusual.

remedy *vb* cure, palliate, relieve; amend, correct, rectify, redress, repair, restore, retrieve; * *n* antidote, antitoxin, cure, medicine, restorative; redress, reparation, restitution, restoration; aid, assistance, relief.

remind *vb* awaken memories of, bring to mind, prompt.

remiss *adj* behindhand, dilatory, indolent, lax, slack, slow, tardy; careless, dilatory, idle, inattentive, neglectful, negligent, shiftless, slack, slothful, thoughtless.

remorse *n* contrition, penitence, qualm, regret, repentance, reproach, sorrow.

remorseless *adj* cruel, harsh, implacable, inexorable, merciless, pitiless, relentless, ruthless, uncompassionate, unmerciful, unrelenting.

remote *adj* distant, far; inappropriate, unconnected, unrelated; abstracted, separated; inconsiderable, slight; isolated, removed, secluded, sequestrated.

removal *n* displacement, relegation, transference; elimination, extraction, withdrawal; abatement, destruction; discharge, dismissal, ejection, expulsion.

remove *vb* dislodge, displace, shift, transfer; abstract, extract, withdraw; abate, banish, suppress; depose, discharge, dismiss, eject, expel, oust, retire; depart.

render *vb* restore, return, surrender; deliver, give, present; afford, supply, yield; construe, interpret, translate.

renounce *vb* abjure, decline, deny, disclaim, disown, forswear, recant, repudiate, reject; abandon, abdicate, drop, forego, forsake, desert, quit, relinquish, resign.

renovate *vb* reconstitute, refresh, refurbish, restore, revamp; reanimate, recreate, regenerate, reproduce, resuscitate, revive.

renown *n* celebrity, distinction, eminence, fame, glory, honour, greatness, name, note, notability, reputation.

renowned *adj* celebrated, distinguished, eminent, famed, famous, honoured, remarkable.

rent *n* broach, break, crack, cleft, crevice, fissure, flaw, fracture, laceration, rift, rupture, split, tear; schism, separation; income, revenue; * vb hire, lease, let.

renunciation n abandonment, abdication, abjuration, abstention, denial, disavowal, rejection, relinquishment, repudiation, resignation, surrender, waiver.

repair vb mend, patch, refit, retouch, tinker; correct, recruit, restore, retrieve; go, move, resort, turn; * n mending, reparation, restoration.

repay vb refund, reimburse; compensate, recompense, remunerate, reward; avenge, retaliate, revenge.

repeal vb abolish, annul, cancel, rescind, reverse, revoke; * n abolition, annulment, cancellation, rescission, revocation.

repeat vb double, duplicate, iterate; cite, narrate, quote, recite; echo, reproduce; * n duplicate, echo, iteration, reiteration, repetition.

repel vb repulse; check, confront, oppose, parry, rebuff, resist, withstand; decline, refuse, reject; disgust, revolt, sicken.

repellent adj abhorrent, disgusting, forbidding, repugnant, repulsive, revolting.

repentance n compunction, contriteness, contrition, penitence, regret, remorse.

repentant adj contrite, penitent, regretful, remorseful, rueful, sorry.

repetition n harping, iteration, recapitulation, reiteration; redundancy, tautology, verbosity; narration, recital, rehearsal; recurrence, renewal.

replace vb reinstate, reset; refund, restore; succeed, supersede, supplant.

replenish vb refill, re-supply; enrich, furnish, provide, store, supply.

replica n copy, duplicate, facsimile, reproduction.

reply vb answer, echo, rejoin, respond; * n acknowledgement, answer, rejoinder, response, retort.

report vb announce, declare; broadcast, describe, detail, herald, mention, narrate, publish, recite, relate, rumour, state, tell; minute, record; * n account, announcement, declaration, statement; description, detail, narration, narrative, news, recital, story, tale, talk; gossip, hearsay, rumour; clap, detonation, discharge, explosion; fame, reputation, repute; account, bulletin, minute, note, record, statement.

repose vb recline, rest, settle; lie, recline, sleep, slumber; confide, lean; place, put, stake; deposit, lodge, store; * n quiet, recumbence, rest, sleep, slumber; inactivity, leisure, respite, relaxation; calm, ease, peace, quiet, quietness, stillness, tranquillity.

reprehensible adj blameworthy, censurable, condemnable, culpable, reprovable.

represent vb exhibit, express; depict, describe, draw, portray, sketch; act, impersonate, mimic, personify; exemplify, illustrate, image, portray, reproduce, symbolise.

representation n exhibition, show; impersonation; account, description, narration, narrative; image, likeness, portraiture, resemblance; sight, spectacle; expostulation, remonstrance.

representative adj illustrative, symbolic, typical; delegated, representing; * n agent, commissioner, delegate, deputy, emissary, envoy, legate, lieutenant, messenger, proxy, substitute.

repress vb crush, dull, overcome, overpower, silence, smother, subdue, suppress, quell;

RESENTMENT

chasten, check, control, curb, restrain; appease, quiet.

reprimand vb admonish, censure, chide, rebuke, reprehend, reproach, reprove, upbraid; * n admonition, censure, rebuke, reprehension, reproach, reprobation, reproof, reproval.

reproach vb censure, rebuke, reprehend, reprimand, upbraid; condemn, discredit, disparage, revile, traduce, vilify; * n abuse, censure, condemnation, disapprobation, disapproval, invective, rebuke, remonstrance, reprobation, reproof, reviling, scorn, scurrility, upbraiding, vilification; abasement, discredit, disgrace, dishonour, disrepute, indignity, ignominy, offence, scandal, scam, shame, slur, stigma.

reproduce vb copy, duplicate, emulate, imitate, print, repeat, represent; breed, generate, procreate, propagate.

reproof n admonition, censure, chiding, condemnation, correction, criticism, lecture, objurgation, rating, rebuke, reprehension, reprimand, reproach, upbraiding.

repudiate vb abjure, deny, disavow, discard, disclaim, disown, nullify, reject, renounce.

repugnant adj incompatible, irreconcilable; adverse, antagonistic, hostile, inimical, opposed, unfavourable; detestable, distasteful, offensive, repellent, repulsive.

repulse vb check, defeat, refuse, reject, repel; * n repelling.

repulsion n abhorrence, aversion, dislike, disgust, hatred, hostility, loathing, rebuff, rejection, repugnance, spurning.

repulsive adj abhorrent, disagreeable, disgusting, forbidding, harsh, hateful, loathsome, nauseating, nauseous, odious, offensive, repellent, repugnant, revolting, sickening, ugly, unpleasant.

reputation n character, fame, mark, name, repute; celebrity, credit, distinction, esteem, estimation, fame, glory, honour, prestige, regard, renown, respect.

request vb ask, beg, beseech, claim, demand, desire, entreat, pray, supplicate; * n asking, entreaty, importunity, invitation, petition, prayer, requisition, suit, supplication.

require vb beg, beseech, bid, claim, crave, importune, invite, pray, request, summon; need, want; direct, enjoin, exact, order.

requirement n demand, exigency, need, needfulness, requisite, requisition, request, want; behest, bidding, claim, command, exaction, mandate, order, precept.

rescind vb annul, cancel, countermand, invalidate, overturn, quash, recall, repeal, retract, revoke, void.

rescue vb deliver, extricate, free, liberate, preserve, ransom, recover, redeem, release, save; * n deliverance, extrication, liberation, redemption, release, salvation.

research vb analyse, examine, explore, inquire, investigate, probe, study; * n analysis, examination, exploration, inquiry, investigation, scrutiny, study.

resemblance n analogy, likeness, semblance, similarity; counterpart, facsimile, image, likeness, representation.

resemble vb compare, liken; copy, imitate.

resentful adj angry, bitter, hurt, irascible, irritable, malignant, revengeful, sore, touchy.

resentment n acrimony, anger, annoyance, bitterness, displeasure, fury, gall, grudge, indignation, ire, irritation,

RESERVATION

pique, rage, soreness, umbrage, vexation, wrath.

reservation *n* suppression; appropriation, booking, exception, restriction, saving; proviso; custody, park, sanctuary.

reserve *vb* hold, husband, keep, retain, store; * *adj* auxiliary, spare, substitute; * *n* aloofness, coldness, concealment, suppression; retention, restraint, reticence, uncommunicativeness, unresponsiveness; coyness, demureness, modesty, shyness, taciturnity; park, sanctuary.

reserved *adj* coy, demure, modest, shy, taciturn; aloof, cautious, cold, distant, incommunicative, reticent, unsociable; bespoken, booked, held, kept, retained, set apart, taken, withheld.

reside *vb* abide, domicile, dwell, inhabit, live, lodge, remain, sojourn, stay.

residence *n* inhabitance, sojourn, stay; abode, domicile, dwelling, habitation, home, house, lodging, mansion.

resign *vb* abandon, abdicate, cede, disclaim, forego, forsake, leave, quit, relinquish, renounce, surrender, yield.

resignation *n* abandonment, abdication, renunciation, retirement, surrender; acquiescence, compliance, endurance, forbearance, long-sufferance, patience.

resist *vb* block, check, confront, counteract, disappoint, frustrate, hinder, impede, neutralise, obstruct, oppose, rebel, rebuff, stand against, stem, stop, thwart, withstand.

resolute *adj* constant, decided, determined; firm, fixed, hardy, inflexible, persevering, relentless, staunch, steadfast, steady, stouthearted, sturdy, tenacious, undaunted, unflinching, unshaken, unwavering, unyielding.

resolution *n* explication, unravelling; backbone, courage, determination, firmness, fortitude, grit, hardness, inflexibility, pluck, perseverance, purpose, relentlessness, stamina, steadfastness, steadiness, tenacity.

resolve *vb* analyse, disperse, scatter, separate; change, dissolve, transform; decipher, disentangle, elucidate, explain, interpret, unfold, unravel; conclude, decide, determine, fix, intend, purpose, will; * *n* conclusion, decision, determination, intention, will; declaration, determination, resolution.

resort *vb* frequent, haunt; assemble, congregate, convene, repair; * *n* expedient, recourse; haunt, rendezvous, retreat, spa; assembling, concourse, meeting; recourse, reference.

resource *n* dependence, resort; appliance, contrivance, expedient, means, resort.

resources *npl* capital, funds, income, property, reserve, supplies, wealth.

resound *n* echo, fill the air, resonate, reverberate, ring.

respect *vb* admire, esteem, honour, prise, regard, revere, reverence, value, venerate; consider, observe; * *n* attention, civility, courtesy, deference, estimation, honour, politeness, recognition, regard, reverence, veneration; consideration, kind; aspect, bearing, feature, matter, particular, reference, regard, relation.

respectable *adj* considerable, estimable, honourable, proper, upright, worthy; considerable, mediocre.

respectful *adj* ceremonious, civil, courteous, deferential, dutiful, formal, polite.

respond *vb* answer, reply, rejoin; accord, correspond.

responsible *adj* accountable,

answerable, liable, trustworthy.

rest *vb* cease, desist, halt, hold, pause, repose, stop; relax, repose, unbend; repose, sleep, slumber; lean, lie, recline; acquiesce, confide, trust; lean, rely; calm, comfort, ease; be left, remain; * *n* inactivity, motionlessness, quiescence, quiet, repose; hush, peace, peacefulness, quiet, relief, stillness, tranquillity; cessation, intermission, interval, lull, pause, relaxation, respite, stop, stay; siesta, sleep, slumber; death; brace, stay, support; balance, remainder, remnant, residuum; surplus.

restless *adj* disquieted, disturbed, sleepless, uneasy, unquiet; changeable, inconstant, unsettled, unstable, unsteady; active, roving, transient, unsettled, wandering, agitated, fidgety, fretful, turbulent.

restorative *adj* invigorating, recuperative, remedial, stimulating; * *n* corrective, cure, healing, medicine, remedy, stimulant.

restore *vb* refund, repay, return; emend, heal, mend, patch, re-establish, rehabilitate, reinstate, repair, replace, retrieve, tinker; cure, heal, recover, revive; resuscitate, revive.

restraint *n* bridle, check, coercion, control, compulsion, constraint, curb, discipline, repression; arrest, deterrence, inhibition, limitation, repression, restriction, stay; confinement, detention, imprisonment, shackles; constraint, stiffness, reserve.

restrict *vb* bound, circumscribe, confine, limit, qualify, restrain.

restriction *n* confinement, limitation; constraint, restraint; reservation, reserve.

result *vb* accrue, arise, ensue, follow, issue, rise; end, eventuate, terminate; * *n* conclusion, consequence, deduction, inference, outcome; consequence, effect, end, event, eventuality, fruit, issue, outcome, product, sequel, termination; conclusion, decision, finding, resolution, verdict.

resume *vb* continue, renew, restart, summarise.

résumé *n* abstract, curriculum vitae, recapitulation, summary, synopsis.

resurrect *vb* breath new life into, bring back, raise from the dead, reintroduce, restore to life, revive.

retain *vb* detain, hold, keep, preserve, recall, remember, reserve, save, withhold; engage, maintain.

retainer *n* adherent, attendant, dependant, follower, servant.

retaliate *vb* avenge, repay, requite, retort, return.

reticent *adj* close, reserved, secretive, silent, taciturn, uncommunicative.

retinue *n* bodyguard, cortege, entourage, escort, household, ménage, suite, tail, train.

retire *vb* discharge, remove, shelve, withdraw; depart, leave, remove, retreat.

retired *adj* abstracted, removed, withdrawn; apart, private, secret, solitary.

retirement *n* isolation, privacy, retreat, seclusion, solitude, withdrawal.

retiring *adj* coy, demure, diffident, modest, reserved, retreating, shy, withdrawing.

retreat *vb* retire, withdraw; recede; * *n* departure, recession, retirement, withdrawal; privacy, seclusion, solitude; asylum, den, haunt, niche, recess, refuge, resort, shelter.

retribution *n* compensation, judgement, nemesis, penalty, recompense, repayment, requital, retaliation, revenge, reward, vengeance.

retrieve vb recall, recover, recoup, recruit, regain, repair, restore.

return vb reappear, recur, revert; reply, respond; recriminate, retort; convey, communicate, reciprocate, recompense, refund, remit, repay, send, tell, transmit; elect; * n payment, reimbursement, remittance; recompense, recurrence, restitution, restoration, reward; benefit, interest, profit, rent, yield.

reveal vb announce, confess, declare, disclose, discover, display, divulge, expose, open, publish, tell, unmask, unveil.

revel vb carouse, riot, roister, tipple; delight, indulge, luxuriate, wanton; * n carousal, feast, festival.

revelry n bacchanal, carousal, carouse, debauch, festivity, jollification, jollity, orgy, revel, riot.

revenge vb avenge, repay, retaliate; * n rancour, reprisal, retaliation, retribution, vengeance, vindictiveness.

revenue n fruits, income, produce, proceeds, receipts, return, reward, wealth.

revere vb adore, esteem, hallow, honour, venerate, worship.

reverse vb invert, transpose; overturn, quash, undo, unmake; annul, countermand, repeal, rescind, retract, revoke; back, back up, retreat; * adj back, converse, contrary, opposite; * n back, calamity, comedown, contrary, defeat, opposite; change, vicissitude; adversity, hardship, misadventure, mischance, misfortune, mishap, trial.

review vb inspect, overlook, reconsider, re-examine, revise, survey; analyse, criticise, discuss, edit, judge, scrutinise; * n reconsideration, re-examination, retrospect, survey; analysis, digest, synopsis; commentary, critique, criticism, scrutiny.

revile vb abuse, asperse, calumniate, defame, malign, reproach, traduce, upbraid, vilify.

revise vb reconsider, re-examine, review; alter, amend, correct, edit, overhaul, review.

revision n amendment, change, correction, editing, review, rewriting, updating; homework, re-reading, studying.

revive vb reanimate, reinvigorate, resuscitate, revitalise; animate, cheer, comfort, invigorate, quicken, reawaken, recover, refresh, renovate, strengthen; reawake, recall.

revoke vb abolish, annul, cancel, countermand, invalidate, quash, recall, recant, repeal, repudiate, rescind, retract.

revolt vb mutiny, rebel, rise; disgust, nauseate, repel; * n faithlessness, inconstancy; disobedience, insurrection, mutiny, rebellion, sedition, strike, uprising.

revolution n coup, insurrection, mutiny, rebellion, sedition, uprising; change, innovation, reformation, transformation, upheaval; circle, circuit, cycle, lap, orbit, rotation, spin.

revolve vb circle, rotate, swing, turn, wheel; devolve, return; consider, ponder, ruminate, study.

revulsion n abstraction, shrinking; change, reaction, transition; abhorrence, disgust, loathing, repugnance.

reward vb compensate, pay, recompense, remember, remunerate, requite; * n indemnification, pay, requital; bonus, bounty, fee, gratuity, honorarium, premium, tip; punishment, retribution.

rhetoric n eloquence, oratory; bombast, grandiloquence, hot air, hyperbole, pomposity, verbosity, wordiness.

rhythm n lilt, pulsation, swing; measure, metre, rhyme, verse.

rich *adj* affluent, opulent, prosperous, wealthy; costly, gorgeous, luxurious, precious, splendid, sumptuous, superb, valuable; delicious, luscious; abundant, ample, copious, plentiful; fertile, fruitful, luxuriant, productive, prolific; bright, dark, deep, vivid; harmonious, mellow, soft, sweet.

riches *npl* abundance, affluence, fortune, money, opulence, plenty, wealth.

rid *vb* deliver, free, release; clear, disburden, disencumber, sweep; dispatch, dissolve, divorce, finish, sever.

riddle *vb* explain, solve; sieve, sift, permeate, spread; * *n* conundrum, enigma, mystery, puzzle; colander, sieve, strainer.

ridicule *vb* deride, disparage, jeer, mock, lampoon, rally, satirise, taunt; * *n* derision, game, gibe, irony, jeer, mockery, raillery, sarcasm, satire, sneer.

ridiculous *adj* absurd, droll, eccentric, farcical, laughable, ludicrous, nonsensical, odd, outlandish, preposterous, queer, risible, waggish.

right *vb* adjust, correct, settle, straighten, vindicate; * *adj* direct, rectilinear, straight; erect, perpendicular, plumb, upright; equitable, fair, just, justifiable, honest, lawful, legal, legitimate; appropriate, becoming, correct, fitting, orderly, proper, reasonable, suitable; actual, genuine, real, true; dextral; * *adv* equitably, fairly, justly, lawfully; correctly, properly, suitably, truly; actually, exactly, just, really, truly, well; * *n* authority, claim, liberty, permission, power, privilege, title; equity, good, honour, justice, legality, propriety, reason, truth.

righteous *adj* devout, godly, good, holy, honest, incorrupt, just, pious, religious, saintly, virtuous; equitable, fair.

rightful *adj* lawful, legitimate, true; appropriate, correct, deserved, due, equitable, fair, honest, just, lawful, legal, legitimate, merited, proper, reasonable, suitable, true.

rigid *adj* firm, hard, inflexible, stiff, stiffened, unbending, unyielding; erect, steep, stiff; austere, correct, exact, formal, harsh, precise, rigorous, severe, strict, unmitigated; cruel, sharp.

rigour *n* hardness, inflexibility, rigidity, stiffness; austerity, harshness, severity, sternness; evenness, strictness.

rim *n* brim, brink, border, confine, curb, edge, margin, ring, skirt.

ring *vb* circle, encircle, enclose, girdle, surround; chime, clang, knell, peal, reverberate, sound, tingle, toll; call, telephone; * *n* circle, girdle, hoop, round, whorl; clique, confederacy, gang, junta, league, set; chime, knell, peal, toll; call, telephone call.

riot *vb* carouse, revel; * *n* affray, altercation, brawl, commotion, disturbance, pandemonium, quarrel, tumult, uproar; dissipation, excess, luxury, merrymaking, revelry.

riotous *adj* boisterous, revelling, unrestrained, wanton; disorderly, insubordinate, lawless, mutinous, rebellious, refractory, seditious, turbulent, ungovernable, unruly.

ripe *adj* advanced, grown, mature, mellow, seasoned, soft; prepared, ready; accomplished, complete, consummate, finished, perfect, perfected.

ripen *vb* develop, mature.

rise *vb* ascend, climb, levitate, mount; excel, succeed; enlarge, heighten, increase, swell; revive; grow, kindle, wax; begin, flow, originate, spring, start; mutiny, rebel,

RISK

revolt; happen, occur; * n ascension, ascent; elevation, hill, slope; emergence, flow, source, spring; advance, augmentation, expansion, increase.

risk vb bet, endanger, hazard, jeopardise, speculate, venture, wager; * n chance, danger, hazard, jeopardy, venture.

rite n ceremonial, ceremony, form, ministration, observance, ordinance, ritual, rubric, sacrament.

ritual adj ceremonial, formal, habitual, stereotyped; * n ceremonial, ceremony, liturgy, observance, sacrament, service; form, formality, habit, practice, protocol.

rival vb match, oppose; * adj competing, contending, opposing; * n antagonist, competitor, opponent.

road n avenue, carriageway, highway, lane, motorway, route, street, thoroughfare, track, way.

roam vb prowl, ramble, range, rove, straggle, stray, stroll, wander.

roar vb bellow, cry, howl, yell; boom, rattle, resound, thunder; * n bellow, roaring; rage, storm, thunder; cry, outcry, shout; laugh, shout.

rob vb despoil, fleece, pilfer, plunder, rook; appropriate, deprive, embezzle, plagiarise.

robber n bandit, brigand, desperado, highwayman, marauder, pillager, pirate, plunderer, rifler, thief.

robe vb array, clothe, dress, invest; * n attire, costume, dress, garment, gown, habit, vestment; dressing gown, housecoat.

robust adj brawny, firm, forceful, hale, hardy, hearty, iron, lusty, muscular, powerful, seasoned, sinewy, sound, stalwart, stout, strong, sturdy, vigorous.

rock n boulder, crag, reef, stone; defence, foundation, protection; refuge, strength, support; granite, marble, slate; * vb calm, cradle, lull, quiet, soothe; shake, sway, teeter, totter, wobble.

rogue n beggar, vagabond, vagrant; cheat, knave, rascal, scamp, scoundrel, swindler, trickster, villain.

role n character, function, part, task.

roll vb revolve, rotate, turn, wheel; muffle, swathe, wind; bind, involve; flatten, level, smooth, spread; bowl, drive; wheel; lurch, stagger, sway, yaw; billow, swell, undulate; wallow; flow, glide, run; * n document, volume; annals, chronicle, record, rota; catalogue, inventory, list, register, schedule; booming, resonance, reverberation, thunder; cylinder.

rollicking adj boisterous, carefree, cavorting, exuberant, frisky, hearty, jovial, lively, merry, rip-roaring, romping, spirited, sprightly, swash buckling.

romance vb exaggerate, fantasise; * n fantasy, fiction, legend, novel, story; exaggeration; ballad, song.

room n accommodation, capacity, compass, expanse, extent, field, latitude, leeway, play, scope, space, swing; place; apartment, chamber, lodging; opportunity.

roomy adj ample, broad, comfortable, commodious, extensive, large, spacious, wide.

root vb anchor, embed, fasten, implant; confirm, establish; destroy, eradicate, extirpate, exterminate, remove; burrow, dig, grub, rummage; applaud, cheer, encourage; * n base, bottom, foundation; cause, origin, reason, source; etymon, radical, radix, stem.

rosy adj blooming, blushing, favourable, flushed, hopeful, roseate, ruddy.

rot vb corrupt, decay, decompose, degenerate, putrefy, spoil; * n corruption, decay.

rotten adj carious, corrupt, decomposed, fetid, putrefied, putrescent, putrid, rank; defective; corrupt, deceitful, immoral, treacherous, untrustworthy.

rough vb coarsen; manhandle, molest; * adj bumpy, craggy, irregular, jagged, rugged, scratchy, uneven; approximate, cross-grained, crude, formless, incomplete, knotty, shapeless, sketchy, uncut, unfashioned, unfinished, unhewn, unpolished, unwrought, vague; bristly, coarse, disordered, hairy, ragged, shaggy, unkempt; bluff, blunt, brusque, burly, churlish, discourteous, gruff, harsh, impolite, indelicate, rude, surly, uncivil, uncourteous, ungracious, unpolished, unrefined; harsh, severe, sharp, violent; crabbed, hard; discordant, grating, inharmonious, jarring, raucous; boisterous, foul, inclement, severe, stormy, tempestuous, tumultuous, turbulent, untamed, violent, wild; acrimonious, brutal, disorderly, riotous, rowdy, severe, uncivil, unfeeling, ungentle; * n bully, rowdy; draft, outline; unevenness.

round vb curve; circuit, encircle; * adj circular, cylindrical, globular, orbed, rotund, spherical; complete, entire, great, large, unbroken, whole; chubby, plump, stout; flowing, full, harmonious, smooth; brisk, quick; blunt, candid, fair, frank, honest, open, plain; * adv around, circularly, circuitously; * prep about; * n bout, cycle, game, lap, rotation, succession, turn; cannon, catch, dance; ball, circle, circumference, cylinder, globe, sphere; circuit, perambulation, routine, tour, watch.

roundabout adj circuitous, devious, discursive, evasive, indirect, meandering, oblique, tortuous.

rouse vb awaken, raise, wake, waken; animate, bestir, excite, inspire, kindle, rally, stimulate, stir, whet; startle, surprise.

rout vb beat, conquer, defeat, overpower, overthrow, vanquish; chase away, dispel, disperse, scatter; * n defeat, ruin; concourse, multitude, rabble; brawl, disturbance, noise, uproar.

route vb direct, send, steer; * n course, circuit, direction, itinerary, road, passage, path, way.

routine adj familiar, habitual, ordinary, standard, typical, usual; boring, dull, humdrum, predictable, tiresome; * n beat, custom, groove, method, practice, procedure, rut.

row n file, line, queue, rank, series, string, tier; alley, street, terrace; affray, altercation, broil, commotion, dispute, disturbance, quarrel, squabble, tumult, uproar; * vb argue, dispute, fight, quarrel, squabble.

royal adj courtly, generous, grand, imperial, kingly, magnificent, majestic, monarchical, noble, princely, regal, sovereign, splendid, superb.

rub vb abrade, chafe, graze, scrape; clean, massage, polish, wipe; smear, spread; * n caress, massage, polish, shine, wipe; catch, difficulty, drawback, impediment, obstacle, problem.

rubbish n debris, detritus, refuse, waste; dregs, dross, garbage, litter, lumber, refuse, scum, sweepings, trash, trumpery.

rude adj coarse, crude, rough, rugged, shapeless, unfashioned, unformed, unwrought; artless, boorish, ignorant, illiterate, loutish, raw, uncivilised, uncouth, uncultivated, undisciplined, unpolished, ungraceful, unskilful, unskilled, untaught, untrained, untutored; awkward, bluff, blunt, boorish, brusque, churlish, coarse, ill-bred, impertinent, impolite, impudent, insolent, insulting, saucy, uncivil, uncivilised, uncourteous, unrefined; boisterous, harsh, severe, tumultuous, turbulent; artless, crude, inelegant, rustic, unpolished.

rudimentary *adj* elementary, embryonic, fundamental, initial, primary, undeveloped.

ruffian *n* bully, cutthroat, hoodlum, miscreant, monster, rascal, robber, roisterer, rowdy, scoundrel, villain.

ruffle *vb* derange, disarrange, dishevel, disorder, ripple, roughen, rumple; agitate, discompose, disquiet, disturb, excite, harass, irritate, molest, perturb, torment, trouble, vex, worry; pucker, wrinkle; * *n* edging, frill, agitation, bustle, commotion, disturbance, excitement, fluster, flutter, flurry, perturbation, tumult.

rugged *adj* austere, bristly, coarse, crabbed, craggy, hardy, irregular, ragged, robust, rough, rude, severe, seamed, shaggy, uneven, unkempt, wrinkled; inclement, rude, stormy, tempestuous; grating, inharmonious, unmusical.

ruin *vb* crush, damn, defeat, demolish, desolate, destroy, devastate, overturn, shatter, smash, subvert, wreck; beggar, impoverish; * *n* damnation, decay, defeat, demolition, desolation, destruction, devastation, downfall, perdition, rack, shipwreck, subversion, undoing, wreck; bane, destruction, mischief, pest.

ruinous *adj* decayed, demolished; calamitous, damnatory, destructive, disastrous, mischievous, noisome, noxious, pernicious, wasteful.

rule *vb* command, conduct, control, direct, domineer, govern, judge, lead, manage, reign; advise, guide, persuade; adjudicate, decide, determine, settle; obtain, prevail, predominate; * *n* authority, command, control, direction, domination, dominion, empire, government, jurisdiction, lordship, mastery, regency, reign, sway; behaviour, conduct, order, routine, system; convention, criterion, formula, guide, law, maxim, model, precedent, precept, standard, system; decision, order, regulation.

ruler *n* chief, governor, king, lord, master, monarch, regent, sovereign; director, head, manager, president; controller, straightedge.

ruling *n* adjudication, decision, decree, finding, judgement, pronouncement, verdict; * *adj* commanding, controlling, dominant, governing, reigning; chief, dominant,, pre-eminent, prevailing, prevalent, principal, supreme.

rumour *vb* circulate, report, tell; * *n* gossip, hearsay, report, talk; news, report, story, tidings; celebrity, fame, reputation, repute.

rumple *vb* corrugate, crease, crumple, disarrange, dishevel, ruffle, wrinkle; * *n* corrugation, crease, crumple, fold, wrinkle.

run *vb* bolt, course, gallop, haste, hasten, hurry, race, scamper, scour, speed, trip; flow, glide, move, proceed, stream; fuse, liquefy, melt; advance, pass, proceed; extend, lie, spread, stretch; circulate, pass; average, incline, tend; flee; pierce, stab; drive, force, propel, thrust; cast, form, mould, shape; follow, perform, pursue; discharge, emit; direct, maintain, manage; * n race; course, current, flow, motion, passage, progress, wont; continuance, currency, popularity; gallop, journey, trip, trot; demand, pressure; brook, flow, rivulet, streamlet.

rupture vb break, burst, fracture, split; * n breach, break, burst, fracture, split; faction, feud, hostility, quarrel, schism.

rural adj agrarian, country, pastoral, rustic.

rush vb attack, charge, dash, drive, hurtle, precipitate, surge, sweep, tear; * n dash, plunge, precipitance, precipitancy, rout, stampede, tear.

ruthless adj cruel, ferocious, hardhearted, inexorable, inhuman, merciless, pitiless, relentless, remorseless, savage, uncompassionate, unmerciful, unrelenting, unsparing.

S

sabotage v cripple, damage, destroy, disable, disrupt, subvert; * n destruction, disruption, subversion, treachery, treason, wrecking.

sacred adj consecrated, devoted, divine, hallowed, holy; inviolable, inviolate; sainted.

sacrifice vb forgo, immolate, surrender; * n immolation, offering; devotion, loss, surrender.

sacrilegious adj desecrating, impious, irreverent, profane.

sad adj grave, serious; dark, sober, sombre; dejected, depressed, doleful, gloomy, melancholic, miserable, mournful, sorrowful.

saddle vb burden, clog, encumber, load.

safe adj undamaged, unharmed, unhurt, unscathed; guarded, protected, secure; certain, dependable, reliable; good, harmless, sound, whole; * n chest, coffer, strongbox.

safeguard vb guard, protect; * n defence, protection, security; convoy, escort, guard; pass, passport.

sage adj discerning, intelligent, sapient, sensible, shrewd, wise; judicious, well-judged; grave, solemn; * n philosopher, pundit, savant.

saintly adj devout, godly, holy, pious, religious.

sake n cause, purpose, reason; account, cause, consideration, interest, reason, respect.

sale n auction, demand, market, vent.

salt adj saline; pungent, sharp; * n flavour, savour, seasoning, relish, taste; piquancy, poignancy, sarcasm, smartness, wit, zest; mariner, seaman, tar.

salvation n deliverance, escape, preservation, redemption, rescue.

same adj ditto, identical; corresponding, like, similar.

sample vb sip, sup, taste; test, try; demonstrate, exemplify, illustrate; * adj illustrative, representative; * n illustration, instance, piece, specimen; example, model, pattern.

sanctimonious adj affected, devout, holy, hypocritical, pious, self-righteous.

sanction vb authorise; ratify; * n approval, authority, countenance, endorsement, ratification, warranty; ban, boycott, embargo, penalty.

sanctity n devotion, godliness, grace, holiness, piety, purity, religiousness.

sanctuary n church, shrine, temple; asylum, protection, refuge, shelter.

sane adj healthy, lucid, normal, rational, reasonable, sound.

sanitary adj clean, curative, healing, hygienic, remedial, therapeutic.

sarcastic *adj* biting, cutting, mordant, sardonic, satirical, sharp, severe, sneering, taunting.

satellite *n* moon, sputnik; attendant, dependant, follower, lackey, minion, retainer, side-kick; client, dependant, subordinate, tributary, vassal.

satirical *adj* biting, censorious, cutting, invective, ironical, poignant, reproachful, sarcastic, taunting.

satisfaction *n* contentment, enjoyment, gratification, pleasure, satiety; amends, appeasement, atonement, compensation, recompense, redress, reparation, requital, reward.

satisfy *vb* appease, content, gratify, please, sate, satiate, suffice; indemnify, compensate, recompense, remunerate, requite; discharge, settle; assure, convince, persuade; answer, fulfil.

savage *vb* attack, mangle, maul; * *adj* rough, uncultivated, wild; rude, uncivilised, unpolished, untaught; bloodthirsty, feral, ferocious, fierce, rapacious, untamed, wild; beastly, brutal, brutish, inhuman; atrocious, barbarous, bloody, brutal, hardhearted, heathenish, merciless, murderous, pitiless, relentless, ruthless, truculent; rough, rugged, uncivilised; * *n* barbarian, brute, heathen, vandal.

save *vb* liberate, preserve, rescue; salvage, recover, redeem; economise, hoard, husband, reserve, store; hinder, prevent, spare; * *prep* but, deducting, except.

saviour *n* defender, deliverer, guardian, protector, preserver, rescuer.

savour *vb* appreciate, enjoy, relish; flavour, season; * *n* flavour, gust, relish, taste; fragrance, odour, smell, scent.

say *vb* express, pronounce, speak, utter; affirm, allege; recite, rehearse, repeat; assume, presume, suppose; * *n* affirmation, declaration, statement; decision, voice, vote.

saying *n* declaration, expression, observation, remark; adage, aphorism, dictum, maxim, proverb.

scan *vb* examine, investigate, scrutinise, search, sift.

scandalise *vb* offend; calumniate, decry, defame, disgust, libel, reproach, revile, traduce, vilify.

scandalous *adj* defamatory, opprobrious; disgraceful, disreputable, infamous, inglorious, odious, shameful.

scanty *adj* insufficient, meagre, narrow, small; hardly, scarce, short, slender; parsimonious, penurious, scrimpy, skimpy, sparing.

scar *vb* mark, wound; * *n* cicatrice, seam; blemish, defect, disfigurement, flaw, injury; bluff, cliff, crag, precipice.

scarce *adj* deficient, wanting; infrequent, rare, uncommon; * *adv* barely, hardly.

scarcity *n* dearth, deficiency, insufficiency, lack; rareness, rarity, uncommonness.

scare *vb* alarm, daunt, fright, frighten, intimidate, shock, startle, terrify; * *n* alarm, fright, panic, shock, terror.

scatter *vb* broadcast, sprinkle, strew; diffuse, disperse, dissipate, distribute, spread; disappoint, dispel, frustrate.

scent *vb* inhale, nose, smell, sniff; detect, smell out, sniff out; perfume; * *n* aroma, fragrance, odour, perfume, smell.

sceptical *adj* doubtful, dubious, incredulous, questioning, unbelieving.

schedule *vb* list, programme, tabulate; * *n* document, scroll; catalogue, inventory, list, plan, record, register, table, timetable.

scheme vb contrive, design, plan, plot; * n plan, system, theory; cabal, conspiracy, design, device, intrigue, machination, plan, plot, stratagem; arrangement, draught, diagram, outline.

school vb drill, educate, exercise, instruct, teach, train; control, chide, discipline, govern, reprove, tutor; * adj academic, collegiate, institutional, scholastic; * n academy, college, gymnasium, institute, institution, kindergarten, polytechnic, seminary, university; adherents, circle, coterie, disciples, followers; body, order, organisation, sect.

scintillate vb flash, gleam, glisten, glitter, sparkle, twinkle.

scoff vb deride, jeer, mock, ridicule, taunt; gibe, sneer; * n gibe, jeer, sneer, taunt; derision, ridicule.

scold vb berate, blame, censure, chide, reprimand, reprove; brawl, rail, reprimand, upbraid, vituperate; * n shrew, termagant.

scoop n ladle, spoon; coup, exclusive, exposé, revelation, sensation; (with **up**) clear away, lift, pick up, remove, sweep up; bail, dig, empty, excavate, gouge, hollow, scrape.

scope n aim, design, drift, intent, object, purpose, view; amplitude, field, latitude, liberty, margin, range, room, space, sphere, vent; extent, length, span, stretch, sweep.

scorch vb blister, burn, char, roast, sear, singe.

score vb cut, furrow, mark, notch, scratch; note, record; note; enter, register; * n incision, mark, notch; account, bill, debt, reckoning; consideration, motive, reason.

scorn vb condemn, despise, disregard, disdain, slight, spurn; * n contempt, derision, disdain, slight, sneer; derision, scoff.

scoundrel n cheat, knave, miscreant, rascal, rogue, swindler, trickster, villain.

scowl vb frown, glower, lower; * n frown, glower, lower.

scrap vb discard, junk; altercate, bicker, clash, fight, quarrel, row, spat, squabble, tiff, tussle; * n bit, fragment, piece, snippet; bite, crumb, fragment, morsel, mouthful; debris, junk, litter, rubbish, rubble, waste; affray, altercation, bickering, clash, fight, fray, melee, quarrel, row, set-to, squabble, tiff, tussle, wrangle.

scrape vb grind, rasp, scuff; accumulate, collect, gather, save; erase, remove; * n difficulty, distress, perplexity, predicament.

scream vb screech, shriek, squall; * n cry, outcry, screech, shriek, shrill.

screen vb conceal, cover, defend, fence, hide, mask, protect, shelter; * n blind, curtain, partition; defence, guard, protection, shield; cover, veil, disguise; riddle.

screw vb force, pressurise, squeeze, tighten, twist; oppress, rack; distort; * n extortioner, extortionist, miser, skinflint; prison guard; sexual intercourse.

scrupulous adj conscientious, fastidious, precise, rigorous, strict; careful, cautious, circumspect, exact, vigilant.

scrutiny n examination, exploration, inquisition, inspection, investigation, search.

scud vb flee, fly, hasten, post, run, scamper, speed, trip.

scuffle vb fight, strive, struggle; * n altercation, brawl, fight, fray, quarrel, squabble, struggle, wrangle.

scurry vb bustle, dash, hasten,

hurry, scamper; * n burst, bustle, dash, flurry, haste, hurry, scamper, spurt.

seal vb close, fasten, secure; authenticate, confirm, establish, ratify, sanction; confine, enclose, imprison; * n fastening, stamp, wax; assurance, authentication, confirmation, ratification.

search vb examine, explore, inspect, investigate, probe, ransack, scrutinise; delve, hunt, forage, inquire, rummage; * n examination, exploration, hunt, inquiry, inspection, investigation, pursuit, quest, research, scrutiny.

searching adj close, penetrating, trying; examining, exploring, inquiring, investigating, probing, seeking.

season vb acclimatise, accustom, habituate, harden, inure, mature, temper, train; flavour, spice; * n interval, period, spell, term, time.

seasonable adj appropriate, convenient, opportune, suitable, timely.

secluded adj embowered, isolated, private, removed, retired, screened, withdrawn.

seclusion n obscurity, privacy, retirement, separation, solitude, withdrawal.

second n instant, jiffy; minute, moment, trice; another, other; assistant, backer, supporter; * vb abet, advance, aid, assist, encourage, further, help, support, sustain; approve, favour, support; * adj inferior, following, subsequent; additional, extra, other; double, duplicate.

secondary adj inferior, minor, subordinate, subsidiary; * n delegate, deputy, proxy.

secret adj concealed, covered, covert, cryptic, hidden, mysterious, shrouded, veiled; unknown, unrevealed, unseen; stealthy, surreptitious; confidential, private, retired, secluded, unseen; abstruse, latent, mysterious, obscure, occult, recondite, unknown; * n confidence, enigma, key, mystery.

sect n denomination, faction, schism, school.

section n division, fraction, part, piece, portion, segment, slice.

secure vb guard, protect; assure, guarantee, insure; fasten; acquire, gain, obtain, procure; * adj assured, certain, sure; insured, protected, safe; fast, firm, fixed, stable; easy, undisturbed, unsuspecting; inattentive, incautious, negligent, overconfident.

security n bulwark, defence, guard, protection, safeguard, safety, shelter; bond, collateral, deposit, guarantee, pledge, stake, surety, warranty; overconfidence, negligence; assurance, assuredness, certainty, confidence.

sedate adj calm, collected, composed, contemplative, demure, philosophical, placid, quiet, serene, sober, still, thoughtful, tranquil, unruffled.

sedative adj allaying, anodyne, balmy, calming, composing, soothing, tranquillising; * n anaesthetic, anodyne, narcotic, opiate.

sediment n dregs, grounds, precipitate, residue, settlings.

seduce vb allure, attract, corrupt, decoy, ensnare, entice, inveigle, lead.

seductive adj alluring, attractive, enticing, tempting.

see vb behold, contemplate, glimpse, survey; comprehend, conceive, distinguish, espy, notice, observe, perceive, understand; consider, envisage, regard; experience, feel; consider, distinguish, examine, notice, observe; discern, look, penetrate, perceive.

seek vb hunt, look, search; follow, prosecute, pursue; attempt, endeavour, strive, try.

seem vb appear, assume, look, pretend.
seesaw vb alternate, fluctuate, oscillate, pitch, swing.
segment n division, part, piece, portion, section, sector.
segregate vb detach, disconnect, insulate, part, separate.
seize vb capture, catch, clutch, grab, grasp, grip, snatch; confiscate, impound; arrest, capture, take.
seldom adv infrequently, occasionally, rarely.
select vb choose, cull, pick; * adj choice, chosen, excellent, exquisite, good, picked, rare.
selection n choice, election, pick, preference.
self-conscious adj awkward, diffident, embarrassed, insecure, nervous.
selfish adj egoistic, egotistical, greedy, illiberal, mean, narrow, ungenerous.
self-possessed adj calm, collected, composed, cool, placid, sedate, undisturbed, unruffled.
self-willed adj dogged, obstinate, stubborn, uncompliant, wilful.
sell vb barter, exchange, market, peddle, trade, vend.
semblance n likeness, similarity; air, appearance, aspect, bearing, exterior, form, mien, seeming; image, likeness, representation, similitude.
send vb cast, emit, fling, hurl, impel, launch, project, propel, throw, toss; delegate, dispatch; forward, transmit; bestow, confer, grant.
senior adj elder, older; higher, superior.
sensation n feeling, sense, perception; excitement, impression.
sensational adj exciting, melodramatic, thrilling.
sense vb appreciate, notice, perceive, suspect, understand; * n brains, intellect, mind, reason, understanding; appreciation, discernment, feeling, perception, tact, understanding; idea, notion, opinion, sentiment, view; import, interpretation, meaning, significance; judgement, reason, soundness, understanding, wisdom.
sensible adj perceptible; aware, cognisant, conscious; discreet, intelligent, judicious, rational, reasonable, sage, sound, wise; observant, understanding; impressionable, sensitive.
sensitive adj perceptive; impressible, impressionable, responsive, susceptible; delicate, tender, touchy.
sensual adj animal, bodily, voluptuous; lascivious, lewd, licentious, unchaste.
sentence vb condemn, doom, judge; * n determination, opinion; doom, judgement; period, proposition.
sentiment n judgement, notion, opinion; emotion, tenderness; disposition, feeling, thought.
sentimental adj impressible, impressionable, romantic.
sentinel n guard, lookout, picket, sentry, watch, watchman
separate vb detach, disconnect, divide, divorce, part, sever, sunder; remove, withdraw; cleave, open; * adj detached, disconnected, disjointed, dissociated, divided, parted, severed; discrete, distinct, divorced, unconnected; alone, segregated, withdrawn.
sequel n close, conclusion, denouement, termination; consequence, issue, result.
serene adj calm, collected, placid, peaceful, quiet, tranquil, sedate, undisturbed, unperturbed; bright, calm, clear, fair, unclouded.
serenity n calm, collectedness, composure, imperturbability, peacefulness, sedateness, tranquillity; brightness, calmness, clearness, fairness, quietness, stillness.
series n chain, course, order, progression, sequence,

succession, train.
serious *adj* earnest, grave, pious, sedate, solemn, thoughtful; grave, great, important, momentous, weighty.
servant *n* attendant, factotum, helper, henchman, retainer, subaltern, subordinate, underling; domestic, flunky, lackey, menial, scullion, slave.
serve *vb* aid, assist, attend, help, minister, advance, benefit; content, satisfy, supply; handle, officiate, manage, manipulate, work.
service *vb* maintain, overhaul, repair; * *n* labour, work; business, duty, employment office; advantage, benefit, good, gain, profit; avail, purpose, use, utility; ceremony, function, rite, worship.
set *vb* lay, locate, mount, place, put, stand, station; appoint, determine, establish, fix, settle; stake, wager; adapt, adjust, regulate; adorn; arrange, pose, post; appoint, assign, prescribe; estimate, rate, value; contrive, produce; decline, sink; congeal, consolidate, harden, solidify; flow, incline, run; (with **about**) begin, commence; (with **apart**) consecrate, dedicate, devote, reserve; (with **aside**) annul, omit, reject; reserve; (with **before**) display, exhibit; (with **down**) chronicle, record, register, write down; (with **forth**) display, exhibit, explain, expound, manifest, represent, show; (with **forward**) advance, further, promote; (with **free**) acquit, emancipate, liberate, release; (with **off**) adorn, decorate, embellish; define, portion off; (with **on**) incite, prompt, spur, urge; attack, assault; (with **out**) display, issue, proclaim, prove, show; (with **right**) correct, put in order; (with **to rights**) adjust, regulate; (with **up**) erect, exalt, raise; establish, found, institute; (with **upon**) assail, assault, attack, rush upon; * *adj* appointed, established, ordained, prescribed, regular; determined, fixed, firm, obstinate, stiff, unyielding; immovable, predetermined; located, placed, put; * *n* attitude, position, posture; scene, scenery; assortment, collection, suit; class, circle, clique, cluster, company, division, gang, group, party, school.
setting *n* backdrop, background, context, frame, location, mounting, perspective, scene, scenery, set, site, surroundings.
settle *vb* adjust, compose, regulate; balance, close up, conclude, discharge, liquidate, pay, pay up, reckon, satisfy, square; allay, calm, compose, pacify, quiet, rest, tranquillise; confirm, decide, determine, make clear; establish, fix; gravitate, sink, subside; abide, colonise, dwell, establish, people, plant; (with **on**) determine, fix, fix upon; establish.
sever *vb* divide, part, rend, separate, sunder; detach, disconnect, disjoin.
several *adj* single; particular; distinct, independent, separate; different, diverse, manifold, many, sundry, various.
severe *adj* austere, bitter, hard, harsh, inexorable, morose, rigid, rigorous, rough, sharp, stiff, unmitigated, unrelenting, unsparing; accurate, exact, methodical, strict; chaste, plain, restrained, unadorned; biting, bitter, caustic, cruel, cutting, harsh, keen, sharp, trenchant; acute, distressing, intense, sharp, stringent, violent; critical, exact, hard, rigorous.
sew *vb* bind, hem, stitch, tack.
sex *n* gender; coitus, copulation, fornication, lovemaking,

intercourse; desire, libido, reproduction, sexuality.

shabby *adj* faded, ragged, seedy, threadbare, worn, worn-out; mean, paltry, penurious, stingy, ungentlemanly, unhandsome.

shackle *vb* chain, fetter, hamper, manacle; bind, confine, embarrass, encumber, impede, obstruct, restrict, trammel; * *n* chain, fetter, hamper, manacle.

shade *vb* darken, dim, eclipse, obscure; cover, hide, protect, screen, shelter; * *n* darkness, dusk, gloom, obscurity, shadow; cover, protection, shelter; blind, curtain, screen, shutter, veil; degree, kind, variety; colour, complexion, dye, hue, tinge, tint, tone; apparition, ghost, phantom, spectre, spirit.

shadow *vb* cloud, darken, obscure, shade; symbolise, typify; conceal, hide, protect, screen, shroud; * *n* penumbra, umbra; darkness, gloom, obscurity; cover, protection, security, shelter; image, prefiguration, representation; apparition, ghost, phantom, shade, spirit; image, portrait, reflection, silhouette.

shadowy *adj* shady; dark, dim, gloomy, murky, obscure; ghostly, imaginary, impalpable, insubstantial, intangible, spectral, visionary.

shake *vb* quake, quiver, shiver, shudder, tremble, agitate, convulse, jar, jolt, stagger; daunt, frighten, intimidate; weaken; oscillate, vibrate, wave; move, put away, remove, throw off; * *n* agitation, flutter, quaking, shivering, shock, trembling, tremor.

shaky *adj* quaky, shaking, tottering, trembling.

shallow *adj* flimsy, frivolous, trifling, trivial; empty, ignorant, slight, simple, superficial, unintelligent.

sham *vb* feign, imitate, pretend; deceive, delude, dupe, trick; * *adj* assumed, counterfeit, false, feigned, mock, spurious; * *n* delusion, feint, fraud, imposition, imposture, pretence, trick.

shame *vb* debase, discredit, disgrace, dishonour, stain, sully, taint, tarnish; abash, humble, humiliate; deride, flout, jeer, mock, ridicule, sneer; * *n* contempt, derision, discredit, disgrace, dishonour, disrepute, ignominy, infamy, odium, reproach, scandal; abashment, chagrin, confusion, mortification; disgrace, dishonour, reproach, scandal; decorum, modesty, propriety.

shameful *adj* atrocious, base, disgraceful, dishonourable, disreputable, ignominious, nefarious, outrageous, scandalous, villainous, wicked; indecent, scandalous, unbecoming.

shameless *adj* assuming, audacious, brazen, cool, immodest, impudent, indecent, indelicate, insolent, unabashed, unblushing; abandoned, corrupt, depraved, dissolute, graceless, hardened, obdurate, reprobate, sinful, unprincipled.

shanty *n* hovel, hut, lean-to, shack, shed.

shape *vb* create, form, produce; fashion, form, mould; adjust, direct, frame; conceive, figure, image, imagine; * *n* appearance, fashion, figure, form, make; build, cast, cut, fashion, model, mould; apparition, image.

share *vb* apportion, distribute, divide, parcel out, split; partake, participate; receive; * *n* part, portion; allotment, allowance, deal, dividend, division, lot, proportion, quota.

sharp *adj* acute, cutting, keen, trenchant; acuminate, pointed; acute, astute, canny, clear-sighted, clever, cunning,

SHATTER

discerning, discriminating, ingenious, inventive, quick, sagacious, shrewd, smart, subtle, witty; acid, acrid, biting, bitter, burning, hot, piquant, poignant, pungent, sour, stinging; acrimonious, biting, caustic, cutting, harsh, mordant, pointed, sarcastic, severe, tart, trenchant; cruel, hard, rigid, severe; acute, intense, keen, painful, piercing, poignant, severe, sore; biting, nipping, piercing, pinching; ardent, fierce, fiery, impetuous, strong; high, piercing, shrill; attentive, vigilant; keen, penetrating, piercing, severe; close, exacting, shrewd; * adv abruptly, suddenly; exactly, precisely, punctually.

shatter vb break, burst, rend, smash, splinter; derange, disorder, overthrow.

shave vb crop, cut off, mow, pare; slice; graze, skim, touch.

sheen n brightness, gloss, glossiness, shine, splendour.

sheer adj perpendicular, precipitous, steep, vertical; clear, downright, pure, unadulterated, unmingled, unmixed, unqualified, utter; clear; fine, transparent; * adv outright; perpendicularly, steeply; * vb decline, deviate, swerve; * n bow, curve.

shelter vb cover, defend, harbour, hide, house, screen, shroud; * n asylum, cover, harbour, haven, refuge, retreat, sanctuary; cover, defence, safety, screen, security; guardian, protector.

shield vb cover, defend, guard, protect, shelter; repel; avert; * n aegis, escutcheon; cover, defence, guard, palladium, protection, rampart, safeguard, security, shelter.

shift vb alter, change, fluctuate, move, vary; dodge, swerve, veer; devise, manage, plan, scheme; * n change, substitution, turn; contrivance, expedient,

resource; artifice, craft, device, dodge, fraud, ruse, stratagem, subterfuge, trick, wile; chemise, smock.

shimmer vb glimmer, glisten, shine; * n blink, glimmer, glitter, twinkle.

shine vb beam, blaze, flare, glare, gleam, glimmer, glow, lighten, radiate, sparkle; excel; * n brightness, brilliancy, glaze, gloss, polish, sheen.

shiny adj bright, clear, luminous, unclouded; brilliant, glassy, glossy, polished.

shirk vb avoid, dodge, evade, malinger, slack; cheat, trick.

shiver vb shatter, splinter; quake, quiver, shake, shudder, tremble; * n bit, fragment, slice, sliver, splinter; shaking, shivering, shuddering, tremor.

shock vb appal, horrify; disgust, disquiet, disturb, offend, outrage, scandalise; astound, stagger, stun; jar, jolt, shake; encounter, meet; * n agitation, blow, stroke; assault, conflict; blow, clash, collision, impact, percussion, stroke.

shoot vb catapult, expel, hurl, propel; discharge, fire, let off; dart, fly, pass, pelt; extend, jut, project, protrude, put forth, send forth, stretch; bud, germinate, sprout; (with **up**) grow, spring up, start up; * n branch, offshoot, sprout, twig.

shop n boutique, emporium, market, store, supermarket; * vb buy, window-shop.

shore n beach, coast, seaboard, seaside, strand, waterside; beam, brace, buttress, prop, support; * vb brace, buttress, prop, support.

short adj brief, curtailed; direct, near, straight; brief, concise, condensed, pithy, terse, succinct, summary; abrupt, curt, pointed, sharp; defective, deficient, inadequate, scanty; contracted, lacking, limited, wanting; squat, undersised, vertically challenged; brittle,

188

crisp; * *adv* abruptly, at once, forthwith, suddenly.

shortcoming *n* defect, deficiency, error, failing, failure, fault, imperfection, inadequacy, remissness, weakness.

shorten *vb* abbreviate, curtail, cut short; abridge, contract, diminish, lessen, reduce; curtail, cut off, dock, lop, trim; hinder, restrain, restrict.

shot *n* discharge; ball, bullet, missile, projectile; marksman; * *adj* iridescent, moiré, watered; intermingled, interspersed, interwoven.

shoulder *vb* bear, bolster, carry, pack, support, sustain, tote; crowd, elbow, jostle, press forward, push, thrust; * *n* projection, protuberance.

shout *vb* bawl, cheer, clamour, exclaim, halloo, roar, whoop, yell; * *n* cheer, clamour, exclamation, halloo, outcry, roar, whoop, yell.

show *vb* display, exhibit, flaunt, parade, present; indicate, mark, point out; disclose, discover, divulge, explain, make known, proclaim, publish, reveal; demonstrate, evidence, prove, verify; conduct, guide, usher; direct, inform, instruct, teach; explain, expound, elucidate; (with off) display, exhibit, make a show; (with up) expose; * *n* array, exhibition, sight, spectacle; bravery, ceremony, dash, demonstration, display, flourish, pageant, parade, pomp, splendour; likeness, resemblance, semblance; affectation, appearance, illusion, plausibility, pose, pretence, simulation.

showy *adj* dressy, flashy, flaunting, gaudy, gorgeous, loud, ornate, smart, swanky, splendid; grand, magnificent, ostentatious, pompous, pretentious, stately.

shower *n* barrage, deluge, rain, stream, torrent, volley; crew, rabble; * *vb* deluge, inundate, lavish, pour, rain, spray, sprinkle.

shred *vb* tear; * *n* bit, fragment, piece, rag, strip, tatter.

shrewd *adj* artful, astute, crafty, cunning, sly, subtle, wily; astute, canny, discerning, discriminating, ingenious, knowing, penetrating, sagacious, sharp.

shriek *vb* scream, screech, squeal, yell, yelp; * *n* cry, scream, screech, yell.

shrill *adj* acute, high-pitched, piercing, sharp.

shrink *vb* contract, decrease, dwindle, shrivel, wither; blench, flinch, quail, recoil, retire, swerve, wince, withdraw.

shrivel *vb* dry up, parch; contract, decrease, dwindle, shrink, wither.

shroud *vb* cloak, conceal, cover, hide, mask, protect, screen, shelter, veil; * *n* covering, garment; grave clothes, winding sheet.

shudder *vb* quake, quiver, shake, shiver, tremble; * *n* shaking, shuddering, trembling, tremor.

shuffle *vb* disorder, intermix, jumble, mix; dodge, equivocate, evade, prevaricate, quibble; shift, struggle; * *n* artifice, evasion, fraud, pretence, pretext, prevarication, quibble, ruse, subterfuge, trick.

shun *vb* avoid, elude, eschew, escape, evade.

shut *vb* close, close up; confine, enclose, imprison, lock up; (with in) confine, enclose; (with off) bar, exclude; (with up) close up; confine, enclose, fasten in, imprison, lock in, lock up.

shy *vb* cast, fling, hurl, pitch, sling, throw, toss; sheer, start; aside; * *adj* bashful, coy, diffident, reserved, retiring, shrinking, timid; cautious, distrustful, wary; * *n* start; fling, throw.

sick *adj* ailing, ill, unwell, weak; nauseated, queasy; disgusted,

side vb border, bound, edge, flank, frontier, rim, verge; avert, turn aside; (with *with*) favour, join with, second, support; * *adj* flanking; indirect, oblique; odd, off, spare; * *n* border, edge, flank, margin, verge; cause, faction, interest, party, sect.

sift vb part, separate; bolt, screen; analyse, canvass, examine, fathom, investigate, probe, scrutinise, sound, try.

sight vb perceive, see; * *n* cognizance, ken, perception, view; beholding, seeing, vision; exhibition, prospect, scene, show, spectacle; consideration, knowledge, view; examination, inspection.

sign vb indicate, signal; endorse, subscribe; * *n* emblem, index, indication, manifestation, mark, note, proof, signal, symbol, symptom, token; beacon, signal; auspice, foreboding, miracle, omen, portent, presage, prognostic; symbol, type; password.

signal vb flag, hail, nod, nudge, salute, sign, speak, wave, wink; * *adj* conspicuous, eminent, extraordinary, notable, noteworthy, remarkable; * *n* cue, indication, mark, sign, token.

signify vb betoken, express, indicate; denote, imply, mean, purport, suggest; announce, declare, impart, manifest, proclaim; augur, foreshadow, portend, represent, suggest; import, matter, weigh.

silence vb hush, still; allay, calm, quiet; * *interj* be silent, be still, hush, soft, whist; * *n* calm, hush, lull, noiselessness, peace, quiet, quietude, soundlessness, stillness; dumbness, muteness.

silhouette *n* delineation, form, outline, profile, shape; * *vb* delineate, etch, outline.

silly *adj* brainless, childish, foolish, senseless, simple, stupid, witless; absurd, frivolous, imprudent, trifling, unwise; * *n* ass, duffer, idiot, simpleton.

similar *adj* analogous, duplicate, like, resembling; homogeneous, uniform.

similarity *n* agreement, analogy, correspondence, likeness, parallelism, parity, semblance.

simple *adj* elementary, homogeneous, incomplex, unalloyed, unblended, uncombined, uncompounded, unmingled, unmixed; chaste, plain, homespun, unadorned, unaffected, unembellished, unpretentious, unvarnished; artless, downright, frank, guileless, ingenuous, naïve, open, plain, sincere, true, unaffected, unconstrained, undesigning, unsophisticated; credulous, fatuous, foolish, silly, unwise, weak; clear, intelligible, plain, uninvolved, unmistakable.

simplicity *n* chasteness, neatness, plainness; frankness, naïveté, openness, sincerity; clearness, plainness; folly, weakness.

simplify vb abridge, decipher, disentangle, facilitate, streamline.

simultaneous *adj* coincident, concomitant, concurrent, contemporaneous.

sin vb err, transgress, trespass; * *n* depravity, iniquity, misdeed, offence, transgression, unrighteousness, wickedness, wrong.

since *conj* as, because; * *adv* before this; from that time; * *prep* after, subsequently to.

sincere *adj* pure, unmixed; genuine, honest, unaffected, unfeigned, unvarnished; candid, direct, frank, guileless, hearty, honest, ingenuous, open, plain, straightforward, true, truthful, upright.

sincerity *n* candour, earnestness, frankness, genuineness, honesty, ingenuousness, probity, truth, truthfulness, veracity.

sinful *adj* bad, criminal, depraved, immoral, iniquitous, transgressive, unholy, unrighteous, wicked, wrong.

sing *vb* cantillate, carol, chant, hymn, intone, lilt, warble.

singe *vb* burn, scorch, sear.

single *vb* (with **out**) choose, pick, select; * *adj* alone, isolated, one only, sole, solitary; individual, particular, separate; celibate, unmarried, unwedded; pure, uncompounded, unmixed.

singular *adj* extraordinary, rare, remarkable, strange, unusual; exceptional, particular, remarkable, unexampled, unparalleled, unprecedented; strange, unaccountable; bizarre, eccentric, odd, peculiar; individual, single; not complex, uncompounded.

sinister *adj* baleful, untoward; boding ill, inauspicious, ominous; left, on the left hand.

sink *vb* droop, founder, go down, submerge, subside; enter, penetrate; collapse, fail; decay, decline, decrease, dwindle, languish; engulf, immerse, merge, submerge; dig, excavate; bring down, crush, debase, degrade, depress, diminish, lessen, lower; destroy, overthrow, overwhelm, reduce, ruin, swamp, waste; * *n* basin, drain, sewer.

sinless *adj* faultless, guiltless, immaculate, impeccable, innocent, unblemished, undefiled, unspotted, unsullied.

sinner *n* criminal, evildoer, offender, reprobate, wrongdoer.

sip *vb* drink, sup; absorb; * *n* small draught, taste.

sire *vb* father, reproduce; breed, conceive, create, father, generate, produce, propagate; * *n* father, progenitor; sir, sirrah; begetter, creator, father, generator, originator.

sit *vb* remain, repose, rest, stay; lie, rest; dwell, settle; perch; brood, incubate; become, fit.

site *vb* locate, place, position, situate, station; * *n* locality, location, place, position, situation, spot, station.

situation *n* locality, location, place, position, site, spot, whereabouts; case, category, circumstances, condition, juncture, plight, predicament, state; employment, office, place, post, station.

size *n* amplitude, dimensions, expanse, magnitude, mass, volume.

skeleton *n* bare bones, bones, draft, frame, framework, outline, sketch, structure.

sketch *vb* design, draft; delineate, depict, represent; * *n* design, draft, drawing, outline, plan, skeleton.

sketchy *adj* crude, incomplete, unfinished.

skilful *adj* able, accomplished, adept, adroit, apt, competent, conversant, cunning, deft, dexterous, expert, handy, ingenious, masterly, practised, proficient, qualified, trained, versed, well-versed.

skill *n* ability, adroitness, aptitude, aptness, art, deftness, dexterity, expertise, expertness, facility, ingenuity, knack; discernment, discrimination, knowledge, understanding, wit.

skim *vb* brush, glance, graze, kiss, scrape, scratch; coast, flow, fly, glide, sail, whisk; glance at, scan, skip, thumb over, touch upon.

skin *vb* pare, peel; decorticate, excoriate, flay; * *n* cuticle, epidermis, hide, pelt; hull, husk, peel, rind.

skip *vb* bound, caper, gambol, hop, jump, spring; disregard, miss, neglect, omit, pass over,

skim; * n bound, caper, gambol, hop, jump, spring.
skirmish vb battle, combat, contest, fight, scuffle, tussle; * n affray, battle, combat, conflict, contest, encounter, fight, scuffle, tussle.
skirt vb border, bound, edge, fringe, hem, rim; circumvent, flank; * n border, boundary, edge, margin, rim, verge; kilt, overskirt, petticoat.
slack vb ease off, let up; abate, ease up, relax; malinger, shirk; * adj backward, careless, inattentive, lax, negligent, remiss; abated, dilatory, diminished, lingering, slow, tardy; loose, relaxed; dull, idle, inactive, quiet, sluggish; * n excess, leeway, looseness, play; coal dust, residue.
slacken vb abate, diminish, lessen, lower, mitigate, moderate, neglect, remit, relieve, retard, slack; loosen, relax; flag, slow down.
slander vb asperse, backbite, brand, calumniate, decry, defame, libel, malign, reproach, scandalise, vilify; detract from, disparage; * n aspersion, calumny, defamation, libel, scandal, vilification.
slant vb incline, lean, list, slope; * n inclination, slope, tilt.
slap vb clap, smack, spank, strike; * adv instantly, plumply, quickly; * n blow, clap.
slapdash adv haphazardly, hurriedly, precipitately.
slash vb, n cut, gash, slit.
slaughter vb butcher, kill, massacre, murder, slay; * n bloodshed, butchery, carnage, killing, massacre, murder, slaying.
slay vb butcher, dispatch, kill, murder, slaughter; destroy, ruin.
sleek adj glossy, silken, silky, smooth.
sleep vb doze, drowse, nap, slumber; * n dormancy, hypnosis, lethargy, rest, slumber.
sleeping adj dormant, inactive, quiescent.
sleepwalker n night-walker, noctambulist, somnambulist.
sleepwalking n somnambulism.
sleepy adj dozy, drowsy, heavy, lethargic, somnolent; narcotic, slumberous, somniferous, soporific; heavy, inactive, lazy, slow, sluggish, torpid.
slender adj lank, lithe, narrow, skinny, slim, slight, thin; fine, flimsy, slight, tenuous, weak; inconsiderable, moderate, small, trivial; inadequate, insufficient, lean, meagre, pitiful, scanty, small; light, meagre, sparing.
slice vb cut, divide, part, section; sever; * n chop, piece.
slick adj glossy, polished, sleek, smooth; clever, cunning, shrewd, slippery, unctuous; * vb gloss, lacquer, polish, shine, sleek, varnish; grease, lubricate, oil.
slide vb glide, move smoothly, slip; * n glide, skid, slip.
slight vb disdain, disregard, neglect, snub; overlook; skimp, slur; * adj inconsiderable, insignificant, little, petty, small, trifling, trivial, unimportant, unsubstantial; delicate, feeble, frail, weak; careless, cursory, desultory, scanty, superficial; flimsy; slender, slim; * n discourtesy, disregard, disrespect, neglect.
slim vb lose weight, reduce, slenderise; * adj gaunt, lank, lithe, narrow, skinny, slender, spare; inconsiderable, slight, trifling, trivial, unsubstantial; insufficient, meagre.
slimy adj miry, muddy, oozy; clammy, gelatinous, glutinous, gummy, lubricious, mucous, viscous.
slinky adj clinging, close-fitting, feline, figure hugging, sinuous, sleek.
slip vb glide, slide, err, mistake, trip; omit; disengage, throw

SMELL

off, escape, loose, release; * *n* glide, slide; blunder, error, fault, lapse, misstep, mistake, oversight, peccadillo, trip; error, fault, impropriety, indiscretion, transgression; desertion, escape; cord, string; case, covering; cutting, shoot, twig; piece, streak, strip.

slippery *adj* glib, slithery, smooth; changeable, insecure, mutable, perilous, uncertain, unsafe, unstable; cunning, dishonest, elusive, faithless, perfidious, shifty, treacherous.

slit *vb* cut; divide, rend, slash, split, sunder; * *n* cut, gash.

slope *vb* incline, slant, tilt; * *n* acclivity, cant, declivity, gradient, inclination, incline, obliquity, pitch.

slouch *vb* droop, loll, slump; shuffle; * *n* malingerer, shirker, slacker; shuffle, stoop.

slovenly *adj* unclean, untidy; disorderly, dowdy, loose, slatternly, unkempt, untidy; careless, heedless, lazy, negligent, perfunctory.

slow *vb* abate, brake, check, decelerate, mitigate, moderate, weaken; delay, detain, retard; ease, relax, slacken; * *adj* deliberate, gradual; dead, dull, heavy, inactive, inert, sluggish, stupid; behindhand, late, tardy, unready; delaying, dilatory, lingering, slack.

sludge *n* mire, mud; slosh, slush.

sluggish *adj* drowsy, idle, inactive, indolent, inert, languid, lazy, slothful, torpid, slow; dull, stupid, supine, tame.

slumber *vb* doze, nap, repose, rest, sleep; * *n* doze, nap, repose, rest, siesta, sleep.

slump *vb* drop, fall, founder, sag, sink; decline, depreciate, deteriorate, ebb, fail, fall, recede, slide, slip, subside, wane; * *n* droop, drop, fall, lowering; decline, downturn, subsidence, ebb, falling off, wane; crash, recession.

slur *vb* asperse, calumniate, disparage, reproach; conceal, disregard, obscure, slight; * *n* mark, stain; brand, disgrace, reproach, stain, stigma; innuendo.

sly *adj* artful, crafty, cunning, subtle, wily; astute, cautious, shrewd; knowing; clandestine, secret, stealthy, underhand.

smack *vb* smell, taste; slap, strike; crack, snap; kiss; * *n* flavour, savour, tang, taste; dash, little, sprinkling, tinge, touch; smattering; crack, slap, snap; kiss.

small *adj* diminutive, little, miniature, petite, tiny, wee; infinitesimal, microscopic, minute; inappreciable, inconsiderable, insignificant, petty, trifling, trivial; slender; faint, feeble, puny, slight; illiberal, narrow-minded, paltry, selfish, sordid, ungenerous, unworthy.

smarmy *adj* bootlicking, crawling, greasy, ingratiating, obsequious, oily, servile, slimy, smooth, suave, sycophantic, toadying, unctuous.

smart *vb* hurt, pain, sting; * *adj* keen, painful, pricking, pungent, severe, sharp, stinging; agile, brisk, fresh, lively, nimble, quick, sprightly, spry; effective, efficient, energetic, vigorous; adroit, alert, clever, dexterous, expert, intelligent, quick; acute, apt, pertinent, ready, witty; chic, dapper, fine, spruce, trim.

smash *vb* break, dash, shatter; * *n* crash, destruction, ruin; bankruptcy, failure.

smear *vb* bedaub, daub, plaster, smudge; contaminate, pollute, smirch, soil, stain, sully, tarnish; * *n* blot, blotch, daub, patch, smirch, smudge, spot, stain; calumny, defamation, libel, slander.

smell *vb* scent, sniff, stench, stink; * *n* aroma, bouquet, fragrance, odour, perfume, redolence, scent, stench, stink; sniff.

smile *vb* grin, laugh, simper, smirk; * *n* grin, simper, smirk.

smitten *vb* afflicted, beset, laid low, plagued, struck down; beguiled, bewitched, bowled over, captivated, charmed, enamoured, infatuated.

smoke *vb* emit, exhale, reek, steam; fumigate; discover, find out, smell out; * *n* effluvium, exhalation, fume, mist, reek, steam; fumigation.

smooth *vb* flatten, level; ease, lubricate; extenuate, palliate, soften; alleviate, assuage, calm, mitigate, mollify; * *adj* even, flat, level, polished, unruffled, unwrinkled; glossy, satiny, silky, sleek, soft, velvet; flowing, liquid; fluent, voluble; flattering, ingratiating, insinuating, mild, oily, soothing, suave, unctuous.

smother *vb* choke, stifle, suffocate; conceal, deaden, extinguish, hide, repress, suppress, stifle; smoke.

smudge *vb* blur, smear, smut, soil, spot, stain; * *n* blur, blot, smear, smut, spot, stain.

smutty *adj* coarse, gross, immodest, impure, indecent, indelicate, loose; dirty, foul, soiled, stained.

snag *vb* catch, enmesh, entangle, hook, snare, tangle; * *n* knot, projection, protuberance; catch, difficulty, drawback, hitch, rub, shortcoming, weakness; obstacle.

snap *vb* break, fracture; bite, seize; crack; crackle, pop; * *adj* casual, cursory, hasty, offhand, sudden; * *n* bite, catch, nip, seizure; catch, clasp, fastening, lock; crack, flick, flip, smack; briskness, energy, verve, vim.

snare *vb* catch, entangle, entrap; * *n* catch, gin, net, noose, trap, wile.

snarl *vb* grin, gnarl, growl, grumble, murmur; complicate, entangle, knot; confuse, ensnare; * *n* growl; disorder, entanglement, tangle; difficulty, embarrassment, intricacy.

snatch *vb* catch, clutch, grasp, grip, pull, seize, snip, wrest; * *n* bit, fragment, part, portion; catch, effort.

sneak *vb* skulk, slink, steal; truckle; * *adj* clandestine, concealed, covert, hidden, secret, sly, underhand; * *n* informer, telltale.

sneer *vb* gibe, jeer; (with **at**) deride, despise, disdain, laugh at, mock, scoff; * *n* flouting, gibe, jeer, scoff.

snip *vb* clip, cut, nip; snap; * *n* bit, fragment, particle, piece, shred; share.

snub *vb* abash, cold-shoulder, humble, humiliate, mortify, slight, take down; check, clip, cut short, dock, nip, prune, stunt; * *n* check, rebuke, slight; * *adj* squashed, squat, stubby, turned up.

snug *adj* close, concealed; comfortable, compact, convenient, neat, trim.

snuggle *vb* cuddle, nestle, nuzzle.

so *adv* thus; in such a manner; in this way; as it is, as it was, such; for this reason, therefore; be it so; * *conj* in case that, on condition that, provided that.

soak *vb* drench, moisten, saturate, wet; absorb, imbibe; imbue, steep.

soar *vb* ascend, glide, mount, rise, tower.

sober *vb* (with **up**) calm down, collect oneself, compose oneself, cool off, moderate, simmer down; * *adj* abstemious, abstinent, temperate; rational, reasonable, sane, sound; calm, collected, composed, moderate, rational, reasonable, steady, temperate, unimpassioned; demure, grave, quiet, serious, solemn, sombre, staid; dark, drab, quiet, sad, sombre, subdued.

social *adj* civic, civil; affable, communicative, familiar, friendly, hospitable; convivial, festive, gregarious; * *n* gathering, party, reception, soiree.

society *n* association, company, fellowship; the community, the public; the world; elite; association, body, brotherhood, corporation, club, company, fellowship, fraternity, union.

sodden *adj* drenched, saturated, soaked, steeped, wet; boiled, stewed.

soft *adj* impressible, malleable, plastic, pliable, yielding; downy, fleecy, velvety; pulpy, squashy; compliant, weak; mild, gentle, kind, lenient, tender; delicate, tender; easy, gentle, quiet; effeminate, luxurious, unmanly; dulcet, gentle, melodious, smooth; * *interj* hold, stop.

soften *vb* mellow, melt, tenderise; abate, alleviate, appease, assuage, balm, blunt, calm, dull, ease, lessen, mitigate, moderate, mollify, milden, quell, quiet, relent, relieve, soothe, still; extenuate, modify, qualify; enervate, weaken.

soil *n* earth, ground, loam; country, land; blemish, defilement, dirt, filth, foulness; blot, spot, stain, taint, tarnish; * *vb* bedaub, bespatter, contaminate, daub, defile, foul, pollute, stain, sully, taint, tarnish.

sojourn *n* rest, stay, stop, stop over, visit; * *vb* abide, dwell, lodge, reside, rest, stay, stop, tarry.

sole *adj* individual, one, only, single, solitary, unique.

solemn *adj* ceremonial, formal, ritual; devotional, devout, reverential, sacred; grave, serious, sober; august, grand, imposing, impressive, majestic, stately, venerable.

solicit *vb* appeal to, beg, beseech, entreat, implore, importune, petition, pray, press, request, supplicate, urge; arouse, entice, excite, invite, summon; canvass, seek.

solid *adj* congealed, firm, hard, impenetrable; compact, dense, impermeable; sound, stable, strong, substantial; real, valid, weighty; reliable, safe, sound, trustworthy.

solidarity *n* community, consolidation, fellowship, joint interest, mutual responsibility.

solitary *adj* alone, companionless, lone, lonely, only, separate, unaccompanied; individual, single; deserted, desolate: isolated, lonely, remote, secluded, unfrequented; * *n* anchorite, hermit, recluse, solitaire, solitarian.

solution *n* answer, elucidation, explication, explanation, key, resolution, unravelling, unriddling; dissolution, liquefaction, resolution, separation; disconnection, discontinuance, disruption.

solve *vb* clear up, disentangle, elucidate, explain, interpret, resolve, unfold.

sombre *adj* cloudy, dark, dismal, dull, gloomy, overcast, shady, sunless; doleful, funereal, grave, lugubrious, melancholy, mournful, sad, sober.

some *adj* a, an, any, one; about, near; certain, little, moderate, part, several.

somebody *n* one, someone, something; celebrity, VIP.

something *n* thing; somebody; affair, event, matter, thing.

sometime *adj* former, late; * *adv* formerly, once; at one time or other.

sometimes *adv* at times, now and then, occasionally; formerly, once.

somewhat *adv* to some degree, more or less, rather; * *n* a little, more or less, part.

somewhere *adv* in one place or

somnolent *adj* comatose, dozy, drowsy, half awake, heavy-eyed, sleepy, soporific, torpid.

song *n* aria, ballad, canticle, carol, ditty, lullaby; descant, melody; anthem, hymn, lay, poem, psalm, strain; poesy, poetry, verse.

soon *adv* anon, before long, by and by, in a short time, presently, shortly; forthwith, promptly, quick; gladly, readily, willingly.

soothe *vb* cajole, humour; appease, assuage, balm, calm, lull, mollify, pacify, quiet, sober, soften, still, tranquillise; allay, alleviate, blunt, ease, lessen, mitigate, moderate, palliate, qualify, relieve, soften, temper.

soporific *adj* dormitive, hypnotic, narcotic, opiate, sleepy, slumberous, somnific, soporous.

sorcerer *n* charmer, conjurer, diviner, enchanter, magician, necromancer, seer, shaman, thaumaturgist, witch, wizard.

sordid *adj* base, degraded, low, mean, vile; avaricious, covetous, miserly, penurious, stingy, ungenerous.

sore *adj* irritated, painful, raw, tender; aggrieved, galled, grieved, hurt, irritable, pained, tender, vexed; afflictive, distressing, sharp; * *n* abscess, gathering, ulcer; affliction, grief, pain, sorrow, trouble.

sorrow *vb* bewail, grieve, lament, mourn, weep; * *n* affliction, grief, heartache, mourning, sadness, trouble, woe.

sorrowful *adj* dejected, depressed, grieving, heartsore, sad; distressing, lamentable, melancholy, mournful, painful, sad; disconsolate, dismal, doleful, dolorous, dreary, lugubrious, melancholy, rueful, woebegone, woeful.

sorry *adj* dejected, grieved, pained, sorrowful; distressing, pitiful; chagrined, mortified, pained, regretful, remorseful, sad; abject, base, contemptible, despicable, low, mean, paltry, poor, insignificant, miserable, pitiful, worthless, wretched.

sort *vb* arrange, class, classify, order; join, put together; choose, elect, pick out, select; associate, fraternise; accord, fit, suit; * *n* character, class, denomination, description, kind, nature, order, race, species, type; manner, way.

so-so *adj* indifferent, mediocre, middling, ordinary, passable, tolerable.

soul *n* mind, psyche, spirit; being, person; embodiment, essence, spirit, vital principle; ardour, energy, fervour, inspiration, vitality.

sound *adj* entire, intact, unbroken, unhurt, impaired, uninjured, whole; hale, hardy, healthy, vigorous; good, perfect, undecayed; sane, well-balanced; correct, right, solid, valid, well-founded; legal, valid; deep, fast, profound, undisturbed; lusty, severe; * *n* channel, narrows, strait; noise, note, tone, voice, whisper; * *vb* appear, seem; express, utter; announce, celebrate, proclaim, spread; fathom, gauge, measure, test; examine, probe, search, test.

sound out *vb* canvass, examine, probe, pump, question.

sour *vb* acidulate; embitter, envenom; * *adj* acid, astringent, pricked, sharp, tart, vinegary; acrimonious, fretful, glum, ill-humoured, ill-natured, ill-tempered, peevish, petulant; bitter, disagreeable; austere, dismal, gloomy, morose, sad, sullen; bad, curdled, musty, rancid, turned.

source *n* beginning, fountain head, origin, rise, root, spring, well; cause.

souvenir *n* keepsake, memento, remembrance.

sovereign *adj* imperial, princely, regal, supreme; chief, highest, paramount, predominant, principal, supreme; efficacious, effectual; * *n* autocrat, monarch, suzerain; emperor, empress, king, lord, potentate, queen, ruler.

sovereignty *n* authority, dominion, empire, power, rule, supremacy, sway.

sow *vb* scatter, strew; disperse, disseminate, propagate; plant; besprinkle, scatter.

space *n* expanse, proportions, spread; accommodation, capacity, room; place; distance, interval.

spacious *adj* extensive, vast, wide; ample, broad, capacious, commodious, large, roomy.

span *vb* compass, cross, measure, overlay; * *n* brief period, spell; pair, yoke.

spank *vb* belt, cuff, flagellate, slap, smack, tan, wallop, whack.

spare *vb* lay aside, reserve, save, set aside; dispense with, do without, part with; omit, refrain, withhold; exempt, forgive, keep from; afford, allow, grant; preserve, save; economise, pinch; * *adj* frugal, scanty, stinted; parsimonious; emaciated, gaunt, lank, lean, meagre, thin, skinny; extra, supernumerary.

sparing *adj* little, scarce; abstemious, meagre, spare; economical, frugal, saving; compassionate, forgiving, lenient, merciful.

spark *vb* scintillate, sparkle; begin, incite, instigate, kindle, light, start, trigger; * *n* scintilla, scintillation, sparkle; beginning, germ, seed.

sparkle *vb* coruscate, gleam, glisten, glitter, radiate, scintillate, shine, twinkle; bubble, effervesce, foam; * *n* glint, scintillation, spark; lustre.

sparse *adj* dispersed, infrequent, scanty, scattered, sporadic, thin.

spasmodic *adj* erratic, irregular, sporadic; convulsive, violent.

spatter *vb* besprinkle, splash, sprinkle; spit.

speak *vb* articulate, deliver, enunciate, express, pronounce, utter; announce, declare, disclose, mention, tell; announce, declare, make known, proclaim; address, greet, hail; declare, make known; argue, converse, dispute, talk; discourse, hold forth, harangue, mention, orate, plead, spout, tell.

speaker *n* discourse, orator, spokesperson; chairperson, presiding officer.

special *adj* specific; individual, particular, peculiar, unique; exceptional extraordinary, particular, uncommon; appropriate, express, peculiar.

speciality *n* particularity; feature, forte, pet subject.

species *n* class, collection, group; kind, sort, variety; (*law*) fashion, figure, form, shape.

specific *adj* characteristic, especial, particular, peculiar; definite, precise.

specify *vb* define, designate, detail, indicate, individualise, name, show.

specimen *n* copy, example, model, sample.

speck *n* blemish, blot, flaw, spot, stain; bit, corpuscle, mite, mote, particle, scintilla.

spectacle *n* display, exhibition, parade, review, scene, show; curiosity, marvel, phenomenon, sight, wonder.

spectator *n* beholder, bystander, observer, onlooker, witness.

spectre *n* apparition, banshee, ghost, hobgoblin, phantom, shade, shadow, spirit, sprite, wraith.

speculate *vb* cogitate, conjecture, contemplate, imagine, muse, ponder, reflect, theorise, think; bet, gamble, hazard, risk, venture.

speculative *adj* contemplative, philosophical, unpractical; ideal, imaginary, theoretical; hazardous, risky, unsecured.

speech *n* articulation, language, words; dialect, idiom, tongue; conversation, parlance, talk, verbal intercourse; mention, remark, saying, talk; address, declaration, discourse, oration.

speed *vb* hasten, hurry, rush, scurry; prosper, thrive; accelerate, dispatch, expedite, hasten, hurry, quicken, urge on; dispatch, execute; advance, assist, help; favour; * *n* acceleration, celerity, dispatch, expedition, fleetness, haste, hurry, quickness, swiftness, velocity; good fortune, good luck, prosperity; impetuosity.

speedy *adj* fast, fleet, hasty, hurried, hurrying, quick, rapid, swift; expeditious, prompt, quick; approaching, near.

spell *n* charm, exorcism, incantation, jinx, witchery; bewitchment, enchantment, entrancement, fascination; fit, interval, period, season, stint, turn; * *vb* decipher, interpret, unfold, unravel, unriddle.

spend *vb* dispose of, expend, layout; consume, dissipate, exhaust, lavish, squander, use up, wear; apply, bestow, devote, employ.

spendthrift *n* prodigal, waster.

spent *adj* exhausted, fatigued, used up, wearied, worn out.

sphere *n* ball, globe, orb; bound, circle, circuit, compass, department, function, office, orbit, province, range; order, rank; country, domain, quarter, realm, region.

spherical *adj* bulbous, globated, globous, globular, rotund, round; planetary.

spice *n* flavour, flavouring, relish, savour, taste; dash, infusion, particle, sprinkling, tincture.

spicy *adj* aromatic, fragrant; piquant, pointed, pungent, sharp; indelicate, off-colour, risqué, sensational, suggestive.

spill *vb* effuse, pour out, shed; * *n* accident, fall.

spin *vb* twist; draw out, extend; prolong, protract; pirouette, twirl, whirl; * *n* drive, joyride, ride; autorotation, gyration, revolution, rotation, turning; pirouette, reel, turn, whirl.

spiny *adj* prickly, spinous, thorny; difficult, perplexed, thorny, troublesome.

spiral *adj* circular, coiled, corkscrew, helical, whorled, winding; * *n* coil, corkscrew, curlicue, helix, screw, whorl.

spirit *vb* animate, encourage, excite; carry off, kidnap; * *n* immaterial, substance, life; person, soul; angel, apparition, demon, ghost, phantom, shade, spectre, sprite; disposition, humour, mood, temper; ardour, cheerfulness, courage, energy, enthusiasm, fire, force, mettle, resolution, vigour, vivacity, zeal; animation, cheerfulness, enterprise, liveliness, spice, spunk, vivacity, warmth; drift, gist, intent, meaning, sense, significance, tenor; character, characteristic, complexion, essence, nature, quality; alcohol, liquor.

spirited *adj* active, alert, animated, ardent, bold, brisk, courageous, earnest, frisky, lively, mettlesome, sprightly, vivacious.

spiritual *adj* ethereal, ghostly, incorporeal, psychical; ideal, moral, unworldly; divine, holy, sacred; ecclesiastical.

spit *vb* impale, thrust through, transfix; eject, throw out; expectorate, salivate, slobber, splutter; * *n* saliva, spittle, sputum.

spite *vb* mortify, thwart; annoy, offend, vex; * *n* grudge, hatred, ill-will, malevolence, malice, maliciousness, pique, rancour, spleen, venom, vindictiveness.

spiteful *adj* hateful, ill-natured, malevolent, malicious, malign, malignant, rancorous.

splash *vb* dash, spatter, splurge, swash, swish; * *n* blot, daub, spot.

splendid *adj* beaming, bright, brilliant, glowing, lustrous, radiant, resplendent, shining; dazzling, gorgeous, imposing, magnificent, sumptuous, superb; brilliant, celebrated, distinguished, eminent, famous, glorious, illustrious, noble, remarkable, signal; grand, lofty, noble, sublime.

splendour *n* brightness, lustre, radiance; display, éclat, gorgeousness, grandeur, magnificence, showiness, stateliness; celebrity, fame, glory, grandeur, renown; grandeur, loftiness, nobleness, sublimity.

splice *vb* braid, entwine, graft, interlace, intertwine, join, knit, marry, mesh, plait, unite, wed.

splinter *vb* rend, sliver, split; * *n* fragment, piece.

split *vb* cleave; break, burst, rend, splinter; divide, part, separate; * *n* crack, fissure, rent; breach, separation.

splutter *vb* sputter, stammer, stutter.

spoil *vb* loot, pilfer, plunder, ravage, rob, steal, waste; corrupt, damage, destroy, disfigure, harm, impair, injure, mar, ruin; decay, decompose; * *n* booty, loot, pillage, plunder, prey; robbery, waste.

spokesman *n* mouthpiece, prolocutor, speaker.

sponge *vb* cleanse, wipe; efface, expunge, rub out, wipe out.

sponger *n* hanger-on, parasite.

spongy *adj* absorbent, porous; showery, wet; drenched, marshy, saturated, soaked, wet.

sponsor *vb* back, endorse, finance, guarantee, patronise, promote, support, subsidise, underwrite; * *n* angel, backer, guarantor, patron, supporter, surety, underwriter; godparent.

spontaneous *adj* free, gratuitous, impulsive, improvised, instinctive, unconstrained, voluntary, willing.

sport *vb* caper, frolic, gambol, play, romp, skip; trifle; display, exhibit; * *n* amusement, diversion, entertainment, frolic, fun, gambol, game, pastime, pleasantry, prank, recreation; jest, joke, derision, jeer, mockery, ridicule; monstrosity.

sportive *adj* frisky, frolicsome, gamesome, hilarious, lively, playful, sprightly, tricksy; comic, facetious, funny, humorous, jocular, lively, ludicrous, mirthful, vivacious, waggish.

spot *vb* besprinkled, dot, speck, variegate; blemish, disgrace, soil, stain, sully, tarnish; detect, discern, espy, observe, see, sight; * *n* blot, fleck, freckle, mark, mottle, patch, speck, speckle; blemish, blotch, flaw, pock, stain, taint; locality, place, site.

spotless *adj* perfect, undefaced; blameless, immaculate, innocent, irreproachable, pure, stainless, unblemished, untainted, untarnished.

spotlight *vb* accentuate, feature, focus on, highlight, illuminate, throw into relief; * *n* attention, fame, interest, limelight, notoriety.

spouse *n* companion, consort, husband, mate, partner, wife.

spout *vb* gush, jet, spurt, squirt; declaim, mouth, speak, utter, * *n* adjutage, conduit, tube; beak, gargoyle, nose, nozzle, waterspout.

sprain *vb* overstrain, rick, strain, twist, wrench.

spray *vb* atomise, douche, gush, jet, shower, spout, squirt; * *n* aerosol, atomiser, douche, foam, froth, shower, sprinkler; bough, branch, shoot, sprig, twig.

spread *vb* dilate, expand, extend, stretch; diffuse, disperse, distribute, radiate, scatter, strew; broadcast, circulate, disseminate, divulge, promulgate, propagate; unfold, unfurl; cover; * *n* extent, range, reach, scope, stretch; expansion, extension; circulation, dissemination, propagation; cloth, cover; banquet, feast, meal.

spree *n* bacchanal, debauch, frolic, jollification, orgy, revel, revelry.

sprig *n* shoot, spray, twig; youth.

sprightly *adj* airy, animated, blithe, brisk, buoyant, cheerful, frolicsome, joyous, lively, vigorous, vivacious.

spring *vb* bound, hop, jump, leap, prance, vault; arise, emerge, grow, issue, proceed, stem; derive, descend, emanate, flow, originate, rise, start; rebound, recoil; bend, warp; grow, thrive, wax; * *adj* hopping, jumping, resilient; * *n* bound, hop, jump, leap, vault; elasticity, flexibility, resilience; fount, fountain, geyser, well; cause, origin, original, principle, source; seed time.

springy *adj* bouncing, elastic, rebounding, recoiling, resilient.

sprinkle *vb* scatter, strew; bedew, dust, powder, sand, spatter; cleanse, wash; shower.

sprinkling *n* affusion, bedewing, splattering, spraying, wetting; dash, scattering, seasoning, suggestion, tinge, touch, trace, vestige.

sprout *vb* burst forth, germinate, grow, push, put forth, shoot, shoot forth; * *n* shoot, sprig.

spruce *vb* preen; adorn, deck, dress, smarten, trim; * *adj* dandyish, dapper, fine, foppish, jaunty, natty, neat, smart, tidy, trim.

spry *adj* active, agile, brisk, lively, nimble, prompt, ready, smart, sprightly, stirring, supple.

spur *vb* gallop, hasten, press on, prick; animate, drive, goad, impel, induce, rouse, stimulate, urge forward; * *n* goad, point; fillip, goad, impulse, incentive, incitement, inducement, instigation, motive, stimulus, whip; knob, knot, point, projection.

spurious *adj* bogus, counterfeit, deceitful, false, feigned, fictitious, mock, pretended, sham, unauthentic.

spurn *vb* drive away, kick, despise, disregard, flout, slight; disdain, reject, repudiate.

spurt *vb* gush, jet, spout, stream out, well; * *n* gush, jet, spout, squirt; burst, dash, rush.

spy *vb* behold, discern, see; discover, search out; inspect, scrutinise, search; shadow, trail, watch; * *n* agent, detective, mole, scout, secret emissary, undercover agent.

squabble *vb* brawl, fight, quarrel, scuffle, struggle; altercate, bicker, contend, dispute, wrangle; * *n* brawl, dispute, fight, quarrel, rumpus.

squad *n* band, bevy, crew, gang, knot, relay, set.

squalid *adj* dirty, filthy, foul, mucky, unclean, unkempt.

squander *vb* dissipate, expend, lose, misuse, spend, throw away, waste.

square *vb* quadrate; adapt, fit, mould, regulate, shape, suit; adjust, balance, close, settle; accord, cohere, fit, harmonise, quadrate, suit; * *adj* quadrate; equal, equitable, exact, fair, honest, just; adjusted, balanced, even, settled; just, true, suitable; * *n* quadrate, rectangle, tetragon; parade, piazza, plaza.

squat *vb* crouch; occupy, plant, settle; * *adj* crouching; dumpy, pudgy, short, stocky, stubby, thickset.

squawk vb cackle, crow, cry, hoot, screech, yelp; complain, protest, squeal.

squeal vb cry, howl, scream, screech, shriek, yell; betray, inform on; * n cry, howl, scream, screech, shriek, yell.

squeamish adj nauseated, queasy; dainty, delicate, fastidious, finical, nice, particular, priggish.

squeeze vb clutch, compress, constrict, grip, pinch, press; drive, force; crush, oppress; force through, press; (with **out**) extract; * n congestion, crowd, crush.

squirm vb twist, wriggle, writhe.

squirt vb eject, jet, splash, spurt.

stab vb gore, jab, pierce, spear, stick, transfix, transpierce; wound; * n cut, jab, thrust; blow, injury, wound.

stable adj fixed, immovable, immutable, invariable, permanent, unchangeable; constant, firm, staunch, steadfast, steady, unwavering; abiding, durable, enduring, fast, lasting, permanent, secure, sure.

staff n cane, pole, rod, stick wand; bat, club, cudgel, stay, support; employees, personnel, team, workers, work force.

stage vb dramatise, perform, present, produce; * n dais, platform, rostrum, scaffold, stand; arena, field; boards, playhouse, theatre.

stagger vb reel, sway, totter; alternate, fluctuate, overlap; falter, hesitate, waver; amaze, astonish, astound, dumbfound, nonplus, shock, surprise.

stagnant adj close, motionless, standing; dormant, dull, inactive, inert, sluggish, torpid.

stagnate vb decay, deteriorate, languish, rot, vegetate.

staid adj calm, composed, demure, sedate, serious, settled, sober, solemn, unadventurous.

stain vb blemish, blot, discolour, maculate, soil, spot, sully, tarnish; colour, dye, tinge; contaminate, corrupt, defile, dishonour, pollute, taint; * n blemish, blot, discoloration, flaw, imperfection, spot, tarnish; contamination, dishonour, infamy, pollution, shame, taint, tarnish.

stake vb brace, prop, secure, support; finance, pledge, wager; hazard, jeopardise, risk; * n pale, peg, picket, post, stick; bet, pledge, wager; adventure, hazard, risk.

stale adj flat, insipid, mawkish, mouldy, musty, tasteless, vapid; decayed, effete, faded, old; common, commonplace, hackneyed, stereotyped, threadbare, trite.

stalk n culm, pedicel, petiole, shaft, spire, stem, stock; * vb march, pace, stride, strut; follow, hunt, shadow, track.

stall n stable; cell, compartment; booth, kiosk, shop, stand; * vb block, delay, equivocate, filibuster, postpone; arrest, check, die, fail, halt, stop.

stalwart adj athletic, brawny, muscular, powerful, robust, stout, strapping, strong, sturdy, vigorous; brave, daring, gallant, indomitable, intrepid, resolute, valiant, valorous; * n backer, member, partisan, supporter.

stamina n energy, force, power, strength, sturdiness, vigour.

stamp vb brand, impress, imprint, mark, print; * n brand, impress, impression, print; cast, character, complexion, cut, description, fashion, mould, type.

stampede vb charge, flee, panic; * n charge, flight, rout, rush.

stance n bearing, carriage, department, posture; attitude, position, stand, standpoint, viewpoint.

stand vb be erect; abide, continue, endure, remain;

halt, pause, stop; be firm, be resolute, stay; be valid, have force; depend, rest; bear, endure, suffer, sustain, weather; abide, admit, await, submit, tolerate; fix, place, put, set upright; (with **against**) oppose, resist, withstand; (with **by**) be near, be present; aid, assist, defend, help, support; defend, justify, maintain, support; (marine) attend, be ready; (with **fast**) be fixed, be immovable; (with **for**) mean, represent; aid, defend, support; (with **off**) keep aloof; (with **out**) be prominent, jut, project, protrude; not comply, persist; (with **up for**) defend, justify, support, uphold; (with **with**) agree; * n place, position, post, station; halt, stay, stop; dais, platform, rostrum; booth, stall; opposition, resistance.

standard adj average, customary, normal, regular, usual; accepted, approved, received; regulation; * n canon, model, norm, rule, test; gauge, measure, model, scale.

standardise vb assimilate, bring into line, institutionalise, regiment, stereotype.

standing adj established, fixed, settled; lasting, permanent; motionless, stagnant; * n position, station; continuance, duration, existence; footing, ground, hold; position, rank, reputation, status.

standstill n cessation, interruption, stop; deadlock.

staple adj basic, chief, essential, fundamental, main, primary, principal; * n fibre, filament, thread; body, bulk, mass, substance.

star vb act, feature, headline, lead, perform, play; emphasise, highlight, stress; * adj leading, main, paramount, principal; celebrated, illustrious; * n heavenly body, luminary; asterisk; destiny, doom, fate, fortune, lot; diva, headliner, hero, heroine, lead, prima ballerina, prima donna.

stark adj rigid, stiff; absolute, bare, downright, entire, gross, pure, sheer; * adv absolutely, completely, fully, wholly.

starry adj astral, sidereal, stellar; bright, brilliant, shining, sparkling, twinkling.

start vb begin, commence, initiate, institute; discover, invent; flinch, jump, shrink, wince; alarm, disturb, fright, scare; depart, set off; call forth, evoke, raise; dislocate, spring; * n beginning, commencement, inauguration, outset; fit, jump, spasm, twitch; impulse, sally.

startle vb flinch, shrink, wince; alarm, frighten, scare, shock; amaze, astonish, astound.

starve vb famish, perish; lack, want; kill, subdue.

state vb affirm, assert, declare, explain, expound, express, propound, recite, say, set forth, voice; * adj civic, national, public; * n case, circumstances, condition, pass, phase, plight, position, predicament, situation; condition, guise, mode, quality, rank; dignity, glory, magnificence, pageantry, splendour; nation, realm.

stately adj august, dignified, grand, imperial, imposing, magnificent, majestic, noble, princely, royal; ceremonious, formal, magisterial, solemn.

statement n account, allegation, announcement, communiqué, declaration, description, exposition, narrative, recital, report; assertion, predication, proposition, pronouncement, thesis.

static adj changeless, constant, fixed, immobile, inert, motionless, stationary, unmoving, unvarying.

station vb establish, locate, place, post; * n location, place, position, post, seat, situation; business, employment, occupation, office; character, dignity, rank, standing, state, status; depot, stop, terminal.

stationary *adj* fixed, motionless, permanent, quiescent, stable, standing, still.

stature *n* height, physique, size; consequence, elevation, eminence, prominence.

status *n* caste, condition, footing, position, rank, standing.

stay *vb* abide, dwell, rest, sojourn, tarry; halt, remain, stop; attend, delay, linger, wait; arrest, check, curb, hold, prevent, rein in, restrain; delay, detain, hinder, obstruct; prop, shore up, support, sustain, uphold; * *n* delay, rest, sojourn; halt, stand, stop; check, curb, hindrance, impediment, interruption, restraint, stumbling block; buttress, prop, staff, support, supporter.

steady *vb* balance, stabilise, support; * *adj* firm, fixed, stable; regular, undeviating, uniform; constant, resolute, stable, staunch, steadfast, unwavering.

steal *vb* burglarise, burgle, crib, embezzle, filch, pilfer, purloin, poach, shoplift, thieve; creep, sneak.

steam *vb* fume; evaporate, vaporise; cook, poach; navigate, sail; be hot, sweat; * *n* vapour; exhalation, fume, mist, reek.

steamy *adj* misty, moist, vaporous; erotic, voluptuous.

steel *vb* case-harden, edge; brace, fortify, harden, nerve, strengthen.

steep *adj* abrupt, precipitous, sheer, sloping, sudden; * *n* declivity, precipice; * *vb* digest, drench, imbrue, imbue, saturate, soak.

steer *vb* direct, conduct, govern, guide, pilot.

stem *vb* (with **from**) bud, descend, originate, spring, sprout; oppose, resist, withstand; dam, oppose, staunch, stay, stop; * *n* axis, trunk; petiole, stalk; branch, descendant, offspring, progeny, shoot; ancestry, descent, family, generation, line, lineage, pedigree, stock; (marine) beak, bow, cutwater, prow; helm, lookout; etymon, radical, origin, root.

step *vb* pace, stride, tread, walk; * *n* pace, stride; stair, tread; gradation, grade, interval; advance, advancement, progression; act, action, procedure, proceeding; footprint, trace; footfall, pace, walk; expedient, means, measure, method; round, rung.

sterile *adj* barren, unfruitful, unproductive, unprolific; bare, dry, empty; (botanical) acarpous, male, staminate.

sterling *n* authentic, excellent, fine, first-class, genuine, standard, substantial, superlative, true.

stern *adj* austere, dour, severe; cruel, hard, harsh, inflexible, rigid, rigorous, severe, strict, unrelenting; immovable, uncompromising; * *n* behind, hind part, posterior, rear, tail; (marine) counter, poop, tailpost; butt, buttocks, rump.

stew *vb* boil, seethe, simmer; * *n* ragout; difficulty, mess, scrape.

stick *vb* gore, penetrate, pierce, puncture, spear, stab; insert, thrust; attach, cement, glue, paste; set; adhere, cling, hold; persist, remain, stay, stop; doubt, hesitate, scruple, waver; (with **by**) adhere to, be faithful, support; * *n* stab, thrust; birch, rod, switch; bat bludgeon, club, cudgel; cane, staff; cue, pole, stake.

sticky *adj* adhesive, clinging, gluey, glutinous, gummy, tenacious, viscous.

stiff *adj* inflexible, rigid, unbending, unyielding; firm, thick; obstinate, strong, stubborn, tenacious; absolute, austere, dogmatic, inexorable, rigorous, severe, straitlaced, stringent, uncompromising; ceremonious, constrained, formal, frigid, punctilious, stately, starchy, stilted; abrupt, cramped, graceless, harsh, inelegant.

stifle *vb* smother, suffocate; check, deaden, extinguish, quench, repress, stop, suppress; gag, hush, muffle, silence, smother, still.

stigma *n* blot, brand, disgrace, dishonour, shame, spot, stain, taint, tarnish.

still *vb* hush, lull, silence, stifle; appease, calm, compose, pacify, quiet, tranquillise; calm, check, immobilise, quiet, stop, subdue, suppress; * *adj* hushed, mute, noiseless, silent; calm, placid, quiet, serene, tranquil, unruffled; inert, motionless, stagnant, stationary; * *n* hush, lull, peace, quiet, silence, tranquillity; picture, photograph, shot; * *adv, conj* till now, yet; however, nevertheless ; always, continually, ever, habitually, uniformly.

stimulate *vb* animate, arouse, awaken, brace, encourage, excite, fire, impel, incite, inflame, inspirit, instigate, prick, prompt, provoke, rally, rouse, spur, stir up, urge, whet.

stimulus *n* encouragement, fillip, incentive, incitement, motivation, provocation.

sting *vb* hurt, nettle, prick, wound; afflict, pain.

stingy *adj* avaricious, close, close-fisted, grudging, mean, miserly, parsimonious, penurious.

stink *vb* emit a stench, reek, smell bad; * *n* bad smell, offensive odour, stench.

stint *vb* bound, confine, limit, restrain; begrudge, pinch, straiten; cease, desist, stop; * *n* bound, limit, restraint; period, quota, share, stretch, task, time, turn.

stipulate *vb* agree, condition, contract, covenant, engage, settle, terms.

stir *vb* budge, move; agitate, disturb, prod; argue, discuss, raise, start; animate, arouse, awaken, excite, incite, instigate, prompt, provoke, rouse, spur, stimulate; appear, happen; get up, rise; (with **up**) animate, awaken, incite, instigate, provoke, rouse, stimulate; * *n* activity, ado, agitation, bustle, confusion, excitement, fidget, flurry, fuss, hurry, movement; commotion, disorder, disturbance, tumult, uproar.

stock *vb* fill, furnish, store, supply; accumulate, garner, hoard, reposit, reserve, save; * *adj* permanent, standard, standing; * *n* assets, capital, commodities, shares; hoard, inventory, merchandise, provision, reserve, store, supply; ancestry, breed, descent, family, line, lineage, parentage, pedigree, race; cravat; butt; block, pillar, post, stake; stalk, stem, trunk.

stocky *adj* chubby, chunky, plump, short, stout, stubby, thickset.

stodgy *adj* filling, heavy, leaden, starchy, substantial; boring, dull, laboured, staid, tedious, turgid, unexciting.

stoic, stoical *adj* impassive, imperturbable, patient, philosophic, philosophical, phlegmatic, unimpassioned.

stolen *adj* filched, pilfered, purloined; clandestine, furtive, secret, sly, stealthy, surreptitious.

stolid *adj* blockish, heavy, obtuse, stockish, unemotional, wooden.

stomach *vb* abide, bear, brook, endure, stand, suffer, swallow, tolerate; * *n* abdomen, belly, gut, paunch, tummy; appetite, desire, inclination, liking, relish, taste.

stone *vb* stein; brick, cover,

slate, tile; lapidate, pelt; * n boulder, cobble, gravel, pebble, rock, gem, jewel; cenotaph, monument; nut, pit; adamant, agate, flint, granite, marble, slate.

stony adj gritty, hard, lapidose, lithic, rocky; flinty, hard, inflexible, obdurate; cruel, hard-hearted, inexorable, pitiless, unfeeling, unrelenting.

stoop vb bow, lean, sag, slouch, slump; abase, cower, cringe, submit, succumb, surrender; condescend, deign, vouchsafe; sink; * n bend, inclination, sag, slouch, slump; descent, swoop.

stop vb block, blockade, obstruct; arrest, block, halt, hold, pause, stall, stay; bar, delay, embargo, impede, intercept, interrupt, obstruct, prevent, restrain, staunch, stay, suppress, thwart; cease, desist, discontinue, forbear, leave off, refrain from; arrest, intermit, quiet, terminate; lodge, stay, tarry; * n halt, intermission, pause, respite, rest, suspension, truce; block, cessation, check, hindrance, interruption, repression; bar, impediment, obstacle, obstruction; full stop, point.

stoppage n arrest, block, hindrance, interruption, obstruction, prevention.

store vb accumulate, amass, cache, deposit, hoard, husband, put by, reserve, save, stow away; furnish, provide, replenish, stock, supply; * n cache, deposit, fund, hoard, provision, reserve, stock, supply, treasure, treasury; abundance, plenty; storehouse; emporium, market, shop.

storm vb assault, attack; fume, rage, rampage, rant, rave; * n blizzard, gale, hurricane, squall, tempest, tornado, typhoon, whirlwind; agitation, commotion, disturbance, insurrection, tumult, turmoil; adversity, affliction, calamity; assault, attack, brunt, onslaught.

stormy adj blustering, squally, tempestuous, windy; riotous, rough, turbulent, wild; agitated, blustering, furious.

story n chronicle, history, record; account, narrative, recital, record, relation, report, statement, tale; fable, fiction, novel, romance; anecdote, legend, tale; fabrication, falsehood, fib, fiction, invention, lie, untruth.

stout adj athletic, brawny, robust, stalwart, strong, sturdy, vigorous; courageous, hardy, indomitable; obstinate, proud, resolute, stubborn; firm, hardy, solid, staunch, strong, sturdy; bouncing, chubby, corpulent, fat, large, obese, plump, portly, stocky, strapping, thickset.

straight adj direct, rectilinear, right, undeviating, unswerving; erect, perpendicular, plumb, upright, vertical; equitable, fair, honest, honourable, just, straightforward; * adv at once, directly, immediately, without delay.

straightaway, **straightway** adv at once, directly, forthwith, immediately, speedily, suddenly, without delay.

straighten vb arrange, neaten, order, tidy.

strain vb make tense, stretch, tighten; injure, sprain, wrench; overexert, overtax, rack; embrace, fold, hug, press, squeeze; compel, force; drain, filter, filtrate, percolate, purify, separate; fatigue, overwork, tax, tire; * n stress, tenseness, tension; effort, exertion, force, overexertion; burden, tax; sprain, wrench; lay, melody, movement, song, stave, tune; manner, style, vein; disposition, trait, turn; descent, extraction, family, lineage, pedigree, stock.

straits *n* crisis, difficulty, dilemma, distress, emergency, hardship, mess, plight, predicament; channel, narrows.

strand *vb* abandon, beach, be wrecked, cast away, maroon, run aground, wreck; * *n* beach, coast, shore.

strange *adj* alien, exotic, foreign, outlandish, remote; new, novel; curious, exceptional, extraordinary, odd, peculiar, rare, singular, surprising, uncommon, unusual; abnormal anomalous, extraordinary, incredible, marvellous, mysterious, unheard of, unique, unnatural, wonderful; bizarre, grotesque, odd, peculiar, queer; inexperience, unfamiliar, unknown; bashful, distant, distrustful, reserved, shy, uncommunicative.

stranger *n* alien, foreigner; immigrant, newcomer; outsider; guest, visitor.

strangle *vb* choke, smother, suffocate, throttle, tighten; quiet, repress, still, suppress.

strap *vb* beat, thrash, whip; bind, fasten; * *n* thong; band, ligature, strip, tie.

stratagem *n* artifice, dodge, finesse, machination, plan, plot, ruse, scheme, wile.

strategy *n* manoeuvering, plan, policy, tactics.

stray *vb* deviate, digress, err, meander, ramble, roam, straggle, swerve, transgress, wander; * *adj* abandoned, lost, wandering; accidental, erratic, random, scattered.

streak *vb* band, striate, stripe; dart, dash, flash, hurtle, run, sprint, tear; * *n* band, belt, layer, line, strip, stripe, thread, trace; cast, stripe, touch, vein; beam, bolt, dart, dash, flare, flash, ray, stream.

stream *vb* flow, glide, pour, run, spout; emit, shed; emanate, issue, radiate; extend, float, wave; * *n* brook, race, rill, rivulet, run, runlet; course, current, flow, flux, race, rush, torrent, wake, wash; beam, gleam, patch, radiation, ray, streak.

street *n* avenue, boulevard, lane, road, row, thoroughfare.

strength *n* force, might, main, nerve, potency, power, vigour; hardness, solidity, toughness; impregnability, proof; brawn, grit, muscle, robustness, stamina; courage, firmness, fortitude, resolution, spirit; efficacy, soundness, validity; emphasis, force, nerve, vigour; security, stay, support; brilliance, intensity, vitality, vividness; excellence, potency, spirit, virtue; vehemence; boldness, energy.

strengthen *vb* buttress, recruit, reinforce; fortify; brace, harden, nerve, steel; freshen, invigorate, vitalise; animate; clench, confirm, corroborate, establish, justify, sustain, support.

strenuous *adj* ardent, eager, earnest, energetic, resolute, vigorous, zealous; bold, determined, intrepid, resolute, spirited, valiant.

stress *vb* accent, accentuate, emphasise, highlight; bear, pressurise; rack, strain, stretch, tense; * *n* accent, accentuation, emphasis; effort, force, pull, strain, tension, tug; boisterousness, severity; pressure, urgency.

stretch *vb* brace, strain, tense, tighten; elongate, extend, lengthen, protract; display, distend, expand, spread, widen; sprain, strain; distort, exaggerate, misrepresent; * *n* compass, extension, extent, range, reach, scope; effort, exertion, strain.

strict *adj* strained, tense, tight; accurate, exact, literal, particular, precise, scrupulous; austere, harsh, inflexible, puritanical, rigid, rigorous, severe, stern, stringent,

strife *n* battle, combat, conflict, contention, discord, struggle, warfare.

strike *vb* bang, beat, box, cudgel, cuff, hit, knock, lash, pound, punch, slap, slug, smite, thump, whip; impress, stamp; afflict, chastise, deal, inflict, punish, smite; affect, astonish, stun; clash, collide, dash, hit; surrender, yield; mutiny, rebel.

string *n* cord, fibre, rope, twine; chain, file, line, procession, queue, series, succession; hang, link, suspend, thread; (with **out**) disperse, extend, lengthen, protract.

strip *n* piece, ribbon, shred, slip; * *vb* denude, skin, uncover; deprive, deforest, desolate, despoil, devastate, disarm, dismantle, disrobe, expose, loot; plunder, pillage, ransack, rob, sack; disrobe, uncover, undress.

strive *vb* attempt, endeavour, labour, strain, struggle, toil; contend, fight, wrestle; compete, cope, struggle.

stroke *n* blow, glance, hit, knock, lash, pat, percussion, shot, thump; attack, paralysis; affliction, damage, hardship, hurt, injury, misfortune, reverse; dash, feat, touch; * *vb* caress, feel, pet; massage, nuzzle, rub, touch.

stroll *vb* ramble, rove, saunter, stray, wander; * *n* excursion, promenade, ramble, rambling, roving, tour, trip, walk, wandering.

strong *adj* powerful, robust, sturdy; able, enduring; cogent, firm, valid.

structure *vb* arrange, construct, make, organise; * *n* form, formation, organisation; anatomy, composition; arrangement, building, edifice, fabric, framework.

struggle *vb* endeavour, labour, strive, toil; battle, contend, fight, wrestle; agonise, flounder, writhe; * *n* effort, endeavour, labour, pains; battle, conflict, contention, fight, strife; agony, contortions, distress.

stubborn *adj* dogged, headstrong, inflexible, intractable, obdurate, obstinate, perverse, refractory, ungovernable, unmanageable, unyielding, wilful; constant, enduring, firm, hardy, persevering, persistent, steady, stoical, unremitting; firm, hard, inflexible, stiff, strong, tough, unpliant.

studious *adj* contemplative, meditative, reflective, thoughtful; assiduous, attentive, diligent, lettered, scholarly.

study *vb* cogitate, meditate, muse, ponder, reflect; analyze, contemplate, examine, investigate, ponder, probe, scrutinise, search; * *n* exercise, inquiry, investigation, reading, research; cogitation, consideration, contemplation, examination, meditation, reflection, thought; model, representation, sketch; den, library, office.

stung *vb* angered, hurt, incensed, nettled, piqued, resentful, wounded.

stupendous *adj* amazing, astonishing, astounding, marvellous, surprising, wonderful; enormous, huge, immense, monstrous, vast.

stupid *adj* brainless, doltish, dull, foolish, idiotic, inane, inept, obtuse, senseless, simple, slow, sluggish, tedious, tiresome, witless.

sturdy *adj* bold, determined, firm, hardy, persevering, pertinacious, resolute, stiff; brawny, forcible, muscular, powerful, robust, stalwart, stout, strong, thickset, vigorous, well-set.

style *vb* address, characterise,

denominate, designate, dub, entitle, name, term; * n expression, turn; cast, character, fashion, form, genre, make, manner, mode, model, shape, vogue; appellation, denomination, designation, name, title; chic, elegance, smartness; pen, pin, point, stylus.

stylish adj chic, courtly, elegant, fashionable, polished, smart.

suave adj affable, agreeable, amiable, bland, courteous, debonair, delightful, gracious, mild, pleasant, smooth, sweet, urbane.

subdue vb beat, break, bow, conquer, control, defeat, discomfit, foil, master, overbear, overcome, overpower, overwhelm, quell, rout, subjugate, surmount, vanquish, worst; allay, curb, mellow, moderate, mollify, repress, restrain, soften.

subject vb master, overcome, subdue, subjugate, tame; enslave, enthral; refer, submit, surrender; * adj beneath, underneath; dependent, enslaved, inferior, servile, subordinate, subservient; conditional, obedient, submissive; disposed, liable, prone; * n henchman, liegeman, slave, subordinate; matter, point, theme, thesis, topic; premise; case, object, patient, recipient; ego, self.

sublime adj aloft, high, sacred; eminent, exalted, grand, great, lofty, noble; august, eminent, glorious, magnificent, majestic, noble, stately; elate, exhilarated, raised.

submission n capitulation, surrender, yielding; obedience, resignation; deference, homage, humility, obeisance, passiveness, prostration.

submissive adj amenable, compliant, docile, pliant, tame, yielding; acquiescent, obedient, passive, patient, resigned, unassertive; humble, lowly, meek, obsequious, prostrate, self-abasing.

submit vb defer, resign, surrender, yield; commit, propose, refer; offer; acquiesce, bend, comply, stoop.

subordinate adj ancillary, inferior, junior, secondary, subservient, subsidiary; * n assistant, dependant, inferior, underling.

subscribe vb accede, approve, agree, assent, consent, yield; contribute, donate, give, offer; promise.

subsequent adj after, ensuing, later, latter, following, sequent, succeeding.

subside vb settle, sink; abate, decline, decrease, diminish, ebb, lapse, lessen, lower, lull, wane.

subsidiary adj assistant, auxiliary, cooperative, subordinate, subservient.

subsidise vb aid, finance, fund, sponsor, support, underwrite.

subsist vb be, breathe, exist, live; abide, continue, endure, persist, remain; feed, maintain, ration, support.

substance n actuality, element, reality; burden, content, core, drift, essence, gist, heart, import, meaning, sense, significance, solidity, soul, weight; estate, income, means, property, resources, wealth.

substantial adj considerable, essential, existent, hypostatic, real; concrete, durable, positive, solid, tangible, true; corporeal, material; bulky, firm, heavy, large, massive, notable, significant, sizable, solid, sound, stable, stout, strong; cogent, efficient, influential, valid, weighty.

subterfuge n artifice, evasion, excuse, expedient, mask, pretence, pretext, sophistry, trick.

subtle adj artful, astute, crafty, cunning, designing, intriguing, sly, tricky, wily; clever, ingenious; acute, deep, discerning, profound, shrewd; airy, delicate, ethereal, light, nice, rare, refined, slender, thin, volatile.

subtract *vb* deduct, detract, diminish, remove, take, withdraw.

subvert *vb* overthrow, overturn, reverse, upset; demolish, destroy, extinguish, ruin, overthrow; confound, corrupt, injure, pervert.

succeed *vb* ensue, follow, inherit, replace; flourish, prevail, prosper, thrive, win.

success *n* attainment, issue, result; fortune, luck, triumph.

successful *adj* auspicious, felicitous, fortunate, lucky, prosperous, victorious, winning.

succession *n* chain, concatenation, procession, progression, sequence, series; descent, entail, inheritance, lineage, race, reversion.

succinct *adj* brief, compact, concise, condensed, curt, pithy, short, summary, terse.

succulent *adj* juicy, luscious, lush, mouth watering, rich.

sudden *adj* abrupt, hasty, hurried, immediate, instantaneous, rash, unexpected; brief, momentary, quick, rapid.

sue *vb* charge, indict, prosecute, summon; appeal, beg, demand, entreat, implore, petition, plead, pray, supplicate.

suffer *vb* undergo; bear, endure, support, sustain, tolerate; admit, allow, indulge, let, permit.

sufficient *adj* adequate, ample, competent, enough; able, equal, qualified, responsible.

suffocate *vb* asphyxiate, choke, smother, stifle, strangle.

suffuse *vb* bathe, cover, imbue, infuse, mantle, permeate, pervade, steep, transfuse.

suggest *vb* advise, allude, hint, indicate, insinuate, intimate, move, prompt, propose, propound, recommend.

suggestion *n* allusion, hint, indication, insinuation, intimation, presentation, prompting, proposal.

suit *vb* accommodate, adapt, adjust, fashion, fit, match; accord, become, befit, gratify, harmonise, please, satisfy, tally; * *n* appeal, entreaty, invocation, petition, request, solicitation, supplication; courtship, wooing; action, case, process, prosecution, trial; clothing, costume.

suitable *adj* adapted, accordant, apposite, applicable, apt, becoming, befitting, congruous, convenient, consonant, correspondent, decent, due, eligible, expedient, fit, fitting, just, pertinent, proper, relevant, worthy.

sulky *adj* churlish, cross, dogged, grouchy, ill-humoured, ill-tempered, moody, morose, perverse, sour, spleenish, sullen, surly, vexatious.

sullen *adj* cross, glum, grumpy, ill-tempered, moody, morose, sore, sulky; cheerless, cloudy, dark, depressing, dismal, funereal, gloomy, lowering, melancholy, mournful, sombre; dull, gloomy, heavy, sluggish; intractable, perverse, refractory, stubborn, vexatious; baleful, evil, inauspicious, malign, malignant, sinister, unlucky.

sully *vb* blemish, contaminate, deface, defame, dirty, disgrace, dishonour, foul, soil, slur, spot, stain, tarnish.

sultry *adj* close, hot, humid, muggy, oppressive, stifling, stuffy, sweltering.

sum *vb* add, compute, reckon; collect, comprehend, condense, summarise; * *n* aggregate, amount, total, totality, whole; compendium, substance, summary; acme, completion, summit.

summary *adj* brief, concise, curt, pithy, short, succinct, terse; brief, quick, rapid; * *n* abridgement, abstract, brief, compendium, digest, epitome, precis, résumé, syllabus, synopsis.

summit *n* apex, cap, climax, top.

summon *vb* arouse, bid, call, invite, invoke, rouse; convene, convoke; charge, indict, prosecute, subpoena, sue.

sundry *adj* diverse, various.

sunny *adj* bright, brilliant, clear, fine, radiant, shining, unclouded, warm; cheerful, genial, happy, joyful, smiling.

superb *adj* beautiful, elegant, exquisite, gorgeous, grand, imposing, magnificent, majestic, noble, rich, showy, splendid, stately, sumptuous.

superficial *adj* external, flimsy, shallow, untrustworthy.

superintend *vb* administer, control, inspect, manage, overlook, oversee, supervise.

superior *adj* better, greater, high, higher, finer, supreme, ultra, upper; chief, foremost, principal; distinguished, noble, pre-eminent, surpassing, unrivalled, unsurpassed; predominant, prevalent; * *n* chief, director, head, higher-up, leader, manager, principal, senior, supervisor.

supernatural *adj* marvellous, metaphysical, miraculous, other-worldly, unearthly.

supersede *vb* annul, obviate, overrule, suspend; displace, replace, succeed, supplant.

supervise *vb* administer, conduct, control, direct, inspect, manage, overlook, oversee, superintend.

supplant *vb* displace, oust, remove, replace, supersede, undermine, unseat.

supple *adj* elastic, flexible, lithe, pliable, pliant; compliant, humble, submissive, yielding; fawning, flattering, grovelling, obsequious, parasitical, slavish, sycophantic, servile.

supplement *vb* add, augment, reinforce; * *n* addendum, addition, appendix, codicil, complement, postscript.

supply *vb* equip, furnish, minister, outfit, provide, replenish, stock; afford, accommodate, contribute, furnish, give, grant; * *n* hoard, provision, reserve, stock, store.

support *vb* brace, cradle, prop, sustain, uphold; bear, endure, suffer, tolerate; cherish, keep, maintain, nourish, nurture; assume, carry, perform, play, represent; corroborate, substantiate, confirm, verify; abet, advocate, aid, approve, assist, back, champion, countenance, encourage, favour, float, held, patronise, reinforce, succour, uphold; * *n* bolster, brace, buttress, foothold, guy, hold, prop, shore, stay, substructure, underpinning; groundwork, mainstay, staff; base, bed, foundation; keeping, living, livelihood, maintenance, subsistence, sustenance; evidence; aid, assistance, behalf, championship, comfort, encouragement, favour, help, patronage, succour.

suppose *vb* believe, conceive, conclude, consider, conjecture, deem, imagine, presume, think; assume, hypothesise; believe, imagine, posit, predicate, think; fancy, opine, surmise, suspect, theorise.

suppress *vb* crush, overwhelm, overpower, quash, quell, quench, smother, stifle, subdue, withhold; arrest, inhibit, repress, stop; conceal, extinguish, retain, secret, silence, stifle, strangle.

supreme *adj* chief, dominant, greatest, highest, leading, paramount, predominant, pre-eminent, principal, sovereign.

sure *adj* certain, confident; dependable, effective, infallible,

precise, reliable, trustworthy, undeniable, undoubted, well-proven; assured, guaranteed, inevitable, irrevocable; fast, safe, secure, stable, steady.
surfeit *vb* gorge, overfeed, sate, satiate; nauseate, pall; * *n* excess, glut, oppression, plethora, satiation, satiety, superabundance, superfluity.
surge *vb* rise, rush, sweep, swell, swirl, tower; * *n* breaker, roller.
surly *adj* churlish, crabbed, cross, crusty, discourteous, gruff, grumpy, harsh, ill-natured, ill-tempered, peevish, perverse, petulant, rough, rude, snappish, snarling, sour, sullen, testy, touchy, uncivil, ungracious; rough, sullen, tempestuous.
surpass *vb* beat, eclipse, exceed, excel, outdo, outmatch, outnumber, outstrip, outshine, surmount, transcend.
surplus *adj* leftover, remaining, spare, superfluous; * *n* balance, excess, remainder, residue, superabundance, surfeit.
surprise *vb* amaze, astonish, astound, confuse, disconcert, dumbfound, startle; * *n* amazement, astonishment, shock, wonder.
surrender *vb* cede, sacrifice, yield; abdicate, abandon, relinquish, renounce, resign, waive; capitulate, succumb; * *n* abandonment, cession, renunciation, resignation, yielding.
surreptitious *adj* clandestine, covert, furtive, secret, stealthy, underhand, veiled.
surround *vb* beset, circumscribe, embrace, encircle, encompass, environ, girdle, hem, invest.
survey *vb* observe, overlook, reconnoitre, scan, scout, view; examine, inspect, scrutinise; oversee, supervise; measure, plan, plot, prospect; * *n* prospect, view; examination, prospect, reconnaissance, review; estimating, measuring, planning, plotting, prospecting, work, study.
survive *vb* endure, last, outlast, outlive.
susceptible *adj* capable, excitable, impressible, predisposed, receptive, sensitive.
suspect *vb* believe, conjecture, fancy, guess, imagine, suppose, surmise, think; distrust, doubt, mistrust; * *adj* doubtful, dubious, suspicious.
suspend *vb* hang, sling, swing; adjourn, defer, delay, discontinue, hinder, interrupt, postpone, stay, withhold; debar, dismiss, rusticate.
suspicion *n* conjecture, guess, hint, inkling, suggestion, supposition, surmise, trace; apprehension, distrust, doubt, jealousy, misgiving, mistrust.
suspicious *adj* distrustful, jealous, suspect; doubtful, questionable.
sustain *vb* bear, bolster, fortify, support, uphold; nourish, preserve, support; aid, assist, comfort, relieve; brave, endure, suffer; confirm, ratify, sanction, validate; confirm, establish, justify, prove.
swallow *vb* devour, drink, eat, engorge, gobble, gorge, gulp, imbibe, ingurgitate; absorb, appropriate, devour, engulf, submerge; consume, occupy; brook, digest, endure, pocket, stomach; recant, renounce, retract; * *n* gullet, oesophagus, throat; inclination, liking, palate, taste; draught, gulp, ingurgitation, mouthful, taste.
swamp *vb* engulf, overwhelm, sink; capsize, ruin, sink, upset, wreck; * *n* bog, fen, marsh, morass, quagmire, slough.
swanky *n* de luxe, exclusive, expensive, fancy, fashionable, flashy, glamorous, gorgeous, grand, lavish, luxurious, ostentatious, plush, posh, rich, showy, smart, stylish, sumptuous, swish.
swarm *vb* abound, crowd, teem; * *n* cloud, concourse, crowd,

flock, hive, horde, host, mass, multitude, shoal, throng.

sway vb brandish, move, rock, roll, swing, wave, wield; bias, influence, persuade, turn, urge; control, direct, govern, guide, manage, rule; hoist, raise; incline, lean, yaw; * n ascendency, authority, command, domination, dominion, empire, government, mastership, omnipotence, predominance, power, rule, sovereignty; bias, direction, influence, weight; oscillation, sweep, swing, wave.

swear vb affirm, attest, avow, declare, promise, state, testify, vow; blaspheme, curse.

sweep vb clean, brush; brush, touch; rake, scour, traverse; * n amplitude, compass, movement, range, reach, scope; destruction, havoc, ravage; curvature, curve.

sweet adj candied, honeyed, luscious, nectarous, sugary; balmy, fragrant, odorous, redolent; harmonious; dulcet, mellifluous, melodious, pleasant, tuneful, silver-toned, silvery; beautiful, fair, lovely; charming, delightful, pleasant; affectionate, amiable, lovable, winning; benignant, gentle, serene, soft; clean, fresh, pure, sound; * n fragrance, perfume; delight, joy, pleasure.

swell vb bloat, bulge, dilate, distend, expand, inflate, puff, swell, tumefy; augment, enlarge, increase; rise, surge; strut, swagger; * n swelling; augmentation, excrescence, protuberance; ascent, hill, rise; force, intensity, power; billows, surge, undulation, waves; blade, buck, coxcomb, dandy, exquisite, fop, popinjay.

swift adj fast, fleet, flying, quick, rapid, speedy; eager, forward, prompt, ready; instant, speedy, sudden.

swindle vb cheat, con, deceive, defraud, diddle, dupe, embezzle, forge, hoax, steal, trick; * n cheat, con, deceit, deception, fraud, hoax, imposition, roguery, trickery.

swing vb oscillate, sway, vibrate, wave; brandish, flourish, wave, whirl; * n oscillation, sway, undulation, vibration; freedom, margin, play, range, scope, sweep; bias, tendency.

swoop vb descend, pounce, rush, seize, sweep; * n clutch, pounce, seizure; descent.

symbol n badge, emblem, figure, mark, picture, representation, representative, sign, token.

symbolic, **symbolical** adj emblematic, figurative, representative, significant.

symmetry n balance, congruity, evenness, harmony, order, proportion, regularity.

sympathetic adj commiserating, compassionate, condoling, kind, pitiful, tender.

sympathy n accord, affinity, agreement, communion, concord, congeniality, correspondence, harmony, reciprocity, union; condolence, fellow-feeling, kindliness, tenderness, thoughtfulness.

symptom n indication, mark, note, sign, token.

symptomatic adj characteristic, indicative, symbolic.

system n method, order, plan.

systematic adj methodical, orderly, regular.

T

table vb move, propose, submit, suggest. * n slab, tablet; board, counter, desk, stand; bench, catalogue, chart, index, list, schedule, synopsis, tabulation; diet, fare, food.

taboo vb forbid, prohibit, proscribe; * adj forbidden, outlawed, prohibited; * n ban, prohibition, proscription.

tackle vb grapple, seize; attempt,

try, undertake; * *n* apparatus, equipment, gear, harness, implements, rigging, tackling, tools, weapons.

tact *n* adroitness, cleverness, diplomacy, discernment, insight, knack, perception, skill, understanding.

tail *vb* dog, follow, shadow, track; * *adj* abridged, limited, reduced. *n* conclusion, end, extremity; flap, skirt; retinue, train.

taint *vb* imbue, impregnate; contaminate, corrupt, defile, inflect, pollute, poison, spoil; blot, stain, sully, tarnish; * *n* stain, tinge; contamination, corruption, defilement, infection, pollution; blemish, defect, fault, flaw, stain.

take *vb* obtain, procure, receive; clasp, clutch, grasp, grip, seize; filch, misappropriate, pilfer, purloin, steal; abstract, apprehend, appropriate, arrest, bag, capture; attack, befall; capture, carry off, conquer, gain, win; allure, attract, bewitch, captivate, charm, enchant, engage, fascinate, interest; consider, hold, suppose, regard; choose, elect, select; employ, expend, use; claim, demand, require; bear, endure, experience, perceive, tolerate; deduce, derive, detect, discover; carry, conduct, convey; clear, surmount; drink, eat, imbibe, inhale, swallow; * *n* proceeds, profits, return, revenue, yield.

tale *n* account, fable, legend, narration, novel, recital, rehearsal, relation, romance, story, yarn; account, catalogue, reckoning, tally.

talent *n* ability, aptitude, capacity, cleverness, faculty, forte, genius, gift, knack.

talk *vb* chatter, communicate, confess, converse, declaim, discuss, gossip, speak; * *n* chatter, communication, conversation, diction, gossip, language, rumour, speech, utterance.

talkative *adj* chatty, garrulous, loquacious, voluble.

tame *vb* domesticate, train; conquer, master, overcome, subdue, subjugate; * *adj* amenable, docile, domestic, domesticated, gentle; broken, crushed, meek, subdued, unresisting, submissive; dull, feeble, flat, insipid, jejune, languid, prosaic, prosy, spiritless, uninteresting.

tamper *vb* alter, dabble, damage, interfere, meddle; intrigue.

tang *n* aftertaste, flavour, relish, savour, taste; nip, sting.

tangible *adj* corporeal, material, palpable, tactile, touchable; actual, certain, evident, obvious, open, perceptible, positive, real, sensible, solid, substantial.

tangle *vb* complicate, intertwine, interweave, mat, snarl; catch, ensnare, entrap, involve; embroil, perplex; * *n* disorder, intricacy, jumble, perplexity; dilemma, quandary.

tap *vb* knock, pat, rap, strike, tip, touch; draw off, extract, pierce; draw on, exploit, mine, use; bug, eavesdrop, listen in; * *n* pat, tip, rap, touch; faucet, plug, spout, stopcock, valve; bug, listening device.

tardy *adj* slow, sluggish; backward, behindhand, late, loitering, overdue.

tarnish *vb* blemish, deface, defame, dim, discolour, dull, slur, smear, soil, stain, sully; * *n* blemish, blot, stain.

tart *adj* acid, acrid, piquant, pungent, sharp, sour; caustic, crabbed, curt, harsh, ill-humoured, ill-tempered, petulant, sarcastic, severe, snappish, sharp, testy.

task *n* drudgery, labour, toil, work; charge, chore, duty, employment, enterprise, job, mission, undertaking, work, assignment, exercise.

taste *vb* experience, perceive, undergo; relish, savour; * *n* flavour, relish, savour, snack, piquancy; bit, dash, fragment, hint, morsel, mouthful, sample, shade, sprinkling, suggestion; appetite, desire, fondness, liking, partiality, predilection; cultivation, culture, delicacy, discernment, discrimination, judgment, refinement; manner, style.

taunt *vb* chaff, deride, jeer, mock, scoff, sneer, revile, ridicule, upbraid; * *n* derision, gibe, insult, jeer, ridicule, scoff.

taut *adj* strained, stretched, tense, tight.

tawdry *adj* flashy, gaudy, garish, glittering, loud, ostentatious, showy.

tax *vb* burden, demand, exact, load, strain; accuse, charge; * *n* assessment, custom duty, excise, levy, toll, tribute; burden, demand, strain; accusation, censure.

teach *vb* coach, drill, educate, enlighten, inform, instruct, ground, prime, school, train, tutor; communicate, explain, expound, impart, inculcate, infuse, instil, interpret, preach, propagate; advise, counsel, direct, guide, show.

teacher *n* coach, educator, inculcator, instructor, don, master, pedagogue, preceptor, trainer, tutor; counsellor, guide, mentor; pastor, preacher.

tear *vb* slit, rive, rend, rip; claw, lacerate, rend, wound; sever, sunder; * *n* fissure, laceration, rent, rip, wrench.

tease *vb* annoy, badger, bother, chafe, harass, harry, hector, irritate, molest, pester, plague, provoke, tantalise, torment, trouble, vex, worry.

tedious *adj* dull, fatiguing, irksome, monotonous, tiresome, uninteresting, wearisome; dilatory, slow, sluggish.

teem *vb* abound, overflow, swarm.

tell *vb* count, enumerate, number, reckon; describe, narrate, recount, relate, report; announce, betray, confess, disclose, divulge, inform, reveal; acquaint, communicate, teach; discern, distinguish; communicate, express, mention, publish, speak, state, utter.

temper *vb* modify, qualify; appease, assuage, calm, mitigate, moderate, pacify, restrain, soften, soothe; accommodate, adapt, adjust, fit; * *n* character, constitution, nature, structure, type; disposition, humour, mood, spirits, tone, vein; calmness, composure, equanimity, moderation, tranquillity; anger, irritation, passion.

temporary *adj* brief, ephemeral, fleeting, impermanent, momentary, short-lived, transient, transitory.

tempt *vb* test, try; allure, decoy, entice, induce, inveigle, seduce; dispose, incite, incline, instigate, lead, prompt, provoke.

tenacious *adj* retentive; clinging, cohesive, firm, resisting, retentive, sticky, strong, tough, unyielding; dogged, fast, obstinate, opinionated, pertinacious, persistent, resolute, stubborn, unwavering.

tend *vb* accompany, attend, guard, keep, protect, shepherd, watch; gravitate, head, incline, influence, lead, lean, point, trend, verge; conduce, contribute.

tendency *n* aptitude, bearing, bent, bias, disposition, direction, drift, gravitation, inclination, leaning, liability, predisposition, proneness, propensity, susceptibility.

tender *vb* bid, offer, present, proffer, propose, suggest; * *n* bid, offer, proffer, proposal; currency, money; * *adj* delicate, feeble, feminine, fragile, immature, infantile, soft, weak, young; affectionate, compassionate, gentle, humane, kind, loving, merciful, mild, sensitive, sympathetic, tender-hearted; affecting, disagreeable, painful, touching.

tense *vb* flex, strain, tauten, tighten; * *adj* rigid, strained, stretched, taut, tight; excited, highly strung, intent, nervous.

tentative *adj* experimental, provisional, testing, toying.

term *vb* call, christen, designate, dub, entitle, name, phrase; * *n* bound, boundary, confine, limit, terminus; duration, period, season, semester, spell, time; expression, locution, name, phrase, word.

terminal *adj* bounding, limiting; final, ultimate; * *n* end, extremity; bound, limit; airport, depot, station.

terminate *vb* bound, limit; end, finish, close, complete, conclude; prove.

termination *n* ending, suffix; bound, limit; end, completion, conclusion, consequence, effect, outcome, result.

terms *npl* conditions, provisions, stipulations.

terrible *adj* appalling, dire, dreadful, formidable, frightful, gruesome, hideous, horrible, shocking, terrific, tremendous; alarming, awe-inspiring, awful, dreadful; great; excessive, extreme, severe.

terrify *vb* affright, alarm, daunt, dismay, fright, frighten, horrify, scare, shock, terrorise.

terror *n* affright, alarm, anxiety, awe, consternation, dismay, shock, dread, fear, horror, intimidation, panic.

test *vb* assay; examine, prove, try; * *n* attempt, examination, experiment, or deal, proof, trial; criterion, standard; exhibition, proof; distinction, judgement.

testify *vb* affirm, assert, attest, avow, certify, corroborate, declare, evidence, state, swear.

testimonial *n* certificate, credential, recommendation; monument, record.

testimony *n* affirmation, confession, confirmation, corroboration, declaration, deposition; evidence, proof, witness.

testy *adj* captious, choleric, cross, fretful, hasty, irascible, irritable, peevish, peppery, pettish, petulant, snappish, touchy, waspish.

text *n* copy, subject, theme, thesis, treatise.

texture *n* fabric, web; character, coarseness, composition, fibre, fineness, grain, make-up, organisation, structure.

thankful *adj* appreciative, beholden, grateful, obliged.

thaw *vb* liquefy, melt, soften.

theatrical *adj* dramatic; affected, ceremonious, ostentatious, pompous, showy, stagy, stilted, unnatural.

theft *n* embezzlement, fraud, larceny, pilfering, purloining, robbery, stealing, thieving.

theme *n* composition, essay, subject, text, thesis, topic, treatise.

theoretical *adj* abstract, conjectural, doctrinaire, ideal, hypothetical, pure, speculative, unapplied.

theory *n* assumption, conjecture, hypothesis, plan, postulation, principle, scheme, surmise, system; doctrine, philosophy, science; explanation, rationale.

therefore *adv* accordingly, consequently, hence, so, then, thence, whence.

thick *adj* bulky, chunky, dumpy, plump, solid, squat, stubby; clotted, coagulated, dense, dull, heavy, viscous, cloudy, dirty, foggy, hazy, misty, obscure, vaporous; muddy, turbid; abundant, frequent, multitudinous, numerous; close, compact, crowded, set; guttural, hoarse, inarticulate, indistinct; dim, dull; familiar, friendly, intimate; * *adv* fast, frequently, quick; closely, densely; * *n* centre, midst.

thief *n* depredator, filcher, pilferer, marauder, purloiner, robber, stealer; burglar, corsair, defrauder, embezzler, highwayman, house breaker, kidnapper, pickpocket, pirate, poacher, privateer, sharper, swindler.

thieve *vb* embezzle, peculate, pilfer, plunder, filch, purloin, rob, steal, swindle.

thin *vb* attenuate, dilute, diminish, prune, reduce, refine; * *adj* attenuated, bony, emaciated, fine, flimsy, gaunt, lank, lanky, lean, meagre, pinched, scanty, scrawny, slender, slight, slim, sparse, spindly.

thing *n* being, body, contrivance, creature, entity, object, substance; action, affair, arrangement, circumstance, concern, deed, event, matter, occurrence, transaction.

think *vb* cogitate, contemplate, dream, meditate, muse, ponder, reflect, speculate; consider, deliberate, reason; apprehend, believe, conceive, conclude, deem, determine, fancy, hold, imagine, judge, opine, presume, reckon, suppose, surmise; design, intend, purpose; account; compass, design, plan, plot; * *n* assessment, reasoning, reflection.

thirst *n* appetite, craving, desire, hunger, longing, yearning; drought, dryness.

thirsty *adj* arid, dry, parched; eager, greedy, hungry, longing, yearning.

thorough *adj* arrant, complete, entire, exhaustive, finished, perfect, sweeping, unmitigated, total; accurate, correct, reliable, trustworthy.

thought *n* absorption, cogitation, meditation, musing, reflection, rumination; contemplation, intellect, thinking; idea, pondering, speculation; consciousness, imagination, perception, understanding; fancy, notion; conclusion, judgement, motion, opinion, sentiment, supposition, view; attention, care, consideration, deliberation, provision, solicitude; design, expectation, intention, purpose.

thoughtful *adj* absorbed, contemplative, deliberative, dreamy, engrossed, pensive, philosophic, reflecting, reflective; attentive, careful, cautious, circumspect, heedful, kindly, mindful, provident, prudent, regardful, watchful, wary; quiet, serious, sober, studious.

thoughtless *adj* careless, casual, flighty, heedless, improvident, inattentive, inconsiderate, neglectful, negligent, rash, reckless, regardless, remiss, unmindful; blank, dull, insensate, vacant, vacuous.

thrash *vb* beat, bruise, conquer, defeat, drub, flog, lash, pommel, punish, thwack, trounce, wallop, whip.

thread *vb* course, direction, drift, tenor; * *n* cord, fibre, filament, line; pile, staple.

threadbare *adj* old, seedy, worn; common, shabby, hackneyed, stale, trite, worn-out.

threat *n* defiance, fulmination, intimidation, menace, thunder, thunderbolt.

threaten *vb* endanger, fulminate, intimidate, menace; augur, forebode, foreshadow, indicate, portend, presage, warn.

thrift *n* economy, frugality, parsimony, saving; gain, profit, prosperity, success.

thrifty *adj* careful, economical, frugal, provident, saving, sparing; flourishing, thriving, vigorous.

thrill *vb* affect, agitate, electrify, inspire, move, penetrate, rouse, touch; * *n* excitement,

sensation, shock, tingling, tremor.
throng *vb* congregate, crowd, fill, flock, pack, press; * *n* assemblage, concourse, congregation, crowd, horde, host, mob, multitude.
throw *vb* cast, chuck, fling, hurl, lance, launch, overturn, pitch, send, sling, toss, whirl; * *n* cast, launch, pitch, sling, whirl; chance, gamble, try, venture.
thrust *vb* clap, dig, drive, force, impel, plunge, poke, propel, push, ram, shove; * *n* dig, jab, lunge, pass, plunge, poke, propulsion, push, stab, tilt.
thump *vb* bang, batter, beat, knock, punch, strike, thwack, whack; * *n* blow, knock, punch, strike.
ticklish *adj* risky, uncertain, unstable, unsteady; delicate, difficult, nice.
tidy *vb* clean, neaten, order, straighten; * *adj* neat, orderly, shipshape, spruce, trim.
tie *vb* bind, confine, fasten, knot, lock, manacle, secure, shackle, fetter, yoke; entangle, interlace, knit; connect, hold, join, link, unite; constrain, oblige, restrain, restrict; * *n* fastening, knot, ligament, ligature; allegiance, bond, obligation; bow, cravat.
tight *adj* close, compact, fast, firm; taut, tense, stretched; impassable, narrow.
tilt *vb* cant, incline, slant, slope, tip; forge, point, thrust; joust, rush; * *n* canopy, tent; lunge, pass, thrust; cant, inclination, slant, slope, tip.
time *vb* clock, control, measure, regulate, schedule; * *n* duration, interim, interval, season, span, spell, term; aeon, age, date, epoch, eon, era, period, term; cycle, dynasty, reign; parturition; measure, rhythm.
timely *adj* appropriate, apropos, early, opportune, prompt, punctual, seasonable.
timid *adj* afraid, faint-hearted, fearful, irresolute, nervous, pusillanimous, timorous, unadventurous; bashful, coy, diffident, modest, shrinking, retiring.
tinge *vb* colour, dye, stain, tint; imbue, impregnate, infuse; * *n* cast, colour, dye, hue, shade, stain, tint; flavour, smack, quality, taste.
tint *n* cast, colour, complexion, dye, hue, shade, tone.
tiny *adj* diminutive, Lilliputian, little, microscopic, miniature, minute, puny, small, wee.
tip *n* apex, cap, end, extremity, peak, point, top, vertex; donation, fee, gratuity, reward; slant; hint, pointer, suggestion; strike, tap; * *vb* incline, overturn, tilt; dispose of, dump.
tire *vb* exhaust, drain, fatigue, harass, jade, weary; bore, bother, irk.
tiresome *adj* annoying, arduous, boring, dull, exhausting, fatiguing, humdrum, irksome, laborious, monotonous, tedious, wearisome, vexatious.
tissue *n* cloth, fabric; membrane, structure, texture, web; chain, collection, conglomeration, mass, network, series, set.
title *vb* call, designate, name, style, term; * *n* caption, legend, head, heading; appellation, denomination, designation, epithet, name; claim, ownership, possession, prerogative, privilege, right.
toast *vb* brown, dry, heat; honour, pledge, salute; * *n* compliment, drink, pledge, salutation, salute; favourite, pet.
toil *vb* drudge, labour, strive, work; * *n* drudgery, effort, exertion, labour, pains, travail, work; net, noose, snare, spring.
token *adj* nominal, superficial, symbolic; * *n* badge, indication, manifestation, mark, note,

sign, symbol, trace, trait; keepsake, memento, reminder, souvenir.

tolerable *adj* bearable, endurable, sufferable, supportable; fair, indifferent, ordinary, passable.

tolerate *vb* allow, indulge, let, permit; abide, brook, endure, suffer.

toll *n* charge, customs, demand, duty, fee, impost, levy, tax, tribute; cost, damage, loss; chime, peal, ring, ringing, tolling; * *vb* chime, peal, ring, sound.

tomb *n* catacomb, crypt, grave, mausoleum, sepulchre, vault.

tone *vb* blend, harmonise, match, suit; * *n* note, sound; accent, cadence, inflection, intonation; mood, strain, temper; force, health, strength, tension; cast, colour, hue, shade, style, tint; drift, tenor.

too *adv* additionally, also, further, likewise, moreover.

top *vb* cap, head, tip; ride; outgo, surpass; * *adj* apical, chief, culminating, finest, first, foremost, highest, leading, prime, principal, uppermost; * *n* apex, crest, crown, head, pinnacle, summit, surface, zenith.

topic *n* business, question, subject, theme, thesis; division, head; dictum, precept, principle, rule; arrangement, scheme.

topple *vb* fall, overturn, tumble, upset.

torment *vb* annoy, agonise, distress, rack, torture; badger, harass, harry, irritate, nettle, plague, tease, trouble, vex, worry; * *n* agony, anguish, pang, rack, torture.

tortuous *adj* crooked, curved, curvilineal, curvilinear, serpentine, sinuate, sinuated, sinuous, twisted, winding; circuitous, indirect, perverse, roundabout.

torture *vb* afflict, agonise, distress, excruciate, pain, rack; * *n* agony, pain, pang, rack, torment.

toss *vb* cast, fling, hurl, pitch, throw; rock, shake; harass; roll, writhe; * *n* cast, fling, pitch, throw.

total *vb* add, amount to, reckon; * *adj* complete, entire, full, whole; integral, undivided; * *n* aggregate, all, gross, mass, sum, whole.

touch *vb* feel, handle, hit, pat, strike, tap; concern, regard; affect, impress, move, stir; grasp, stretch; mollify; move, soften; afflict, distress, hurt, injure, molest, wound; * *n* hint, suggestion, suspicion, taste, trace; blow, contract, hit, pat, tap.

touchy *adj* choleric, cross, fretful, hot-tempered, irritable, peevish, petulant, snappish, splenetic, tetchy, testy, waspish.

tough *adj* cohesive, flexible, tenacious; leathery; sticky, viscous; inflexible, intractable, rigid, stiff; hard, obdurate, stubborn; difficult, formidable, hard, troublesome; * *n* brute, bully, hooligan, ruffian, thug.

tour *vb* journey, perambulate, travel, visit; * *n* circuit, excursion, expedition, journey, pilgrimage, round.

tow *vb* drag, draw, haul, pull; * *n* drag, lift, pull.

tower *vb* rise, soar, transcend; * *n* belfry, column, minaret, spire, steeple, turret; castle, citadel, fortress, stronghold; pillar, refuge.

toy *vb* play, sport, trifle; * *n* bauble, doll, gewgaw, gimmick, knick-knack, plaything, puppet, trinket; trifle; play, sport.

trace *vb* follow, track; copy, delineate, derive, describe, draw, sketch; * *n* evidence, footprint, impression, remains, sign, track, trail, vestige, wake; memorial, record; bit, dash, hint,

TRANSPORT

suspicion, streak, tinge.
track *vb* follow, pursue, scent, track, trail; * *n* footmark, footprint, spoor, trace, vestige; course, pathway, rails, road, trace, trail, wake, way.
trade *vb* bargain, barter, deal, exchange, interchange, sell, traffic; * *n* bargaining, barter, business, commerce, dealing, traffic; craft, employment, occupation, profession, pursuit, vocation.
traditional *adj* accustomed, apocryphal, customary, established, legendary, old, transmitted, unverified, unwritten.
traffic *vb* barter, deal, exchange, trade; * *n* barter, business, commerce, exchange, trade, transportation.
tragedy *n* drama, play; calamity, catastrophe, disaster.
tragic *adj* dramatic; calamitous, catastrophic, disastrous, dreadful, grievous, mournful, sad, sorrowful.
trail *vb* follow, hunt, trace, track, shadow; draw, flow, haul; * *n* footmark, footprint, footstep, mark, trace, track.
train *vb* drag, haul, trail; allure, entice; drill, educate, exercise, instruct, school, teach; accustom, break in, prepare, rehearse, use; * *n* trail, wake; entourage, cortege, followers, retinue, staff; chain, series, succession; course, method, order, process; allure, artifice, device, enticement, lure, persuasion, trap.
traitor *n* betrayer, Judas, renegade, turncoat; deserter, insurgent, mutineer, rebel, revolutionary.
traitorous *adj* faithless, false, perfidious, treacherous; perfidious, treasonable.
tramp *vb* hike, march, plod, trudge, walk; * *n* journey, march, walk; stroller, tramper, vagabond, vagrant.
trample *vb* crush, run over, squash, infringe, stamp, encroach upon.
trance *n* dream, hypnosis, rapture; catalepsy, coma.
tranquil *adj* calm, hushed, peaceful, placid, quiet, serene, still unperturbed, unruffled, untroubled.
tranquillise *vb* allay, appease, assuage, calm, hush, lay, lull, moderate, pacify, quell, quiet, soothe.
transact *vb* conduct, dispatch, enact, execute, manage, negotiate, perform.
transcend *vb* exceed, overlap, overstep, pass; excel, outstrip, outrival, surmount, surpass.
transfer *vb* convey, dispatch, move, translate, transmit, transplant, transport; assign, cede, confer, convey, consign, deed, displace, forward, grant, pass, transmit; * *n* assignment, bequest, carriage, cession, change, conveyance, copy, demise, move, relegation, removal, shift, shipment, transference, transferring, transit, transmission, transportation.
transform *vb* alter, change, metamorphose, transfigure; convert, translate, transmute.
translate *vb* transfer, transport; decipher, decode, interpret, render, turn.
transmit *vb* forward, send; communicate, conduct, radiate; bear, carry, convey.
transparent *adj* clear, diaphanous, lucid; hyaline, pellucid, translucent, unclouded, open; evident, obvious, manifest, obvious, patent.
transpire *vb* chance, happen, occur; evaporate, exhale.
transport *vb* bear, carry, cart, conduct, convey, remove, ship, take, transfer, truck; banish, expel; beatify, delight, enrapture, entrance, ravish; * *n* carriage, conveyance, movement, transportation; beatification, beatitude, bliss,

ecstasy, felicity, happiness, rapture; passion.

trap *vb* catch, ensnare, noose, snare; ambush, deceive, dupe, trick; enmesh, tangle; * *n* gin, snare, toil; ambush, artifice, pitfall, stratagem, trepan.

trappings *npl* adornments, decorations, embellishments, gear, livery, paraphernalia, rigging; accoutrements, equipment, gear.

trash *n* dregs, dross, garbage, refuse, rubbish, waste; balderdash, nonsense.

travel *vb* journey, peregrinate, ramble, roam, rove, tour, voyage, wander; move, pass; * *n* excursion, expedition, journey, tour, trip, voyage.

traveller *n* explorer, globetrotter, itinerant, pilgrim, rover, tourist, trekker, tripper, voyager, wanderer, wayfarer.

treacherous *adj* deceitful, disloyal, faithless, false, insidious, recreant, traitorous, treasonable, unfaithful, unreliable, unsafe.

treason *n* betrayal, lese-majesty, perfidy, sedition, traitorousness, treachery.

treasonable *adj* disloyal, traitorous, treacherous.

treasure *vb* collect, husband, save, store; cherish, idolise, prize, value; * *n* cash, funds, jewels, money, riches, savings, valuables, wealth; abundance, reserve, stock, store.

treat *vb* entertain, gratify; doctor, dose, handle, manage, serve; bargain, covenant, negotiate; * *n* banquet, entertainment, feast; delight, enjoyment, entertainment, gratification, luxury, pleasure.

treatment *n* usage, use; dealing, handling, management, manipulation; therapy.

treaty *n* agreement, alliance, bond, bargain, concordat, convention, covenant, entente, pact.

tremble *vb* quake, quaver, shake, shiver, shudder, tremble, vibrate; * *n* quake, quiver, shake, shiver, shudder, tremor, vibration.

tremendous *adj* appalling, dreadful, frightful, horrible, terrible; wonderful, great.

tremor *n* quaking, shaking, trembling, trepidation, vibration.

trend *vb* drift, incline, lean, run, sweep, tend, turn; * *n* bent, course, direction, drift, inclination, set, leaning, tendency.

trespass *vb* encroach, infringe, intrude, trench; offend, sin, transgress; * *n* encroachment, infringement, injury, intrusion, invasion; error, sin, misdeed, misdemeanour, offence, transgression.

trial *adj* experimental, testing; * *n* examination, experiment, test; knowledge; attempt, effort, endeavour, exertion, struggle; assay, ordeal, proof, test, touchstone; affliction, burden, chagrin, distress, grief, hardship, heartache, misery, pain, sorrow, suffering, tribulation, unhappiness, woe, wretchedness; action, case, cause, hearing, suit.

tribulation *n* adversity, affliction, distress, grief, misery, pain, suffering, trial, trouble, unhappiness.

tribute *n* tax; custom, duty, excise, tax, toll; contribution, grant, offering.

trice *n* flash, instant, jiffy, moment, twinkling.

trick *vb* cheat, circumvent, deceive, defraud, delude, diddle, dupe, gull, hoax; * *n* artifice, blind, deceit, deception, fake, feint, fraud, game, hoax, manoeuvre, ruse, swindle, stratagem, wile; antic, caper, craft, deftness, sleight; habit, peculiarity, practice.

trickle *vb* dribble, drip, ooze, percolate, seep; * *n* dribble, drip, percolation, seepage.

tricky *adj* artful, cunning, deceitful, deceptive, subtle; delicate.

trifle *vb* dally, dawdle, fool, fribble, play, potter, toy; * *n* bagatelle, bauble, fig, triviality; iota, jot, modicum, particle.

trifling *adj* frippery, frivolous, inconsiderable, insignificant, petty, shallow, slight, trivial, unimportant, worthless.

trill *vb* shake; quaver, warble; * *n* quaver, tremolo, warbling.

trim *vb* adjust, arrange, prepare; balance, equalise; adorn, bedeck, decorate, dress, embellish, garnish, ornament; clip, curtail, lop, mow, prune, shave, shear; berate, chastise, chide, rebuke, reprimand, reprove; balance, fluctuate, hedge, shift, shuffle; * *adj* compact, neat, nice, shapely, tidy, well-adjusted, well-ordered; chic, elegant, smart, spruce; * *n* dress, trappings; case, condition, plight, state.

trip *vb* caper, dance, hop, skip; misstep, stumble; bungle, blunder, mistake; overthrow, upset; convict, detect; * *n* hop, skip; lurch, misstep, stumble; blunder, bungle, error, fault, lapse, mistake, oversight, slip, stumble; circuit, excursion, expedition, jaunt, journey, ramble, tour.

triumph *vb* exult, rejoice; prevail, succeed, win; flourish, prosper, thrive; boast, gloat, swagger, vaunt; * *n* exultation, joy, jubilation; accomplishment, achievement, conquest, success, victory.

triumphant *adj* boastful, conquering, exultant, exulting, jubilant, successful, victorious.

trivial *adj* frivolous, immaterial, inconsiderable, insignificant, little, nugatory, paltry, petty, small, slight, slim, trifling, unimportant.

troop *vb* crowd, flock, muster, throng; * *n* company, crowd, multitude, number, throng; band, body, company, party, squad; company.

trouble *vb* agitate, confuse, disarrange, disorder; afflict, ail, annoy, badger, concern, disquiet, distress, disturb, fret, harass, molest, perplex, perturb, pester, plague, torment, vex, worry; * *n* adversity, calamity, distress, grief, hardship, misfortune, misery, sorrow, suffering, tribulation, woe; anxiety, bother, care, discomfort, fuss, inconvenience, irritation, pains, perplexity, plague, vexation, worry; disturbance, row; bewilderment, perplexity.

troublesome *adj* annoying, distressing, disturbing, galling, harassing, perplexing, vexatious, worrisome; irksome, tiresome, wearisome; intrusive; arduous, difficult, hard, inconvenient, trying, unwieldy.

truce *n* armistice, cessation, delay, intermission, lull, pause, recess, reprieve, respite, cease-fire.

truck *vb* barter, deal, exchange, trade; * *n* lorry, van, wagon.

true *adj* actual, unaffected, authentic, genuine, legitimate, real, rightful, sincere, sound, truthful, veritable; constant, faithful, loyal, staunch, steady; equitable, honest, honourable, just, trustworthy, virtuous; accurate, correct, even, exact, right, straight, undeviating; * *adv* good, well.

trust *vb* confide, depend, expect, hope, rely; believe; commit; * *n* belief, confidence, faith; credit, charge, deposit; commission, duty, errand; assurance, belief, confidence, expectation, faith, hope.

trustworthy *adj* confidential, constant, dependable, faithful, firm, honest, incorrupt, upright, reliable, responsible, straightforward, staunch, true, upright.

truth *n* fact, reality, veracity;

actuality, authenticity; cannon, law, principle; right, veracity; candour, fidelity, honesty, ingenuousness, integrity, sincerity, virtue; constancy, devotion, faith, loyalty, steadfastness; accuracy, correctness, exactitude, exactness, nicety, precision, regularity.

truthful *adj* correct, reliable, trustworthy, veracious; candid, frank, guileless, honest, ingenuous, open, sincere, true, trustworthy, trusty.

try *vb* examine, prove, test; attempt; adjudicate, adjudge, hear; purify, refine; sample, smell, taste; aim, attempt, endeavour, strain; * *n* attempt, effort, endeavour, experiment, trial.

trying *adj* difficult, fatiguing, hard, irksome, tiresome, wearisome; afflicting, dire, distressing, grievous, hard, painful, severe.

tug *vb* drag, haul, pull, tow, wrench; labour, strive; * *n* drag, haul, pull, tow, wrench.

tuition *n* education, instruction, schooling, teaching.

tumble *vb* pitch, roll, toss; sprawl, stumble, topple, trip, derange, disarrange, dishevel, disorder, rumple, tousle; * *n* collapse, fall, plunge, spill, stumble, trip.

tumult *n* ado, affray, agitation, altercation, brawl, disturbance, ferment, feud, fray, fuss, hubbub, huddle, melee, noise, perturbation, quarrel, racket, riot, row, squabble, turbulence, turmoil, uproar.

tumultuous *adj* bustling, confused, disorderly, disturbed, riotous, turbulent, unruly.

tune *vb* accord, harmonise, modulate; adapt, adjust; * *n* air, aria, melody, strain, tone; agreement, concord, harmony; accord, order.

tuneful *adj* harmonious, melodious, musical.

turbulent *adj* agitated, restless, tumultuous, wild; blustering, boisterous, disorderly, tumultuous, uproarious; disorderly, insubordinate, insurgent, mutinous, raging, rebellious, refractory, riotous, seditious, stormy, violent.

turmoil *n* activity, agitation, bustle, commotion, confusion, disorder, disturbance, ferment, hubbub, noise, trouble, tumult, turbulence, uproar.

turn *vb* revolve, rotate; bend, defect, spin, sway, swivel, twirl, twist, wheel; crank, grind, wind; deflect, divert, transfer, warp; mould, shape; adapt, manoeuvre, suit; alter, change, metamorphose, transform, transmute, vary; convert, persuade, prejudice; construe, render, translate; depend, hinge, pivot; issue, result, terminate; acidify, curdle, ferment; * *n* cycle, gyration, revolution, rotation; bending, deflection, deviation, diversion, flexion, reel, slew, spin, sweep, swing, swirl, swivel, turning, twist, twirl, winding; alteration, change, variation, bend, circuit, drive, round; bout, hand, innings, opportunity, round, shift, spell; act, action, deed; occasion, purpose; cast, fashion, form, manner, mould, phase; aptitude, bent, bias, faculty, genius, inclination, proclivity, proneness, propensity, talent, tendency.

tussle *vb* conflict, scuffle, struggle, wrestle; * *n* conflict, contest, fight, scuffle, struggle.

tutor *vb* coach, educate, instruct, teach; discipline, train; * *n* coach, governess, governor, instructor, teacher.

tweak *vb*, *n* jerk, pinch, squeeze, twinge, twitch.

twin *vb* couple, link, match, pair; * *adj* double, duplicate, geminate, identical, matched, second, twain; * *n* corollary,

double, duplicate, fellow, likeness.
twine *vb* embrace, encircle, interlace, surround; bend, meander, wind; coil, twist; * *n* convolution, coil, twist; embrace, winding; cord, string.
twinge *vb* pinch, tweak, twitch; * *n* pinch, tweak, twitch; pang, spasm.
twinkle *vb* blink, wink; glimmer, scintillate, sparkle; * *n* blink, gleam, glimmer, scintillation, sparkle; flash, instant, jiffy, moment, second, tick, trice.
twirl *vb* revolve, rotate, spin, turn, twist; * *n* convolution, revolution, turn, twist, whirling.
twist *vb* curl, rotate, spin; contort, convolute, distort, pervert, screw, wring; coil, writhe; wind, wreathe; * *n* coil, curl, spin, twine; braid, coil, curl; change, complication, variation; bend, convolution; defect, distortion, flaw, imperfection; pull, sprain, wrench; aberration, oddity, peculiarity, quirk.
twitch *vb* jerk, pluck, snatch; * *n* jerk; contraction, quiver, spasm, twitching.
type *n* emblem, mark, stamp; image, representation, representative, sign, symbol, token; exemplar, model, original, pattern, standard; character, form, kind, nature, sort; figure, letter, text, typography.
typical *adj* exemplary, figurative, ideal, indicative, model, representative, symbolic.
typify *vb* betoken, embody, exemplify, figure, image, represent, signify.
tyrannical *adj* absolute, arbitrary, autocratic, cruel, despotic, dictatorial, domineering, imperious, severe, unjust; cruel, galling, inhuman, oppressive, severe.
tyranny *n* absolutism, autocracy, despotism, dictatorship, harshness, oppression.
tyrant *n* autocrat, despot, dictator, oppressor.

U

ubiquitous *adj* omnipresent, universal.
ugly *adj* crooked, homely, plain, ordinary, unlovely, unshapely, unsightly; forbidding, frightful, gruesome, hideous, horrible, loathsome, monstrous, shocking, repellent, repulsive; bad-tempered, cantankerous, churlish, cross, quarrelsome, spiteful, surly.
ultimate *adj* conclusive, decisive, eventual, extreme, farthest, final, last; * *n* consummation, culmination, height, peak, quintessence, summit.
umbrage *n* shadow, shade; anger, displeasure, dissatisfaction, injury, offence, resentment.
umpire *vb* adjudicate, judge, referee; * *n* adjudicator, arbiter, judge, referee.
unaccommodating *adj* disobliging, non-compliant, uncivil, ungracious.
unanimity *n* accord, agreement, concert, concord, harmony, unity.
unbalanced *adj* unsound, unsteady, shaky; unadjusted, unsettled.
unbecoming *adj* improper, inappropriate, indecent, indecorous, unbefitting, unseemly, unsuitable.
unbelief *n* disbelief, dissent, distrust, incredulity, miscreance, nonconformity; freethinking, infidelity, scepticism.
unbeliever *n* agnostic, deist, disbeliever, doubter, heathen, infidel, sceptic.
unbending *adj* inflexible, rigid, stiff, unyielding; firm, obstinate, resolute, stubborn.
unbridled *adj* dissolute, lax,

licentious, loose, uncontrolled, ungovernable, unrestrained, violent.

uncanny *adj* inopportune, unsafe; eerie, ghostly, unearthly, unnatural, weird.

uncertain *adj* ambiguous, doubtful, dubious, equivocal, indefinite, indeterminate, indistinct, questionable, unsettled; insecure, precarious; changeable, fitful, fluctuating, irregular, shaky, slippery, unreliable, variable.

unchecked *adj* uncurbed, unhampered, unhindered, unobstructed, unrestrained.

uncommon *adj* exceptional, extraordinary, infrequent, noteworthy, odd, queer, rare, remarkable, scarce, singular, strange, unfamiliar, unusual, unwonted.

uncomplaining *adj* long-suffering, meek, patient, resigned, tolerant.

uncompromising *adj* inflexible, narrow, obstinate, orthodox, rigid, stiff, unyielding.

unconditional *adj* absolute, complete, entire, free, full, unlimited, unqualified, unreserved, unrestricted.

uncouth *adj* boorish, clownish, clumsy, gawky, inelegant, loutish, rough, rude, rustic, uncourtly, ungainly, unrefined, unseemly; outlandish, strange, unfamiliar, unusual.

unctuous *adj* greasy, oily, fat, oleaginous, sebaceous; bland, lubricious, smooth, slippery; fawning, glib, obsequious, plausible, servile, suave, smooth, sycophantic; fervid, gushing.

under *prep* below, beneath, inferior to, lower than, subordinate to; * *adv* below, beneath, down, lower.

underestimate *vb* belittle, underrate, under value.

undergo *vb* bear, endure, experience, suffer, sustain.

underhand *adj* clandestine, deceitful, disingenuous, hidden, secret, sly, stealthy, underhanded, unfair; * *adv* clandestinely, secretly, stealthily, fraudulently, unfairly.

undermine *vb* excavate, sap; demoralise, foil, thwart, weaken.

understand *vb* apprehend, catch, comprehend, conceive, discern, grasp, know, penetrate, perceive, see, twig; assume, take; imply.

understanding *adj* compassionate, considerate, kind, patient, sympathetic, tolerant; * *n* brains, comprehension, discernment, intellect, intelligence, judgement, knowledge, reason.

undertake *vb* assume, attempt, embark on, engage in, enter upon; agree, contract, engage, guarantee, promise, stipulate.

undertaking *n* adventure, affair, attempt, business, effort, endeavour, engagement, enterprise, project, task, venture.

undo *vb* annul, cancel, frustrate, invalidate, neutralise, nullify, reverse; disengage, loose, unfasten, unravel, untie; destroy, overturn, ruin.

undue *adj* illegal, illegitimate, improper, unlawful, excessive, disproportionate, unsuitable; unfit.

undying *adj* deathless, endless, immortal, imperishable.

unearthly *adj* preternatural, supernatural, uncanny, weird.

uneasy *adj* disquieted, disturbed, fidgety, impatient, perturbed, restless, restive, worried; awkward, ungainly, ungraceful; cramping, disagreeable, uncomfortable.

unending *adj* eternal, everlasting, interminable, perpetual, unceasing.

unequal *adj* disproportionate, ill-matched, inferior, irregular, insufficient, uneven.

unequalled *adj* incomparable, inimitable, matchless, nonpareil, novel, paramount, peerless, pre-eminent, superlative, surpassing, transcendent, unparalleled, unrivalled.

unexpected *adj* abrupt, sudden, unforeseen.

unfair *adj* dishonest, faithless, false, hypocritical, inequitable, insincere, one-sided, partial, unequal, unjust, wrongful.

unfaithful *adj* deceitful, dishonest, disloyal, faithless, perfidious, treacherous, unreliable; negligent; faithless, inconstant.

unfeeling *adj* callous, heartless, insensible, numb, obdurate, unconscious; cold-blooded, cruel, hard, merciless, pitiless, stony, unkind, unsympathetic.

unfit *vb* disable, disqualify; * *adj* improper, inappropriate, incompetent, unsuitable; inadequate, incapable, unqualified, useless; feeble, flabby, unhealthy, unsound.

unfold *vb* expand, open, separate, unfurl, unroll; disclose, reveal, tell; decipher, develop, disentangle, evolve, explain, illustrate, resolve, unravel.

ungainly *adj* awkward, boorish, clumsy, gawky, inelegant, loutish, lumbering, slouching, uncourtly, uncouth, ungraceful.

uniform *adj* alike, constant, even, equal, smooth, steady, regular, unbroken, unchanged, undeviating, unvaried; * *n* costume, dress, livery, outfit, suit.

union *n* coalescence, coalition, combination, conjunction, coupling, fusion, incorporation, joining, junction, unification; concurrence, harmony, unanimity; alliance, club, confederacy, federation, guild, league.

unique *adj* choice, exceptional, matchless, only, peculiar, single, sole, singular, unexampled, unmatched.

unison *n* accord, agreement, concord, harmony.

unite *vb* amalgamate, attach, blend, coalesce, confederate, consolidate, fuse, incorporate, merge, weld; associate, connect, couple, link, marry, blend; combine, conjoin, join; harmonise, reconcile; concert, concur, cooperate, fraternise.

universal *adj* all-reaching, catholic, general, ubiquitous, unlimited; all, complete, entire, total, whole.

unjust *adj* inequitable, unequal, unfair, unwarranted, wrong, wrongful; flagitious, heinous, iniquitous, unrighteous, wicked, wrong; biased, partial, prejudiced, unfair.

unknown *adj* unascertained; undiscovered, unexplored, uninvestigated; concealed, dark, enigmatic, mysterious, mystic; anonymous, incognito, inglorious, nameless, obscure, unnoted.

unlimited *adj* boundless, infinite, interminable, limitless, measureless, unbounded; absolute, unconfined, unconstrained, unrestricted; undefined.

unmanageable *adj* awkward, cumbersome, inconvenient, unwieldy; intractable, unruly, unworkable; difficult.

unmitigated *adj* absolute, complete, consummate, perfect, sheer, thorough, unqualified, utter.

unnatural *adj* cold, heartless, inhuman, unfeeling, unusual; affected, constrained, forced, insincere, self-conscious, strained; aberrant, abnormal, irregular, uncommon.

unprincipled *adj* crooked, dishonest, immoral, iniquitous, knavish, lawless, profligate, rascally, roguish, thievish, trickish, unscrupulous, villainous, wicked.

unqualified *adj* incompetent, ineligible, unadapted, unfit; absolute, consummate, direct, downright, unconditional, unmeasured, unmitigated, unrestricted; sweeping.

unreal *adj* chimerical, dreamlike, fanciful, ghostly, illusory, insubstantial, nebulous, shadowy, spectral.

unreserved *adj* absolute, entire, unlimited; above-board, candid, communicative, frank, guileless, honest, ingenuous, open, sincere, undesigning; demonstrative, emotional, open-hearted.

unrighteous *adj* evil, sinful, ungodly, unholy, wicked, wrong; heinous, inequitable, iniquitous, nefarious, unjust.

unripe *adj* crude, green, hard, immature, premature, sour; incomplete, unfinished.

unrivalled *adj* incomparable, inimitable, matchless, peerless, unequalled, unique, unparalleled.

unroll *vb* develop, discover, evolve, open, unfold; lay open.

unruly *adj* disorderly, fractious, headstrong, insubordinate, mutinous, obstreperous, rebellious, riotous, seditious, turbulent, ungovernable, unmanageable, wanton, wild; lawless, obstinate, rebellious, vicious.

unsafe *adj* dangerous, hazardous, insecure, perilous, precarious, treacherous, uncertain, unprotected.

unsavoury *adj* flat, insipid, savourless, tasteless, unflavoured, unpalatable; disagreeable, disgusting, distasteful, nasty, nauseating, offensive, rank, revolting, uninviting, unpleasing.

unscrupulous *adj* dishonest, ruthless, unconscientious, unprincipled, unrestrained.

unseasonable *adj* ill-timed, inappropriate, inopportune, untimely; too late; ungrateful, unsuitable, untimely.

unseasoned *adj* inexperienced, unaccustomed, unqualified, untrained; immoderate, inordinate; green; fresh, unsalted.

unseeing *adj* blind, sightless.

unseemly *adj* improper, indecent, inappropriate, indecorous, unbecoming, uncomely, unfit, unmeet, unsuitable.

unseen *adj* undiscerned, undiscovered, unobserved, unperceived; imperceptible, indiscoverable, invisible.

unselfish *adj* altruistic, devoted, disinterested, generous, impersonal, magnanimous, selfless, self-sacrificing.

unsettle *vb* confuse, disarrange, disconcert, disorder, disturb, unbalance, unhinge, upset.

unshaken *adj* constant, firm, resolute, steadfast, steady.

unsightly *adj* disagreeable, hideous, repellent, repulsive, ugly.

unsociable *adj* distant, reserved, shy, solitary, standoffish, taciturn, uncommunicative, uncompanionable, ungenial; inhospitable, misanthropic, morose.

unsound *adj* defective, impaired, imperfect, rotten, thin, weak; broken, disturbed, restless; diseased, feeble, infirm, poorly, sickly, unhealthy, weak; deceitful, erroneous, fallacious, false, faulty, illogical, incorrect, invalid, questionable, unsubstantial, untenable, wrong; deceitful, dishonest, false, insincere, unfaithful, untrue; unreal; defective, heretical.

unsparing *adj* bountiful, generous, lavish, liberal, ungrudging; harsh, relentless, ruthless, severe, unforgiving.

unspeakable *adj* indescribable, ineffable, inexpressible, unutterable.

unstable *adj* infirm, insecure, precarious, tottering, unsafe,

unsettled, unsteady; erratic, fickle, inconstant, mercurial, unsteady, vacillating, variable, volatile, wavering.

unsteady *adj* fluctuating, oscillating, unsettled; insecure, precarious, unstable; changeable, fickle, inconstant, irresolute, unstable, variable, wavering; drunken, tottering, vacillating, wavering, wobbly; tipsy.

unstrung *adj* overcome, shaken, unnerved, weak.

unsuccessful *adj* abortive, fruitless, futile, ineffectual, profitless, unavailing, vain; ill-fated, luckless, unfortunate, unlucky, unprosperous.

unsuitable *adj* ill-adapted, inappropriate, malapropos, unfit, unsatisfactory, unsuited; improper, inapt, incongruous, infelicitous, unbecoming, unfitting.

unsuited *adj* unadapted, unfitted, unqualified.

unsurpassed *adj* matchless, peerless, unequalled, unexcelled, unmatched, unparalleled, unrivalled.

unsuspecting *adj* confiding, credulous, trusting, unsuspicious.

unswerving *adj* direct, straight, undeviating; constant, determined, firm, resolute, steadfast, steady, stable, unwavering.

untamed *adj* fierce, unbroken, wild; feral.

untangle *vb* disentangle, explain.

untenable *adj* indefensible, unmaintainable, unsound; fallacious, insupportable, unjustifiable, weak.

unthinking *adj* careless, heedless, inconsiderate, unreasoning, unreflecting; automatic, mechanical.

untidy *adj* careless, disorderly, dowdy, frumpy, slovenly, unkempt.

untie *vb* free, loose, unbind, unfasten, unknot, unloose; clear, resolve, unfold.

until *adv*, *conj* till, to the time when; to the place, point, state or degree that; * *prep* till, to.

untiring *adj* persevering; incessant, indefatigable, patient, tireless, unceasing, unflagging, unremitting, unwearying.

untoward *adj* adverse, perverse, refractory, unfortunate; annoying, inconvenient, vexatious; awkward, uncouth, ungainly.

untroubled *adj* calm, careless, composed, peaceful, serene, tranquil, undisturbed, unvexed.

untrue *adj* contrary, inaccurate, wrong; disloyal, faithless, false, perfidious, treacherous, unfaithful.

untrustworthy *adj* deceitful, dishonest, inaccurate, slippery, treacherous, undependable, unreliable; disloyal, false; deceptive, fallible, questionable.

unusual *adj* abnormal, curious, exceptional, extraordinary, odd, peculiar, rare, recherché, remarkable, singular, strange, unaccustomed, uncommon.

unutterable *adj* incommunicable, indescribable, inexpressible, unspeakable.

unvarnished *adj* unpolished; candid, plain, unadorned, unembellished.

unveil *vb* expose, reveal, show, uncover, unmask.

unversed *adj* inexperienced, undisciplined, undrilled, unexercised, unpractised, unprepared, unschooled; unskilful.

unwary *adj* careless, heedless, imprudent, incautious, indiscreet, precipitate, rash, reckless, unguarded.

unwelcome *adj* disagreeable, unacceptable, unpleasant, unpleasing.

unwell *adj* ailing, diseased, ill, indisposed, sick, poorly.

unwholesome adj deleterious, injurious, noisome, noxious, poisonous, unhealthy; injudicious, pernicious, unsound; corrupt, tainted, unsound.

unwieldy adj bulky, cumbersome, cumbrous, elephantine, heavy, hulking, large, ponderous, unmanageable, weighty.

unwilling adj averse, disinclined, indisposed, loath, opposed, recalcitrant, reluctant; forced, grudging.

unwise adj foolish, ill-advised, ill-judged, imprudent, indiscreet, injudicious, silly, stupid, unwary, weak.

unwittingly adv ignorantly, inadvertently, unconsciously, unintentionally, unknowingly.

unwritten adj oral, traditional, unrecorded; conventional, customary.

unyielding adj constant, determined, indomitable, inflexible, resolute, staunch, steadfast, uncompromising, unwavering; intractable, obstinate, perverse, self-willed, stubborn, wilful; adamantine, firm, grim, hard, immovable, inexorable, relentless, rigid, stubborn, unbending.

upheaval n cataclysm, disorder, eruption, explosion, outburst, overthrow.

uphill adj ascending, upward; arduous, difficult, hard, laborious, strenuous, toilsome.

uphold vb elevate, raise; bear up, support; advocate, aid, champion, countenance, defend, justify, maintain, support, sustain, vindicate.

upon prep on top of, over; about, concerning, relating to; immediately after, with.

uppermost adj foremost, highest, loftiest, supreme, topmost.

upright adj erect, vertical; conscientious, fair, faithful, good, honest, honourable, incorruptible, just, pure, righteous, trustworthy, upstanding, virtuous.

uproar n clamour, commotion, din, disturbance, fracas, hubbub, noise, pandemonium, racket, riot, tumult, turmoil.

uproarious adj boisterous, clamorous, loud, obstreperous, riotous, tumultuous.

uproot vb eradicate, extirpate, root out.

upset vb capsize, invert, overthrow, overturn, spill, tip over, topple; agitate, confound, disconcert, distress, disturb, embarrass, fluster, overwhelm, perturb, shock, startle, trouble, unnerve, unsettle; defeat, overthrow, revolutionise, subvert; foil, frustrate, thwart; * adj exposed, overthrown; bothered, disconcerted, flustered, mixed-up, perturbed; shocked, startled, unsettled; beaten, defeated, overpowered, overthrown; distressed, discomposed, overcome, overexcited, overwrought, perturbed, shaken, troubled, unnerved; * n overturn, revolution; capsize, overthrow; refutation; foiling, frustration, ruin, thwarting.

upshot n conclusion, effect, event, issue, outcome, result.

upside down adj bottom up, confused, head over heels, inverted, topsy-turvy.

upstart n adventurer, parvenu, snob, social climber, yuppie.

upturned adj raised, uplifted; retroussé.

upward adj ascending, climbing, rising, uphill; * adv above, aloft, overhead; heavenwards, skywards.

urbane adj civil, courtly, elegant, mannerly, polished, polite, refined, smooth, suave, well-mannered.

urge vb drive, force on, impel, press, push; beg, beseech, entreat, exhort, importune, ply, solicit, tease; animate, egg on, encourage, goad, hurry, incite, quicken, spur, stimulate; * *n* compulsion, desire, drive, impulse, longing, wish, yearning.

urgency *n* drive, emergency, haste, press, pressure, stress; clamorousness, entreaty, importunity, insistence, instance; goad, incitement, spur, stimulus.

usage *n* treatment; custom, fashion, habit, method, mode, practice, prescription, tradition.

use *vb* administer, apply, employ, handle, improve, manipulate, occupy, operate, ply, put into action, take advantage of, turn to account, wield; exert, exploit, profit by, utilise; absorb, consume, exhaust, expend, waste, wear out; accustom, habituate, harden, inure, train; behave toward, deal with, handle, manage, treat; be accustomed, be wont; * *n* appliance, application, consumption, disposal, employment, practice, utilisation; avail, benefit, convenience, profit, service, utility, wear; exigency, necessity, need, occasion; custom, exercise, habit, handling, method, practice, treatment, way.

useful *adj* advantageous, available, availing, beneficial, convenient, effective, good, helpful, operative, practical, profitable, remunerative, salutary, suitable, serviceable, utilitarian; helpful, valuable.

useless *adj* abortive, fruitless, futile, idle, ineffective, impractical, nugatory, null, unavailing, unprofitable, unproductive, valueless, worthless; unserviceable, valueless, waste, worthless.

usher *vb* announce, forerun, herald, introduce, precede; conduct, direct, shepherd, show; * *n* attendant, conductor, escort, shepherd.

usual *adj* accustomed, common, customary, everyday, familiar, frequent, habitual, normal, prevailing, prevalent, regular.

usurp *vb* appropriate, arrogate, assume, seize.

utility *n* avail, benefit, profit, service, use, usefulness; happiness, welfare.

utilise *vb* employ, exploit, put to use, turn to account, use.

utmost *adj* extreme, farthest, highest, last, main, most distant; greatest; * *n* best, extreme, maximum.

utter *adj* complete, entire, perfect, total; absolute, downright, final, sheer, stark, unconditional, unqualified; * *vb* articulate, deliver, disclose, divulge, emit, enunciate, express, give forth, pronounce, reveal, speak, talk, tell; announce, declare, issue.

utterance *n* articulation, expression, pronouncement, pronunciation, publication, speech.

V

vacant *adj* blank, empty, unfilled, void; disengaged, free, unemployed, unoccupied; thoughtless, unthinking; uninhabited, untenanted.

vacate *vb* abandon, evacuate, relinquish, surrender; abolish, annul, cancel, invalidate, nullify, quash, rescind.

vagabond *adj* idle, rambling, roving, roaming, strolling, vagrant, wandering; * *n* beggar, castaway, loafer, lounger, outcast, tramp, vagrant, wanderer.

vagrant *adj* erratic, itinerant, roaming, roving, strolling, unsettled, wandering; * *n* beggar, castaway, loafer, lounger, outcast, tramp, vagabond, wanderer.

vague *adj* ambiguous, confused,

vain *adj* delusive, empty, false, imaginary, suppositional, unsubstantial, unreal, void; abortive, fruitless, futile, ineffectual, profitless, unavailing, unprofitable; trivial, unessential, useless, worthless; arrogant, inflated, opinionated, ostentatious, overweening, proud, self-confident, self opinionated, vainglorious; glittering, gorgeous, ostentatious, showy.

valiant *adj* brave, chivalrous, courageous, daring, dauntless, fearless, gallant, heroic, intrepid, redoubtable, valorous.

valid *adj* cogent, conclusive, efficacious, efficient, good, important, just, logical, solid, sound, strong, substantial, sufficient, weighty.

valour *n* boldness, bravery, courage, daring, gallantry, heroism, spirit.

valuable *adj* precious, profitable, useful; costly, expensive; admirable, estimable, worthy; * *n* heirloom, treasure.

value *vb* account, appraise, assess, estimate, price, rate, reckon; appreciate, esteem, prize, regard, treasure; * *n* importance, usefulness, utility, worth; cost, price, rate; estimation, excellence, importance, merit, worth.

vandal *n* barbarian, destroyer, savage.

vanish *vb* disappear, dissolve, fade, melt.

vanity *n* emptiness, foolishness, futility, triviality, unreality, worthlessness; arrogance, conceit, egotism, ostentation, self-conceit.

vanquish *vb* conquer, defeat, outwit, overcome, overpower, overthrow, subdue, subjugate; crush, foil, master, quell, rout, worst.

vapour *n* cloud, exhalation, fog, fume, mist, smoke, steam; daydream, dream, fantasy, phantom, vision, whim, whimsy.

variable *adj* changeable, mutable, shifting; alterable, capricious, fickle, floating, fluctuating, inconstant, protean, restless, unsteady, vacillating, wavering.

variance *n* disagreement, difference, discord, dissension, incompatibility, strife.

variation *n* alteration, change, modification; deviation, difference, discrepancy; discordance.

variety *n* diversity, medley, miscellany, mixture, variation; kind, sort.

various *adj* different, diverse, manifold, numerous, several, sundry.

varnish *vb* enamel, lacquer; adorn, decorate, embellish, gild, polish; disguise, excuse, extenuate, gloss over, palliate; * *n* enamel, lacquer; cover, extenuation, gloss.

vary *vb* alter, metamorphose, transform; alternate, exchange, rotate; modify, depart, deviate, swerve.

vast *adj* boundless, infinite, measureless, spacious, wide; colossal, enormous, gigantic, huge, immense, prodigious, tremendous; extraordinary, remarkable.

vault *vb* bend, curve, span; tumble, turn; * *n* dome; catacomb, cell, cellar, crypt, dungeon, tomb; depository, strong-room; bound, jump, leap, spring.

veer *vb* change, shift, turn.

vegetate *vb* blossom, develop, flower, germinate, grow, shoot, sprout; bask, hibernate, idle, stagnate.

vehement *adj* furious, impetuous, passionate, rampant, violent; ardent, burning, eager, earnest, enthusiastic, fiery, keen, passionate, zealous; forcible,

veil vb cloak, conceal, cover, envelop, hide, mask, screen, shroud; * n cover, curtain, shade, screen; blind, cover, disguise, mask, muffler.
vein n course, current, seam, streak, thread; bent, character, faculty, humour, mood, talent, turn.
vend vb dispose, flog, hawk, retail, sell.
venerable adj respected, revered, sage, wise; awful, dreadful; aged, old, patriarchal.
veneration n adoration, devotion, esteem, respect, reverence, worship.
vengeance n retaliation, retribution, revenge.
venom n poison; acerbity, acrimony, bitterness, gall, hate, malevolence, malice, rancour, spite, virulence.
venomous adj deadly, poisonous, toxic, virulent; caustic, malignant, mischievous, noxious, spiteful.
vent vb emit, express, release, utter; * n air-hole, hole, mouth, opening, orifice; air-pipe, aperture, blowhole, plug, spout, tap; emission, escape, outlet, passage; discharge, expression, utterance.
ventilate vb aerate, air, freshen, oxygenate, fan; comment, discuss, examine, publish, review, scrutinise.
venture vb dare, hazard, imperil, jeopardise, presume, speculate, test, try, undertake; * n chance, hazard, jeopardy, peril, risk speculation, stake.
verdict n answer, decision, finding, judgement, opinion, sentence.
verge vb incline, lean, slope, tend; approach, border, skirt; * n rod, staff; border, boundary, brink, confine, edge, extreme, limit, margin; edge, eve.
verify vb attest, authenticate, confirm, corroborate, prove, substantiate.

versatile adj capricious, mobile, variable; mercurial unsteady; adaptable, plastic, varied.
versed adj able, accomplished, acquainted, conversant, practised, proficient, qualified, skilled, trained.
version n interpretation, reading, rendering, translation.
vertical adj erect, perpendicular, plumb, upright.
vertigo n dizziness, giddiness.
verve n animation, ardour, energy, enthusiasm, rapture, spirit.
very adv absolutely, enormously, excessively, remarkably, surpassingly; * adj actual, exact, identical, precise; bare, plain, pure, simple.
vestige n evidence, footprint, mark, record, relic, sign, token.
veteran adj aged, experienced, disciplined, seasoned; * n campaigner; master, old-timer, old soldier, past master.
veto vb ban, embargo, forbid, interdict, prohibit; * n ban, embargo, prohibition, refusal.
vex vb annoy, badger, bother, chafe, cross, distress, gall, harass, harry, hector, pester, plague, tease, torment, trouble, worry; affront, displease, irk, irritate, nettle, offend, provoke; agitate, disquiet, disturb.
vexation n agitation, chagrin, discomfort, displeasure, disquiet, distress, irritation, sorrow, trouble; affliction, annoyance, nuisance, plague, torment; damage, troubling.
vibrate vb oscillate, swing, undulate, wave; quiver, sound, thrill; fluctuate, hesitate, vacillate, waver.
vice n defect, failing, fault, imperfection, infirmity; badness, corruption, depravity, error, immorality, iniquity, laxity, obliquity, sin, vileness, wickedness.
vicinity n nearness, proximity; locality, neighbourhood.

vicious *adj* atrocious, corrupt, degenerate, depraved, devilish, diabolical, evil, flagrant, iniquitous, mischievous, profligate, shameless, sinful, unprincipled, wicked; spiteful; foul; corrupt, debased, faulty, impure; contrary, refractory.

victim *n* martyr, sacrifice, sufferer; prey; cull, cully, dupe, gull, gudgeon, puppet.

victimise *vb* bamboozle, beguile, cheat, cozen, deceive, defraud, diddle, dupe, fool, gull, hoax, hoodwink, swindle.

victor *n* champion, conqueror, vanquisher, winner.

victory *n* achievement, conquest, mastery, triumph.

view *vb* behold, contemplate, eye, inspect, survey; consider, inspect, regard, study; * *n* observation, regard, sight; outlook, panorama, scene, survey, vista; aim, intent, design, drift, purpose, scope; belief, conception, judgement, notion, opinion, sentiment, theory; appearance, aspect, show.

vigilant *adj* alert, careful, cautious, circumspect, observant, unsleeping, watchful.

vigorous *adj* lusty, powerful, strong; active, alert, energetic, vehement, vivid, virile; brisk, hardy, robust, sound, sturdy, healthy; flourishing, fresh; bold, emphatic, impassioned, lively, piquant, pointed, severe, spirited, trenchant.

vigour *n* activity, efficacy, energy, force, might, potency, power; dash, spirit, strength; elasticity, health, heartiness, pep, punch, robustness, soundness, tone, vitality; enthusiasm, fire, freshness, intensity, liveliness, verve, raciness.

vile *adj* base, beastly, brutish, contemptible, despicable, disgusting, ignoble, low, mean, odious, repulsive, shabby, slavish, sorry, ugly; bad, evil, foul, gross, impure, iniquitous, lewd, obscene, sinful, wicked; cheap, mean, miserable, valueless, worthless.

vilify *vb* abuse, berate, blacken, blemish, brand, decry, defame, disparage, libel, malign, revile, scandalise, slander, slur, traduce, vituperate.

villain *n* blackguard, knave, miscreant, rascal, reprobate, rogue, ruffian, scoundrel.

vindicate *vb* defend, justify; avenge, assert, maintain, right, support.

vindictive *adj* avenging, grudging, implacable, malevolent, malicious, retaliative, spiteful, unforgiving, unrelenting, vengeful.

violate *vb* hurt, injure; break, disobey, infringe, invade; desecrate, pollute, profane; abuse, deflower, outrage, ravish, transgress.

violent *adj* forceful, frenzied, furious, hot, impetuous, insane, intense, stormy, tumultuous, turbulent, vehement, wild; fierce, fiery, fuming, strong, raging, rampant, rapid, raving, roaring, rough, tearing, ungovernable; accidental, unnatural; desperate, extreme, outrageous, unjust; acute, exquisite, intense, sharp.

virile *adj* forceful, manly, masculine, robust, vigorous.

virtual *adj* constructive, equivalent, essential, implicit, implied, indirect.

virtue *n* chastity, goodness, grace, morality, purity; efficacy, honesty, integrity, justice, probity, quality, worth.

virtuous *adj* blameless, equitable, good, honest, moral, noble, righteous, upright, worthy; chaste, immaculate, innocent, modest, pure, undefiled; efficacious, powerful.

virulent *adj* deadly, malignant, poisonous, toxic, venomous;

acrid, acrimonious, bitter, caustic.

visible *adj* perceivable; apparent, clear, conspicuous, distinct, evident, manifest, noticeable, obvious, open, palpable, patent, plain, revealed, unhidden.

vision *n* eyesight, seeing, sight; apparition, chimera, dream, ghost, hallucination, illusion, phantom, spectre.

visionary *adj* imaginative, quixotic, romantic; chimerical, dreamy, fancied, fanciful, fantastic, ideal, illusory, wild; * *n* dreamer, enthusiast, idealist, optimist, theorist.

vital *adj* basic, cardinal, essential, indispensable, necessary; animate, alive, existing, living; essential, paramount.

vitality *n* animation, life, strength; energy, vigour, virility.

vivacious *adj* active, animated, breezy, brisk, cheerful, gay, light-hearted, lively, merry, mirthful, spirited, sportive, sprightly.

vivid *adj* active, bright, brilliant, clear, intense; fresh, lively, lucid, sprightly, strong; expressive, graphic, striking, telling.

vocation *n* call, citation, injunction, summons; business, calling, occupation, profession, pursuit, trade.

vogue *adj* fashionable, modish, stylish, trendy; * *n* custom, fashion, mode, practice, repute, style, usage.

voice *vb* declare, express, say, utter; * *n* speech, utterance; noise, sound; opinion, suffrage, vote; accent, articulation, enunciation, inflection, intonation, pronunciation; expression, language, words.

void *vb* clear, eject, emit, empty, evacuate; * *adj* blank, empty, hollow, vacant; clear, lacking, wanting, without; invalid, nugatory, null; unreal, vain; * *n* abyss, blank, chasm, emptiness, hole, vacuum.

volatile *adj* gaseous; airy, buoyant, frivolous, lively, sprightly, vivacious; capricious, changeable, fickle, flighty, giddy, inconstant, light-headed, mercurial, reckless, unsteady, whimsical, wild.

volume *n* turn, whirl; book, tome; amplitude, bulk, compass, dimension, size, substance, vastness; fullness, power, quantity.

voluminous *adj* ample, big, bulky, great, large; copious, diffuse, discursive, flowing.

voluntary *adj* free, spontaneous, unbidden, unforced; deliberate, designed, intended; optional, willing.

volunteer *vb* offer, present, proffer, propose, tender.

voracious *adj* devouring, greedy, hungry, rapacious, ravenous.

vote *vb* ballot, elect, opt, return; judge, propose, suggest; * *n* ballot, franchise, poll, referendum, suffrage, voice.

vow *vb* consecrate, dedicate, devote; * *n* oath, pledge, promise.

voyage *vb* journey, navigate, ply, sail; * *n* crossing, excursion, journey, passage, sail, trip.

vulgar *adj* common, ignoble, lowly, plebeian; boorish, coarse, discourteous, flashy, garish, gaudy, ill-bred, inelegant, loud, showy, tawdry, uncultivated, unrefined; ordinary, popular; base, broad, gross, loose, low, mean, ribald, vile; inelegant, unauthorised.

vulnerable *adj* accessible, assailable, defenceless, exposed, weak.

W

wad *n* block, bundle, chunk, lump, mass, roll.

WAFT

waft vb bear, carry, float, transmit, transport; * n breath, breeze, draught, puff.

wag vb shake, sway, waggle; oscillate, vibrate, waver; advance, progress, stir; * n flutter, nod, oscillation, vibration; humorist, jester, joker, wit.

wage vb bet, hazard, lay, stake, wager; conduct, undertake.

wager vb back, bet, gamble, risk, stake; * n bet, gamble, risk, stake.

wages npl compensation, earnings, hire, pay, payment, remuneration, salary, stipend.

wail vb bemoan, deplore, lament; cry, howl, weep; * n complaint, cry, lamentation, moan.

wait vb delay, linger, pause, rest, tarry; attend, minister, serve; abide, expect, look for; * n delay, halt, hold-up, pause, rest, stay, stop.

waive vb defer, forego, surrender, relinquish, renounce; reject.

wake vb arise; activate, animate, arouse, excite, kindle, provoke, stimulate; * n vigil, watch, watching; course, path, rear, track, trail, wash.

wakeful adj sleepless, restless; alert, observant, vigilant, wary, watchful.

walk vb advance, depart, go, march, move, pace, saunter, step, stride, stroll, tramp; * n amble, gait, step; beat, career, course, province; conduct, procedure; alley, avenue, cloister, footpath, path, pavement, promenade, way; constitutional, excursion, hike, ramble, saunter, stroll.

wan adj ashen, bloodless, colourless, haggard, pale.

wander vb prowl, range, roam, rove, stroll; deviate, digress, straggle, stray; ramble, rave; * n amble, cruise, excursion.

wane vb abate, decrease, ebb, subside; decline, fail, sink; * n decrease, diminution; decay, decline, failure.

want vb crave, desire, need, require, wish; fail, lack, neglect; * n absence, defect, default, deficiency, lack; inadequacy, insufficiency, meagreness, paucity, poverty, scantiness, scarcity; necessity, need, requirement; craving, desire, longing, wish; distress, necessity, need, penury, poverty, privation.

war vb battle, campaign, combat, contend, crusade, fight; * n contention, enmity, hostility, strife.

warble vb sing, trill, yodel; * n chant, hum, hymn.

ward vb guard, watch; defend, fend, protect, repel; * n care, charge, guard, watch; defender, guardian, keeper, protector; custody; defence, garrison; minor, pupil; district, division, precinct; apartment, cubicle.

warehouse n depot, repository, store, storehouse.

warfare n battle, conflict, contest, engagement, fray, hostilities, strife, war.

warm vb heat, roast, toast; animate, excite, rouse; * adj tepid; genial, mild, sunny; close, muggy; affectionate, ardent, cordial, eager, fervent, glowing, hearty, hot; excited, fiery, flushed, furious, hasty, keen, lively, passionate, quick, vehement, violent.

warmonger n belligerent, hawk, jingo, militarist, sabre-rattler.

warmth n glow, tepidity; ardour, fervour, zeal; cordiality, eagerness, enthusiasm, excitement, fever, fire, flush, heat, intensity, passion, spirit, vehemence.

warn vb caution; admonish, advise; inform, notify; bid, call, summon.

warning adj admonitory, cautionary, cautioning; * n admonition, advice, caveat, caution; notice; augury, indication, intimation, omen, portent, presage, prognostic, symptom; call, summons; example, lesson.

warrant *vb* certify, guarantee, secure; affirm, assure, attest, declare, justify; authorise, license, maintain, sanction, sustain, uphold; * *n* guarantee, pledge, security, surety; authentication, authority, commission, verification; pass, permit, subpoena, writ.

warrior *n* champion, fighter, hero, soldier.

wary *adj* careful, cautious, circumspect, discreet, guarded, heedful, prudent, vigilant, watchful.

wash *vb* purge; moisten, wet; bathe, clean, flush, irrigate, rinse, sluice; colour, stain, tint; * *n* ablution, bathing, cleansing; bog, fen, marsh, swamp, quagmire; bath, embrocation, lotion; laundry.

waste *vb* consume, corrode, decrease, diminish, emaciate, wear; absorb, deplete, dissipate, drain, empty, exhaust, expend, lavish, misspend, misuse, squander; demolish, desolate, destroy, devastate, dilapidate, pillage, plunder, ravage, ruin, scour; damage, impair, injure; decay, dwindle, wither; * *adj* desolated, destroyed, empty, ravaged, ruined, spoiled, stripped, void; dismal, dreary, forlorn; abandoned, barren, uncultivated, unimproved, uninhabited, wild; useless, valueless, worthless; * *n* consumption, diminution, dissipation, expenditure, loss; destruction, dispersion, extravagance, squandering; decay, desolation, destruction, devastation, havoc, pillage, ravage, ruin; chaff, debris, detritus, dross, husks, junk, matter, refuse, rubbish, trash, worthlessness; barrenness, desert, expanse, wilderness.

wasteful *adj* destructive, ruinous; extravagant, improvident, lavish, prodigal, squandering, thriftless.

watch *vb* attend, guard, keep, oversee, protect, superintend, tend; eye, mark, observe; * *n* guard, outlook, vigil, ward; alertness, observation, surveillance; guard, picket, sentinel, sentry; ticker, timepiece.

watchful *adj* alert, attentive, awake, careful, circumspect, guarded, heedful, observant, vigilant, wary.

waterfall *n* cascade, cataract, chute, fall.

watery *adj* diluted, thin, weak; insipid, spiritless, vapid; moist, wet.

wave *vb* flutter, heave, shake, sway, undulate; brandish, flaunt, flourish, swing; beckon, signal; * *n* billow, breaker, ripple, roll, surge, swell, tide, undulation; flourish, gesture, sway; curl, roll, unevenness.

waver *vb* flicker, undulate; reel, totter; falter, fluctuate, flutter, hesitate, oscillate, quiver, vacillate.

wax *vb* become, grow, increase, mount, rise.

way *n* journey, passage, transit, trend; access, alley, avenue, channel, course, highway, passage, path, road, route, street, track, trail; fashion, manner, means, method, mode, system; distance; behaviour, custom, fashion, form, guise, habit, manner, practice, process, style, usage; device, plan, scheme.

wayward *adj* capricious, contrary, forward, headstrong, intractable, obstinate, perverse, stubborn, unruly, wilful.

weak *adj* debilitated, delicate, exhausted, faint, feeble, fragile, frail, infirm, invalid, languid, languishing, shaky, sickly, unhealthy, unsound; defenceless, vulnerable; soft, unstressed; boneless; pliable, pliant, unsettled, unstable, unsteady, vacillating, yielding; childish, foolish, senseless, shallow, silly, simple; foolish, indiscreet, injudicious, unwise; faint, feeble, indistinct, low, small; attenuated, diluted, insipid, tasteless, thin, watery; feeble, flimsy, frivolous, poor, slight, trifling; futile, illogical, inconclusive, ineffective, inefficient, lame, unconvincing, unsatisfactory, unsupported, unsustained, vague; unsafe, unsound, unsubstantial, untrustworthy; helpless, impotent, powerless; breakable, delicate, frangible; inconsiderable, puny, slender, slight, small.

weaken vb cripple, debilitate, devitalise, enfeeble, invalidate, relax, sap, shake, stagger, undermine, unman; adulterate, attenuate, depress, dilute, exhaust, impair, impoverish, lessen, lower, reduce.

weakness n debility, feebleness, fragility, frailty, languor; defect, fault, flaw; fondness, inclination, liking.

wealth n assets, capital, cash, fortune, funds, money, possessions, property, riches, treasure; abundance, affluence, opulence, plenty.

wear vb bear, carry, don; endure, last; consume, impair, use, waste; * n corrosion, erosion; consumption, use; apparel, array, attire, clothes, clothing, dress, gear.

wearisome adj annoying, boring, dull, exhausting, fatiguing, irksome, monotonous, slow, tedious, tiresome, troublesome, trying, uninteresting.

weary vb debilitate, exhaust, fatigue, harass, jade, tire; * adj drowsy, exhausted, jaded, spent, tired, worn; irksome, tiresome.

web n cobweb; lattice, mesh, net, network, tangle, weave.

wed vb contract, couple, espouse, marry.

wedding n bridal, espousal, marriage, nuptials.

weep vb bemoan, bewail, cry, lament, sob.

weigh vb balance, lift, raise; consider, deliberate, esteem, examine.

weight vb ballast, burden, fill, freight, load; * n gravity, heaviness, heft, tonnage; burden, load, pressure; consequence, emphasis, importance, impressiveness, influence, significance, value.

weighty adj heavy, massive, ponderous, unwieldy; grave, important, influential, serious, significant.

weird adj eerie, ghostly, strange, supernatural, uncanny, unearthly.

welcome vb embrace, greet, hail, receive; * adj agreeable, gratifying, pleasing, satisfying; * n greeting, reception, salutation.

welfare n affluence, benefit, happiness, prosperity, success, wellbeing.

well vb flow, gush, issue, jet, spring; * n fount, fountain, reservoir, spring; origin, source; hole, pit, shaft; * adj hale, healthy, hearty, sound; fortunate, good, happy, satisfactory; * adv accurately, correctly, efficiently, properly, suitably; abundantly, fully, thoroughly; agreeably, commendably, favourably.

wellbeing n comfort, good, happiness, health, welfare.

wet vb dampen, drench, moisten, soak, sprinkle, water; * adj clammy, damp, dank, dewy, dripping, humid, moist; rainy, showery; * n dampness, humidity, moisture.

wheel vb gyrate, revolve, roll, rotate, spin, turn, twist, whirl, wind; * n circle, revolution, roll, rotation, spin.

whim n caprice, fancy, freak,

humour, notion, quirk, vagary, whimsy, wish.

whimsical *adj* capricious, crotchety, eccentric, erratic, fanciful, odd, peculiar, quaint, singular.

whine *vb* cry, grumble, moan, wail, whimper; * *n* complaint, cry, grumble, moan, wail, whimper.

whip *vb* beat, lash, strike; flagellate, flog, lash, scourge; hurt, sting; jerk, snap, snatch, whisk; * *n* cane, crop, lash, scourge, switch, thong.

whirl *vb* gyrate, pirouette, roll, revolve, rotate, turn, twirl, twist, wheel; * *n* eddy, flutter, gyration, rotation, spin, swirl, vortex.

whole *adj* all, complete, entire, intact, total, undivided; faultless, perfect, unbroken, undivided, uninjured; healthy, sound, well; * *adv* entire, in one; * *n* aggregate, all, ensemble, entirety, gross, sum, total, totality.

wholesome *adj* healthy, helpful, invigorating, nourishing, nutritious, salutary; beneficial, good, helpful, improving; fresh, sound.

wicked *adj* abandoned, abominable, depraved, devilish, graceless, immoral, infamous, irreverent, profane, sinful, unprincipled, unrighteous, vicious, vile, worthless; atrocious, bad, criminal, dark, evil, heinous, iniquitous, monstrous, nefarious, unjust, villainous.

wide *adj* broad, comprehensive, distended, expanded, large, spacious, vast; remote; prevalent; * *adv* farthest, fully.

wield *vb* brandish, flourish, handle, manipulate, ply; control, manage, sway.

wild *adj* feral, undomesticated, untamed; desert, desolate, rough, uncultivated; barbarous, ferocious, fierce, savage, uncivilised; luxuriant, rank; disorderly, frantic, frenzied, furious, impetuous, irregular, mad, outrageous, raving, turbulent, ungoverned, uncontrolled, violent; fast, flighty, foolish, giddy, heedless, ill-advised, inconsiderate, reckless, unwise; boisterous, rough, stormy; crazy, fanciful, imaginary, strange; * *n* desert, waste, wilderness.

wilful *adj* cantankerous, dogged, headstrong, heady, inflexible, obdurate, obstinate, perverse, pig-headed, refractory, unruly, unyielding; capricious; deliberate, intended, planned, premeditated.

will *vb* bid, command, decree, direct, ordain; choose, desire, wish; bequeath, devise, leave; * *n* decision, determination, resolution; desire, disposition, inclination, intent, purpose, volition, wish; behest, command, decree, demand, direction, order, request, requirement.

willing *adj* amenable, compliant, disposed, inclined, minded; deliberate, free, intentional, unasked, unbidden, voluntary; cordial, eager, ready.

wily *adj* artful, crafty, crooked, cunning, deceitful, designing, insidious, intriguing, politic, sly, subtle, treacherous, tricky.

win *vb* accomplish, achieve, acquire, catch, earn, gain, gather, get, make, realise, reclaim, recover; gain, succeed, surpass, triumph; arrive, reach; attract, convince, influence, persuade; * *n* conquest, success, triumph, victory.

wince *vb* cower, cringe, flinch, quail, recoil, shrink; * *n* cringe, flinch, start.

wind *n* air, breeze, draught, gust, hurricane, whiff, zephyr; breath, expiration, inspiration, respiration; flatulence, gas; bend, curve, meander, twist, zigzag; * *vb* coil, encircle, roll, turn, twine, twist; bend, curve, meander, zigzag.

windy *adj* breezy, blowy, draughty, gusty, squally; airy, empty, hollow, inflated.

wipe *vb* clean, mop, rub; * *n* hit, strike; gibe, jeer, sneer, taunt.

wisdom *n* depth, discernment, farsightedness, insight, judgement, judiciousness, prescience, sagacity, sapience, understanding; enlightenment, erudition, knowledge, lore, scholarship; reason, sense.

wise *adj* deep, discerning, enlightened, intelligent, judicious, rational, sensible, sage, sapient, solid; erudite, informed, knowing, learned, scholarly; crafty, cunning, designing, foxy, knowing, politic, subtle, wary, wily.

wish *vb* covet, desire, hanker, long; bid, command, desire, intend, mean, want; * *n* behest, desire, intention, pleasure, want, will; craving, desire, hankering, inclination, longing, want, yearning.

wistful *adj* contemplative, engrossed, meditative, musing, pensive, reflective, thoughtful; desirous, longing.

wit *n* genius, intellect, reason, sense, understanding; banter, cleverness, facetiousness, fun, humour, jocularity, point, raillery, satire, sparkle; conceit, jest, joke, pleasantry, quip, repartee, sally; humorist, joker, wag.

witch *n* enchantress, fascinator, sorceress; crone, hag, sibyl.

witchcraft *n* conjuration, magic, necromancy, sorcery.

withdraw *vb* abstract, deduct, remove, retire, separate, sequester, subtract; disengage, wean; recall, recant, resign, retract, revoke; abdicate, decamp, depart, retire, shrink, vacate.

wither *vb* contract, droop, dry, shrivel, wilt, wizen; decay, decline, droop, languish, waste.

withhold *vb* check, detain, hinder, repress, restrain, retain.

withstand *vb* confront, defy, face, oppose, resist.

witness *vb* corroborate, note, notice, observe, see; * *n* attestation, corroboration, evidence, proof, testimony; bystander, corroborator, onlooker, spectator, testifier.

witty *adj* clever, droll, facetious, funny, humorous, jocose, jocular, waggish; alert, penetrating, quick, sparkling.

wizard *n* charmer, diviner, conjurer, enchanter, magician, necromancer, seer, sorcerer.

wizened *adj* dried up, gnarled, lined, shrivelled, shrunken, withered, wrinkled.

woe *n* affliction, agony, anguish, bitterness, depression, distress, grief, heartache, melancholy, misery, sorrow, tribulation, unhappiness.

wonder *vb* admire, marvel; ponder, query, question, speculate; * *n* amazement, astonishment, awe, curiosity, marvel, prodigy, surprise.

wonderful *adj* amazing, awesome, extraordinary, marvellous, miraculous, portentous, prodigious, surprising.

word *vb* express, phrase, put, say, state, term; * *n* expression, name, phrase, term; account, information, intelligence, message, news, report, tidings; affirmation, assertion, avowal, declaration, statement; speech; assurance, parole, pledge, promise; behest, bidding, command, direction, order, precept; countersign, password, signal.

work *vb* operate; drudge, grind, labour, slave, toil; move, perform, succeed; aim, attempt, strive, try; ferment, leaven, rise; accomplish, beget, cause, effect, engender, manage, produce; exert, strain; embroider, stitch; * *n* exertion, drudgery, grind, labour, pain, toil; employment, function, occupation, task; action, accomplishment, achievement, composition, deed, feat, opus, performance, production, fabric; ferment, leaven; treatment.

worldly *adj* common, earthly, human, mundane, terrestrial; carnal, secular, temporal; ambitious, grovelling, irreligious, selfish, proud, sordid, unspiritual.

worn *adj* frayed, ragged, shiny, tattered, threadbare; drawn, haggard, lined, wizened; exhausted, fatigued, spent, tired, wearied.

worry *vb* annoy, badger, bait, beset, bother, disquiet, disturb, fret, harass, harry, hector, infest, irritate, molest, persecute, pester, plague, tease, torment, trouble; * *n* annoyance, anxiety, care, concern, disquiet, fear, misgiving, trouble, uneasiness.

worship *vb* adore, esteem, honour, revere, venerate; deify, idolise; pray; * *n* adoration, devotion, esteem, homage, respect, reverence; exultation, laud, praise, prayer.

worst *vb* beat, conquer, crush, defeat, foil, master, overpower, overthrow, quell, rout, subdue, vanquish.

worth *n* account, character, credit, excellence, importance, integrity, merit, nobleness, virtue; cost, estimation, price, value.

worthless *adj* futile, meritless, paltry, poor, trifling, unsalable, unserviceable, useless, valueless, wretched; base, corrupt: ignoble, low, mean.

worthy *adj* deserving, fit, suitable; excellent, exemplary, good, honest, reputable, righteous, upright, virtuous; * *n* celebrity, dignitary, personage, somebody, VIP.

wound *vb* damage, harm, hurt, injure; cut, harrow, lacerate, pain, prick, stab; mortify, offend; * *n* blow, hurt, injury; damage; anguish, grief, pain, pang, torture.

wrap *vb* cloak, cover, encase, envelope, muffle, swathe; * *n* blanket, cape, cloak, overcoat, shawl.

wreath *n* chaplet, curl, festoon, garland, ring.

wreathe *vb* encircle, festoon, garland, intertwine, surround, twist.

wreck *vb* founder, shipwreck, strand; blast, break, devastate, ruin, spoil; * *n* crash, ruin, shipwreck, smash, undoing.

wrench *vb* distort, twist, wrest; sprain, strain; extort, extract; * *n* twist; sprain, strain; monkey wrench, spanner.

wrest *vb* force, pull, strain, twist, wrench, wring.

wrestle *vb* contend, contest, grapple, strive, struggle.

wretched *adj* comfortless, distressed, forlorn, unhappy, woebegone; afflicting, pitiable, sad, saddening, sorrowful; bad, contemptible, mean, paltry, pitiful, sorry, vile, worthless.

wring *vb* twist, wrench; extort, force, wrest; distress, harass, rack, torture.

wrinkle *vb* corrugate, crease, gather, pucker, rumple; * *n* corrugation, crease, crimp, crinkle, crumple, furrow, ridge, rumple; caprice, fancy, notion, quirk; device, trick.

writ *n* court order, decree, document, summons.

write *vb* compose, indite, inscribe, pen, transcribe.

writer *n* author, clerk, penman, scribe, secretary.

wrong *vb* abuse, encroach, injure, maltreat, oppress; * *adj* inequitable, unfair, unjust; bad, criminal, evil, immoral, improper, iniquitous, sinful, wicked; amiss, improper, inappropriate, unsuitable; erroneous, false, inaccurate, incorrect, mistaken, untrue; * *adv* amiss, erroneously, falsely, improperly; * *n* foul, grievance, inequity, injury, injustice, trespass, unfairness; crime, evil, guilt, immorality, iniquity, misdeed, sin, transgression, unrighteousness, vice, wickedness; error, falsity.

wry *adj* askew, contorted, crooked, distorted, twisted.

X, Y, Z

Xmas *n* Christmas, Noel, yule, yuletide.

X-ray *n* roentgen ray, röntgen ray.

xylograph *n* cut, woodcut, wood engraving.

yap *vb* bark, cry, yelp; * *n* bark, cry, yelp.

yard *n* close, compound, courtyard, enclosure, garden.

yarn *n* anecdote, fabrication, narrative, story, tale, untruth.

yawn *vb* gape; * *n* gap, gape, gulf.

yearn *vb* crave, desire, hanker after, long for.

yell *vb* bawl, bellow, cry out, howl, roar, scream, screech, shriek, squeal; * *n* cry, howl, roar, scream, screech, shriek.

yelp *vb* bark, howl, yap; bitch, grouse; * *n* bark, howl.

yet *adv* besides, further, however, over and above, so far, still, thus far, ultimately; * *conj* moreover, nevertheless, notwithstanding, now.

yield *vb* afford, bear, bestow, confer, impart, produce, render, supply; accede, acquiesce, assent, comply, concede, give, grant; abandon, abdicate, cede, forego, give up, let go, quit, relax, relinquish, resign, submit, succumb, surrender, waive; * *n* earnings, income, output, produce, profit, return.

yielding *adj* accommodating, acquiescent, compliant, obedient, passive, submissive, unresisting; bending, flexible, plastic, pliant, soft, supple, tractable; fertile, productive.

yoke *vb* associate, connect, couple, harness, interlink, join, link, unite; * *n* bond, chain, link, tie, union; bondage, enslavement, servitude, subjection; couple, pair.

young *adj* green, ignorant, inexperienced, juvenile, new, recent; * *n* youth; babies, issue, brood, offspring, progeny, spawn.

youth *n* adolescence, childhood, immaturity, juvenile, minority, pupillage, wardship; boy, girl, lad, lass schoolboy, schoolgirl, slip, sprig, stripling, youngster.

youthful *adj* boyish, childish, girlish, immature, juvenile, young.

zany *adj* comic, comical, crazy, eccentric, funny, scatter brained; clownish, foolish, silly; * *n* buffoon, clown, fool, harlequin, jester, punch.

zeal *n* alacrity, ardour, devotion, earnestness, eagerness, energy, enthusiasm, fervour, intensity, passion, soul, spirit, warmth.

zealous *adj* ardent, burning, devoted, eager, earnest, enthusiastic, fervent, fiery, forward, glowing, passionate.

zenith *n* acme, apex, climax, culmination, heyday, pinnacle, prime, summit, top.

zero *n* cipher, naught, nil, nothing, nought.

zest *n* appetite, enjoyment, exhilaration, gusto, piquancy, relish, thrill; flavour, salt, tang, taste; appetiser, sauce.

zip *n* drive, energy, gusto, life, oomph, pep, pizzazz, sparkle, spirit, verve, vigour, vim, vitality, zest, zing; * *n* dash, flash, fly, hurry, rush, shoot, speed, tear, whizz, zoom.

zone *n* band, belt, girdle; circuit, clime, region.